Tarragona

Living History

TRIANGLE ▼ BOOKS

Tarragona

Living History

Passeig de Sant Antoni. The Praetorium and Museu Arqueològic de Tarragona

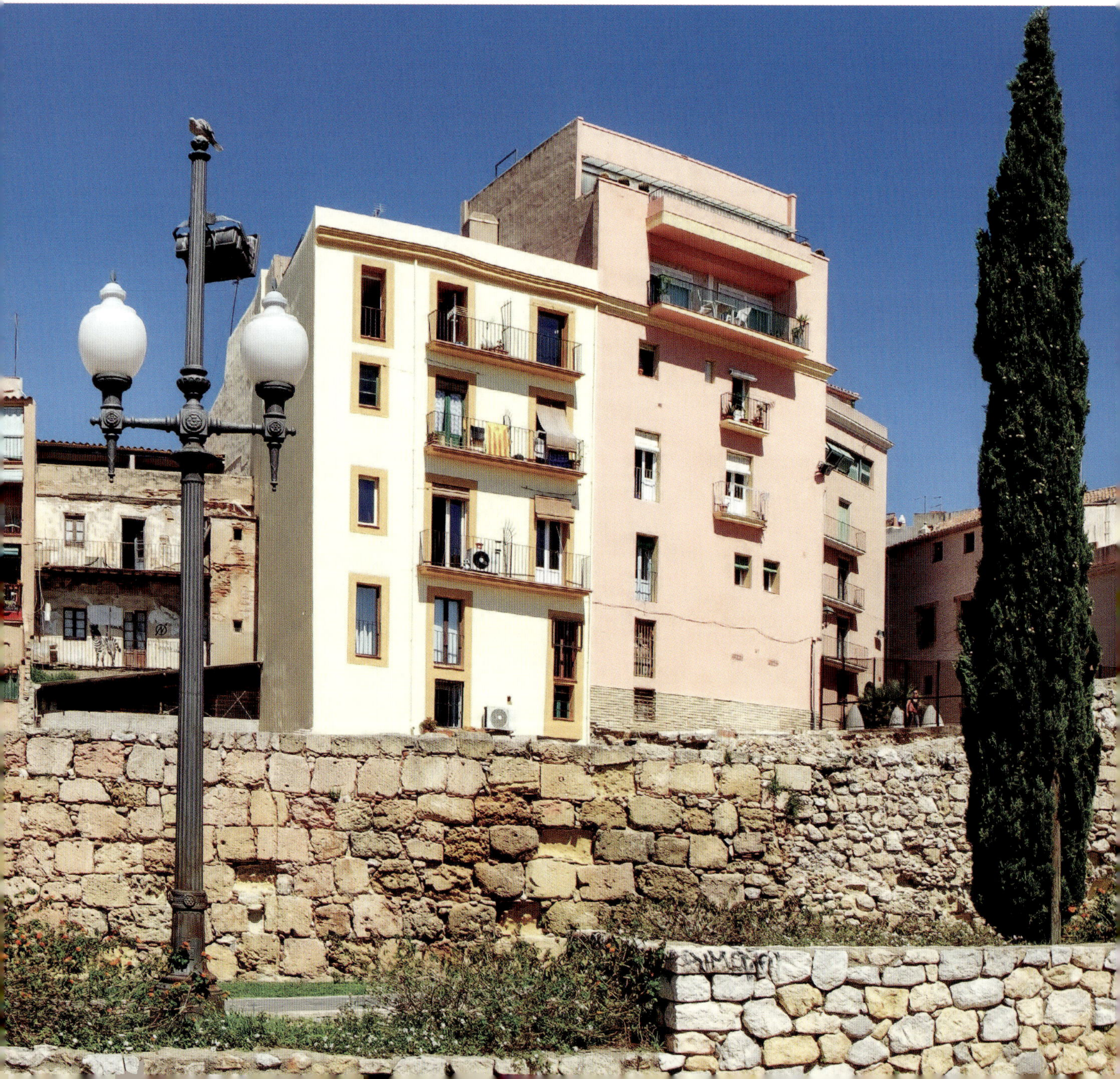

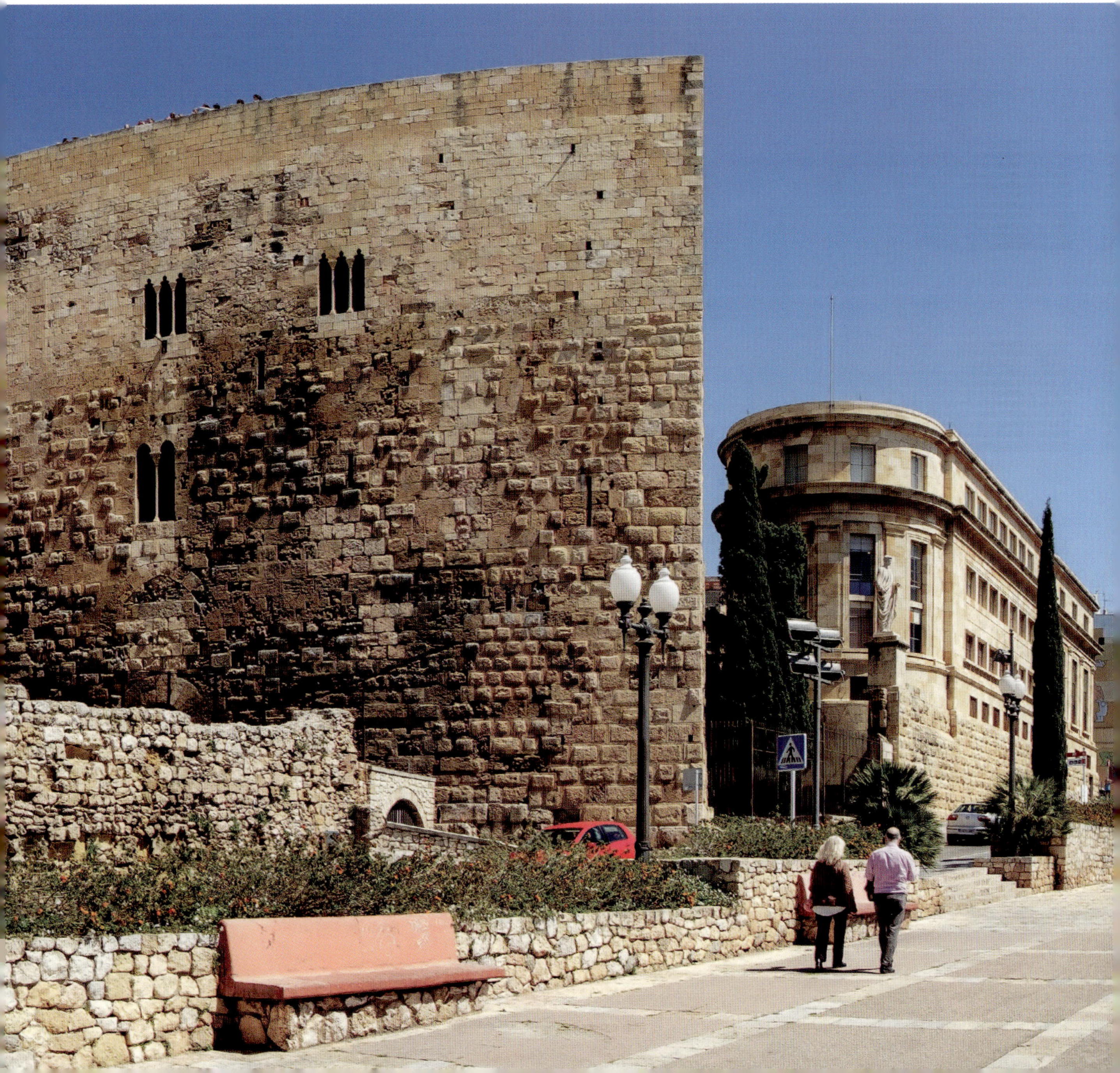

Tarragona was the first Roman city founded outside the Italian peninsula and its neighbouring islands. When the poet Federico García Lorca visited in September 1935 he described it as "pure Rome". Indeed, the Romans spread classical civilisation from here to Hispania and left an important archaeological legacy consisting of 14 landmarks — in the municipalities of Tarragona, Constantí, Altafulla and Roda de Berà — which UNESCO declared World Heritage Sites in the year 2000 and Sites of Outstanding Universal Value in 2015. Around an Iberian settlement, the new inhabitants soon realised that they had found a privileged spot with a series of features that make Tarragona distinctive today: by the sea, with a mild climate all year round, with excellent road and sea connections and fertile land.

So we can safely say that Tarragona is pure Rome, but it is also medieval, modern, art nouveau, with its home-grown offshoot *modernisme*, and contemporary. A city from history, yet with a living history, which emerges from books and stones to be experienced in the streets. A history that comes to life every year during Tàrraco Viva, Europe's leading festival

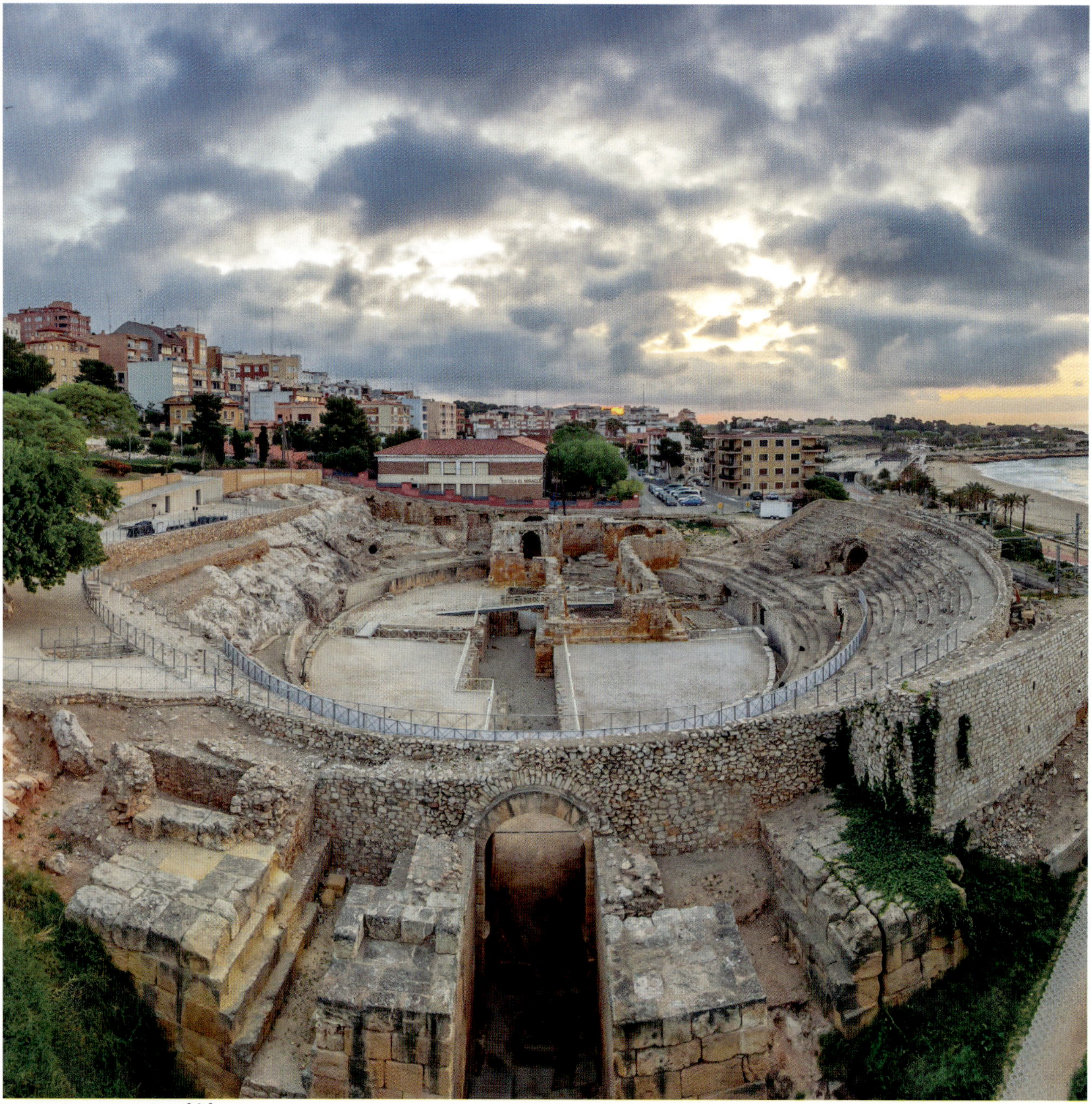

Roman Tarragona. Amphitheatre

celebrating Roman history, or Tarragona Història Viva which is held during the summer and recreates episodes from the city's history. Medieval Tarragona is very much alive in the old town, the Part Alta. Surrounded by the Roman walls with the imposing Cathedral as its centrepiece, it is a warren of narrow streets with squares that shine brightly in the light of thousands of candles every Good Friday with the moving procession of the Holy Burial which is one of the most noteworthy on the Iberian Peninsula. And modern Tarragona which has borne witness to episodes including the siege of Napoleon's troops in 1811 during the Peninsular War, which is commemorated in autumn during Tarragona 1800, an event putting Tarragona's history and culture in the spotlight.

And *modernista* Tarragona, which showcases the city's art nouveau heritage along the Rambla Nova that cuts through the Eixample quarter and includes buildings and unique landmarks that bear the imprint of great architects like Jujol, Domènech i Montaner, Gaudí or Pujol de Barberà, who also left us outstanding examples of their work in other parts of the city. The *modernista* route along the Rambla Nova ends at the spectacu-

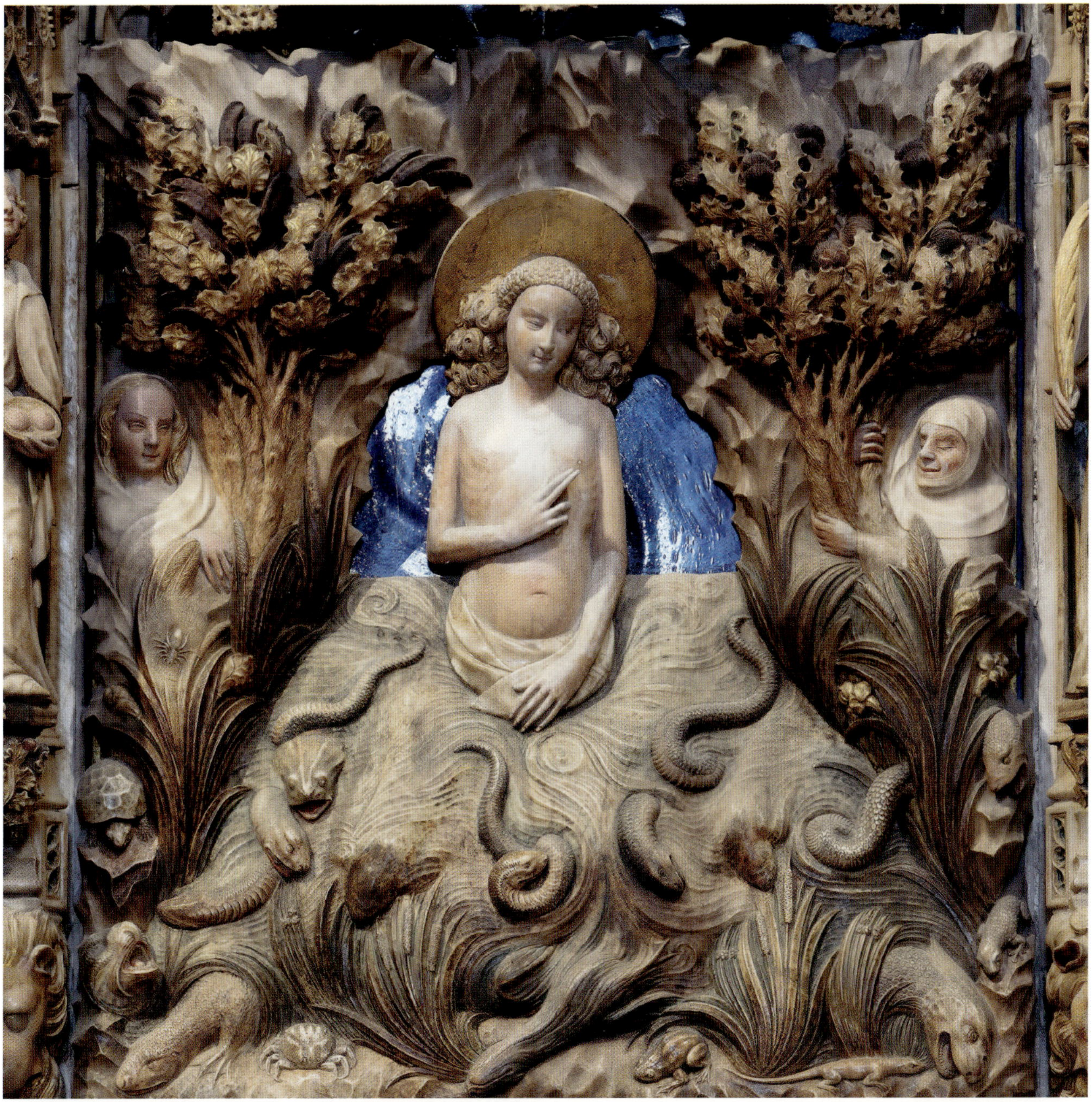

Gothic Tarragona. Cathedral. Detail of the altarpiece of Santa Tecla

lar viewing point, the Balcó del Mediterrani, which juts out over the sea and is the best place to appreciate Tarragona's Mediterranean essence.

A Mediterranean essence that can be seen, smelt, heard, eaten and imbibed every day: right by the sea, in the fishing quarter of El Serrallo, in the working and pleasure harbour, and on the many beaches of fine, golden sand. Or in verdant Tarragona, with its native plant species and farmland which covers 44% of the municipal area and can be discovered bit by bit as you explore the extensive network of more than 100 kilometres of signposted paths.

The celebratory side of Tarragona is also imbued with this essence. Its calendar of events covers the 12 months of the year with the festival held on 23rd September dedicated to its patron saint Santa Tecla as its high point. There are many other red letter days, including *Carnaval*, which is one of the biggest and most crowded in Catalonia, and others, like Sant Magí, in August.

Nearly all the festive calendar is accompanied by one of the most spectacular traditions Catalonia has brought to the world:

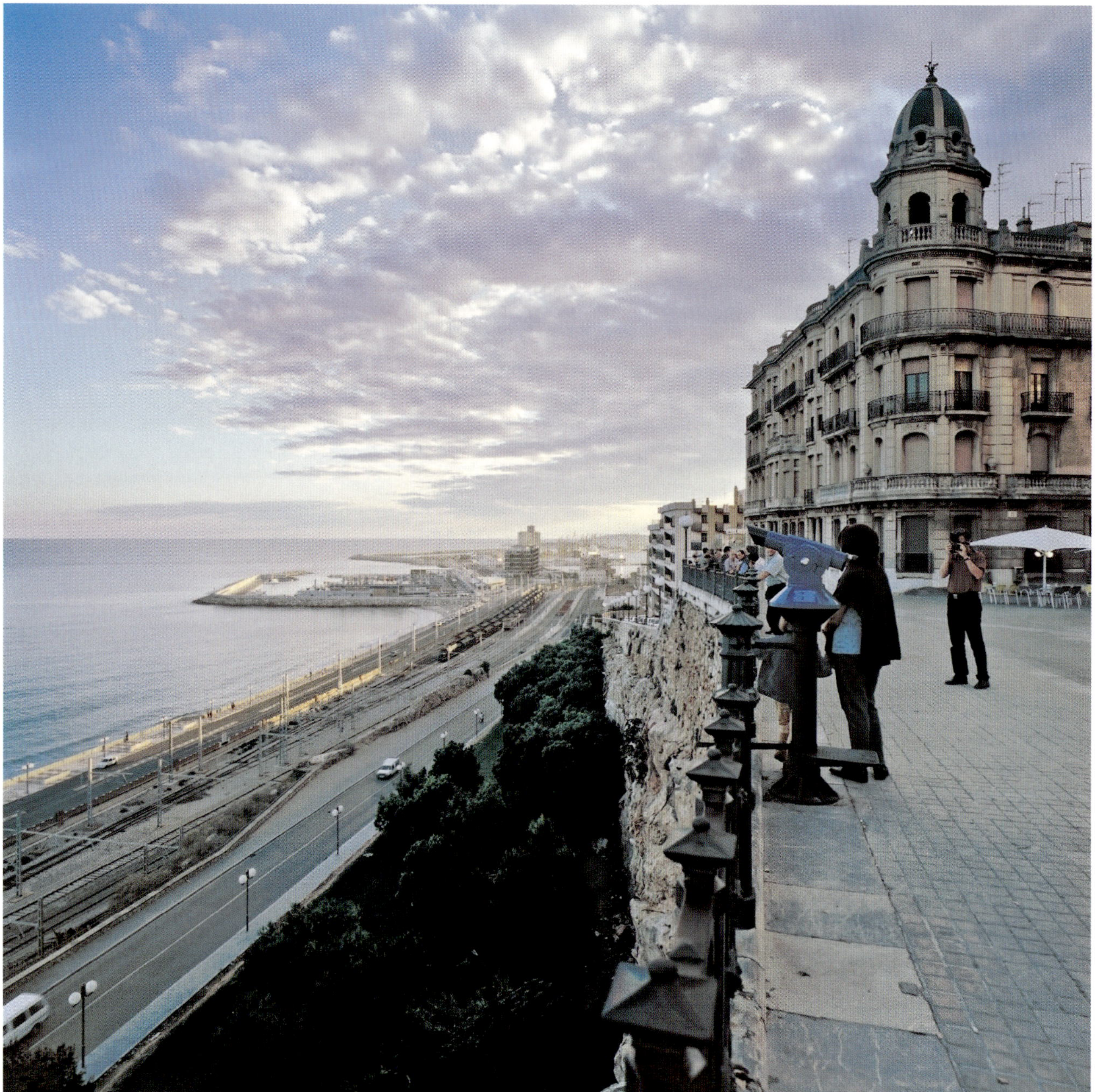

Balcó del Mediterrani

the human towers, or *castells*. Tarragona is known as the *Ciutat de Castells*, meaning that, in addition to hosting the biennial monumental human tower competition, the Concurs de Castells, in October, visitors can take part in workshops run by the human tower groups, or *colles*, and their rehearsals.

Tarragona is steeped in the flavour of Tarragona: of seafood dishes, of prawns and oily fish, of Roman cuisine during the food fair Tàrraco a Taula, of the wines from the DO Tarragona or the other nearby Designations of Origin, of olive oil and popular dishes served up in the El Serrallo quarter, the Part Alta, the Rambla Nova and the Eixample, as well as the downtown area, the Part Baixa, and all the neighbourhoods on the west side of the city, known as the Ponent... You'll also find bars all over town, and in iconic spots like Plaça de la Font, Plaça del Fòrum and Plaça del Rei: pavement cafes built on history.

Not everything is history, but everything is life: retail life, business life, sporting life, congresses, film locations... To experience Tarragona is to experience all these things and much more.

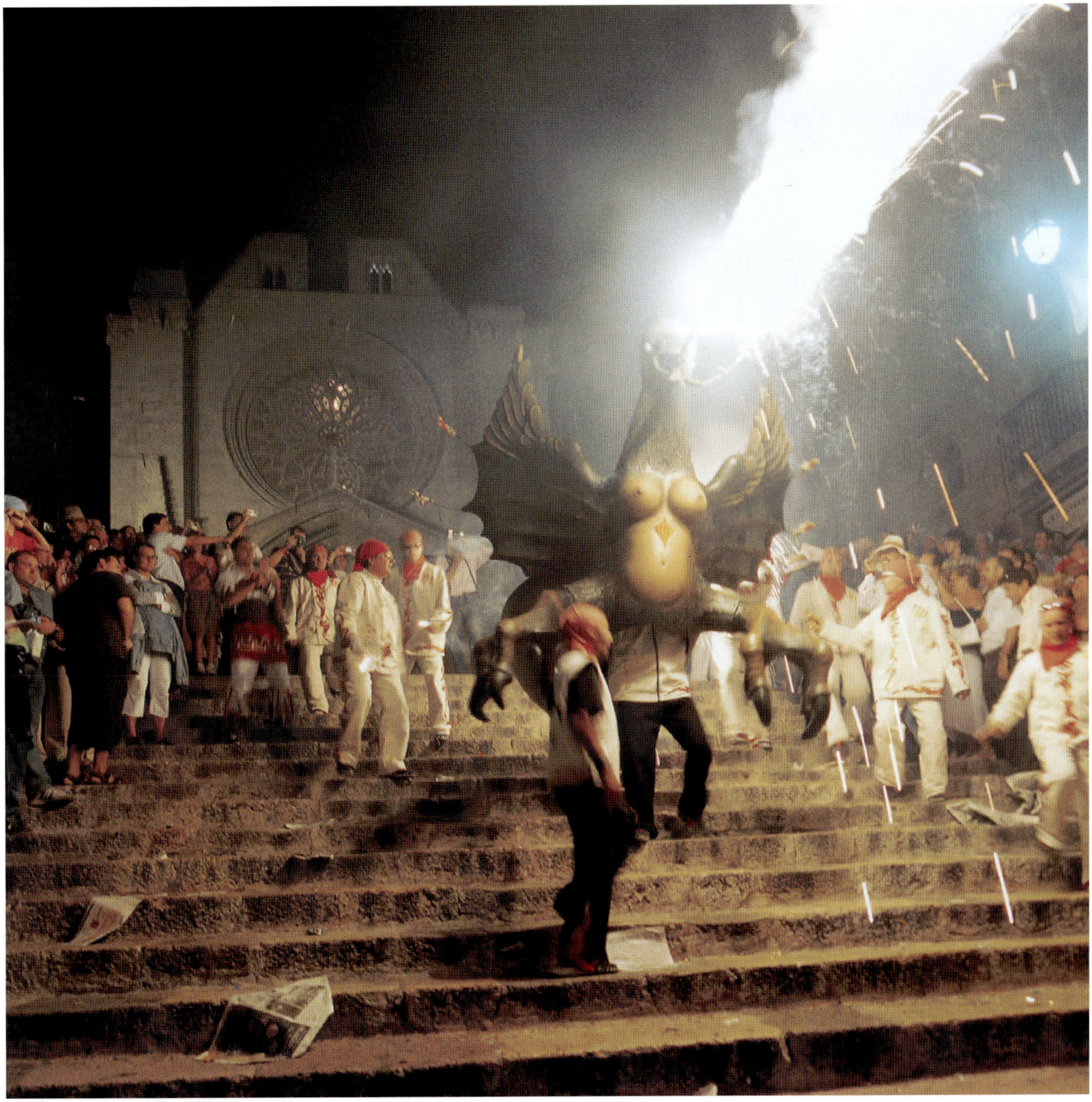

Festivals and traditions. The Wyvern

Roman Tarraco

World Heritage

The lands of the Camp de Tarragona had already been settled in prehistoric times. Proof of this are the archaeological sites such as La Boella, in the municipality of La Canonja, where archaeologists have found traces of flint used in hunting dating back 800,000 to one million years. According to them, the area where they were found provides one of the earliest archives of human evolution in Catalonia and on the Iberian Peninsula.

Not far from here, a rocky hillock close to the river Francolí and its banks, which are ideal for crops, provided a suitable place for human settlements. From the 5th century BC onwards, an Iberian settlement had established itself inside a natural harbour. The settlement was probably known as Kesse and was the main centre of the Kessetan or Cossetan tribe. We don't know if the settlement was partly destroyed or absorbed into the city that was built following the arrival of the Roman troops. The Carthaginian general Hannibal was intending to march on Rome and occupy the city so the troops sought to cut off access and prevent him from getting through. The hillock became the perfect operational base to set up an encampment during the Second Punic War to keep the coast under surveillance and allow the troops to move inland. The general Gnaeus Cornelius Scipio understood the strategic importance of the site and in 218 BC, the settlement the Greeks had named Tarrakon became known as Tarraco.

Tarraco was always one of the most important cities in the Roman Empire from the time it was established as the first permanent military base outside Italy. And it continued in this role during the Cantabrian Wars when it became the home of Emperor Augustus from 26 to 25 BC. For four centuries it was the capital of the largest province in the empire. Today we can still see an extensive collection of Roman inscriptions which is the most complete in existence and gives us an insight into the territorial structure of the empire, with functionaries from Britannia — present-day Great Britain — , Gaul — now the territory comprising France and Belgium — and Pannonia, a province comprising parts of present-day Austria, Hungary, Serbia and Croatia... as well as Egypt, Syria and other places in the Romanised world.

The wealth of the Roman remains in Tarraco is practically unique. These include the walls, which are the oldest and longest Roman monument outside Italy, the Provincial Forum, the largest plaza in the ancient world, and the Circus, part of which has survived in a good state of repair... but the most important thing about the remains of ancient Tarraco is the fact that they symbolise the civic values of a community of cultures and peoples that the Roman Empire went on to become.

Roman route I

→ Appendix p. 1

Roman route II

→ Appendix p. 2

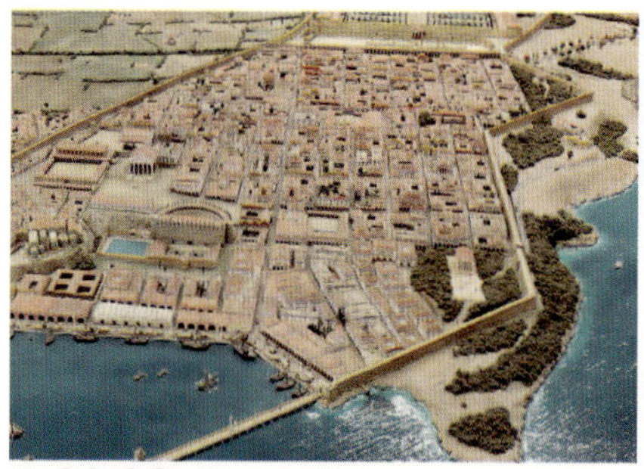

Model of the Roman city

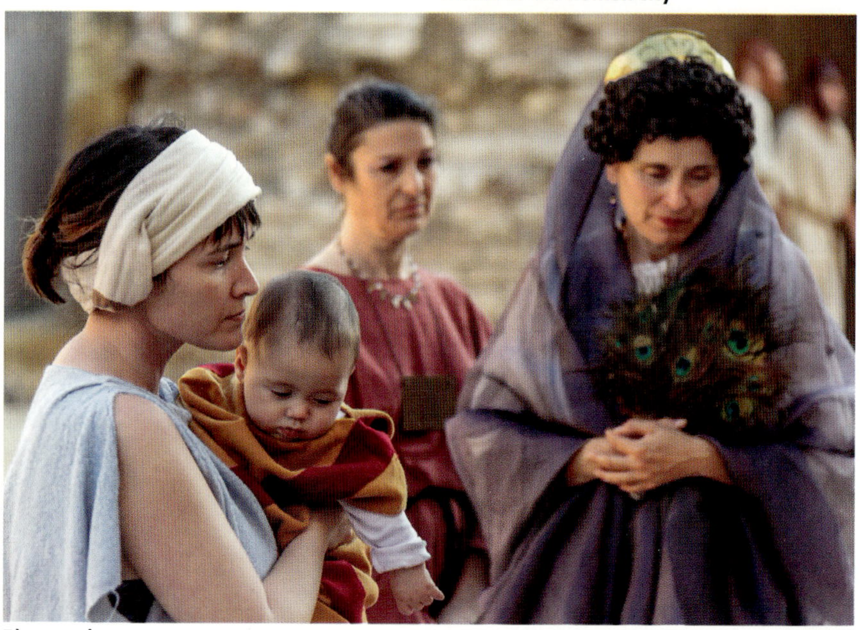

Tàrraco Viva

Emperor Augustus on the Passeig Arqueològic →

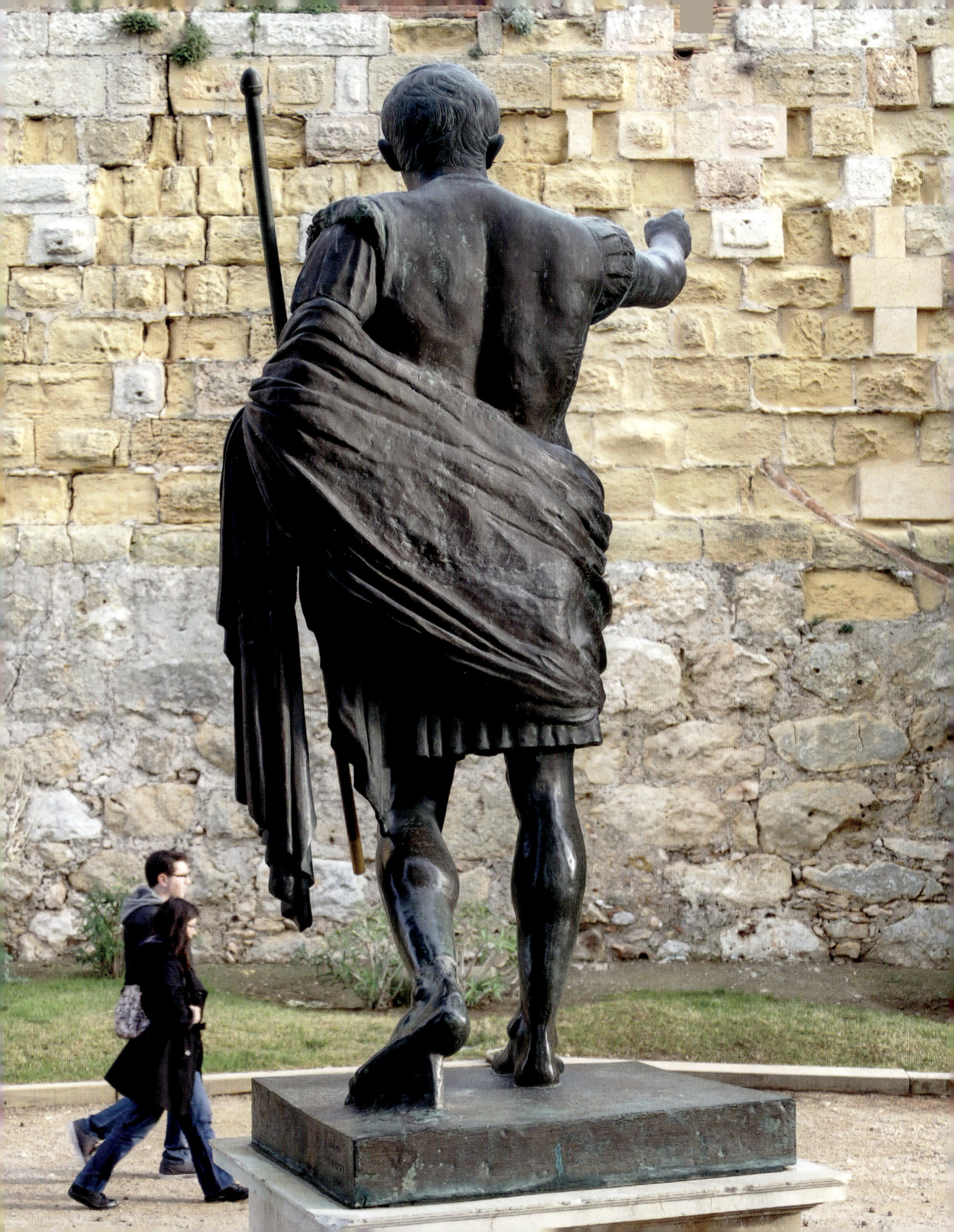

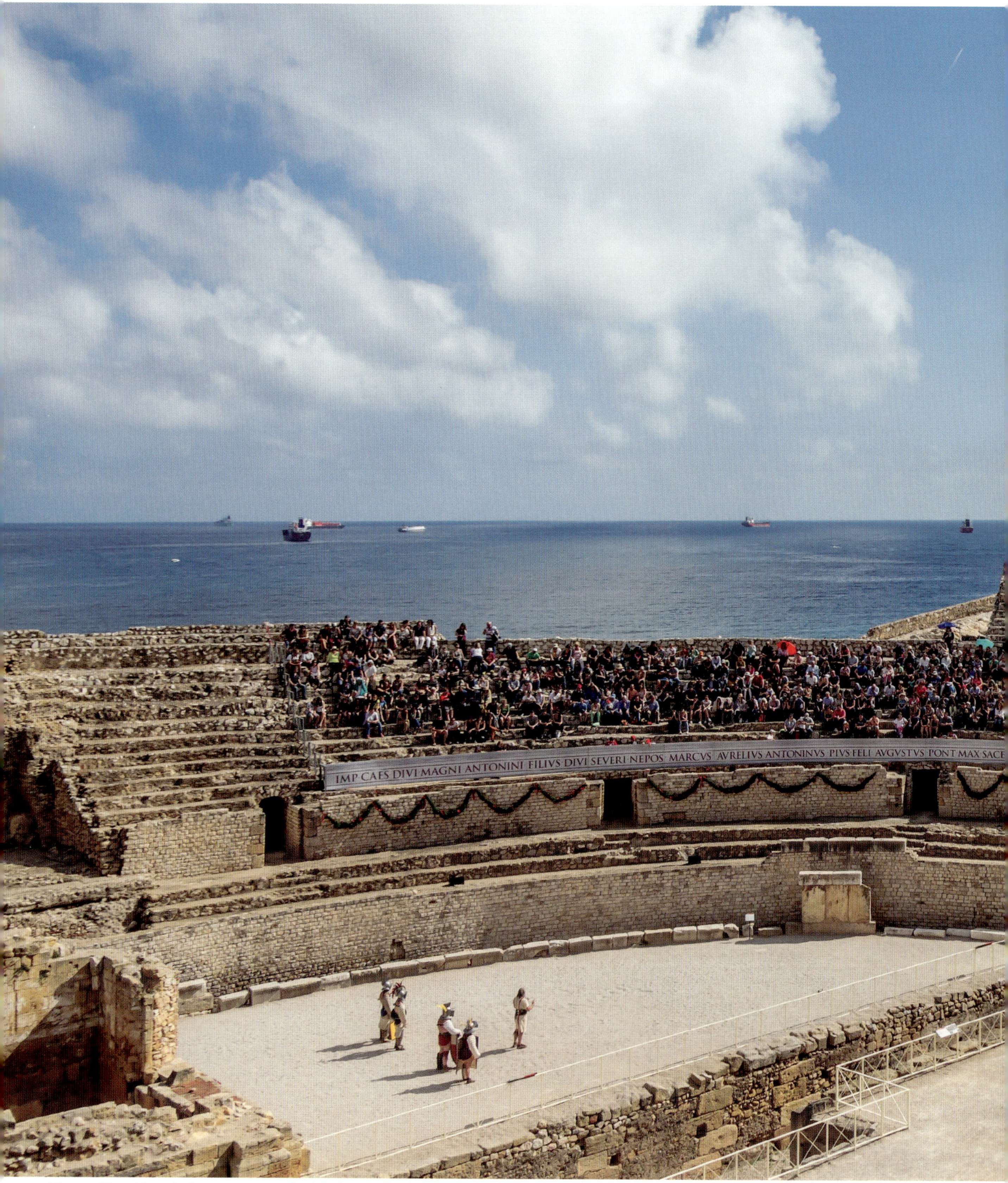

Tàrraco Viva. Historical re-enactment inside the Amphitheatre

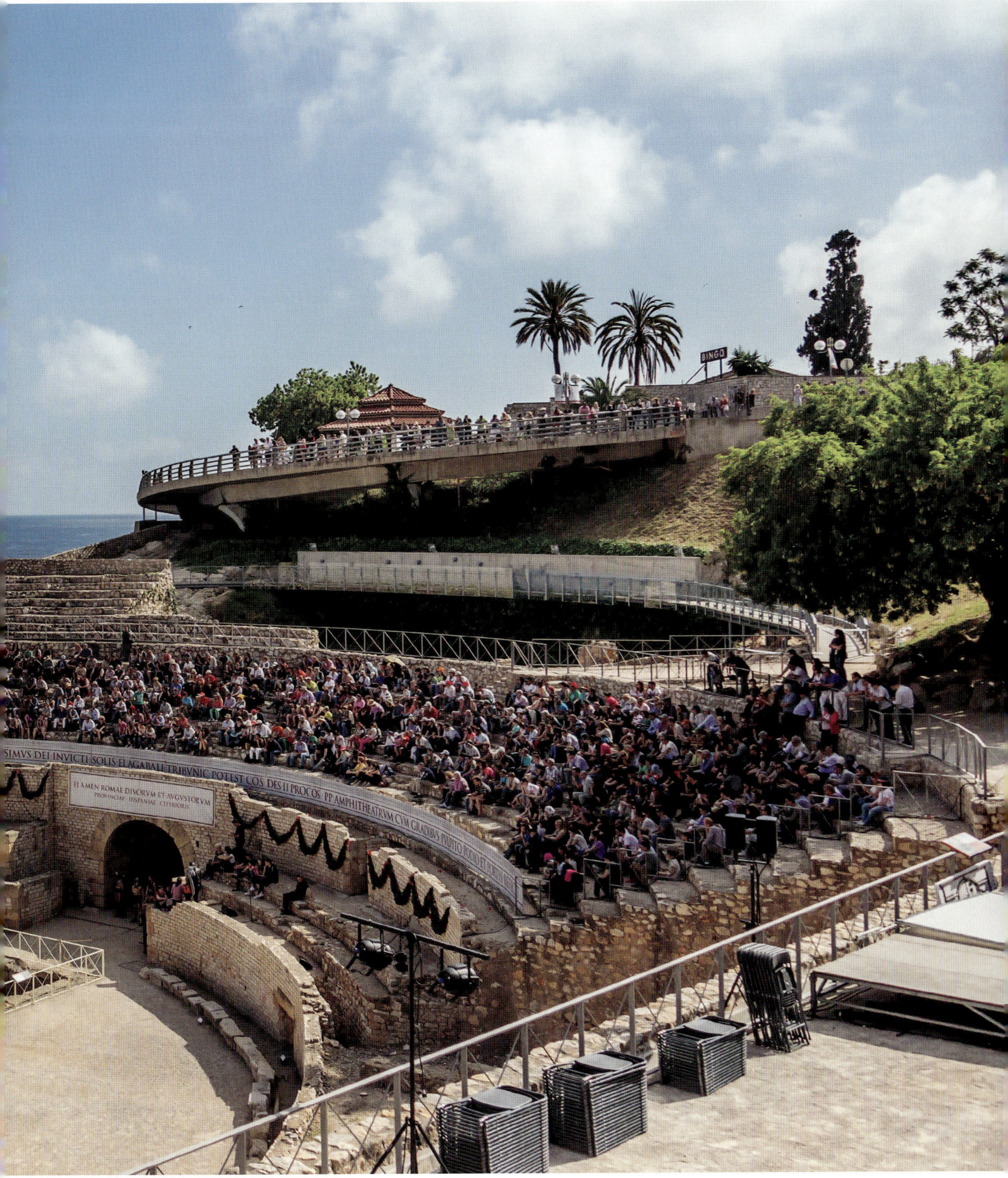
BINGO
SIMVS DEI INVICTI SOLIS ELAGABALI TRIBVNIC POTEST COS DES II PROCOS PP AMPHITHEATRVM CVM GRADIBVS
FLAMEN ROMAE DIVORVM ET AVGVSTORVM
PROVINCIAE HISPANIAE CITERIORIS

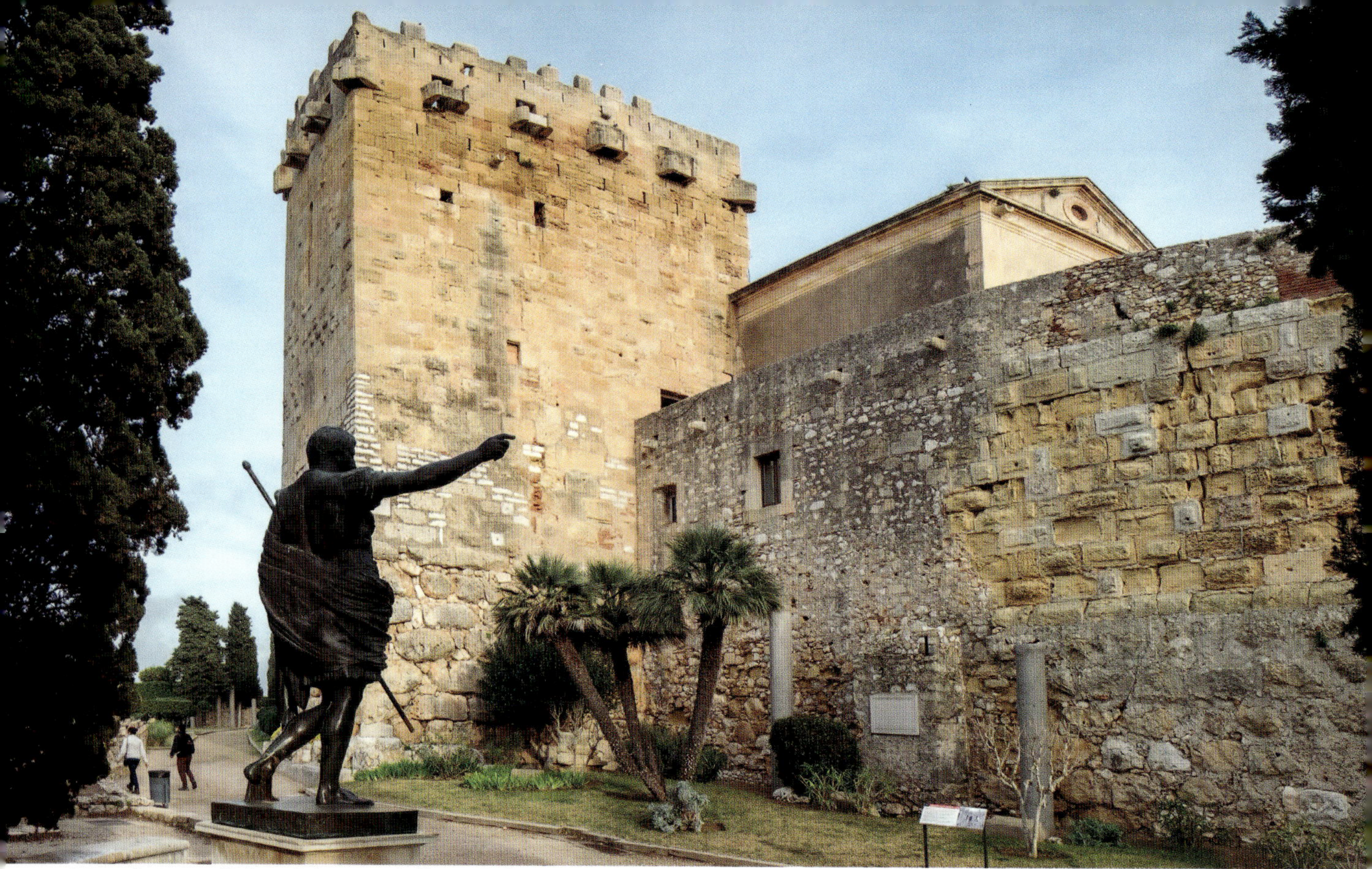

↑ Passeig Arqueològic and the Torre de l'Arquebisbe ↓ Torre de Minerva

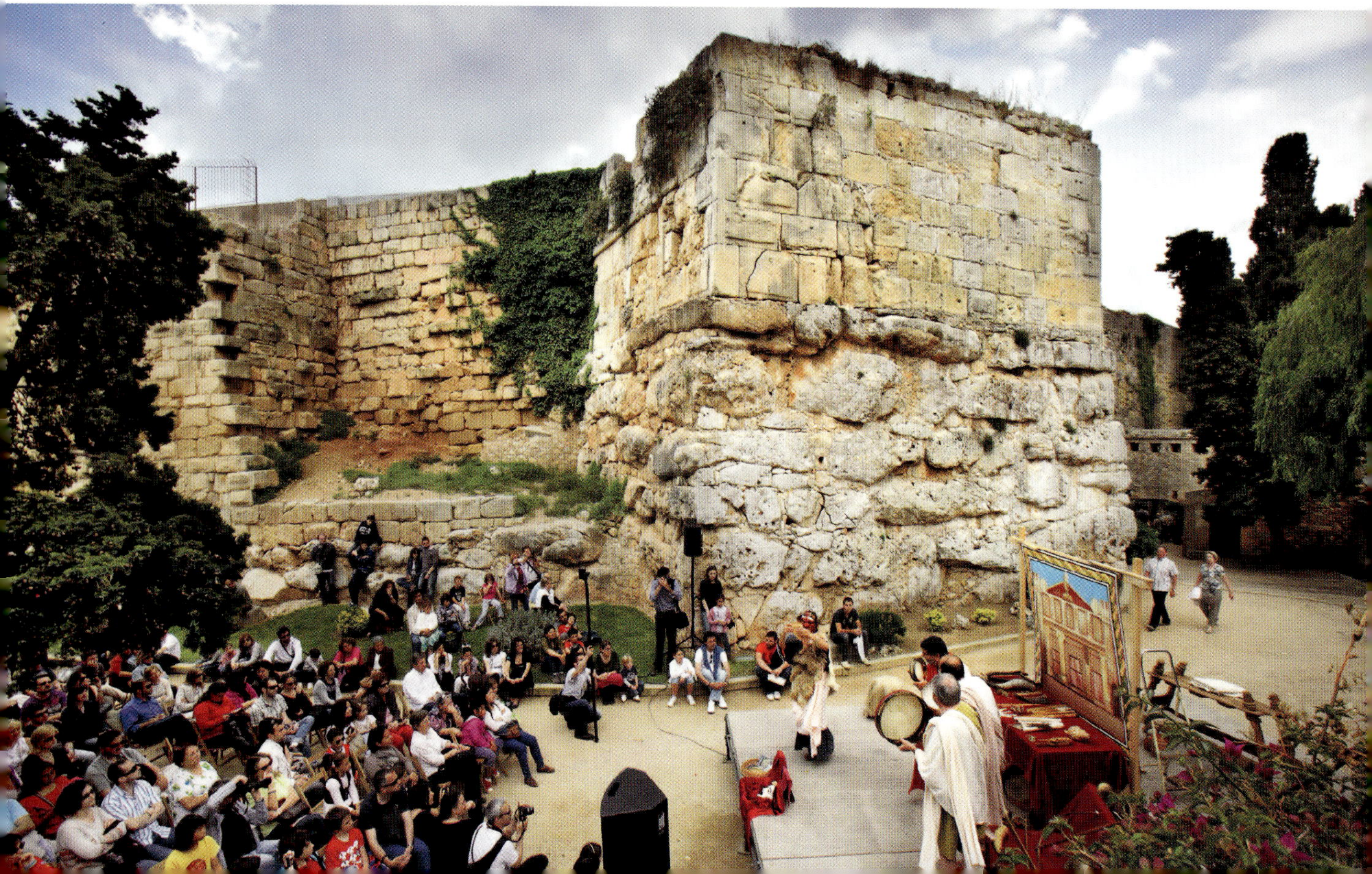

Roman walls

The Roman city walls, which once stretched as far as the port, have always been the city's most iconic landmark. The wide, walled precinct, which covered an area of some 40 hectares, was reduced during the Middle Ages. The magnificent section that survives today shows the walls were built in two phases: the first, measuring 4.5 metres wide and 6 metres high with rectangular towers, and the second, thought to date from 150 to 125 BC, 5 metres wide and 12 metres high. The megalithic base is also Roman.

Passeig Arqueològic

Winding between the Roman walls and the bulwark built by the British and Austrians during the War of the Spanish Succession (1705-1714), the Passeig Arqueològic, or Archaeological Walk, leads us past three Roman towers: the Archbishop's Tower, the Torre de l'Arquebisbe, the Cantor's Tower, the Torre del Cabiscol, the Seminary Tower, the Torre del Seminari, and Minerva's Tower, the Torre de Minerva, also known as the Torre de Sant Magí. At the top of the latter you can see a fragment of a bas-relief of Minerva, in which we can make out her feet, tunic and an escutcheon bearing a wolf's head. The tower contains the most ancient Latin inscription on the Peninsula, carved with a dagger by the centurion Manius Vibius, and dedicated to the goddess.

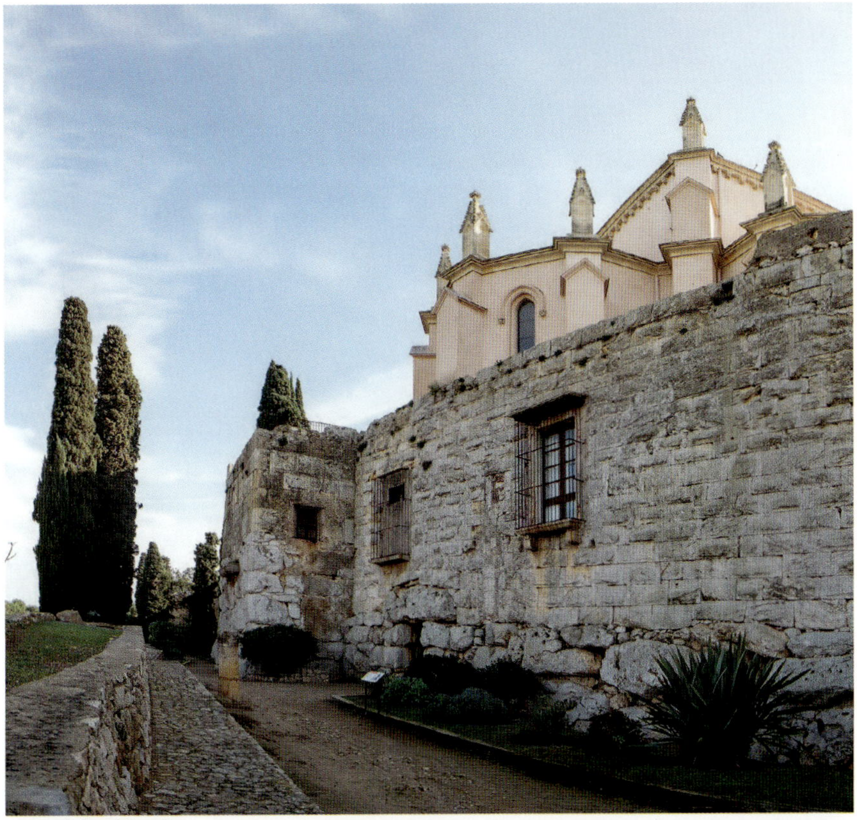

Torre del Cabiscol

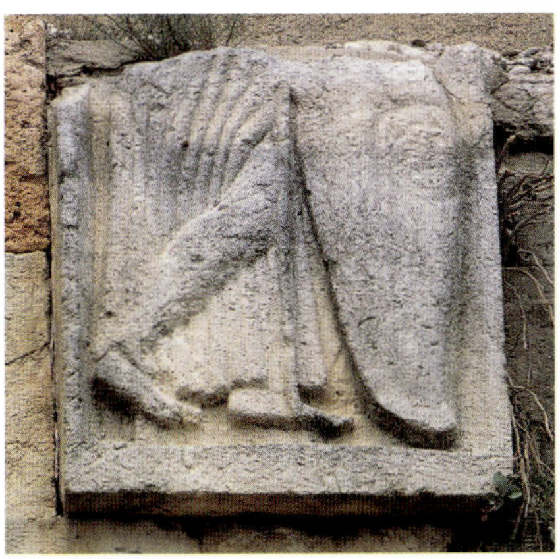

Relief of Minerva

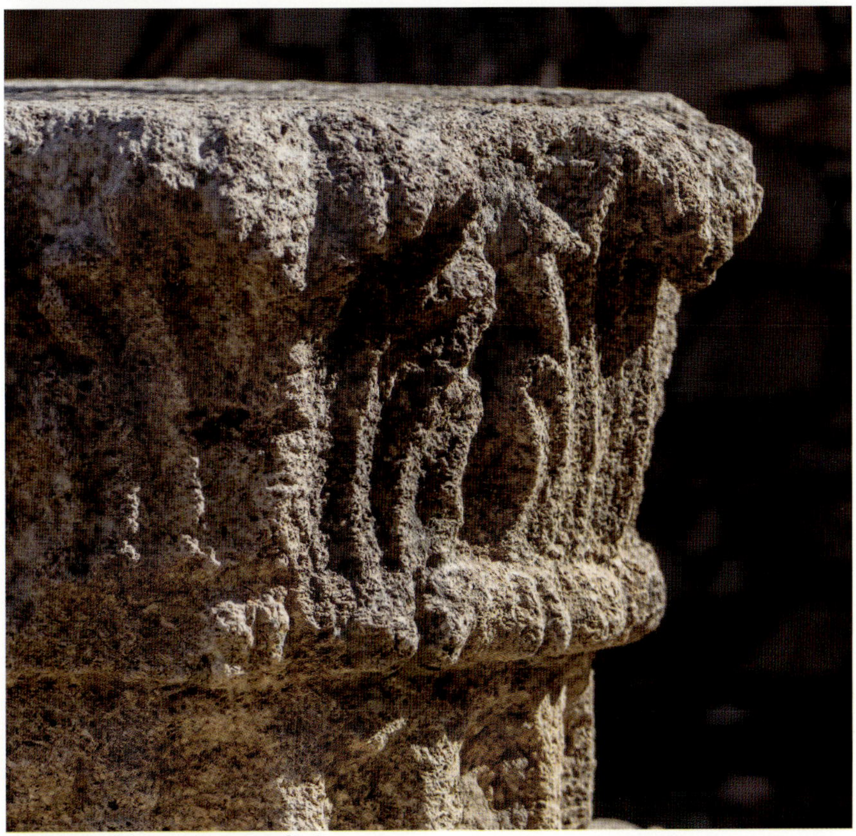

Capital on the Passeig Arqueològic

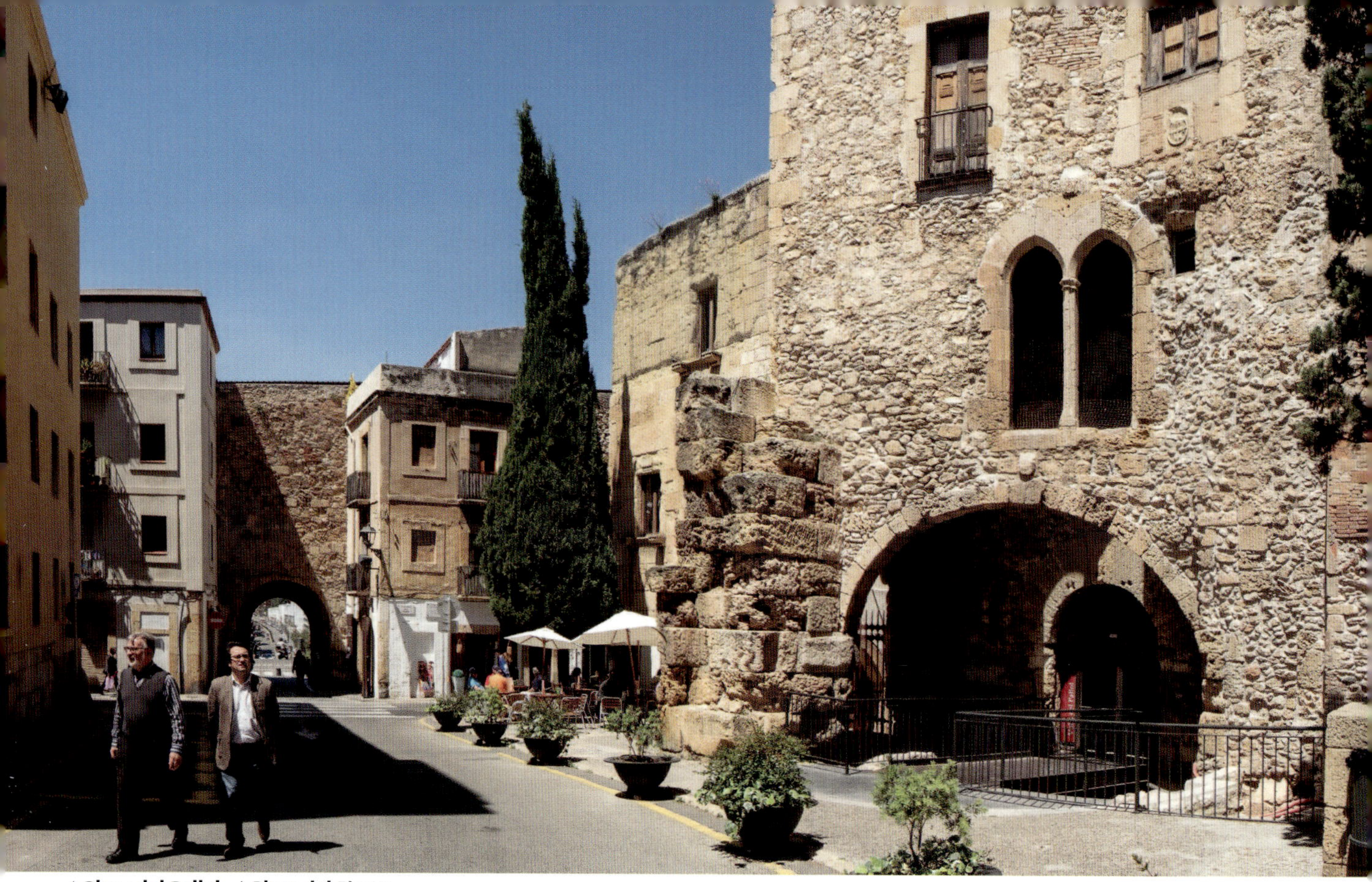

↑ Plaça del Pallol ↓ Plaça del Fòrum

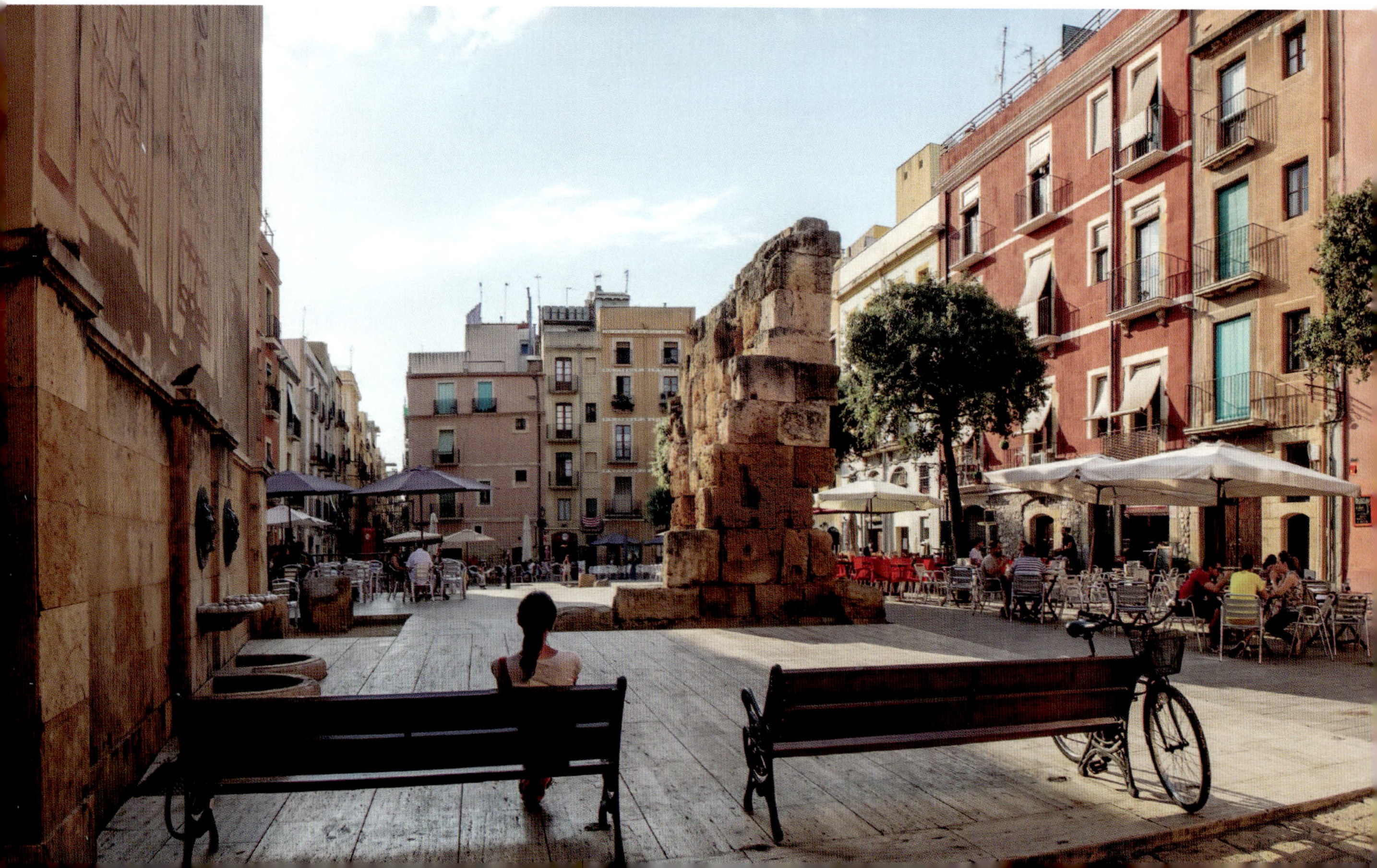

Provincial Forum
Plaça del Pallol

The Provincial Forum was the administrative centre of the province of Hispania Citerior, later known as Tarraconense. The complex was set out on three terraces: at the top, the Temple of Augustus surrounded by the place of worship with its porticoes; in the middle, the administrative building; and at the bottom, the Circus. The plaza itself is usually referred to as the Provincial Forum and is the largest in the Roman world. Measuring 320 metres by 175, it was originally reached by two towers. One of them, the Torre de l'Antiga Audiència, stands in the Plaça de Pallol. It still has the original staircase and monumental doorway inside, both of which survive almost intact. There is also a vault, an archway and a large wall in the square.

Plaça del Fòrum

It retains the foundations and a section of the wall that enclosed the administrative building. Here you can "read" what the great plaza was like in the paving slabs: the lighter strips match the site of the walls and porticoes, and the darker area the part with no buildings. A market is held here on Wednesday and Saturday.

Plaça del Rei - Praetorium
Museu d'Història de Tarragona

The Praetorium was the other tower leading into the administrative building. You can explore the covered passageways, the Roman galleries built on top, and see the sarcophagus of Hippolytus (3rd century) and the statue known as Tecleta (1st-2nd centuries).

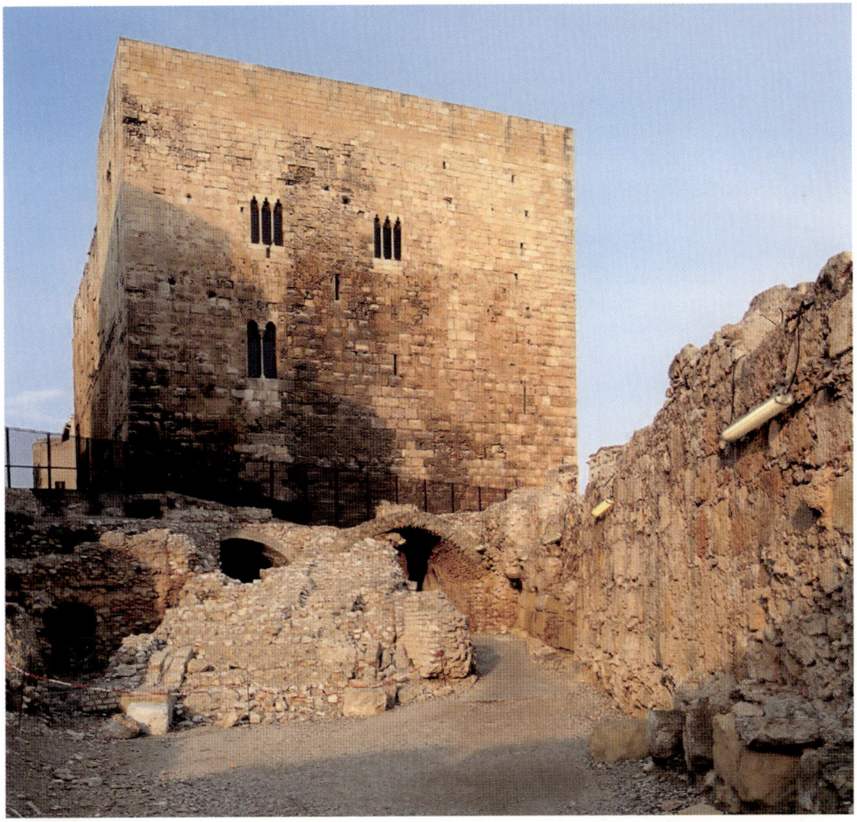

Praetorium

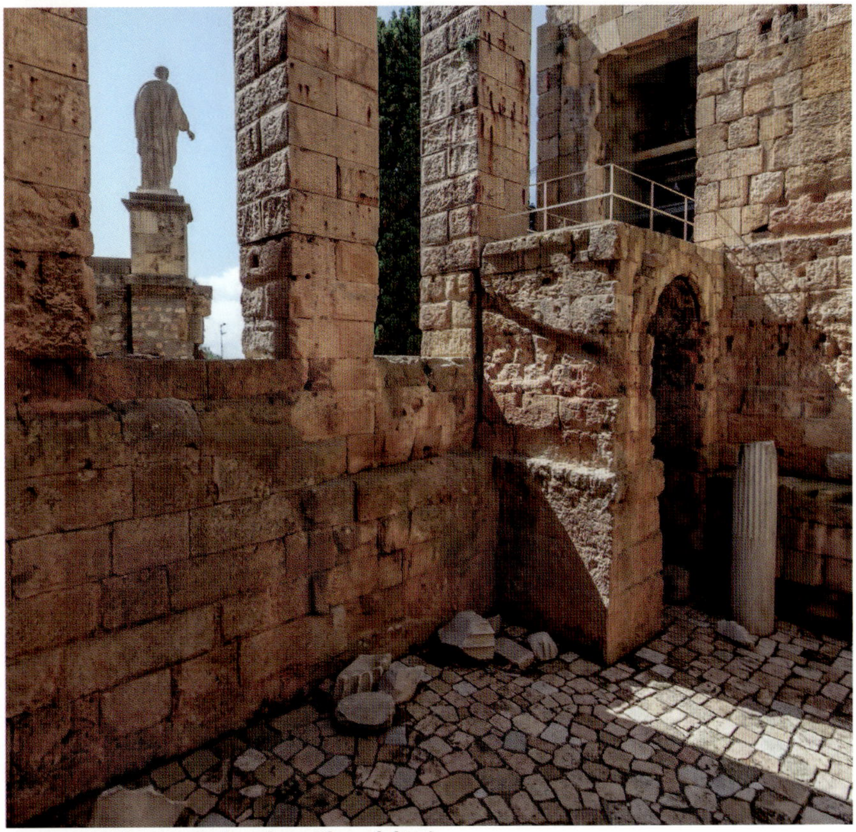

Entrance to the Praetorium from Plaça del Rei

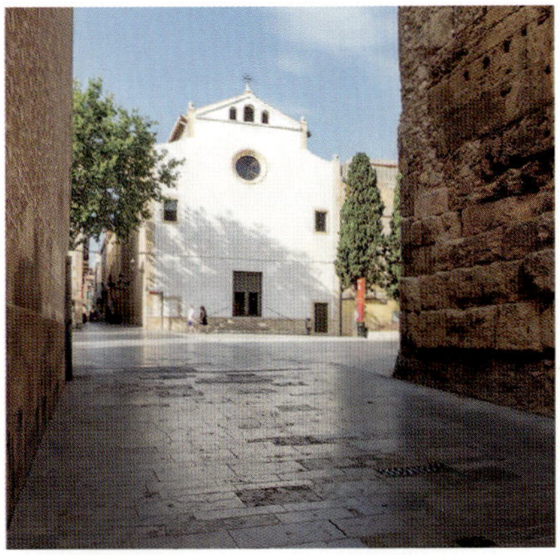

Church of the Santíssima Trinitat, in Plaça del Rei

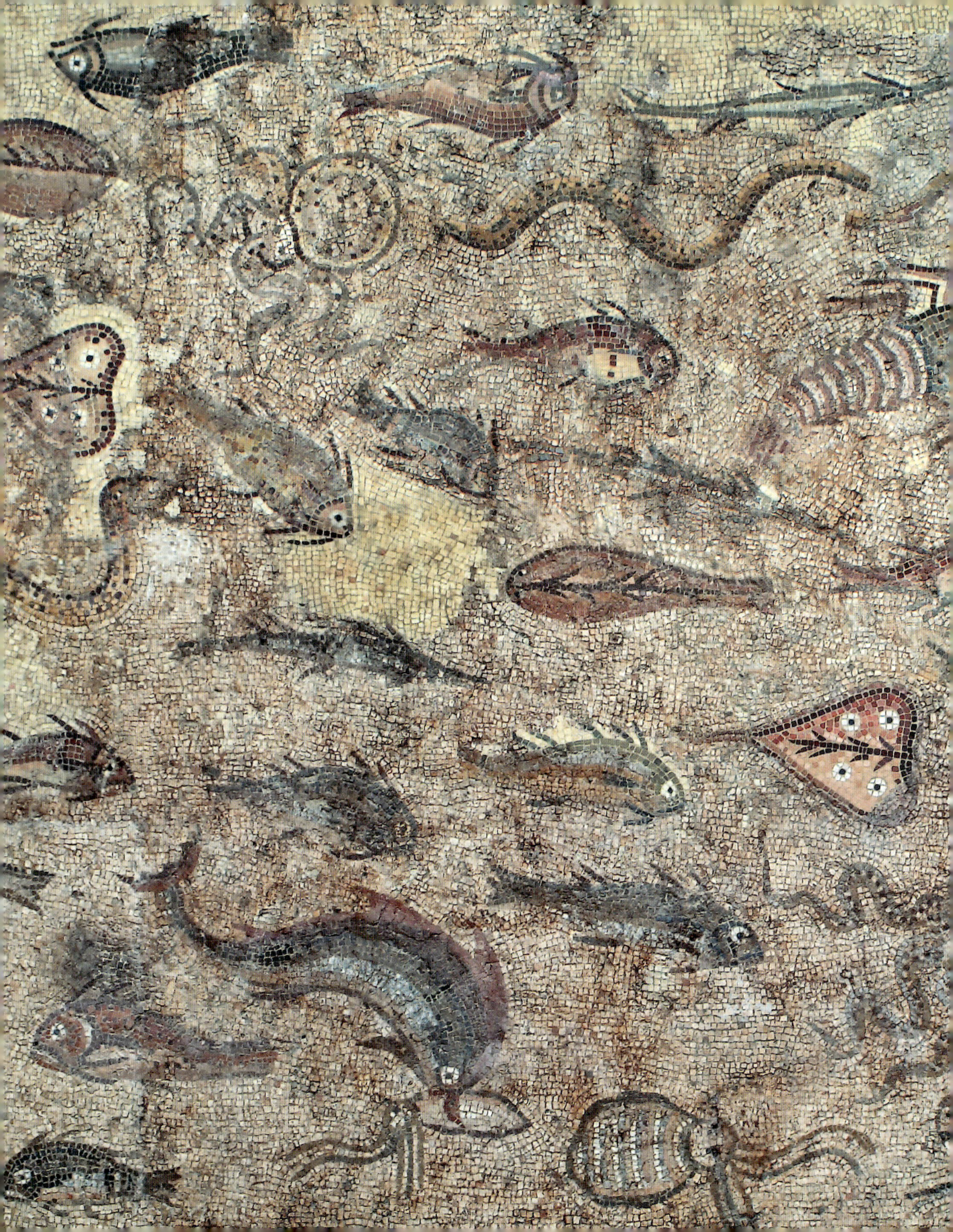

Museu Nacional Arqueològic de Tarragona (MNAT)

Founded in the middle of the 19th century, the MNAT is the oldest archaeological museum in Catalonia. It moved to its current location in 1960. The MNAT is in charge of the Necropolis, the Roman Theatre, the Torre dels Escipions, or Tower of the Scipions, the triumphal archway, the Arc de Berà, and the Roman villas of Centcelles and Els Munts. Highlights include the finest collection of mosaics in Catalonia, including the impressive Medusa and the panel depicting fish and sea creatures; the famous bronze lamp holder in the form of a young slave known as *El Negret*, or Little Black Boy; the six colossal toga-clad figures from the Theatre; the fragment of a marble krater, or mixing vessel, depicting the god Bacchus; paintings, sculptures and mosaics from the villa of Dels Munts, and the collection of plinths and funeral epitaphs.

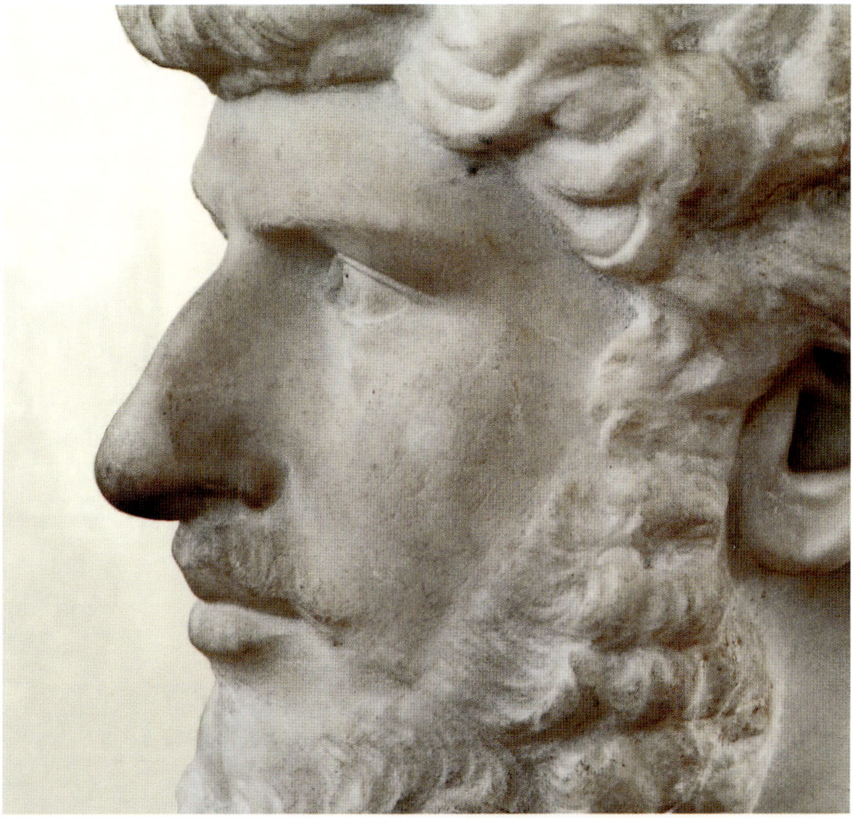

Sculpture of the Emperor Lucius Verus MNAT

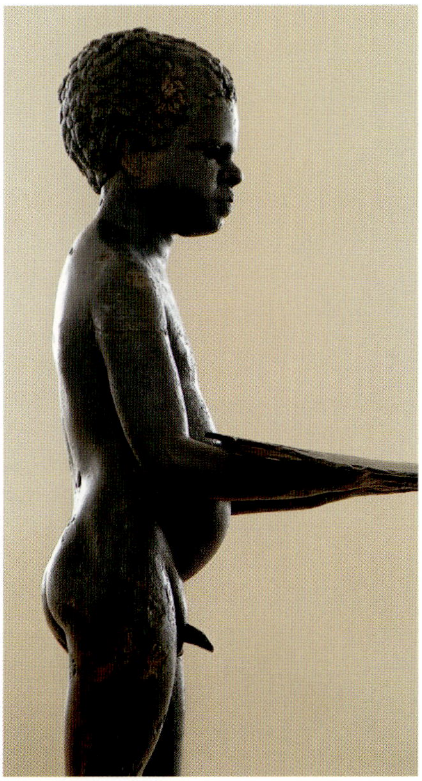

El Negret

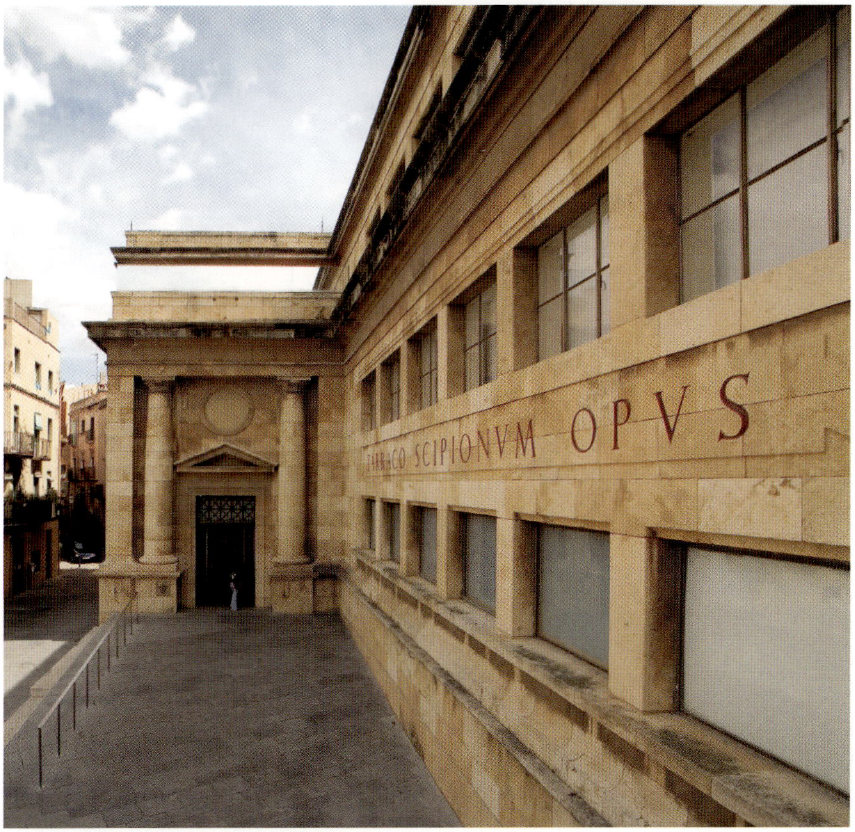

Façade of the MNAT, in Plaça del Rei

← **The fish mosaic**

The Circus

The Circus could accommodate between 25,000 people and was the largest entertainment venue in Tarraco. It is the only surviving example of this type of building in Catalonia. The Circus hosted spectacular races by bigas and quadrigas (two- and four-horse chariots). You can visit the head gate which is part of the Museu d'Història. Archways and vaults have been preserved in different areas of the Part Alta, such as Plaça dels Sedassos, Carrer Ferrers and Carrer Enrajolat (which has an interesting viewing platform overlooking the remains).

The Circus was built during the reign of Emperor Domitian, between 81 and 96 AD. It covered a vast surface area of 325 metres by 115 metres. It formed the lower terrace of the monumental city and consisted of an imposing façade of 57 semi-circular arches that could be seen as you entered the city along the Via Augusta, now the Rambla Vella.

We know the names of some of the charioteers from the surviving funeral inscriptions, including the one dedicated to Eutyches, which is of great poetic beauty and kept at the Museu Diocesà de Tarragona, or the one dedicated to Fuscus, at a private property in Great Britain. In the 12th century, the Circus became an enclosure outside the walled city and the south-facing façade became the inner wall of the new 14th-century city wall.

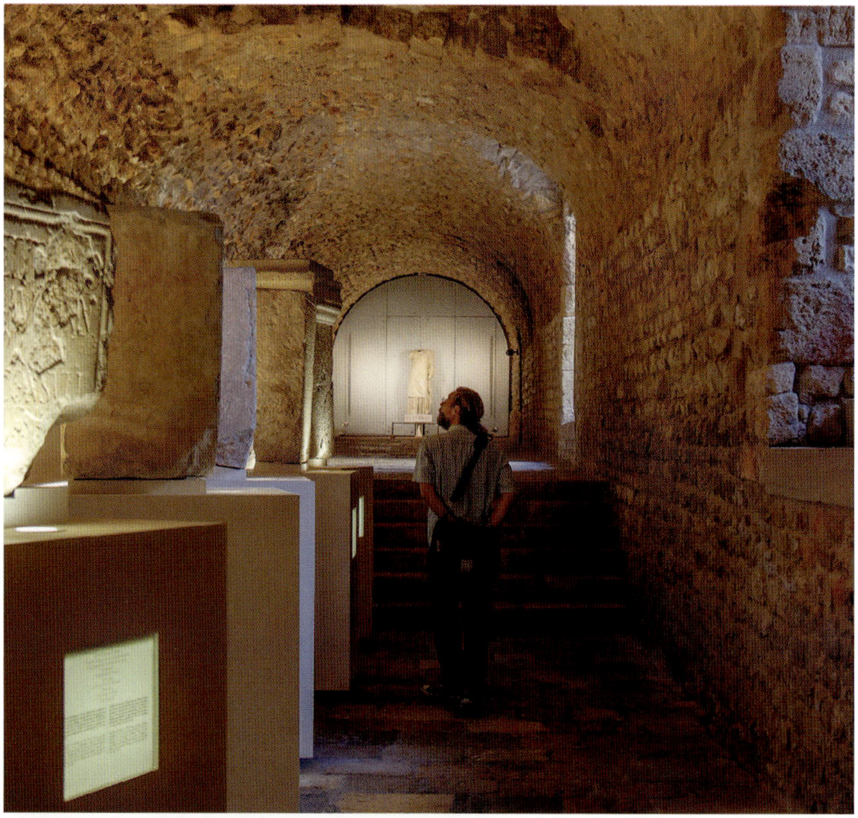

Cryptoporticus of the Praetorium: "Volta de la Tecleta"

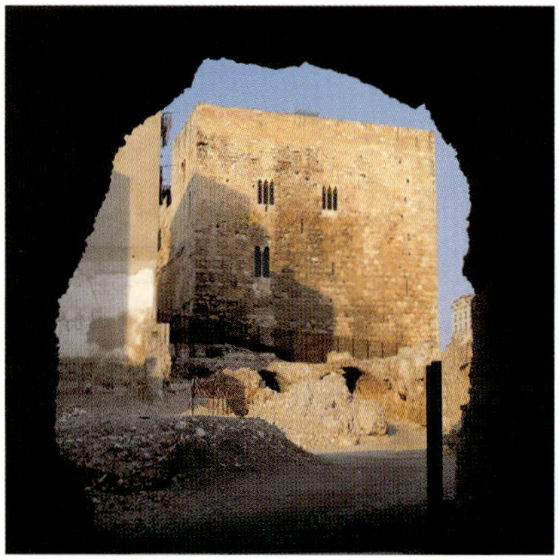

The Praetorium from the head of the Circus

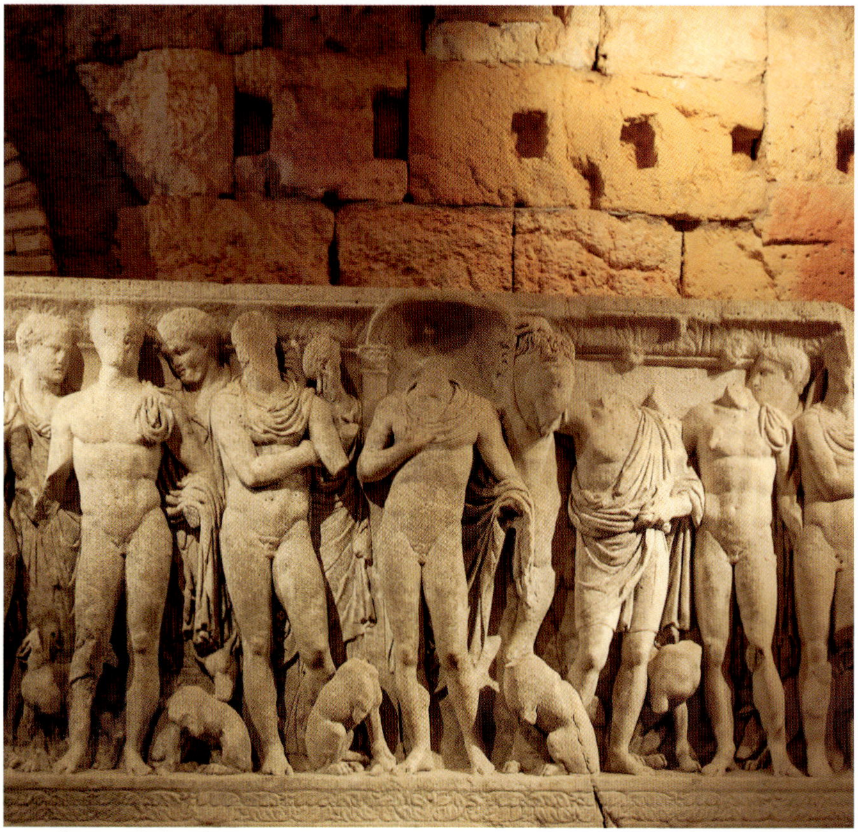

Sarcophagus of Hippolyta

Head of the Circus →

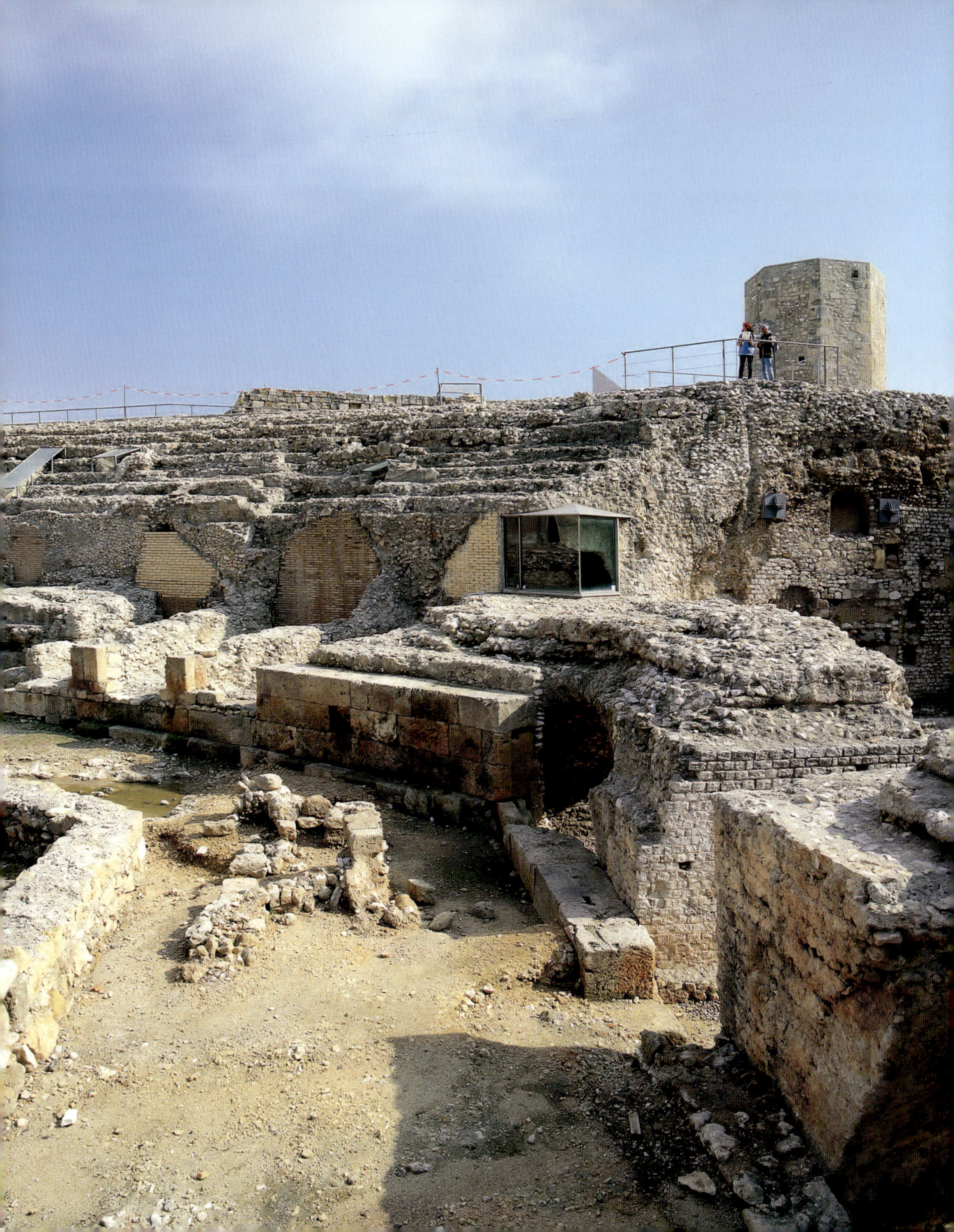

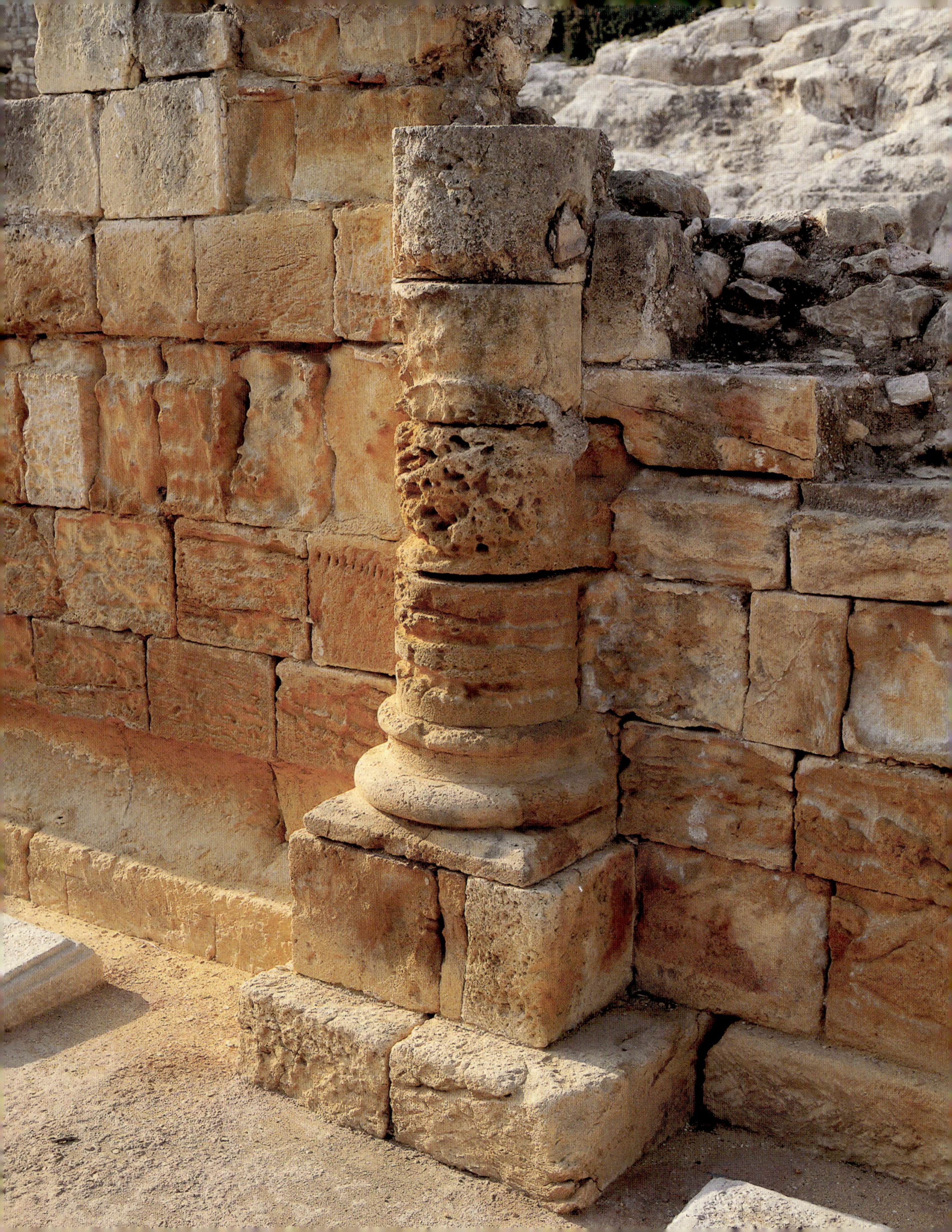

Amphitheatre

The Amphitheatre plays host to gladiator fights — recreated by historical re-enactment groups — on a number of occasions throughout the year as part of the Tàrraco Viva and Tarragona Història Viva festivals. It was built for this purpose in the early 2nd century AD, and refurbished under Emperor Heliogabalus, in 221 AD. This is borne out by an inscription — the longest in the Roman world — that encompassed the entire arena. The arena measured 60 by 40 metres, and included a series of underground pits, the *fossae*, which housed the lifts used to bring the gladiators and wild animals up to the Amphitheatre floor. Inside there was also a little chapel dedicated to the goddess Nemesis, the protector of gladiators.

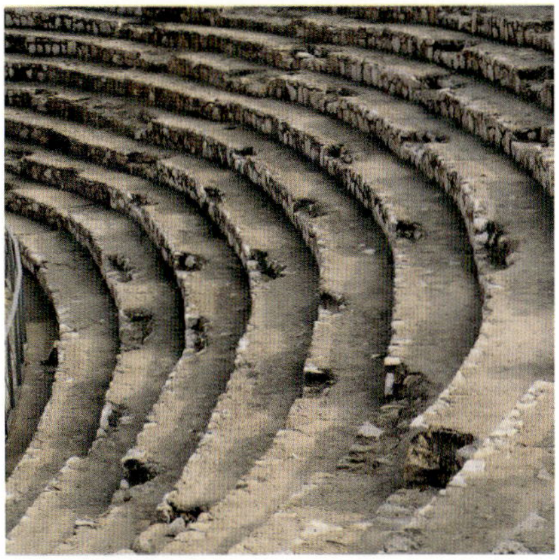

Terrace or *cavea*

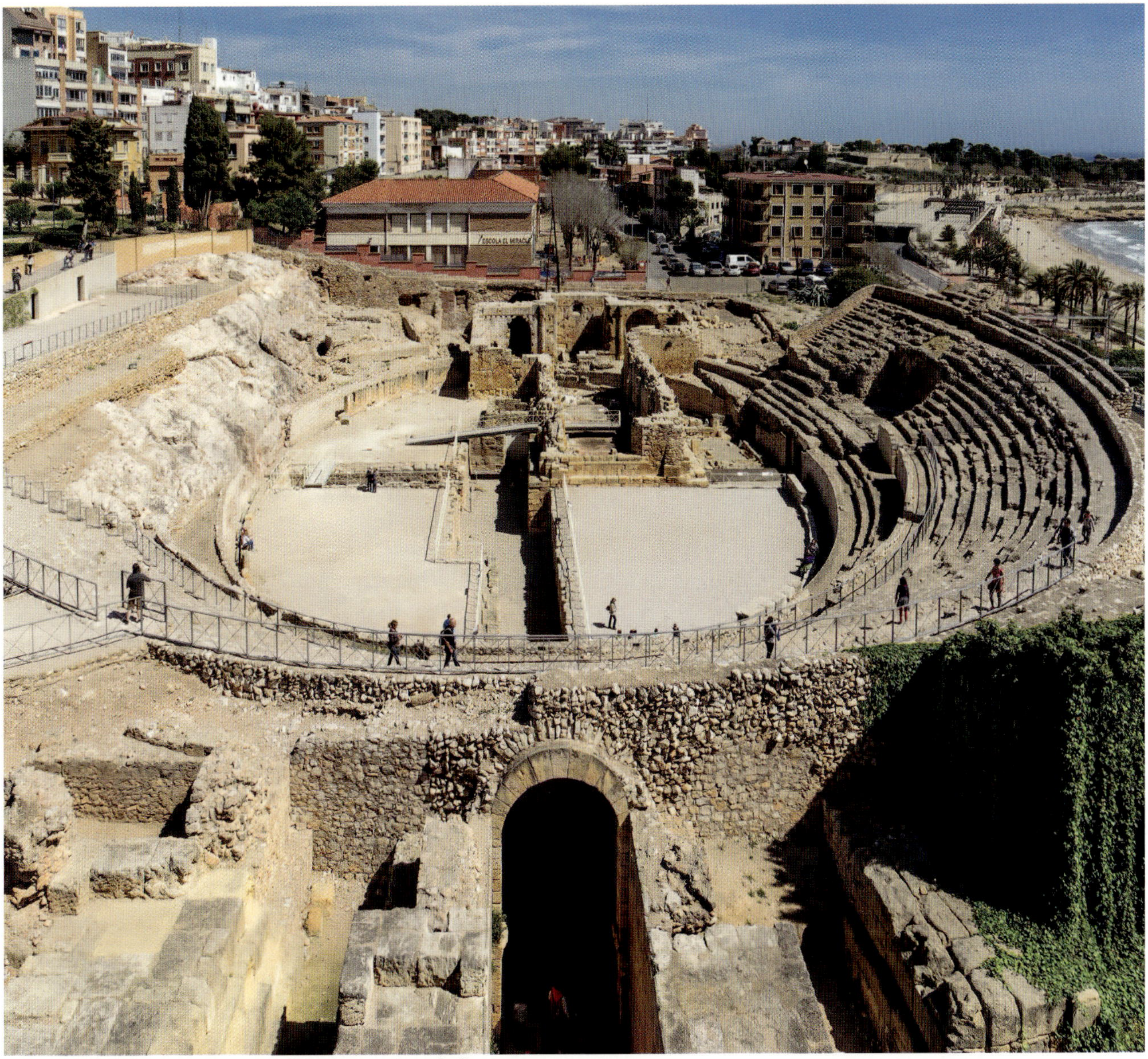

The Amphitheatre from the side of the Porta Triumphalis

← Column from the Romanesque church inside the arena

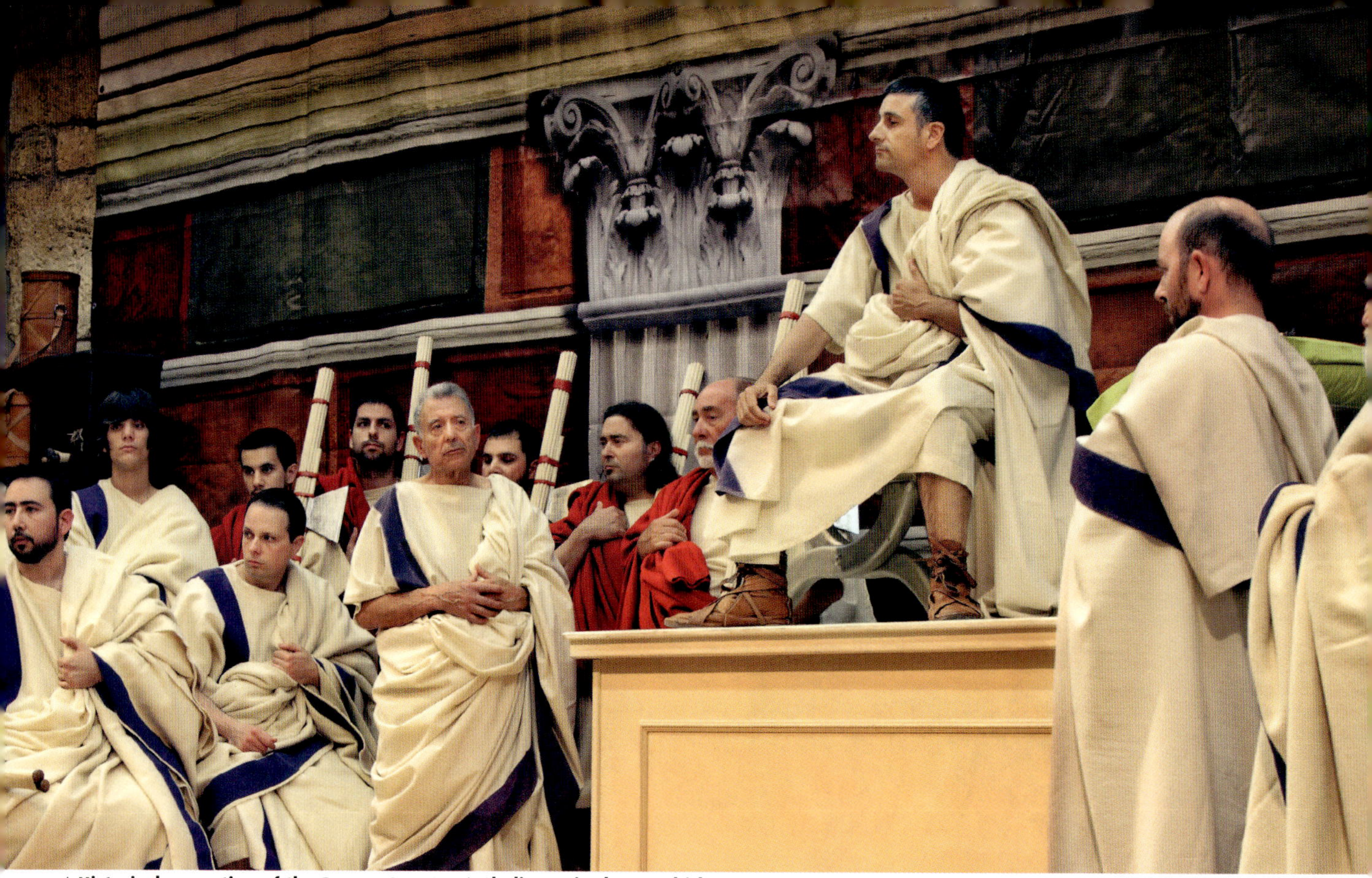

↑ Historical recreation of the Roman Senate ↓ Gladiators in the Amphitheatre

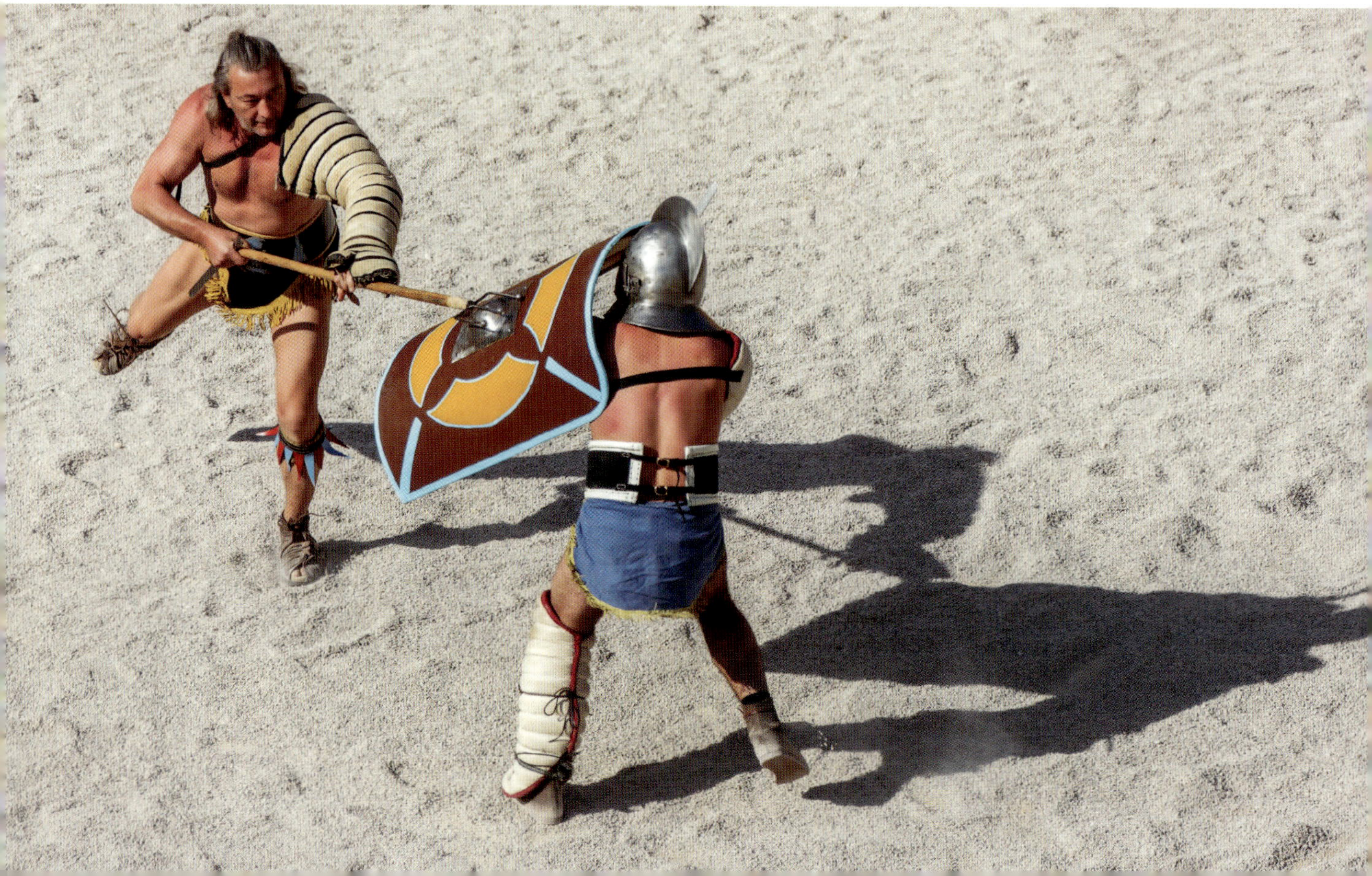

Tàrraco Viva and Tarragona Història Viva

Every May, Tarragona hosts Tàrraco Viva, Europe's leading festival celebrating Roman history. The whole city travels back in time to the period when it was at the pinnacle of its splendour. For a fortnight, locals and visitors can explore the city's Roman past and feel as if they are living in the Roman colony of Tarraco, on rigorous history tours and re-enactments of activities characteristic of Roman civilisation: theatre, politics, gladiatorial battles... against the breathtaking backdrop of the monumental UNESCO World Heritage Sites.

During Tàrraco Viva you can find out how children played during Roman times, explore myths and legends, laugh at popular plays, listen to music or see dance performances, discover the legionnaires' tactics.

In summer it's time for Tarragona Història Viva, which aims to bring the city's Roman history to a wider audience, as a living experience, through large-scale models reconstructing the history of the Roman colony.

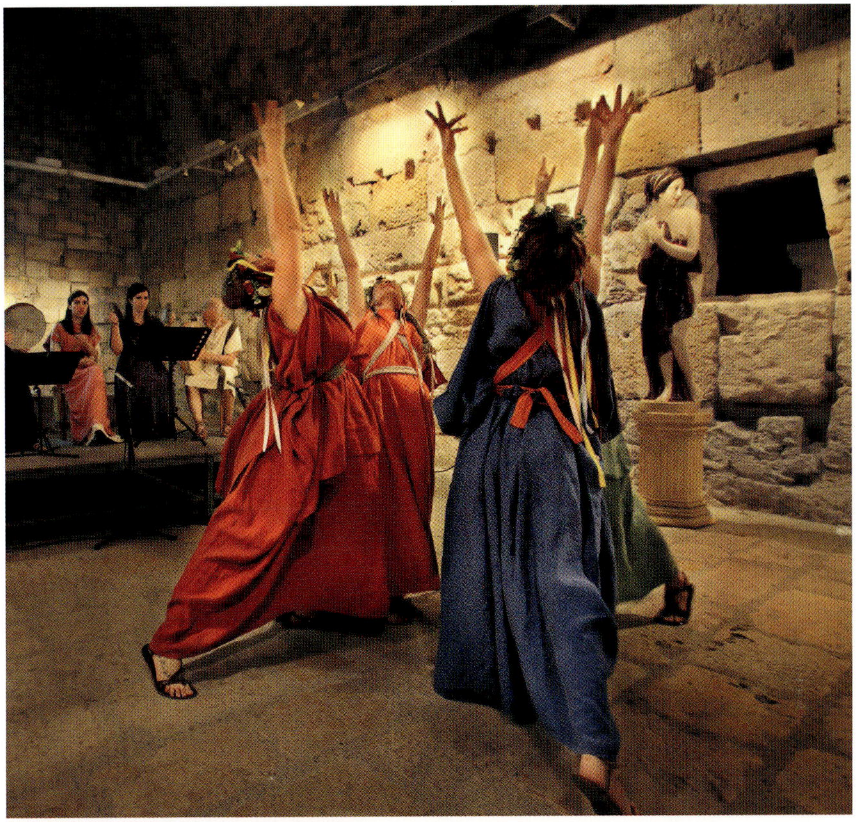

"Carmina canere", the music of Rome

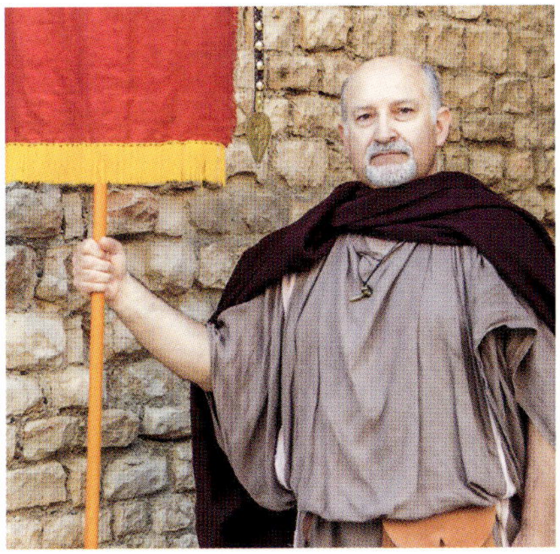

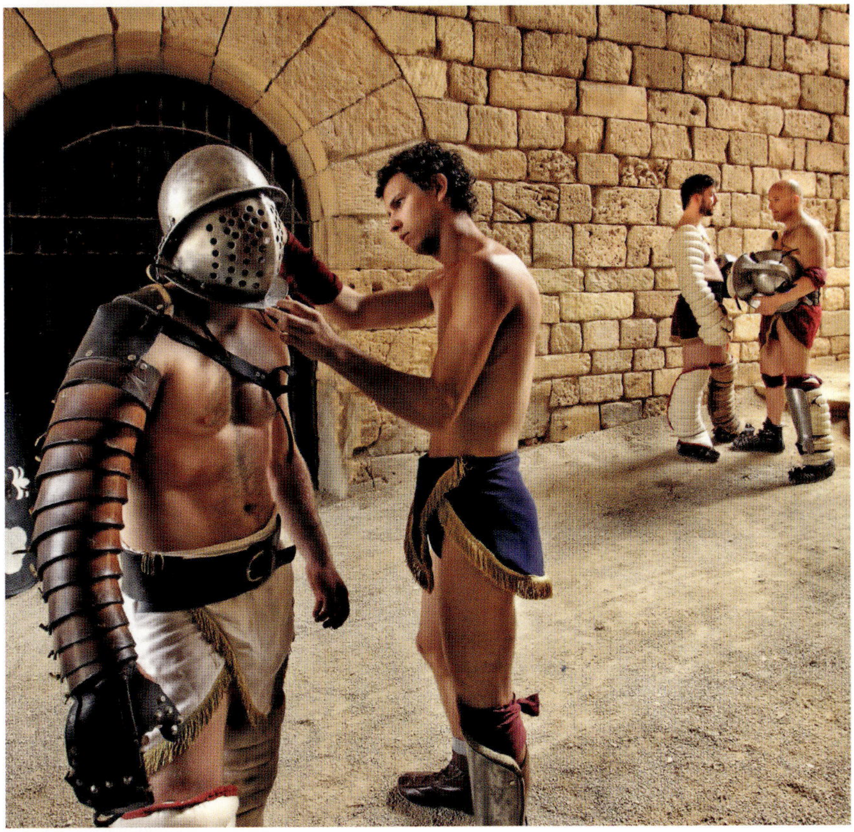

Dressing a gladiator

The Colony Forum

The Local Forum, or Colony Forum, was the focus of daily life in Tarraco. The city council met here, local magistrates were chosen and trade deals were struck… At the end of the Republic, the Forum was set around the Capitoline temple of Jupiter, Juno and Minerva, and had a porticoed square in front. During the reign of Augustus it was expanded with a new square, containing a large basilica, or law court, where the governor meted out justice for the entire province, and a row of shops, or *tabernae*, towards the port. Much of the Forum remains underground or has been destroyed by the modern buildings that have gone up around Carrer Gasòmetre.

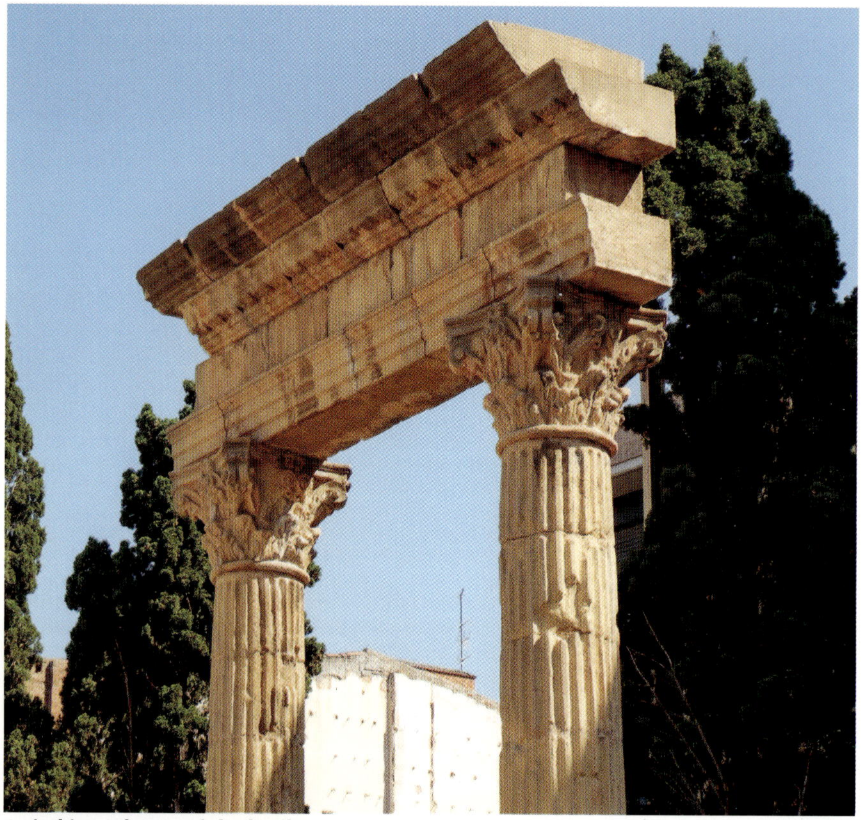

Corinthian columns of the basilica

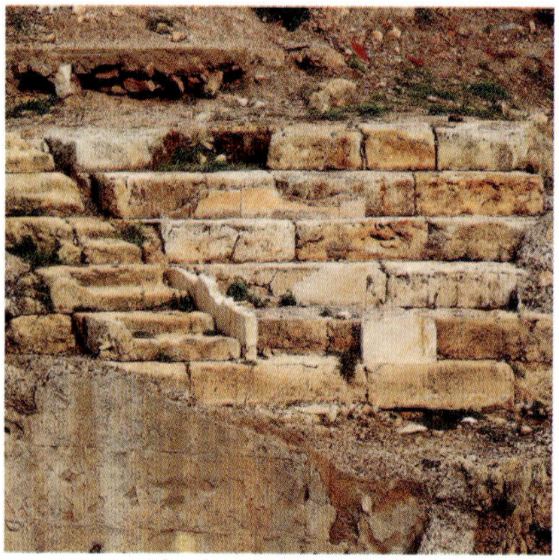

Terraces inside the Theatre

Theatre

The remains of the Theatre, which dates from the time of Augustus, were almost completely demolished in the middle of the 20th century. Public protests in 1977 saved what remained of the original structure. A section of the stage, the lower stands and a monumental fountain survive. The Theatre has undergone restoration work and information panels have been put in place making it a space for the future.

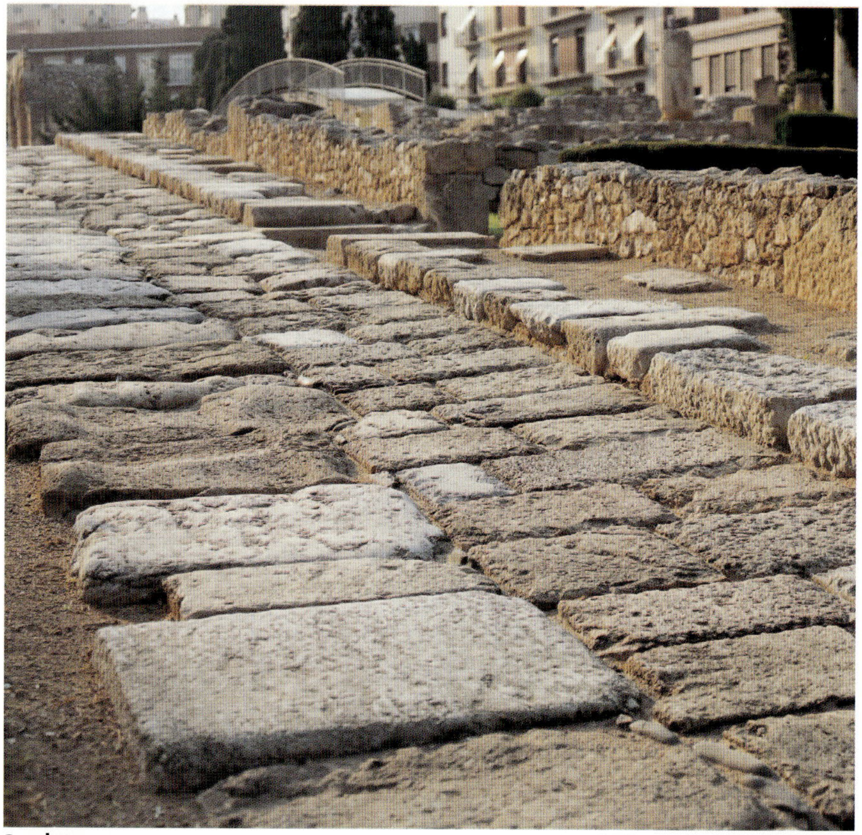

Roadway

Tabernae →

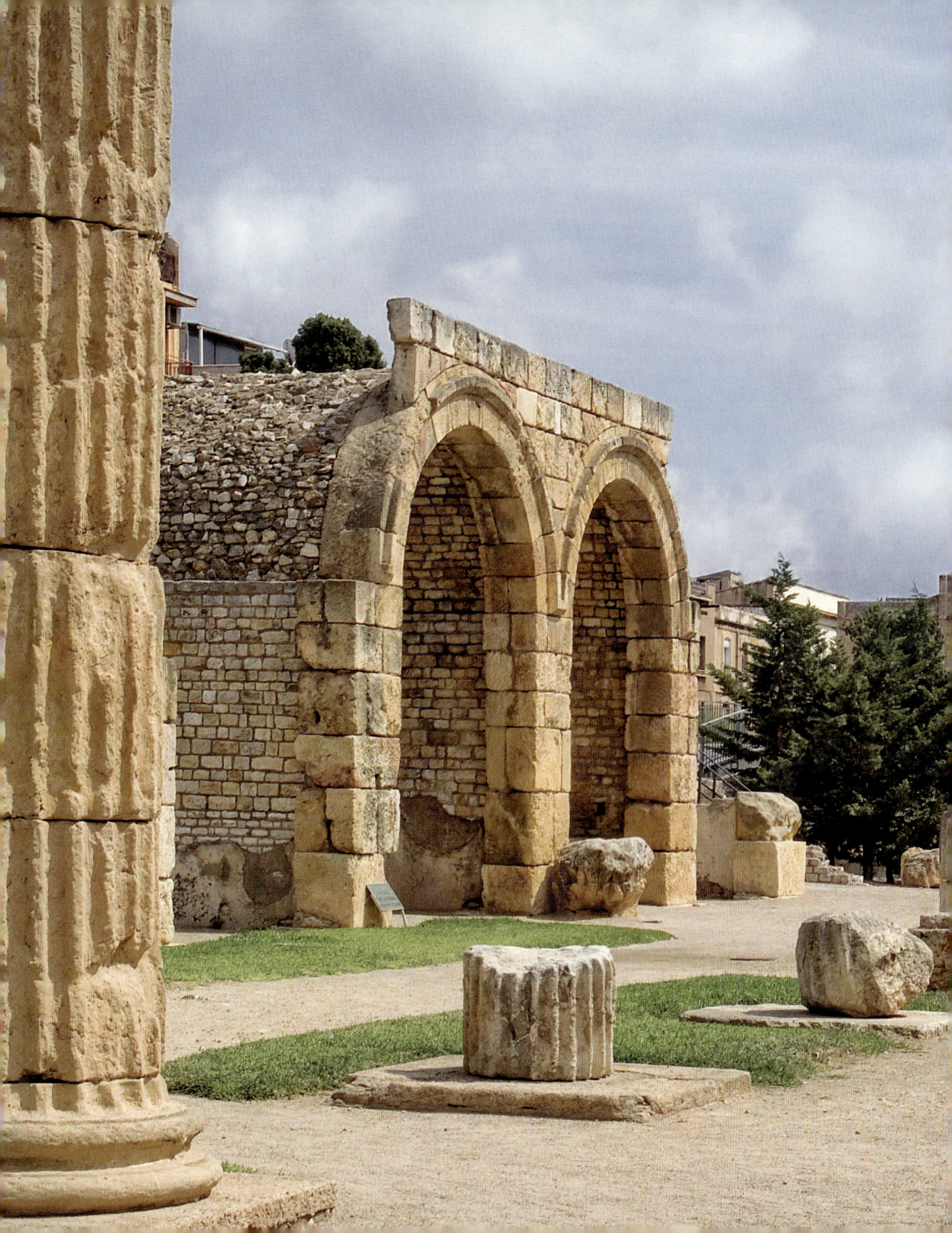

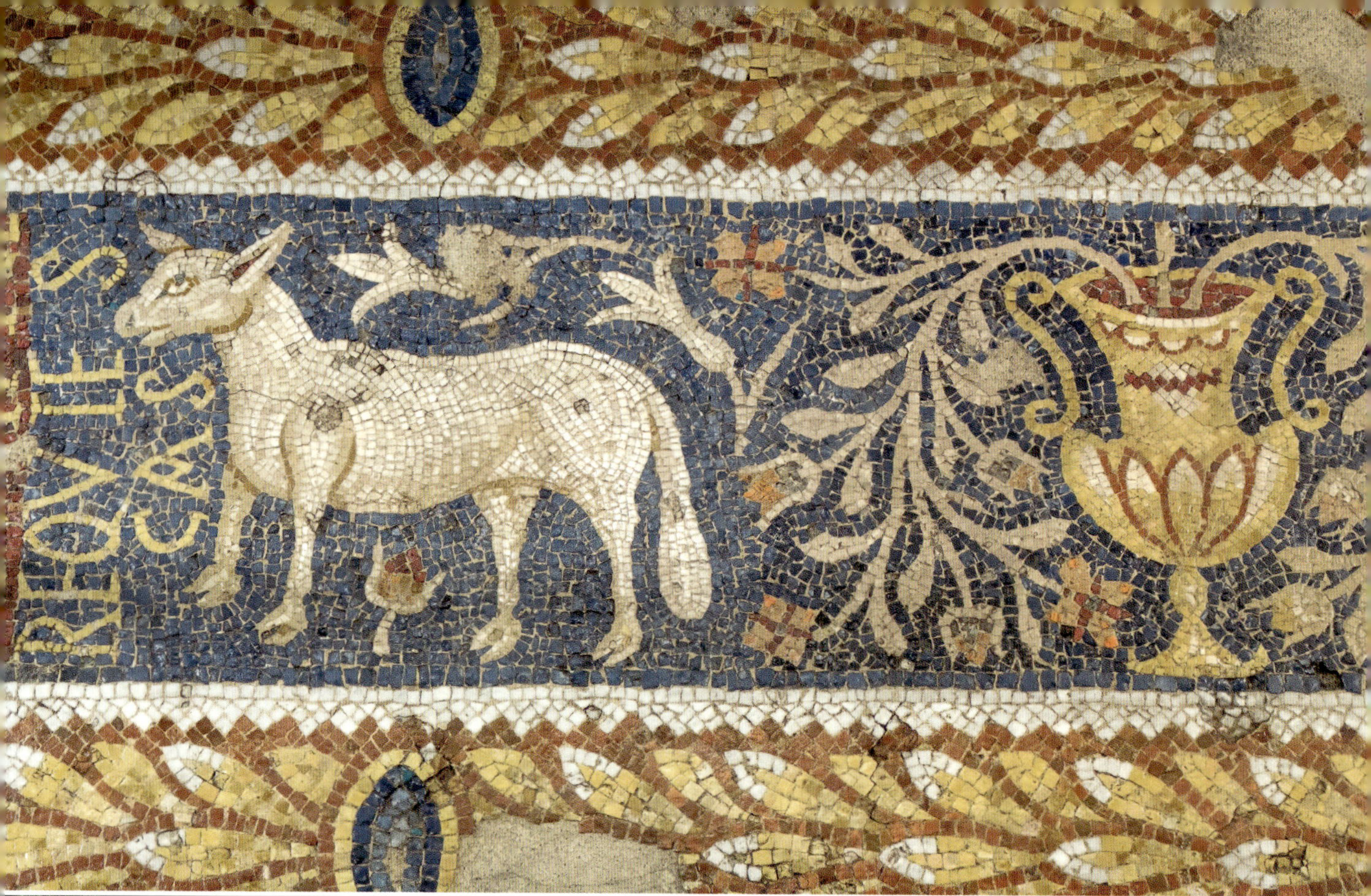

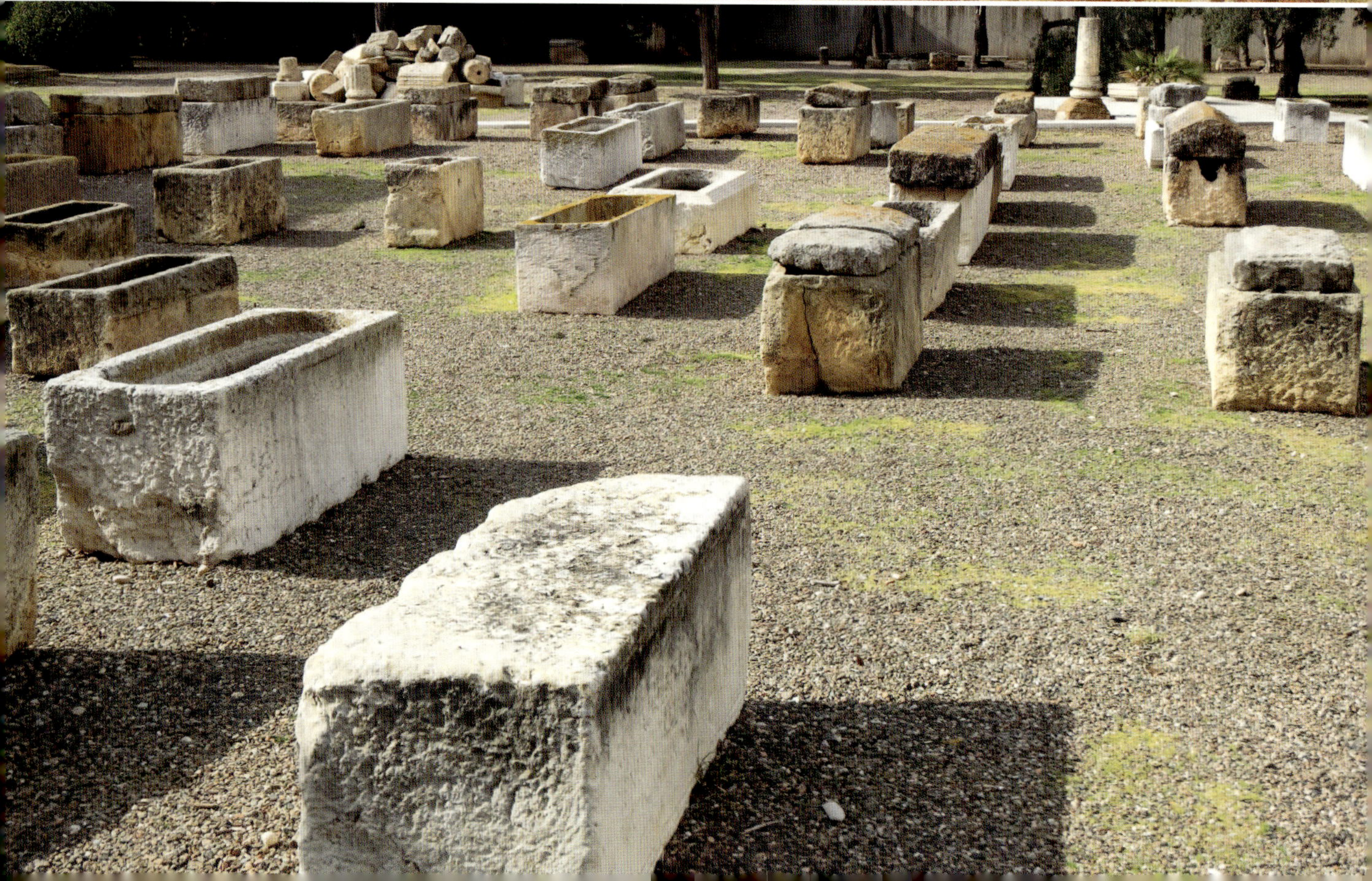

The early Christians

Tarraco was one of the most important Christian metropolises in Hispania. Today Tarragona has a unique early-Christian heritage in terms of its archaeology, art and documents. According to tradition, the arrival of Christianity is thought to coincide with the time the apostle Paul stayed in the colony in 63 AD. The first historical records of the event date from 259 AD, the year the bishop of the city, Fructuosus, and the deacons Augurius and Eulogius were burnt alive in the Amphitheatre.

A basilica was built in the Amphitheatre in the Visigothic era as well as a Romanesque church. Performances of *The Passion of Saint Fructuosus* are staged in the Amphitheatre recreating his imprisonment, trial and martyrdom, based on the earliest records of people martyred on the Iberian Peninsula.

The route of the early-Christians of Tarraco visits the chapel of Sant Pau, the Museu Bíblic Tarraconense (founded in 1930, with its interesting archaeological collection spanning prehistoric times to the Byzantine world, models and Biblical materials), the Cathedral and the Museu Diocesà, the Amphitheatre, the Colony Forum, the Museu Paleocristià, the Early-Christian Necropolis, the basilica in Parc Central and the late-Roman ensemble of Centcelles.

Museum and Early-Christian Necropolis

This vast necropolis, dating from the 3rd to 5th centuries AD, was discovered in 1923, during building work on the tobacco factory. It consists of more than 2,000 tombs and is considered one of the most important examples in the Western Roman Empire due to the type of burials and the period it spans. The necropolis features a wide variety of tombs, from large mausoleums and sarcophaguses to modest graves consisting of tiles and amphoras. The Necropolis is part of a large Christian shrine containing the burial site of the martyred saints Fructuosus, Augurius and Eulogius, who were burnt alive in the Amphitheatre in 259 AD.

← Above, detail of the mosaic of Ampelius Below, sarcophaguses in the garden of the museum

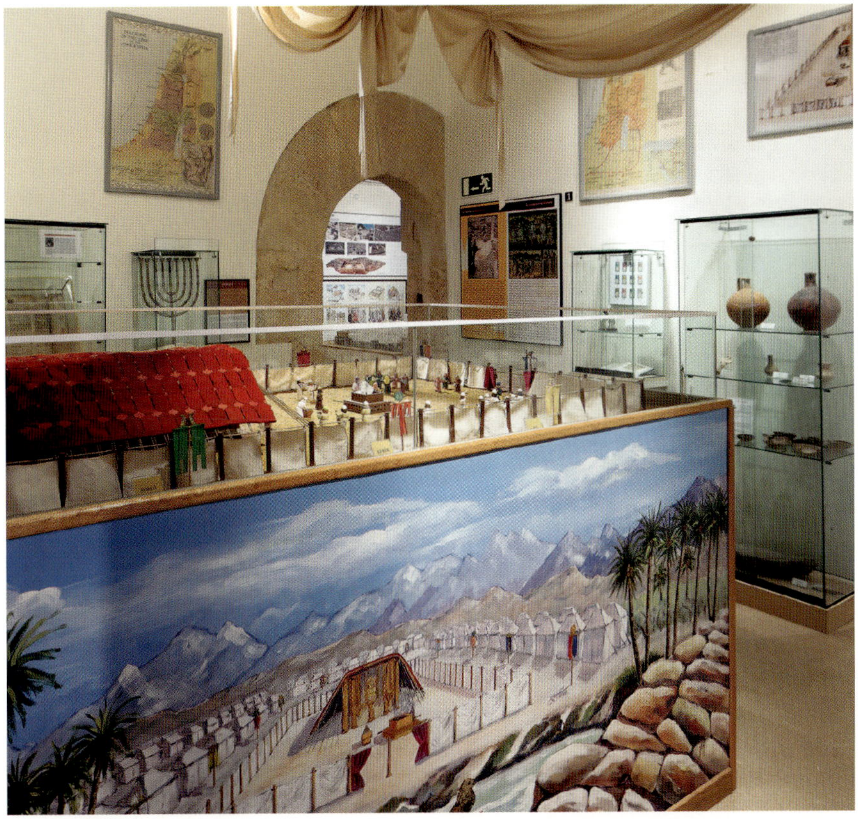

Museu Bíblic Tarraconense

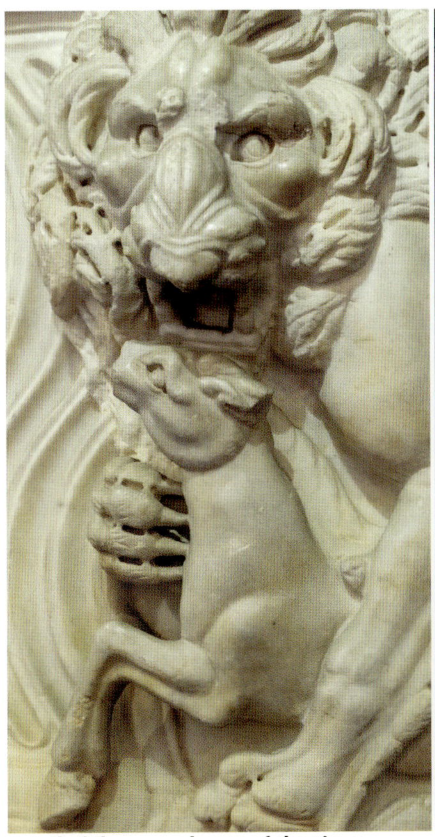

Detail of the sarcophagus of the Lions

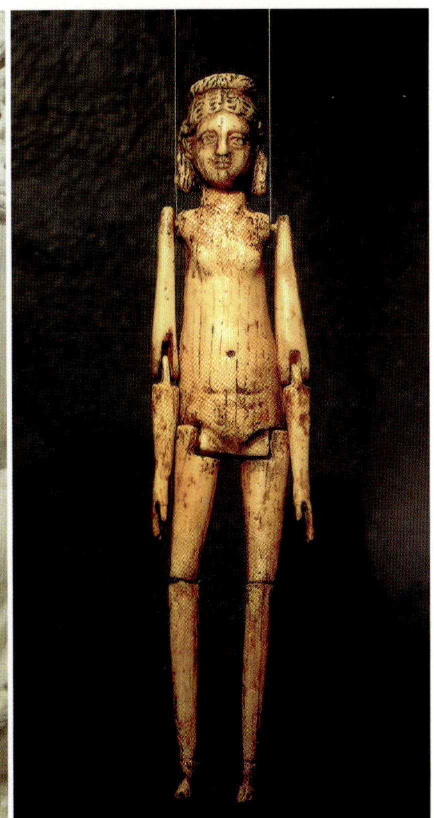

Articulated ivory doll

Pont del Diable Les Ferreres Aqueduct

There can be no life or civilisation without water. And Tarraco's water supply came from three aqueducts, one of which, Gaià, is still in use. The Les Ferreres Aqueduct or Pont del Diable — Devil's Bridge —, is the best-known surviving section of the conduit leading from the river Francolí just 4 kilometres outside the city. The structure is so solid that the settlers who came after the Romans thought it could only be the work of the devil, hence its nickname. The aqueduct was built in the 1st century AD, is 27 metres high and more than 200 metres long, and consists of a double tier of arches, 11 on the lower tier and 25 on the upper tier.

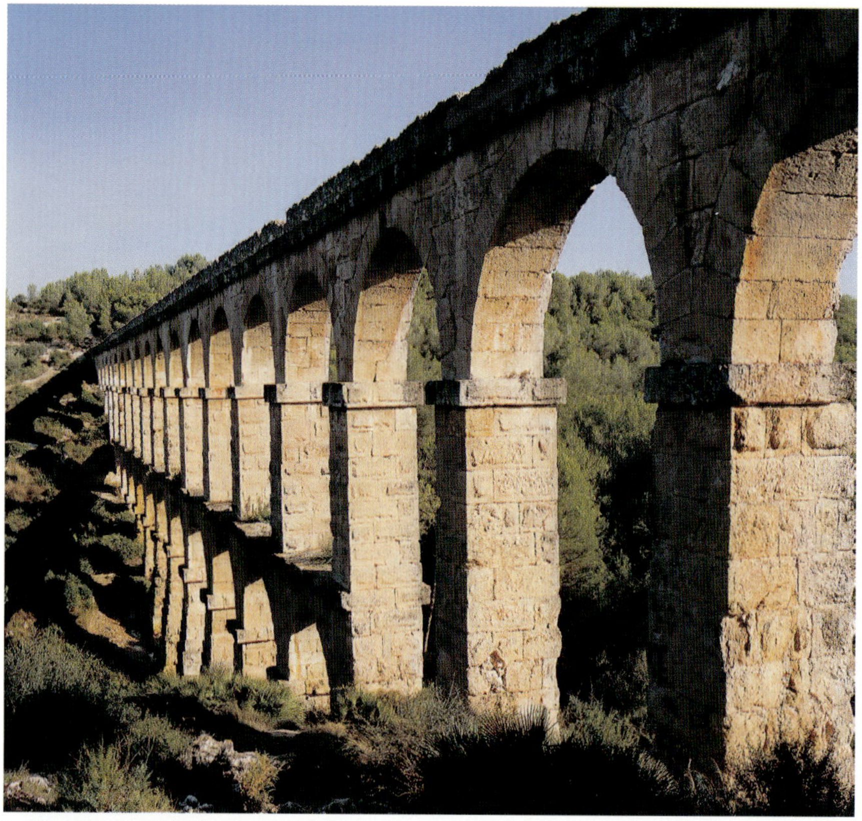

Les Ferreres Aqueduct

El Mèdol

The stone used to construct the buildings and landmarks in Tarraco came from several local quarries. The most impressive of these is El Mèdol, 7,5 kilometres from Tarragona. A column of stone, known as the Agulla, or needle, stands in the centre of a vast hollow measuring 200 metres deep and 50 metres wide. The column has been left untouched since the quarry was in use and marks the actual depth of the stone quarried on the site. Golden limestone, of different shades and hues, was cut into blocks, the marks of which can still be seen on the quarry walls. Nature has tamed the microclimate of the Mèdol hollow and has now been taken over by Mediterranean woodland.

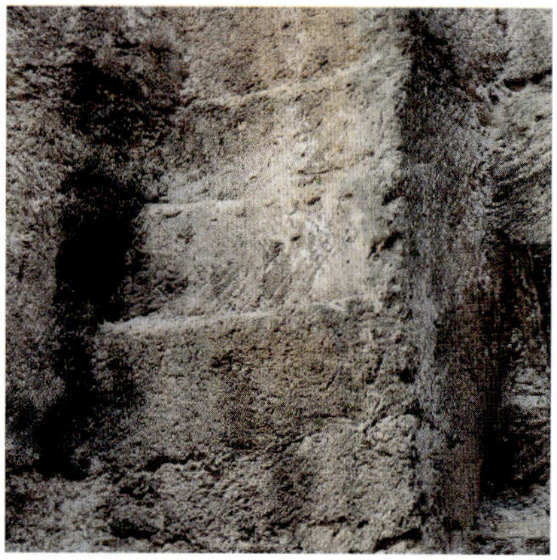

Wall of the quarry

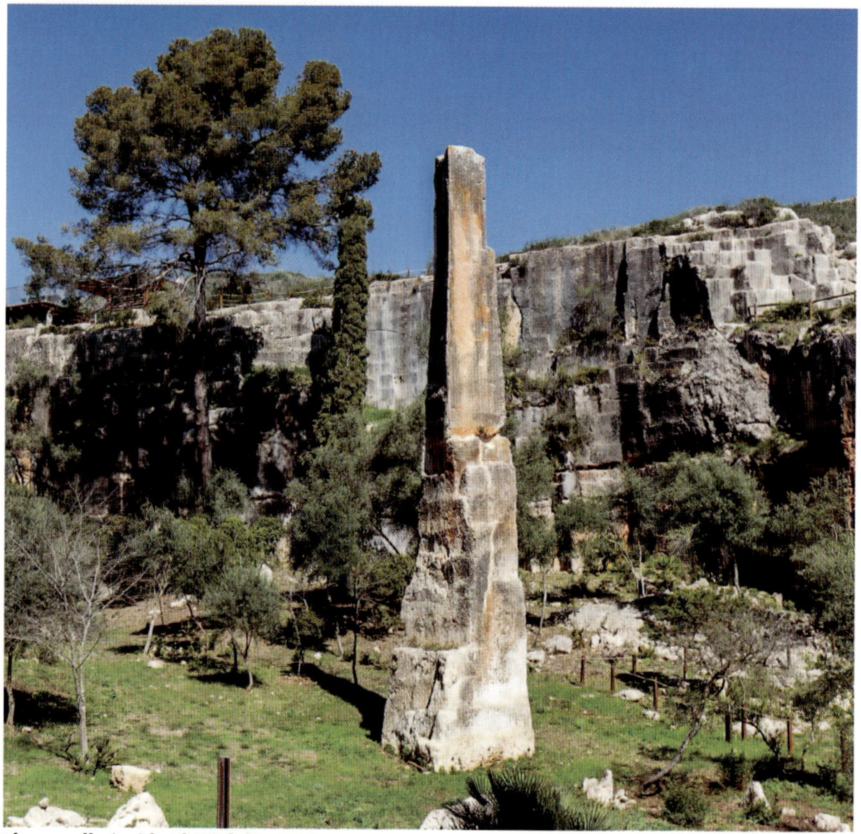

The needle inside El Mèdol quarry

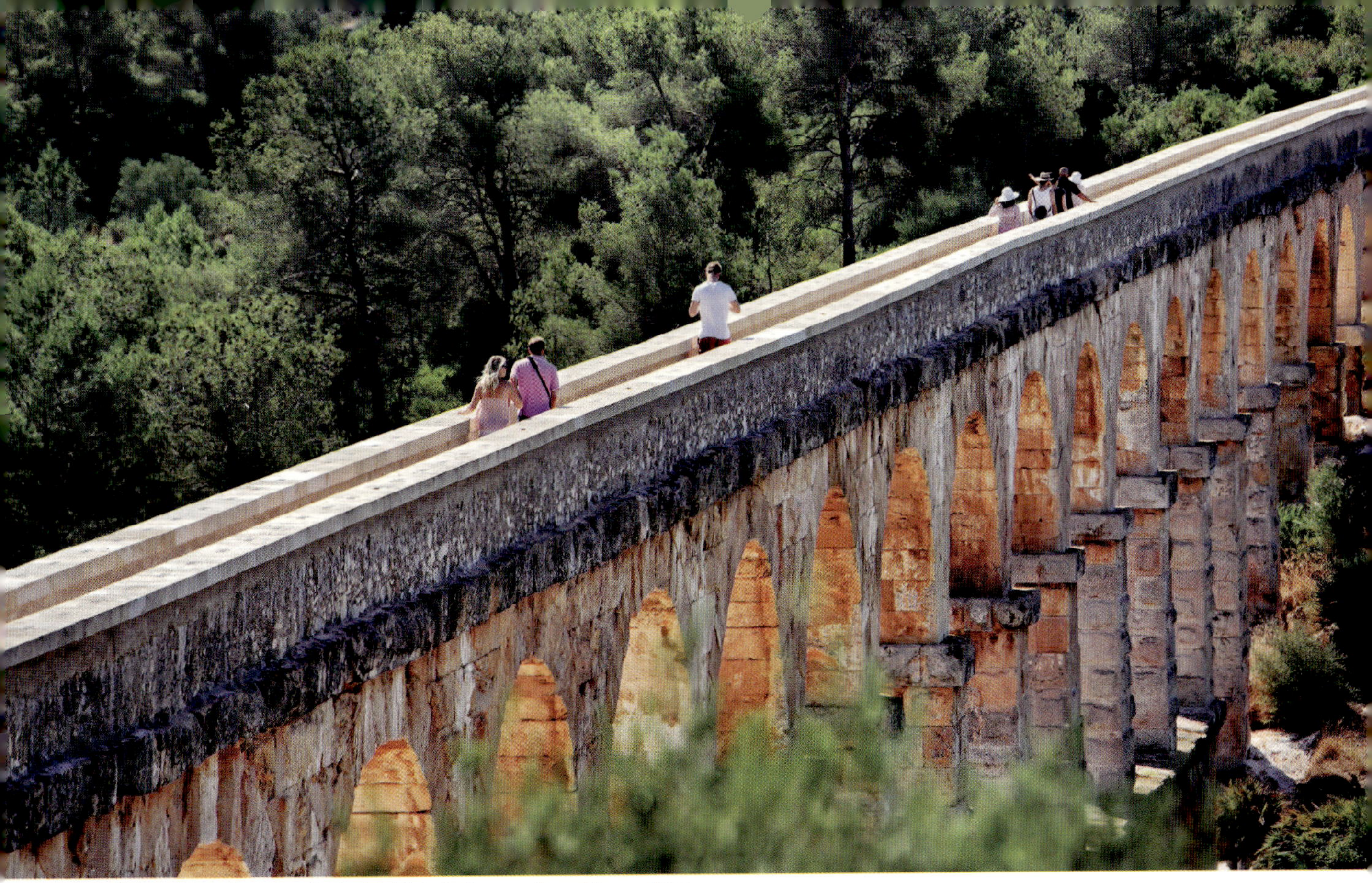

↑ Walking along the aqueduct ↓ A historical scene from Tàrraco Viva

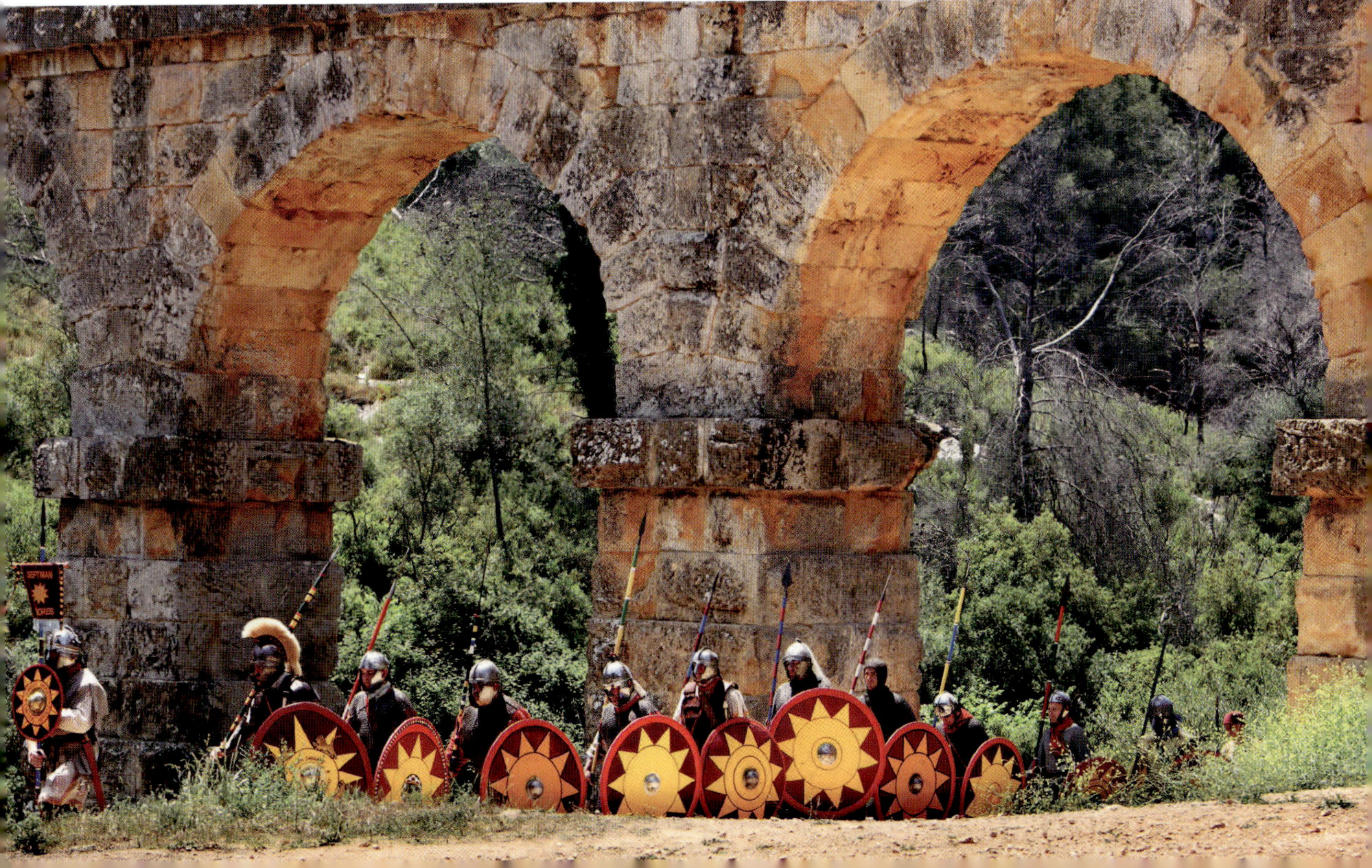

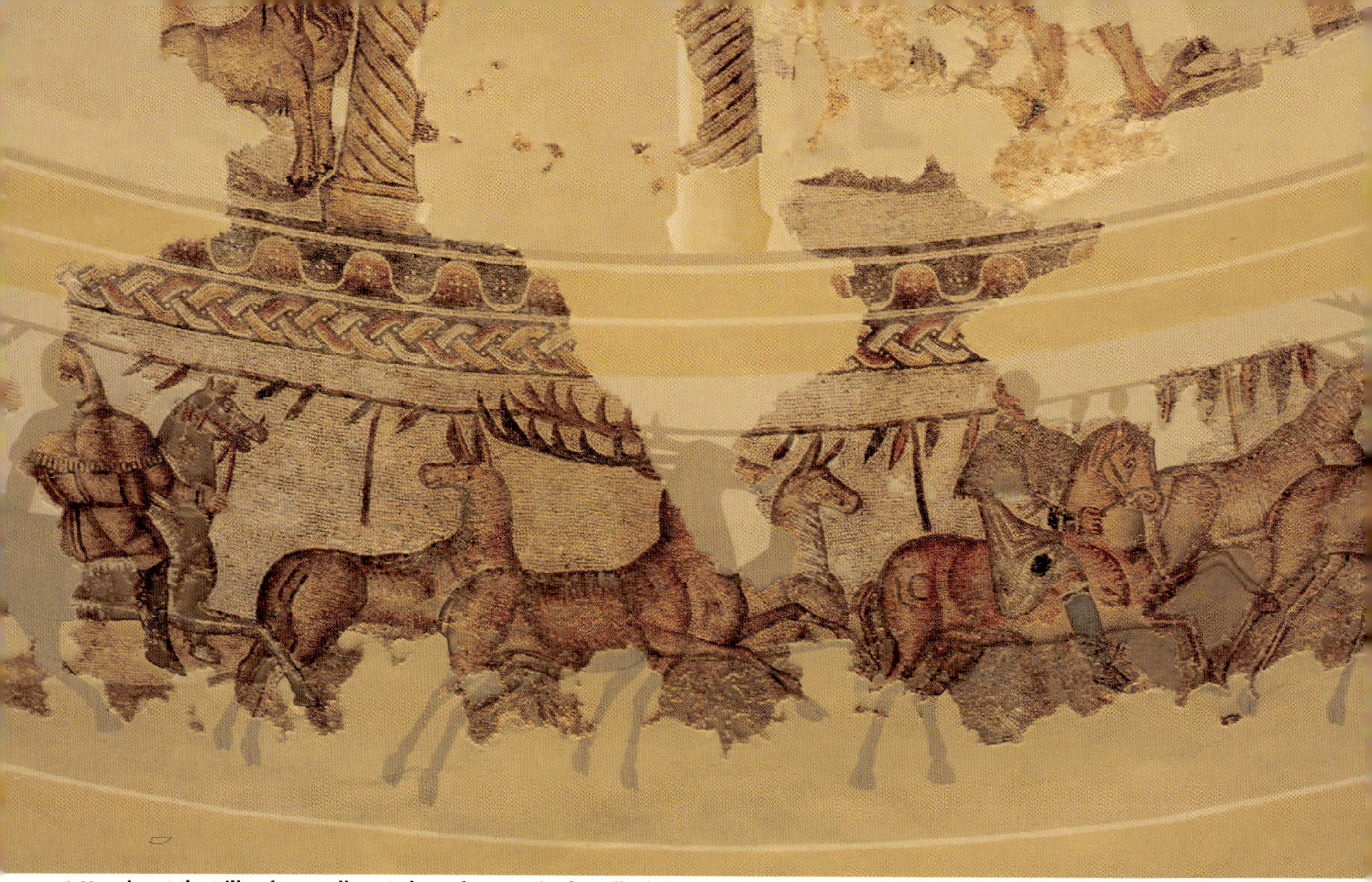

↑ Mosaics at the Villa of Centcelles ↓ Floor of a room in the Villa dels Munts

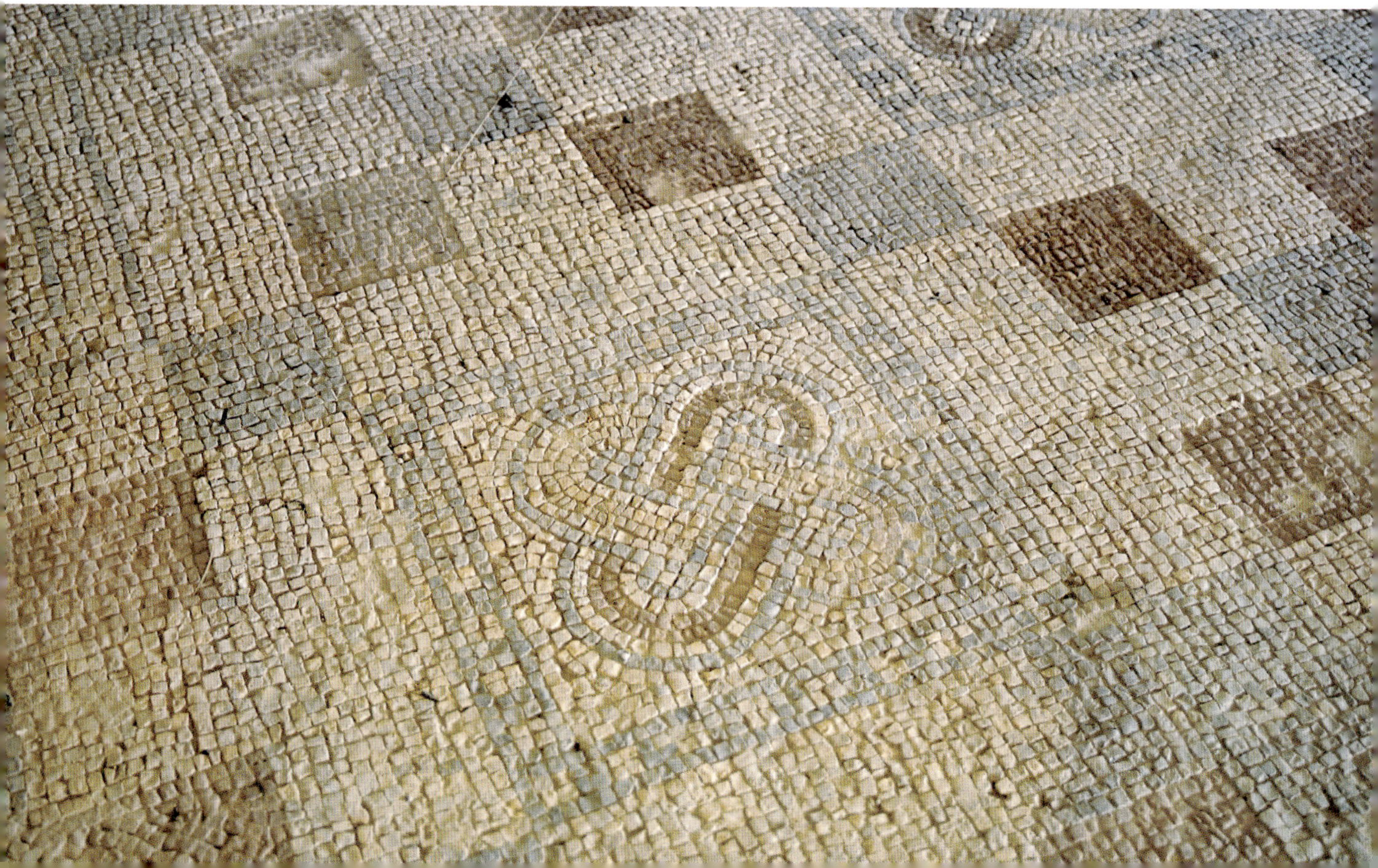

Villa of Centcelles

Located within the municipal boundaries of Constantí, 4 kilometres from Tarragona, the villa of Centcelles was occupied from the 1st to 2nd centuries until late antiquity. A room measuring more than 10 metres in diameter and 13 metres high has a dome decorated with beautiful mosaics depicting scenes from the Bible, such as Adam and Eve and Noah's Ark. They date from the late 4th or early 5th centuries AD. The preserved scenes at the top of the dome have been damaged and sparked debate among scholars who argue that they depict eminent aristocrats or even emperors. Archaeologists from the MNAT maintain that the villa was a base camp for the Imperial armies during the 5th century AD.

Torre dels Escipions

Standing some 6 kilometres outside Tarragona, this early 1st-century funeral monument has no links to the military Scipio family, despite its name. The figures carved on the façade represent the shepherd Attis, who was associated with the burial rites of Asia Minor, and the relief on top shows the couple who owned the tomb. Originally, it would have been painted in bright colours and surmounted by a pyramid-shaped roof.

Villa of Dels Munts

This luxurious villa stands on the small hillock of Dels Munts in the seaside town of Altafulla, 14 kilometres north of Tarragona. It was the home of a high-ranking official from Tarraco in the middle of the 2nd century AD, and Emperor Hadrian is thought to have lived here in the year 123 during his stay in the city. The villa is divided into a residential area and a rustic one. It has two bathing complexes, one of them on the beach.

Arc de Berà

This triumphal arch stands in Roda de Berà, 20 kilometres outside Tarragona. It was built between 15 and 5 AD as stipulated in the will of Lucius Licinius Sura, a wealthy senator from the Colònia Celsa, now in the province of Zaragoza. It was probably surmounted by statues of Augustus depicted as a deity and members of the Imperial family.

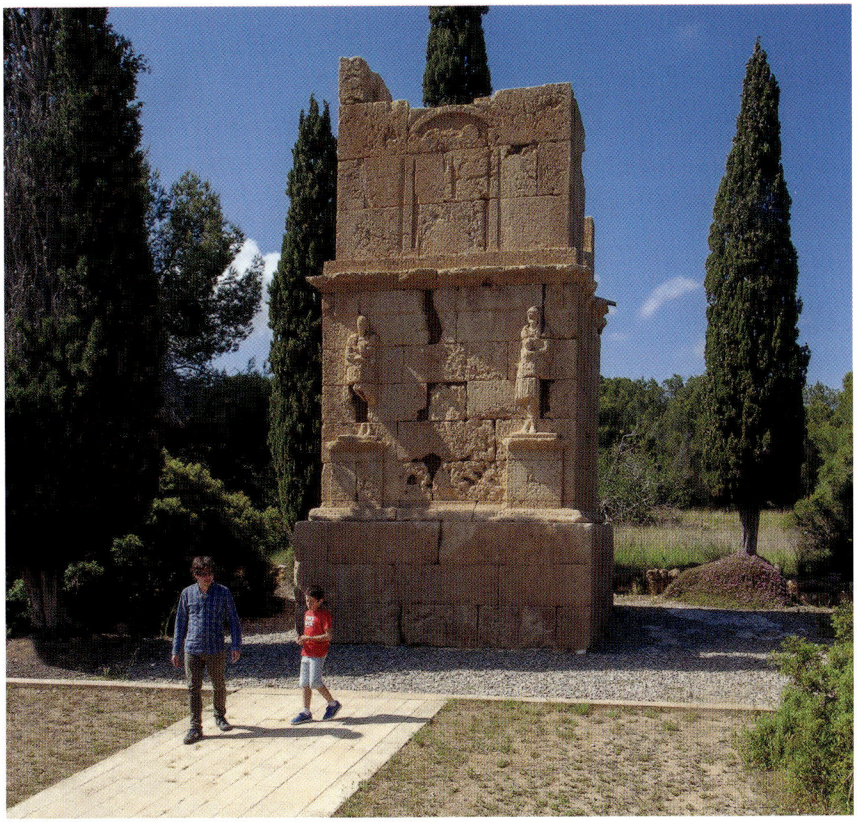

Torre dels Escipions

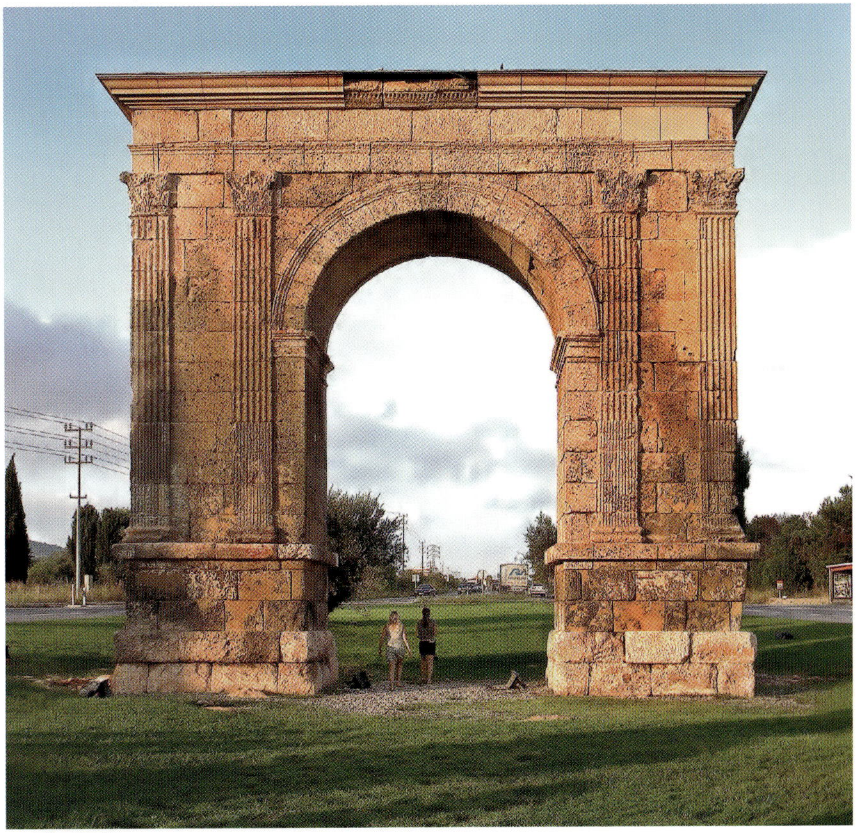

Arc de Berà

Medieval "Terragona"

The Part Alta

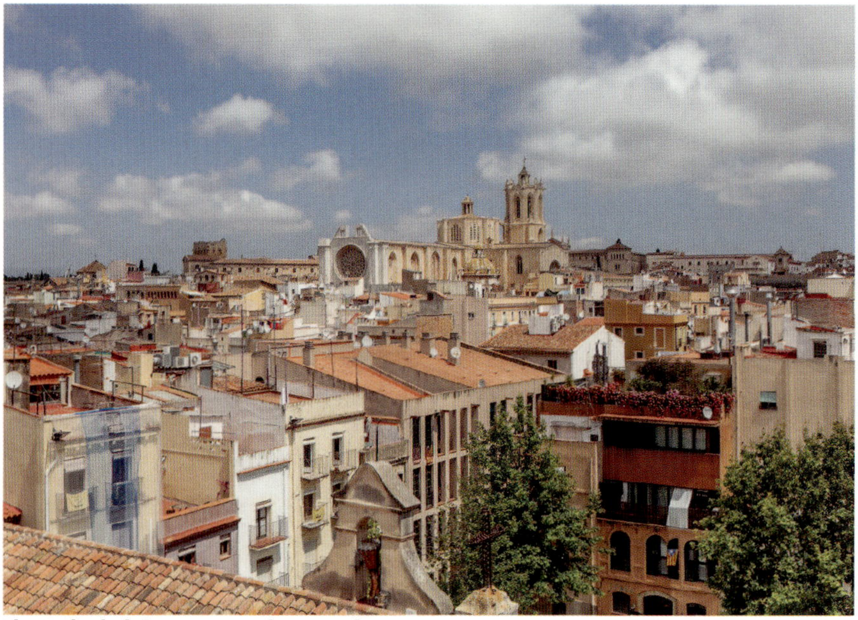
The Cathedral rises up over the Part Alta

In 475 AD, Tarraco became part of the Visigothic kingdom of Toulouse, at more or less the same time as the defeat of the Western Roman Empire. The Islamic incursion of the early 8th century brought about a period of decline in the city and it was gradually abandoned. Despite this, Muslim Tarraquna didn't become completely uninhabited until the fall of the Caliphate of Cordoba, when it became a no man's land. Although the county of Barcelona made several failed attempts to reoccupy Tarragona, it didn't regain its city status until the middle of the 12th century. For several centuries during the Middle Ages it was written as Terragona.

In 1091, a papal bull issued by Urban II invited the Catalan counts to resettle the city and recognised Tarragona as an archbishopric and metropolitan centre, as it had been during the late-Roman and Visigothic periods. However, it took until 1129 for the city to be reoccupied, when the bishop of Barcelona and archbishop of Tarragona, Olegarius Bonestruga, sought the help of a military leader, the Norman, Robert Bordet. Bordet, who was also known as Robert d'Aguiló, was born in the French municipality of Aculley or Culley-sur-Orne, today known as Rabodanges.

The Norman mercenary, who had been awarded the symbolic title of Prince of Tarragona, built the first castle in the new city over the Roman tower known today as the Praetorium, and in 1146 a new archbishop, Bernat Tort, built a new castle, the Castell del Patriarca, on top of another of the Roman towers on the lower right-hand corner of the place of worship. The castle has long since vanished. The Bordet family — who went by the surname Tarragona at the time — was expelled from the city following numerous clashes with members of the archbishop's circle, which included the murder of one of Robert's sons and Archbishop Hug de Cervelló. In 1173, King Alfonso of Aragon and the new archbishop Torroja signed an agreement instating a joint government of royal and ecclesiastical powers subjecting local inhabitants to both while giving them a greater degree of autonomy.

Work on the Cathedral was begun in 1171, in the centre of the upper enclosure, on a site previously occupied by a Roman temple dedicated to Emperor Augustus. The layout of the new city was dictated by the presence of the great episcopal see, the walls around it, the terracing and surviving Roman elements and the construction of the characteristic buildings of the time: castles, the hospital, the market place...

Medieval route

→ Appendix p. 3

Medieval portico in the Pla de la Seu →

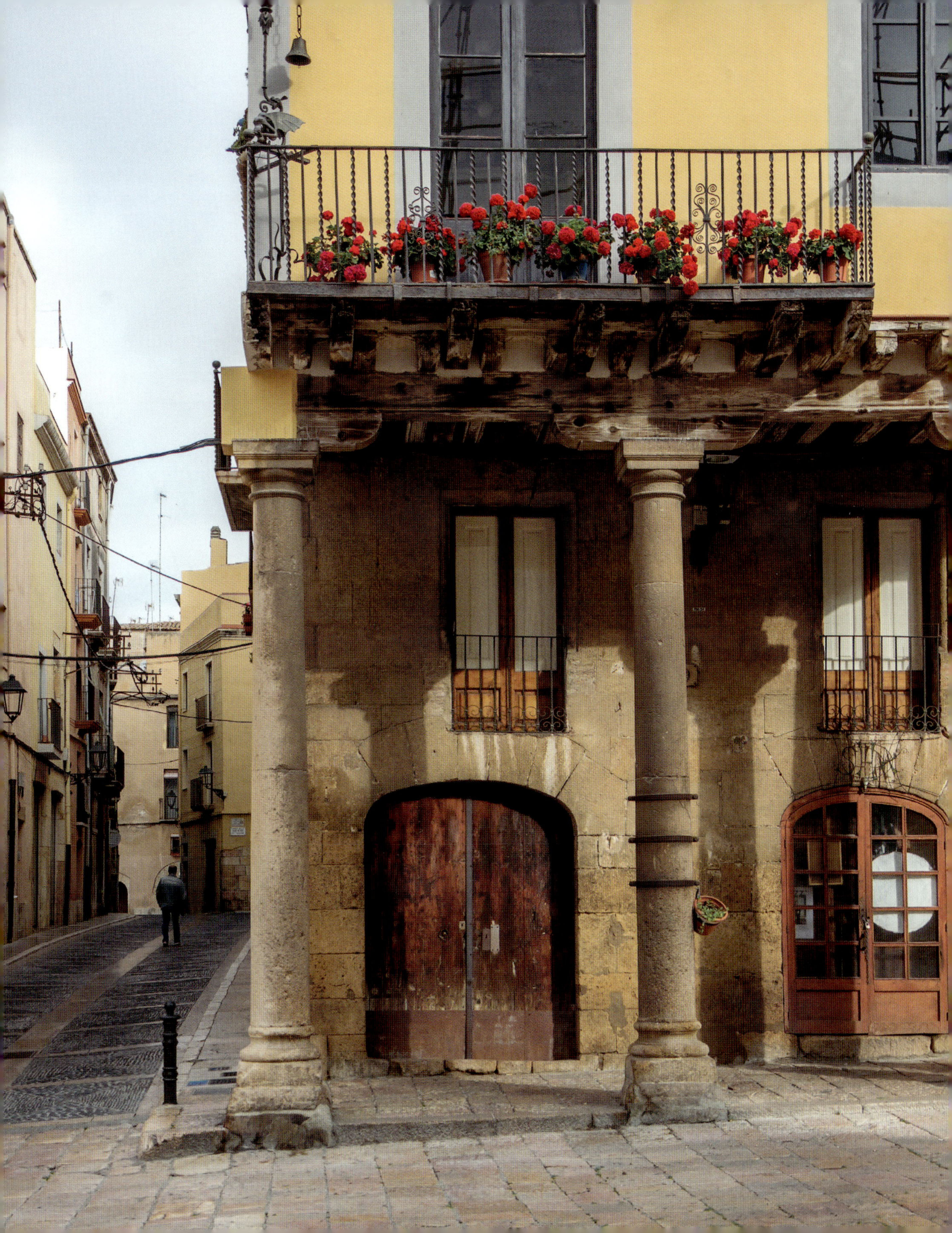

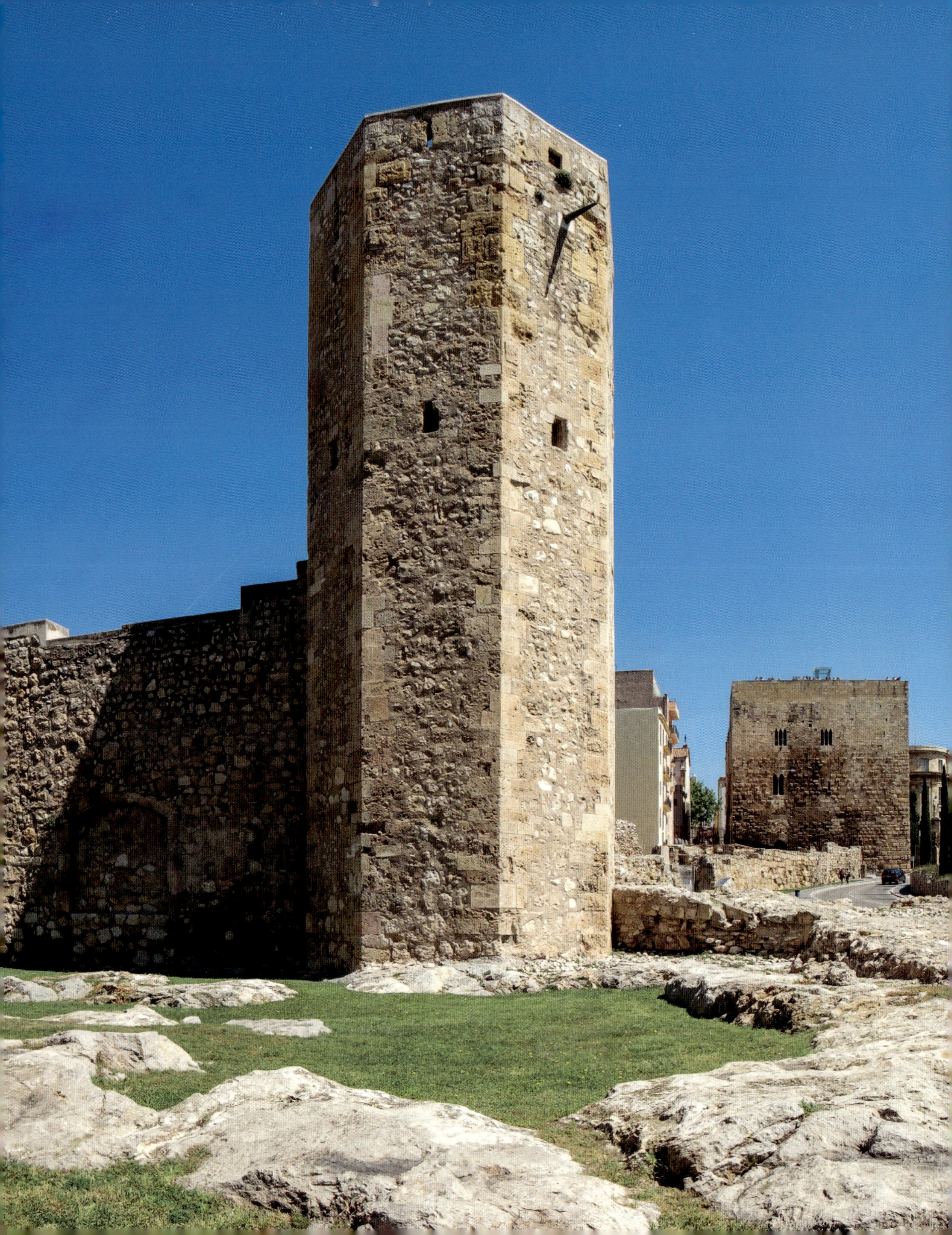

The medieval walls

The walled city was extended in the second half of the 14th century to the area known as El Corral, which stood on the site of the former Circus. A new wall, known as La Muralleta, was built here. A section of this wall can be seen opposite the head gate of the Circus. It has an entrance cut lengthways into one of the sides which affords views of the Roman structures. Four towers were built on the new defence wall and the Roman wall in the current Part Alta (old town) remained in use. Later on, openings were made in the outer walls of the Roman wall for the windows and balconies of houses.

Torre de les Monges

The Torre de les Monges, or Nuns' Tower, in the Rambla Vella, is so named because of the convent of Poor Clares built across the road in the late 13th century. The tower dates from the late 14th century, stands 18 metres high and is built from small ashlars. A bulwark was added to the back of the tower during the reign of Carlos V which is why the tower is also known by the emperor's name. The towers that didn't survive were La Grossa, Framenors and El Bordell.

Torre d'en Tintoré

This tower was first documented in the 15th century, but was probably built at an earlier date. It has a rectangular floor plan and was built on to the Roman wall to protect the Portal de Vilaverd, a gateway to the medieval Corral. Built of masonry with small ashlars on the corners, it retains some of the battlements and a barbican. There is a Roman inscription on one of the sides dedicated to a former slave who made his fortune.

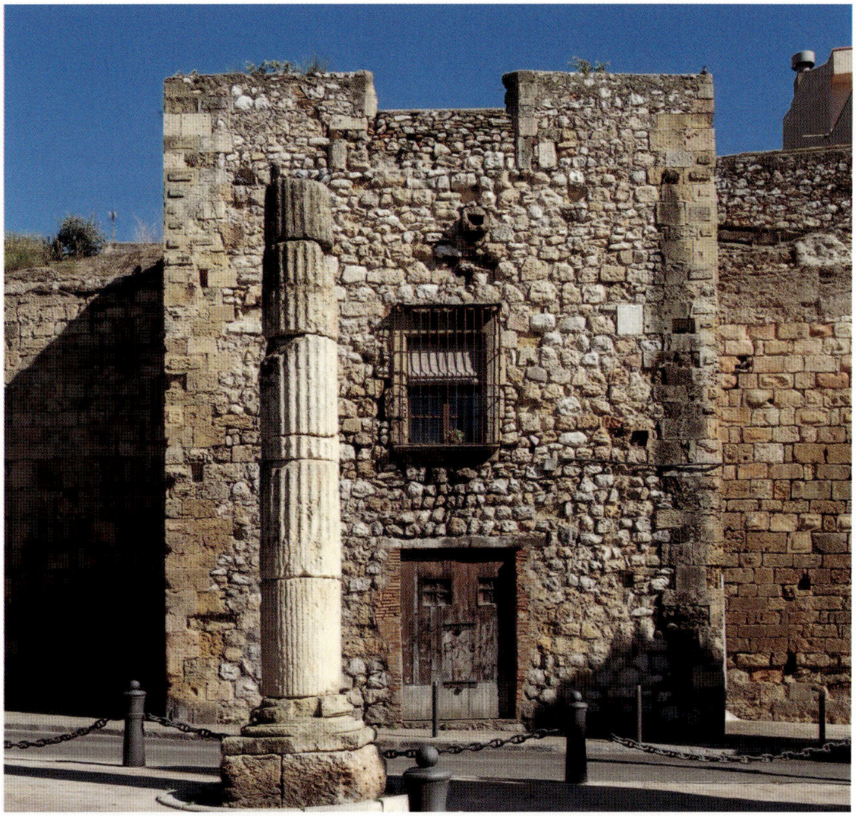

Torre d'en Tintoré, on the Roman Empire Way

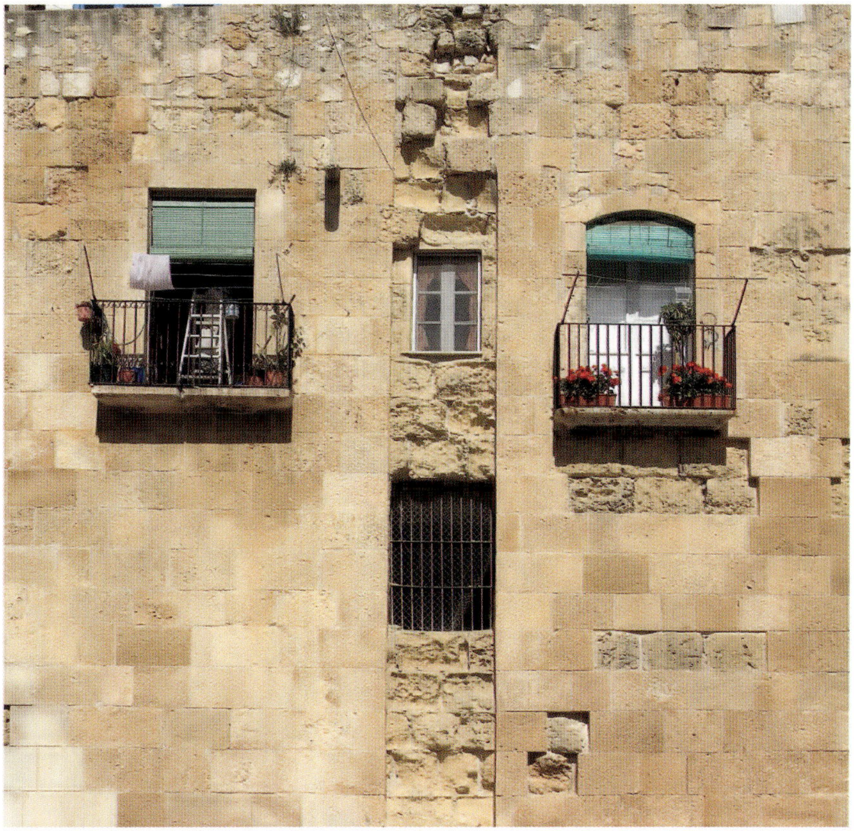

Fragment of the wall, on Passeig de Sant Antoni

← Torre de les Monges

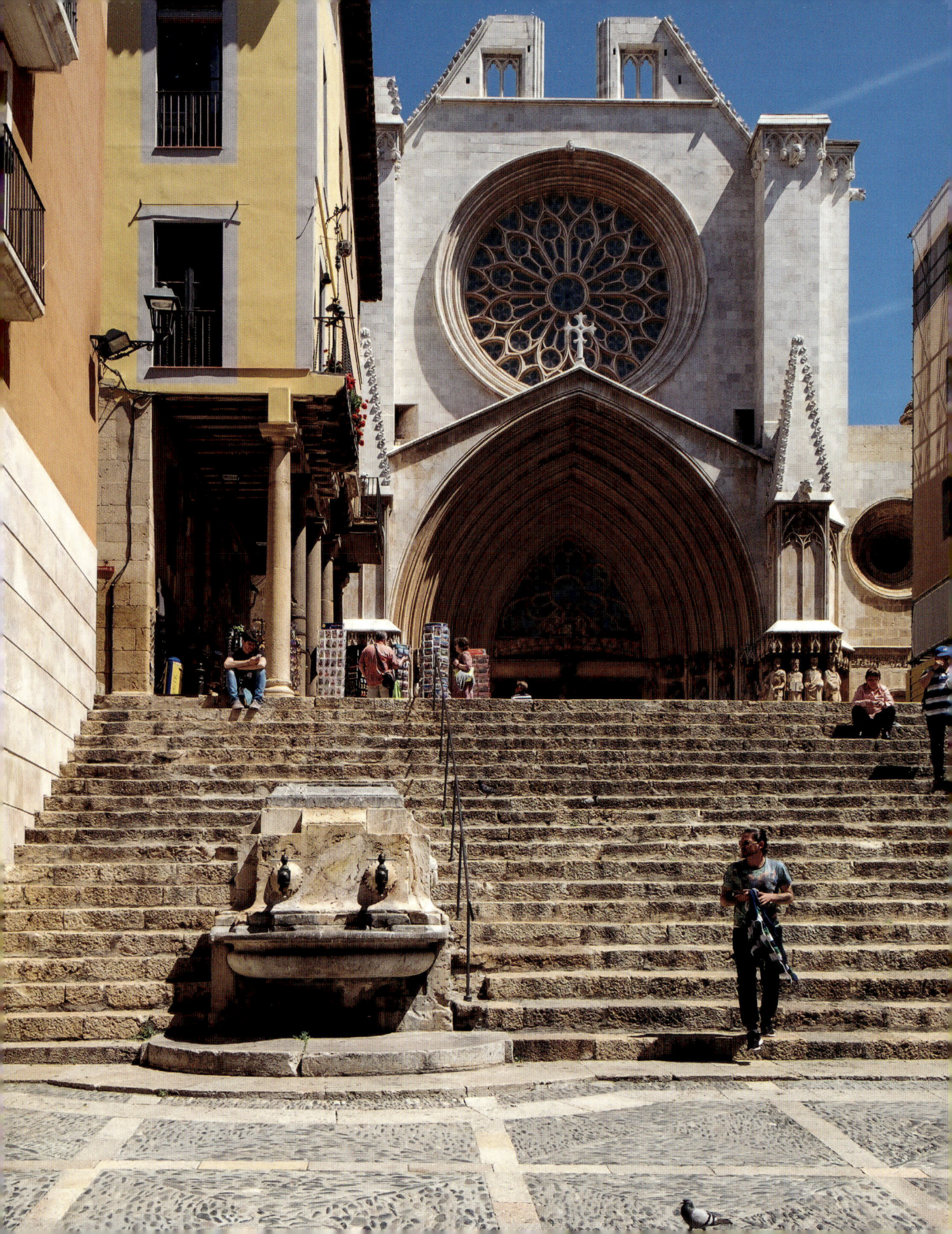

Carrer Major

Carrer Major is a central street lined with shops selling antiques, select foods, wines and drinks. It already served this purpose in the Middle Ages but its layout follows the central section of the Roman administrative building, which connected the Pulvinar, or tribune for the president of the Circus, and the Temple of Augustus. We know of its historic importance because it is home to some of the city's most noteworthy buildings: the former seat of the local government, the Casa de la Generalitat, the old city hall, the Antic Ajuntament, and the Casa de l'Abat de Poblet, which was once the home of the Abbot of Poblet.

The Pla de la Seu

The Pla de la Seu is the medieval acropolis that stands on the site of the Roman temple. With the Cathedral as its centrepiece, it contains splendid palaces that belonged to members of the aristocracy and Church. One of these is the former Palau de la Cambreria, which became known as Casa Balcells, with its Gothic and Renaissance windows, when the papacy abolished the post of *cambrer*, the person who provided the members of the church with their vestments. The monarchs stayed here when they visited the city and Queen Juana Enríquez, the mother of Ferdinand the Catholic, died here. Two future popes also lived here, Gregory X and Benedict XIII. Next door is one of the most unusual and ancient houses, the Casa dels Porxos. Opposite stands the archdeacon's house, Ca l'Ardiaca.

The steps leading to the Pla de la Seu are the perfect vantage point to watch one of the many New Year's festivals held in the streets of the Part Alta. They have been shifted slightly from the site of the original Roman steps that once connected the administrative building with the place of worship. You can see a section of the Roman steps inside a shop along Carrer Major.

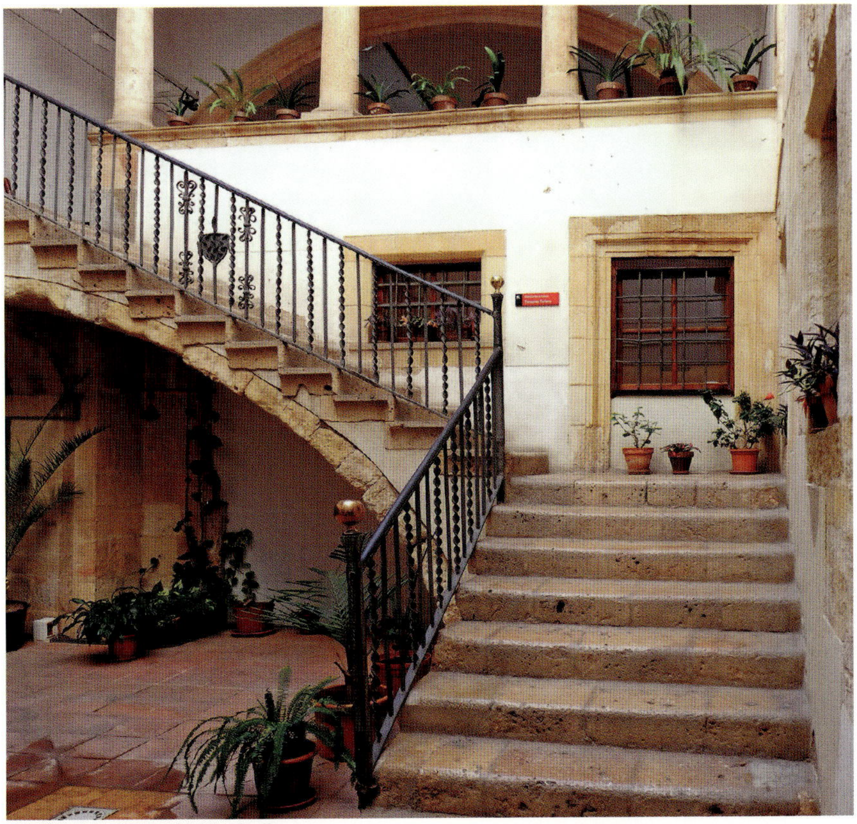

Courtyard of the old city hall

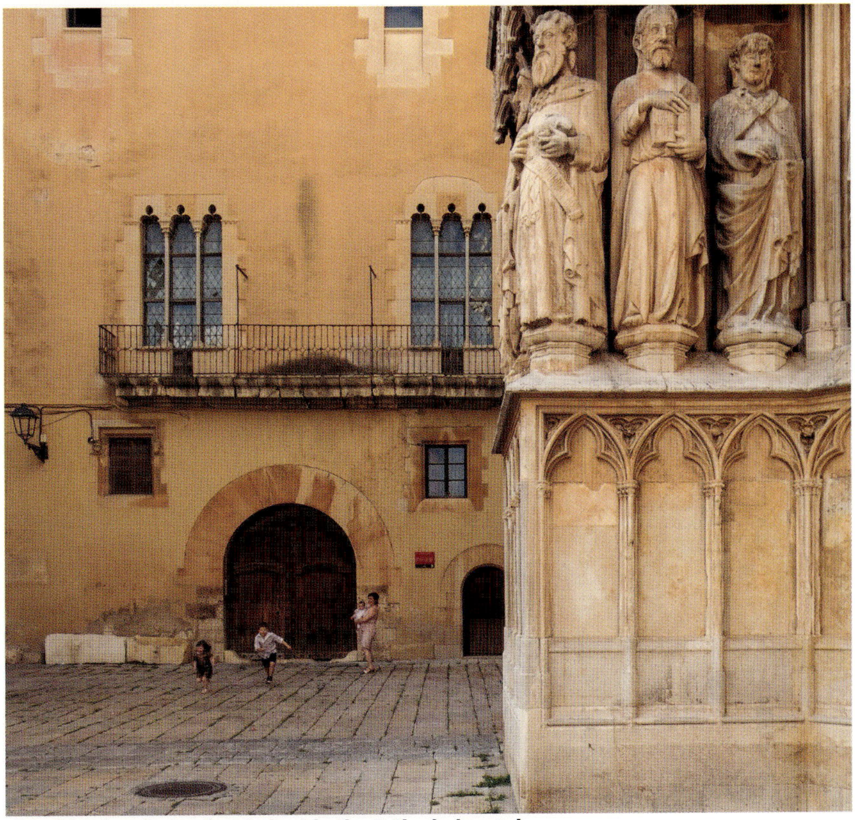

The old Palau de Cambreria beside the Cathedral portal

← The fountains and steps outside the Cathedral

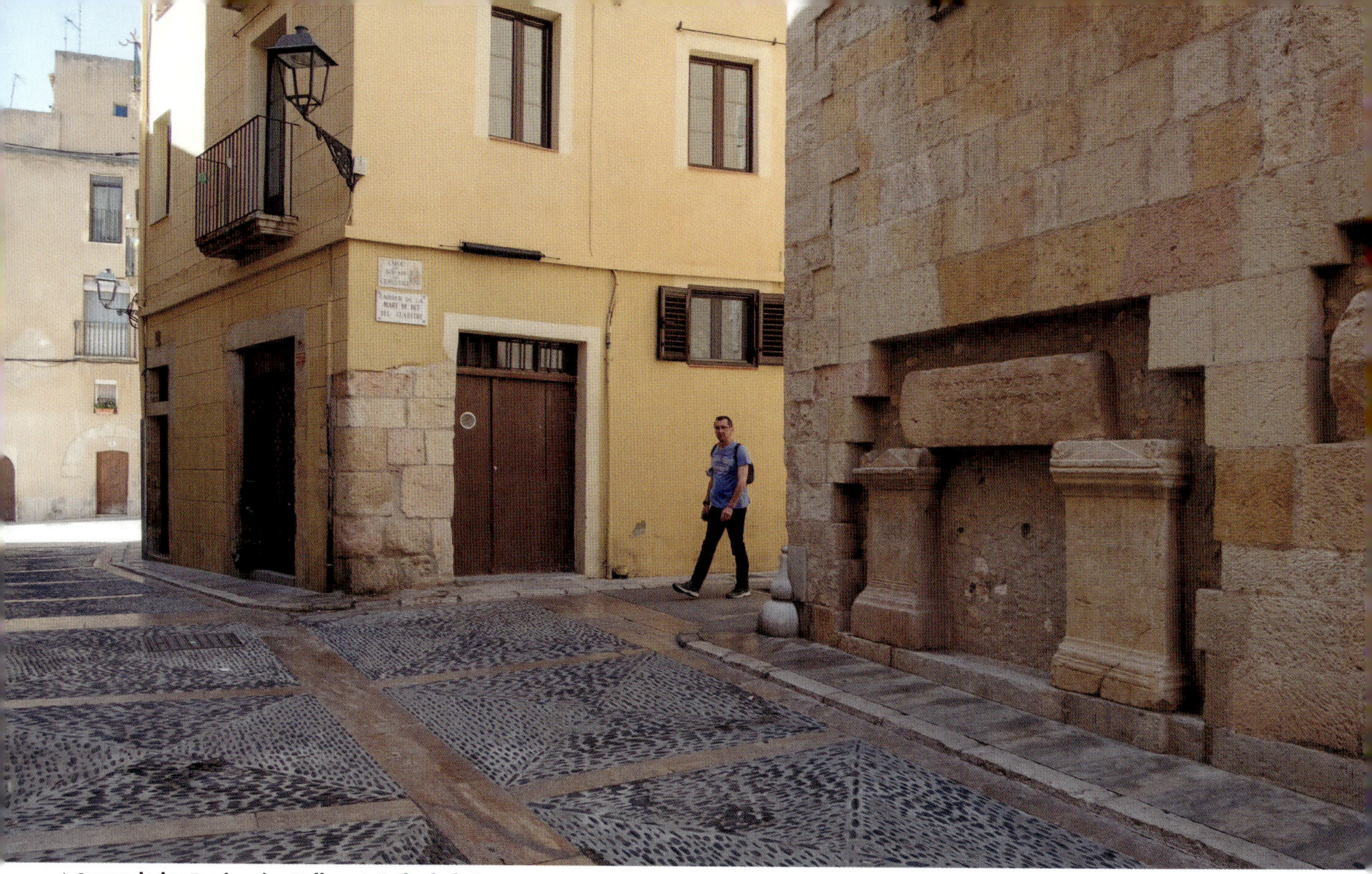

↑ Carrer de les Escrivanies Velles ↓ Cathedral steps

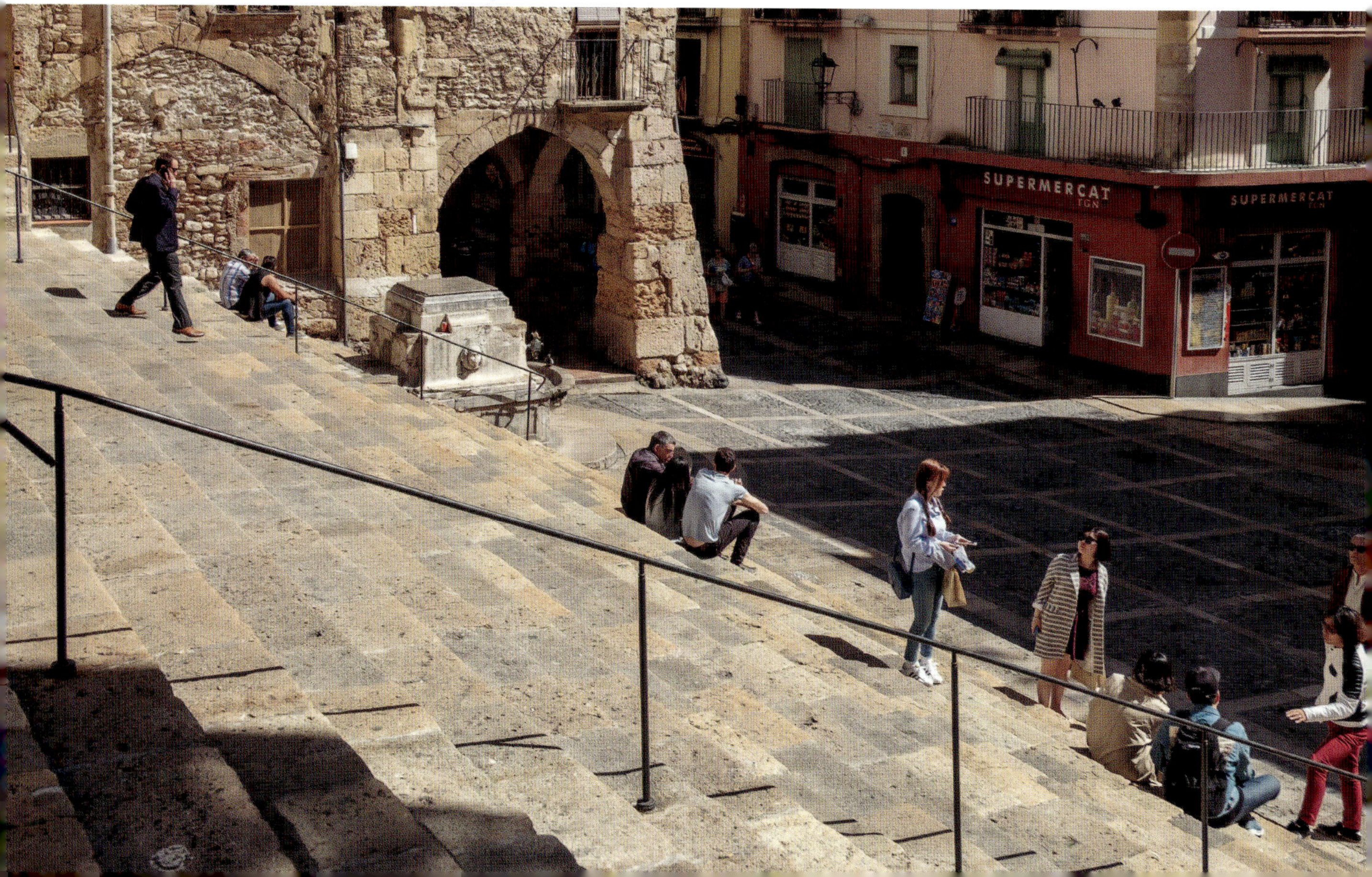

Streets and hidden nooks and crannies

The Part Alta is a maze of streets and surprising hidden nooks and crannies. Everyone has their favourite and you have to explore them on foot to really appreciate them. Here are just a few to begin with: Carrer de la Merceria, with its Gothic arches and centuries-old shops standing alongside more innovative ones, was built on the site of the Roman walls and was a medieval vegetable market. If you go there for a wander on a Sunday morning, you'll find an antiques market selling postcards, books and fossils... Every year, on the nearby Carrer de Comte, local residents and artists paint the fifty bollards in the street in bright colours with a theme of their choice.

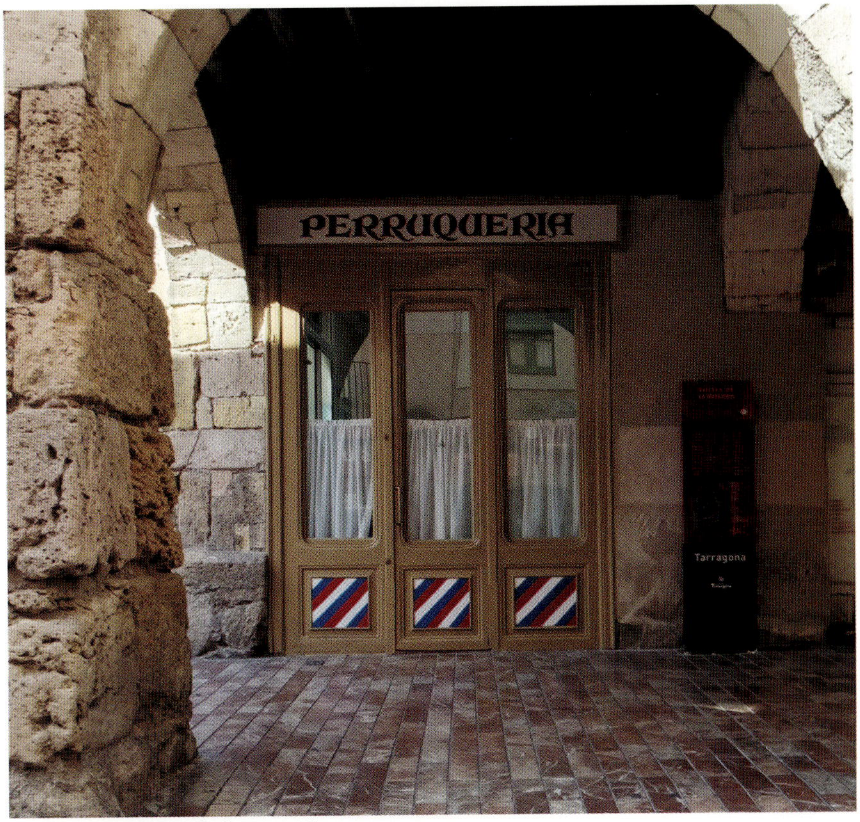

Porticoes on Carrer de la Merceria

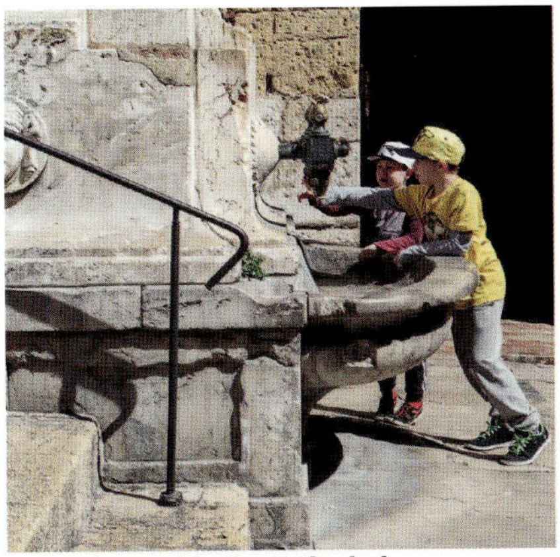
Fountain outside the Cathedral

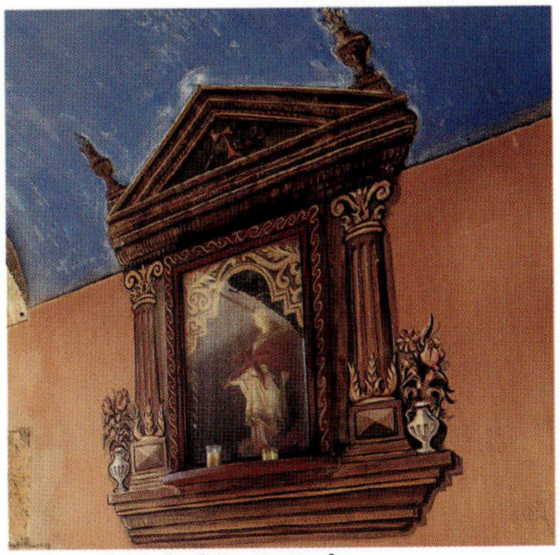
Votive chapel of Santa Tecla

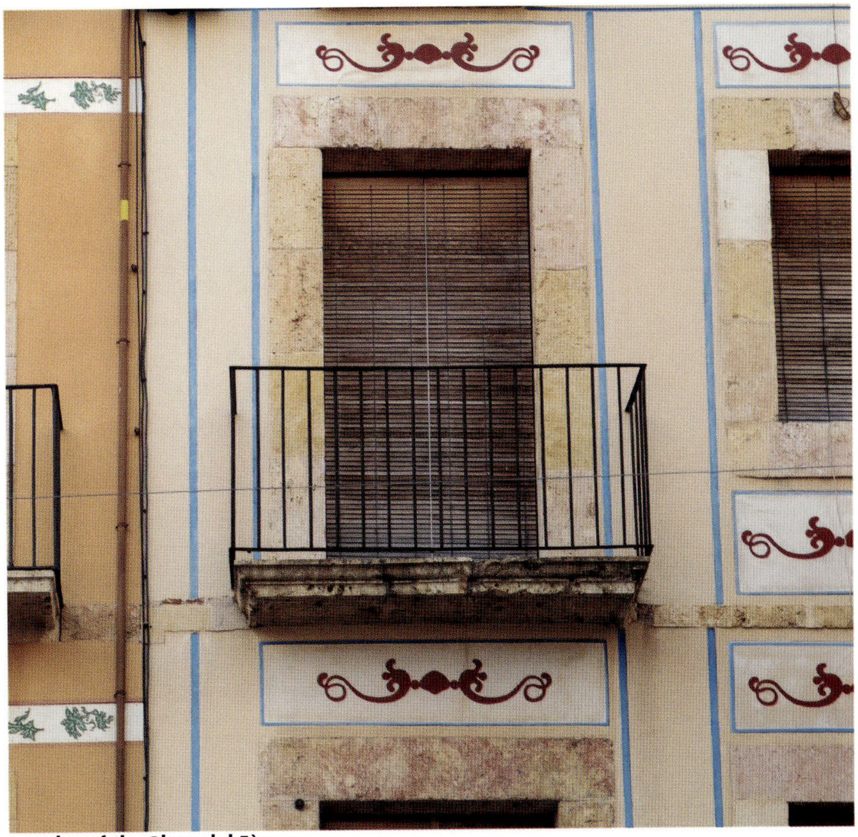
Façades of the Plaça del Fòrum

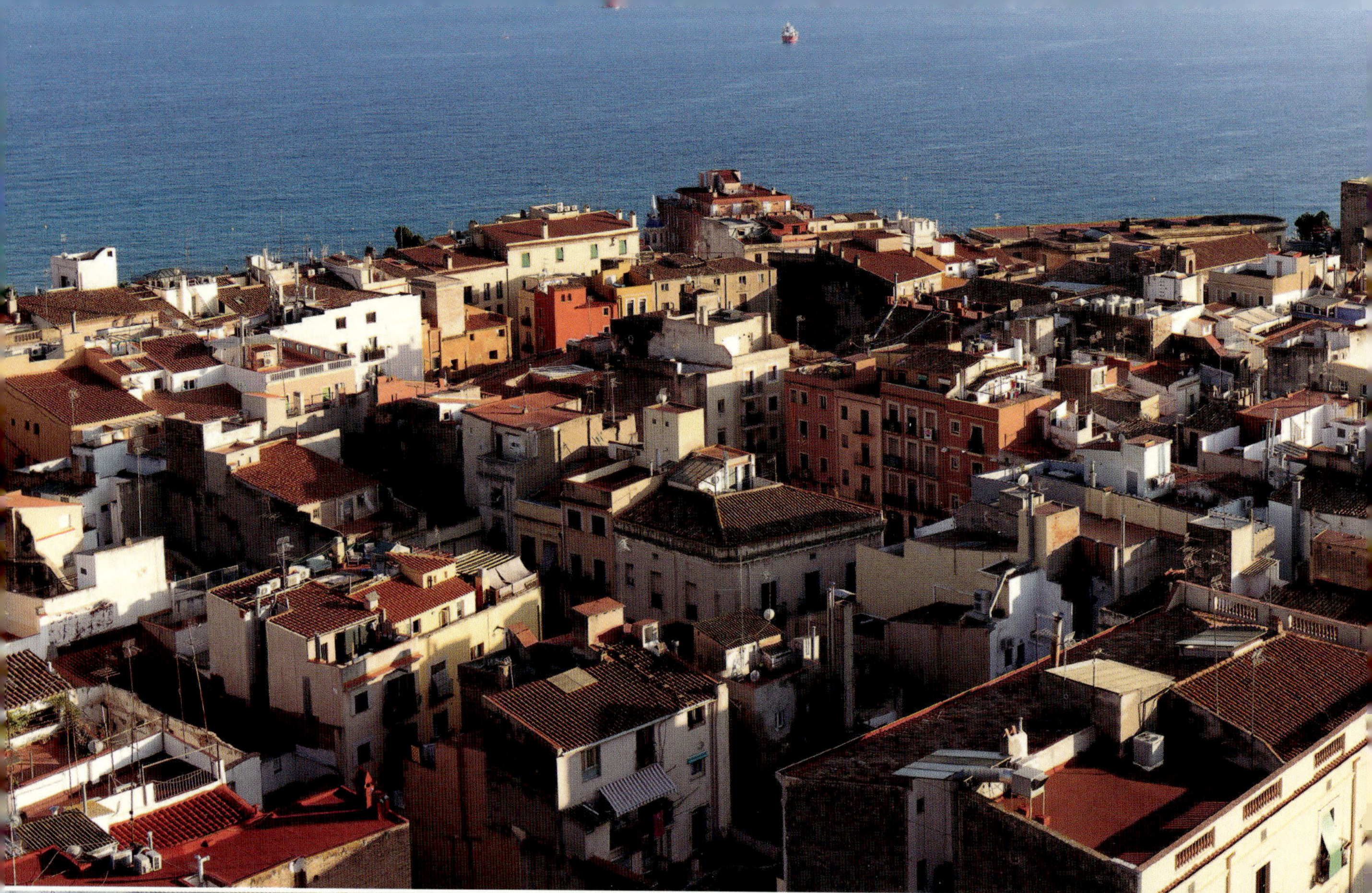
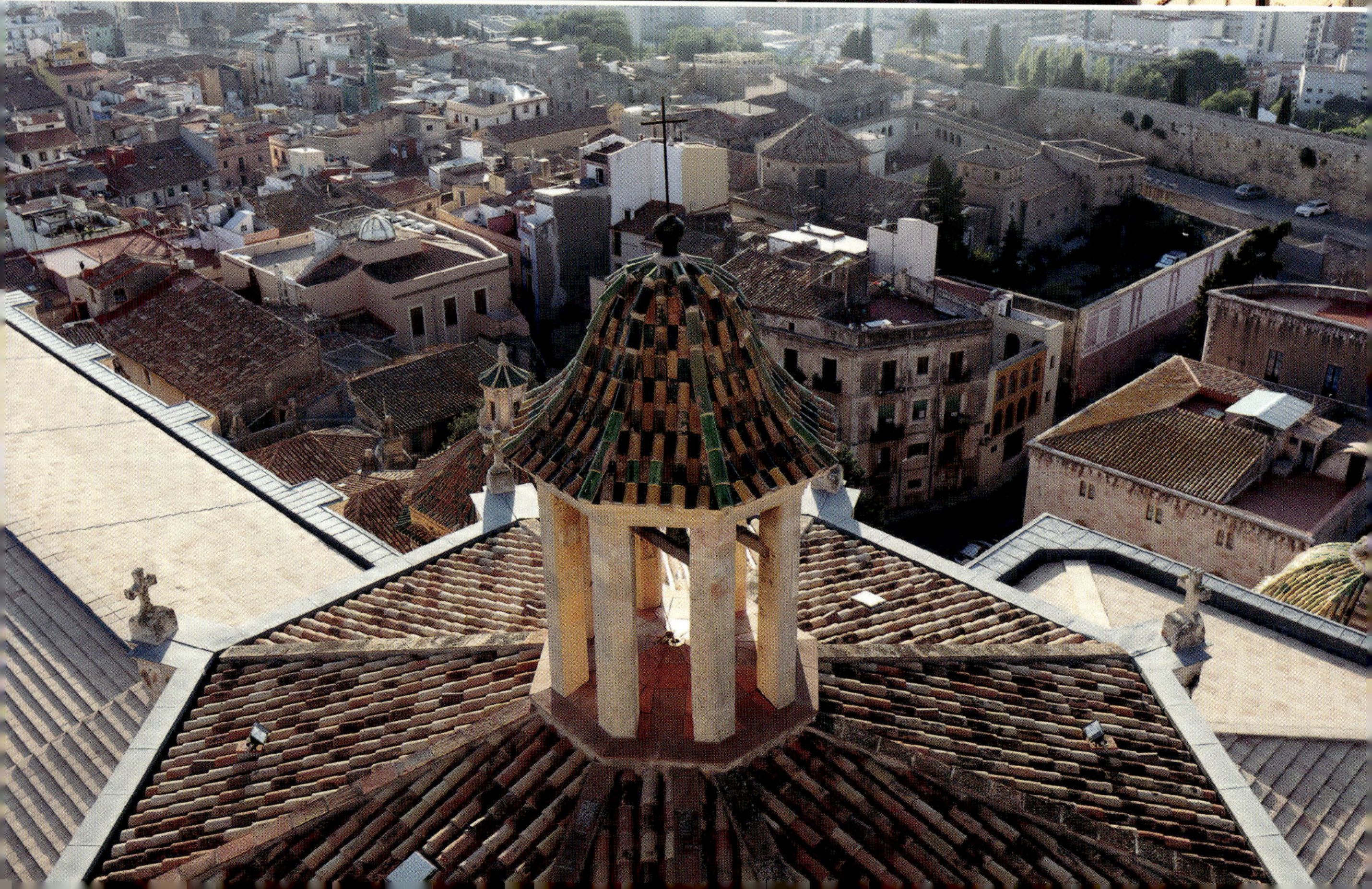

You can see more than 50 Roman inscriptions etched into the façades of many houses in the Part Alta. Some of them are on Carrer Merceria, but you'll also find them on Carrer Mediona, on the Cathedral façade… The building, the Col·legi d'Enginyers Industrials, at number 6, Carrer de les Escrivanies Velles, is a great place to see them. On the wall are two funeral tablets from the late 2nd century BC and two Hebrew inscriptions. They are replicas, the originals being kept inside the college. These are two examples of the way heritage is inextricably linked to daily life. Further down, in Plaça dels Sedassos, you can have dinner next to one of the entrances to the Circus arena. These are two examples of the way heritage can go hand in hand with daily life.

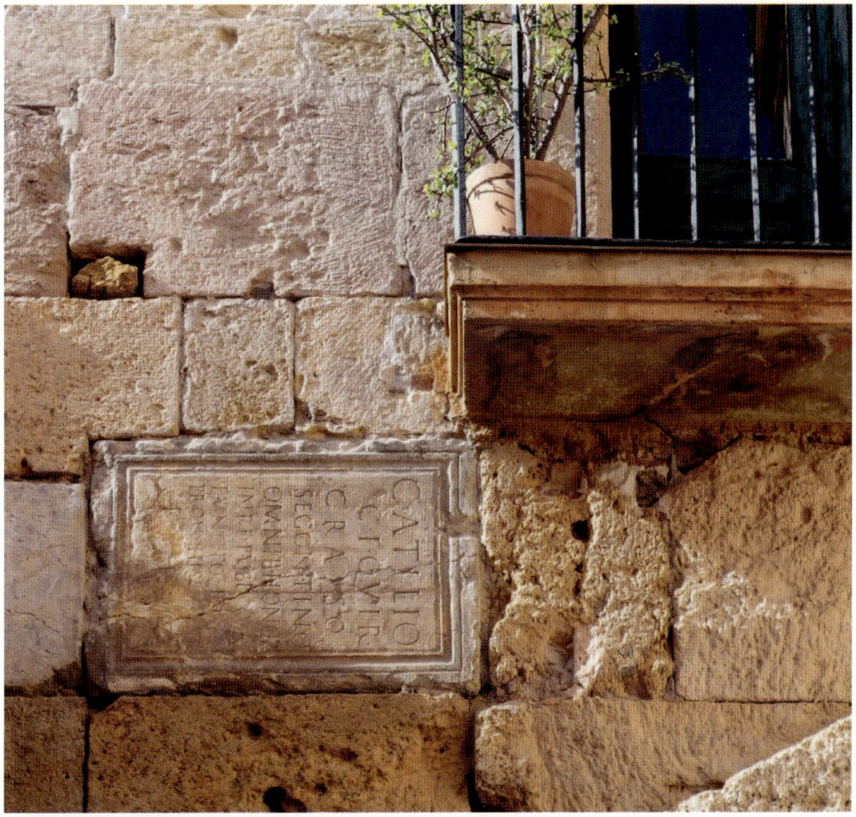

Carrer dels Ferrers

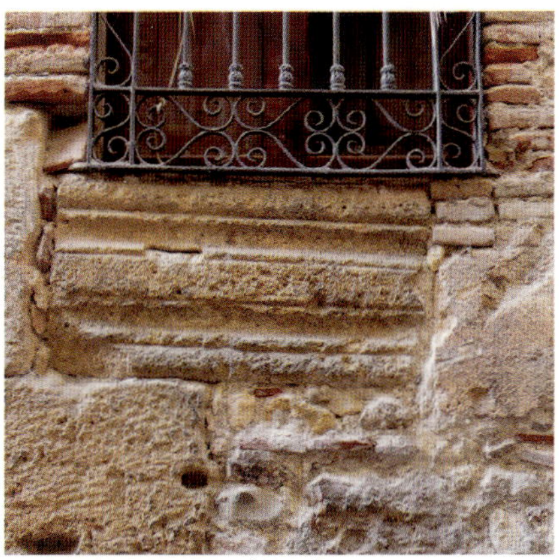

Carrer de Sant Pere i Estubes

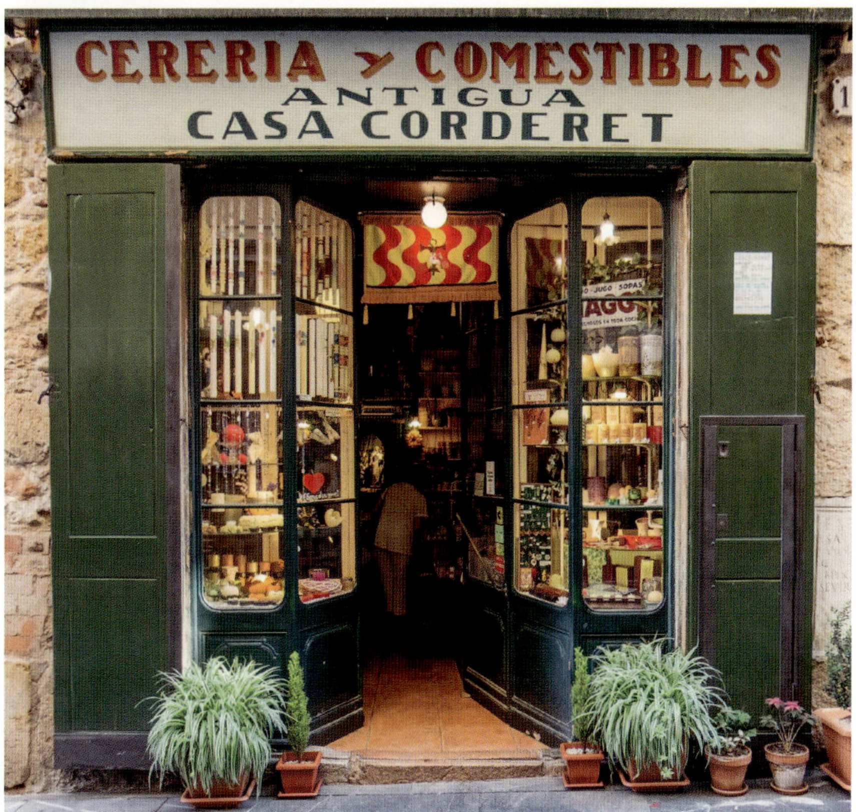

Traditional shop in Carrer de la Merceria

← The top of the Cathedral bell tower

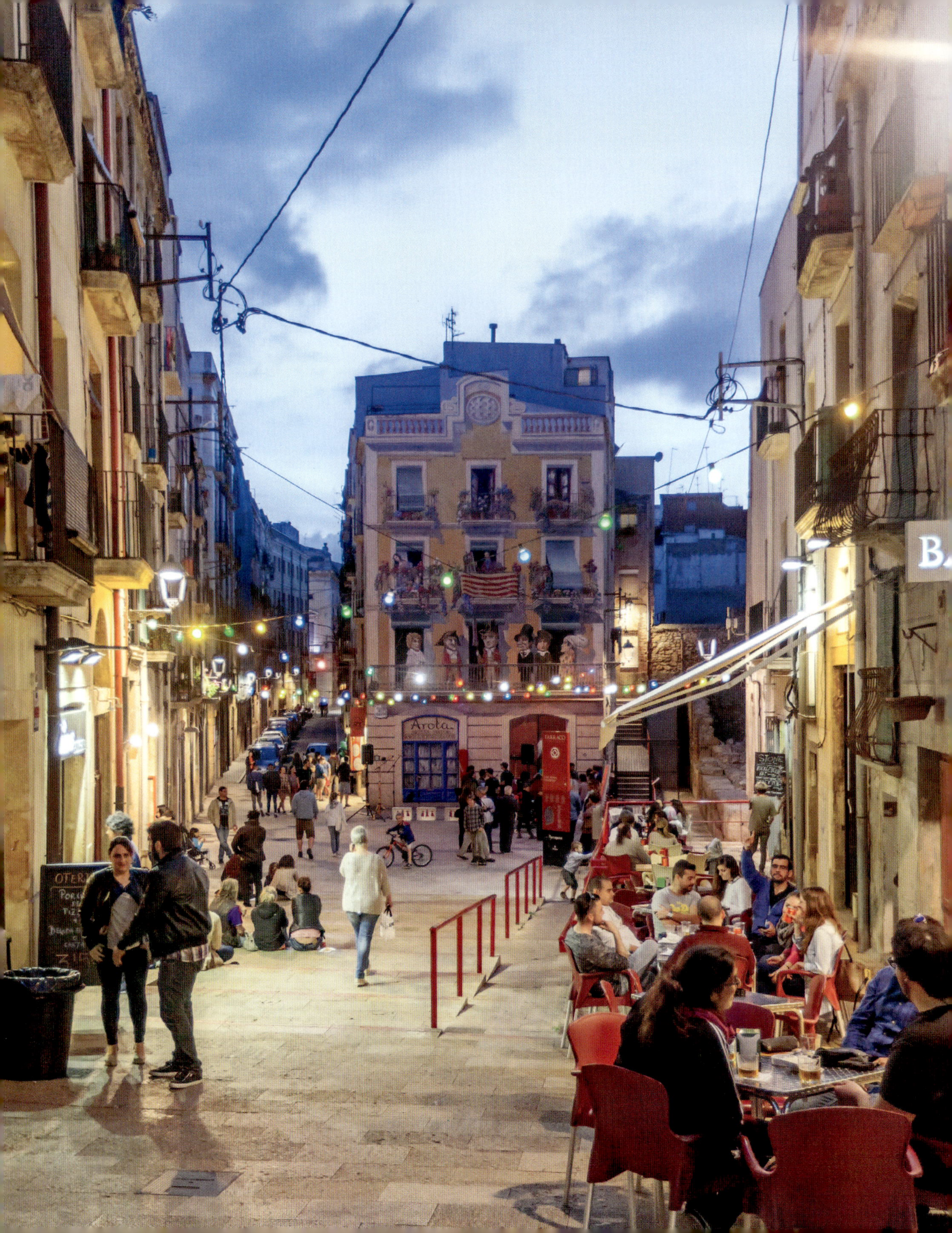
Arola

Church of Sant Llorenç

The current church dates from the 14th century, although it has been refurbished several times: once by the Renaissance architect, Pere Blai, and the last time in 1990. Known as the farmers' church, the architect Jujol created the sculptures and decorative elements for the building, and for the Farmers' Guild, including the casket for the procession of the Holy Sepulchre, the procession of the Pieta, the altar and floor, the images of Saint Lawrence, Saint Isidore, etc.

The Call jueu

The Jewish Quarter, or Call jueu, was situated around the current Plaça dels Àngels, and was made up of streets such as Carrer d'en Granada and squares like Plaça d'en Rovellat. It had a synagogue, school, baths and a small doorway leading out of the walls. You can still see the Gothic arches on Carrer Talavera, and the ones in Ca la Garsa. People from around the world with connections to Tarragona's Jewish community often visit in search of their roots.

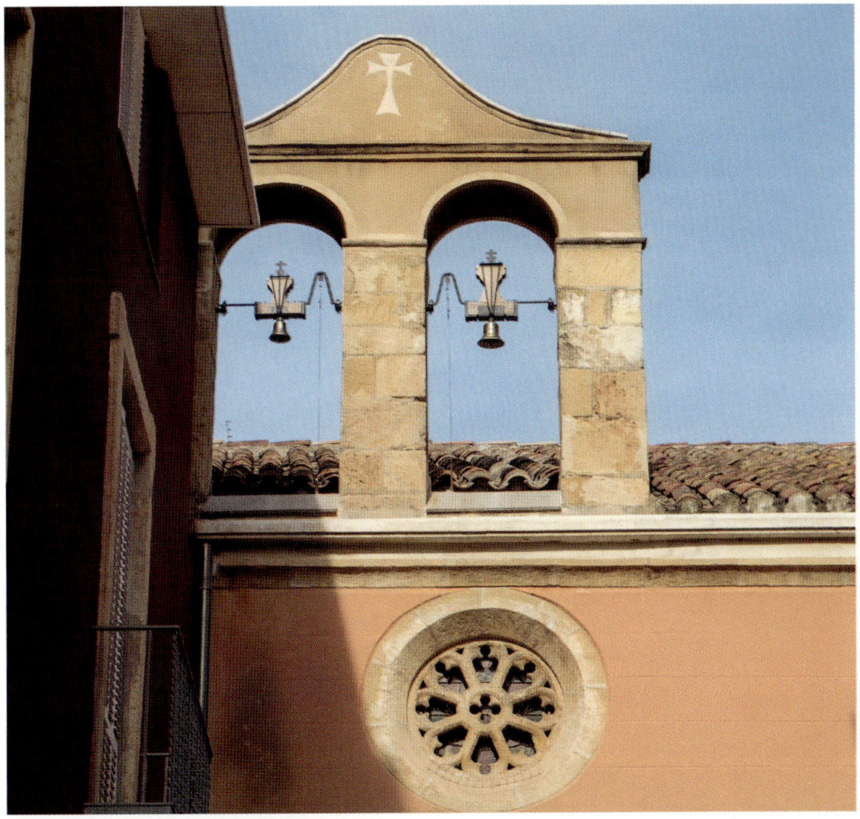

Church of Sant Llorenç bell tower

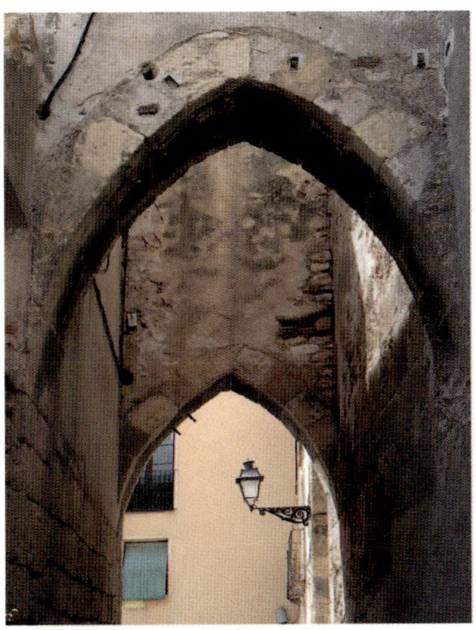

Archways in the Jewish Quarter, near Plaça d'en Rovellat

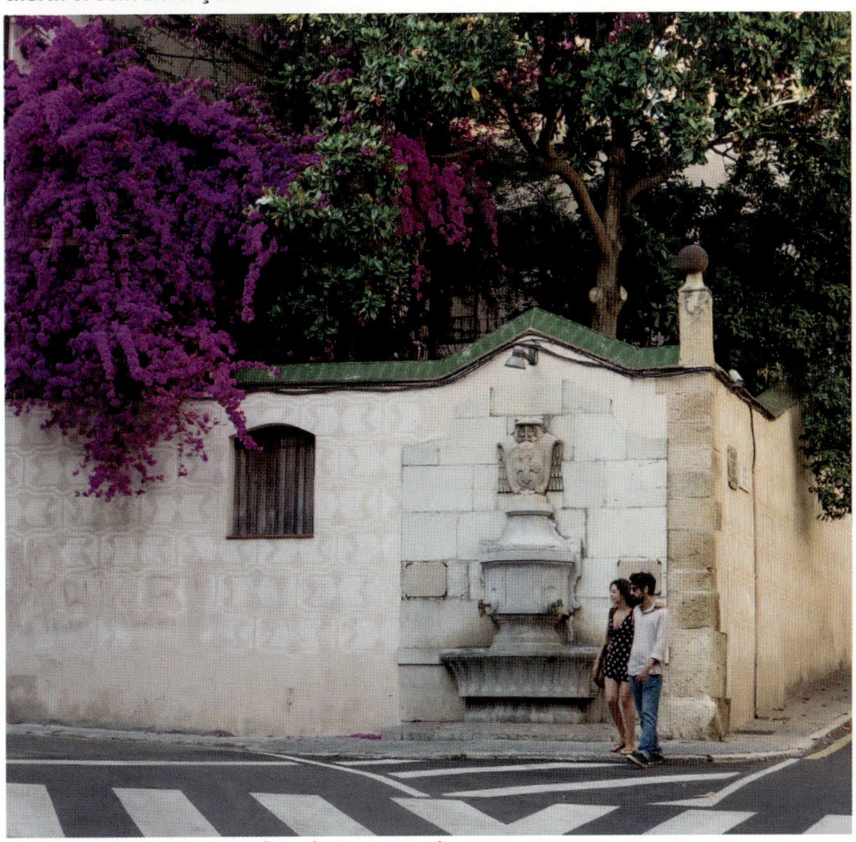

The Armanyà fountain, in Plaça de Sant Antoni

← Plaça dels Sedassos

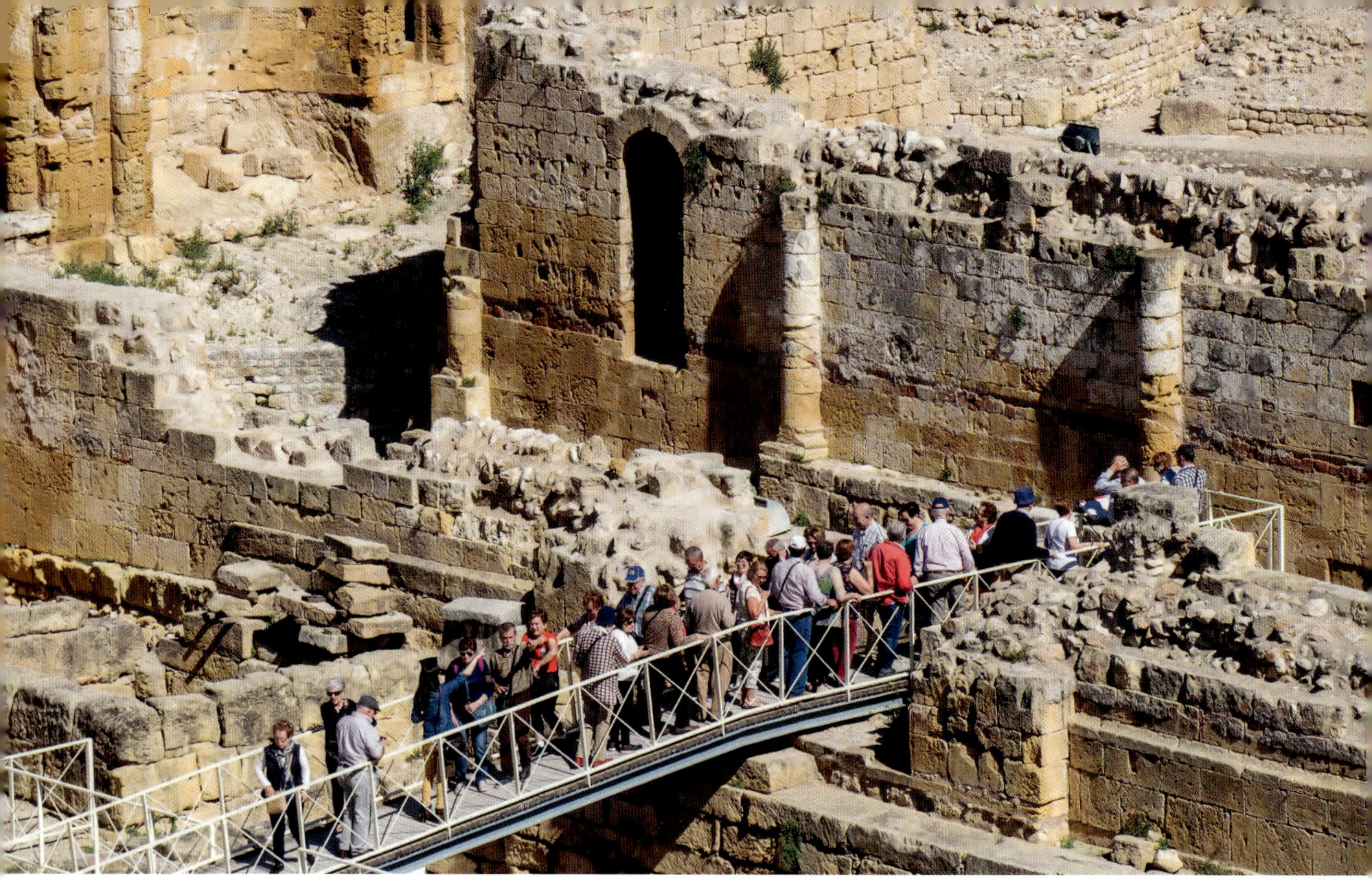

↑ Santa Maria del Miracle in the centre of the Roman Amphitheatre ↓ Chapel of Santa Tecla la Vella | Chapel of Sant Pau

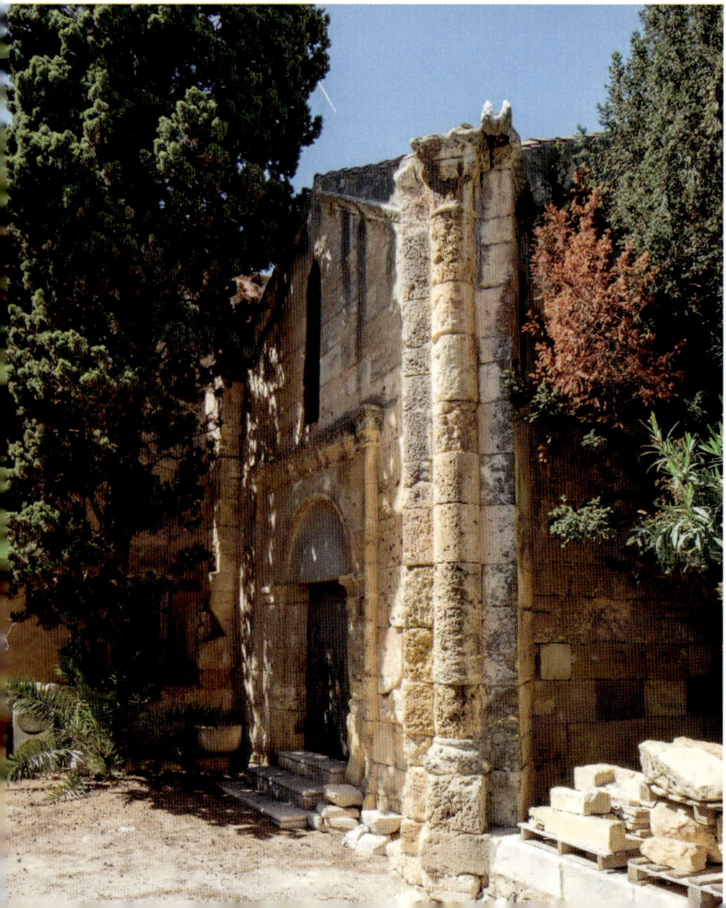

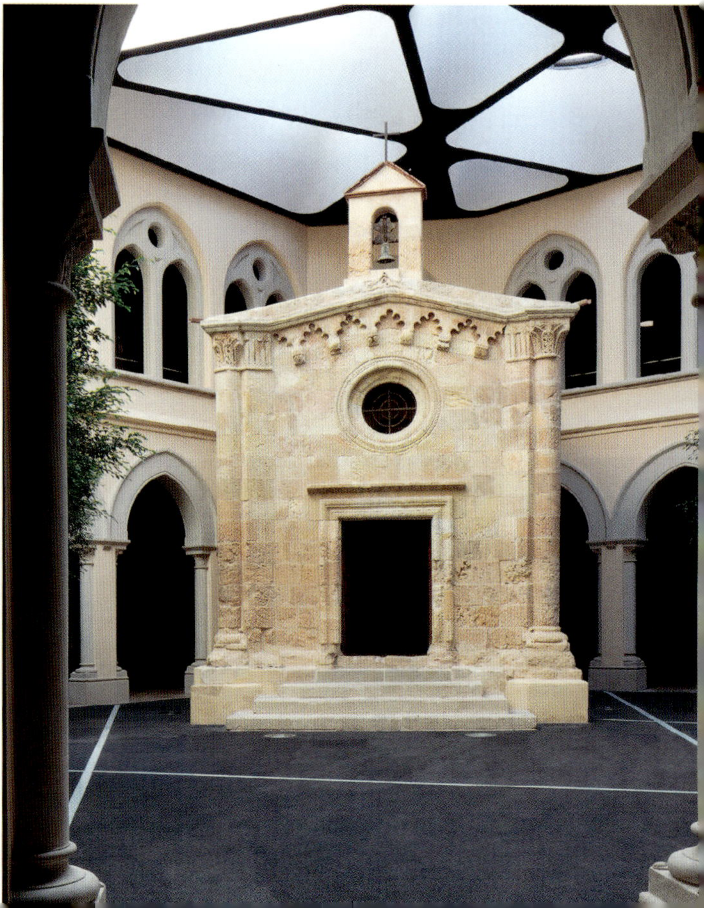

Santa Maria del Miracle

After Bishop Fructuosus and his deacons were martyred there, the Amphitheatre became a place of Christian worship. A Visigothic basilica was built on the site in the late 6th century but it was abandoned some time during the Islamic era. A Romanesque church dedicated to Saint Mary was built here in the 12th century. A Trinitarian convent and a prison, which was closed in 1908, have also stood on the site. The buildings attached to the church were also demolished making it visible but resulting in its collapse. The rest of the medieval remains were demolished in 1930.

Chapel and Old Hospital of Santa Tecla

The chapel of Santa Tecla la Vella is a small 13th-century Romanesque building which was extended in the 15th century using earlier materials. It was the church of the Cathedral cemetery, which stood in what is now Carrer de les Coques. Across the street, the Hospital of Santa Tecla, now the home of the Tarragona Regional Council, housed the poor and orphans and tended the sick in the 12th and 16th centuries.

Chapel of Sant Pau and Seminary

The 13th-century chapel of Sant Pau stands in one of the cloisters of the former Pontifical Seminary. According to a pious belief, it was built on a rock on which the apostle is thought to have preached. The neo-Gothic seminary building dates from 1883 and was designed by the architect Font i Carreras. It was recently refurbished and renamed the Centre Tarraconense El Seminari. It is open to the entire community and has a library with more than 100,000 books.

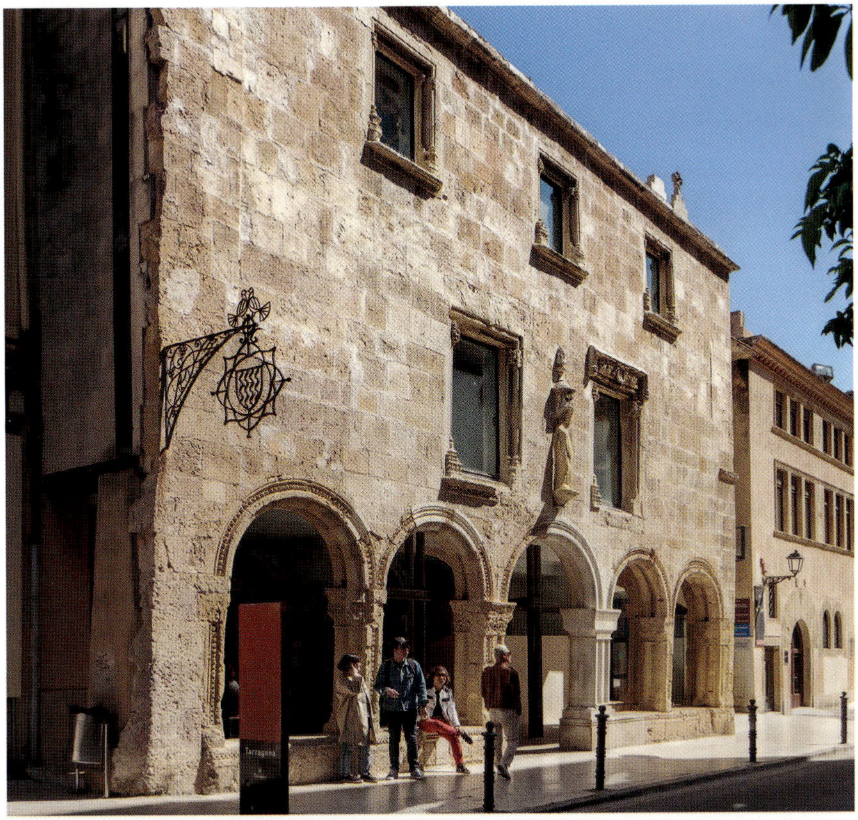

Old Hospital of Santa Tecla on Carrer de les Coques

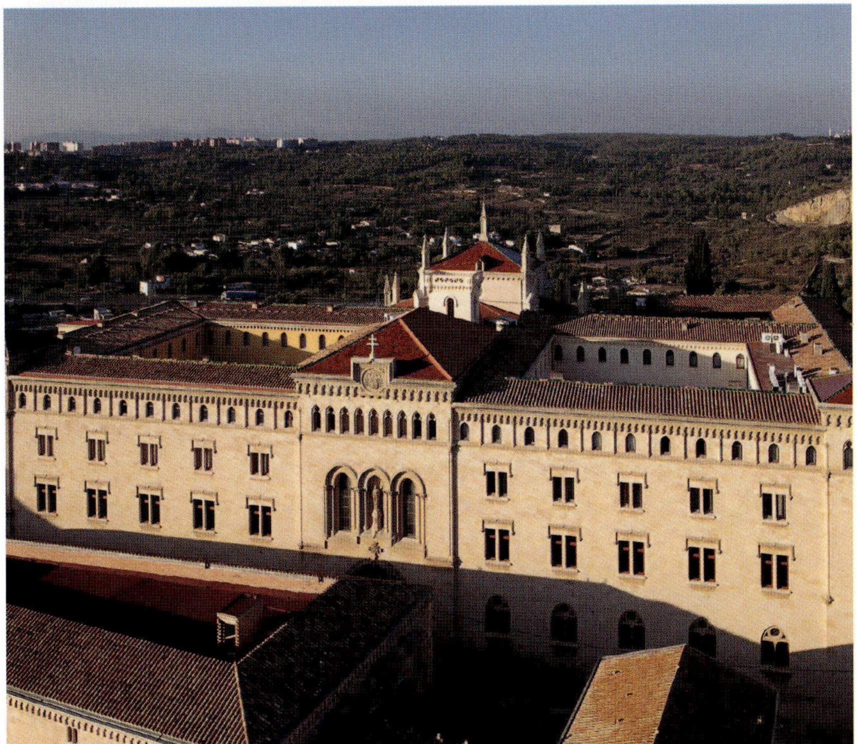

The Seminary, seen from the bell tower of the Cathedral

The Cathedral

The temple of the acropolis

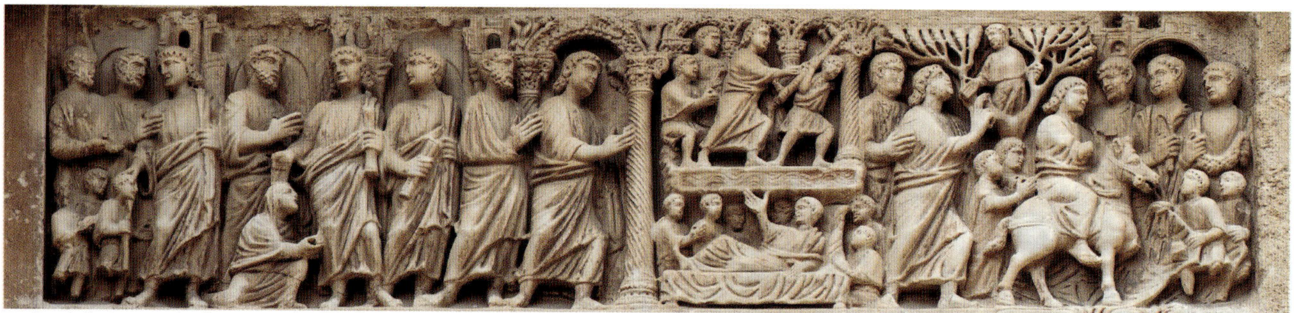

Early-Christian sarcophagus embedded in the façade of the Cathedral (370-400 AD)

The Cathedral was built between the 12th and 14th centuries on the site of the Roman temple dedicated to the Emperor Augustus that stood at the top of the hill overlooking the city. The building reveals the transition from Romanesque to Gothic architecture. When Augustus died in 14 AD, the Roman Senate declared him a divinity, as they had done previously with Julius Caesar. The following year, Emperor Tiberius granted the people of Tarragona permission to dedicate a temple to the new god. According to the Roman historian Tacitus, the temple in Tarraco served as an example for all the capitals of the Empire.

The Roman holy precinct began to be dismantled from the 5th century onwards when Christianity became the dominant faith. A basilica is believed to have been built on the site during the Visigothic period, on the upper terrace of the Roman temple. This 6th-century building would have been the metropolitan episcopal see that replaced a previous one. It was abandoned after the Muslim incursion in the early 7th century. From 1154 onwards, building work commenced on the Cathedral complex comprising a chapter house set around cloisters which used one of the enclosing walls of the holy precinct. The building of the Cathedral proper began with the main apse, which had already been completed by 1184. It has a Latin-cross floor plan with three naves, a transept and three apses, which house the chapel of Santa Maria — also known as the chapel of Els Sastres, or tailors — the high altar and the chapel of Sant Oleguer. It was consecrated in 1331 and Gothic, Renaissance and baroque chapels were added at a later date.

The main façade

The main façade has three portals corresponding to the three naves of the Cathedral. The central one is Gothic and features carvings of the apostles and prophets dating from two different eras, while the portals on either side are Romanesque. The central portal, which dates from the late 13th century, has ogival arches. An early-Christian sarcophagus dating from the end of the 4th century has been set into the wall above the right-hand Romanesque wall; it depicts scenes from the life of Christ. The tympanum dates from the late 14th century and depicts the Final Judgement with Christ judging humanity. The trumeau, or central column of the Gothic portal, features one of the most interesting sculptures on the façade: the Virgin and Child. The façade is surmounted by a large rose window.

Main façade of the Cathedral →

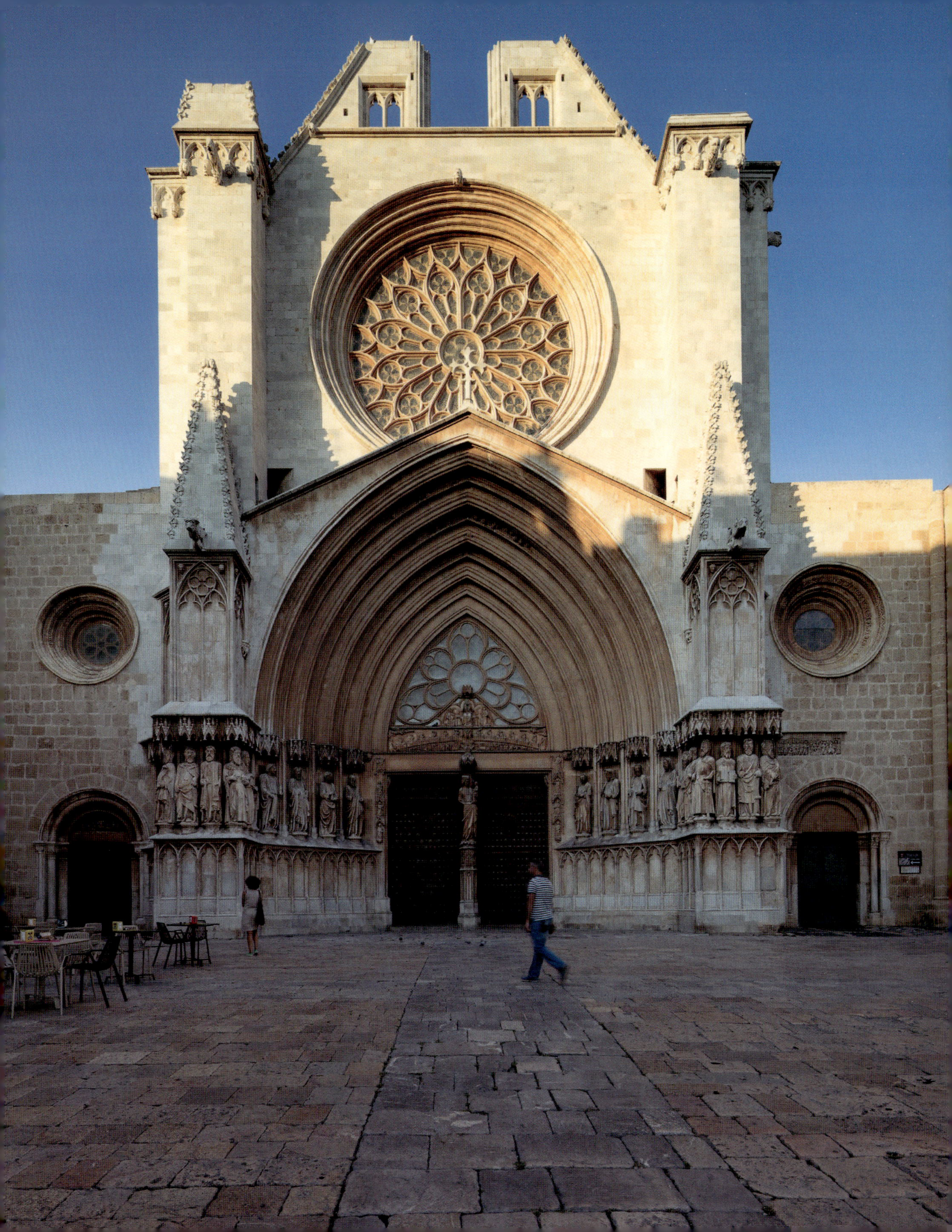

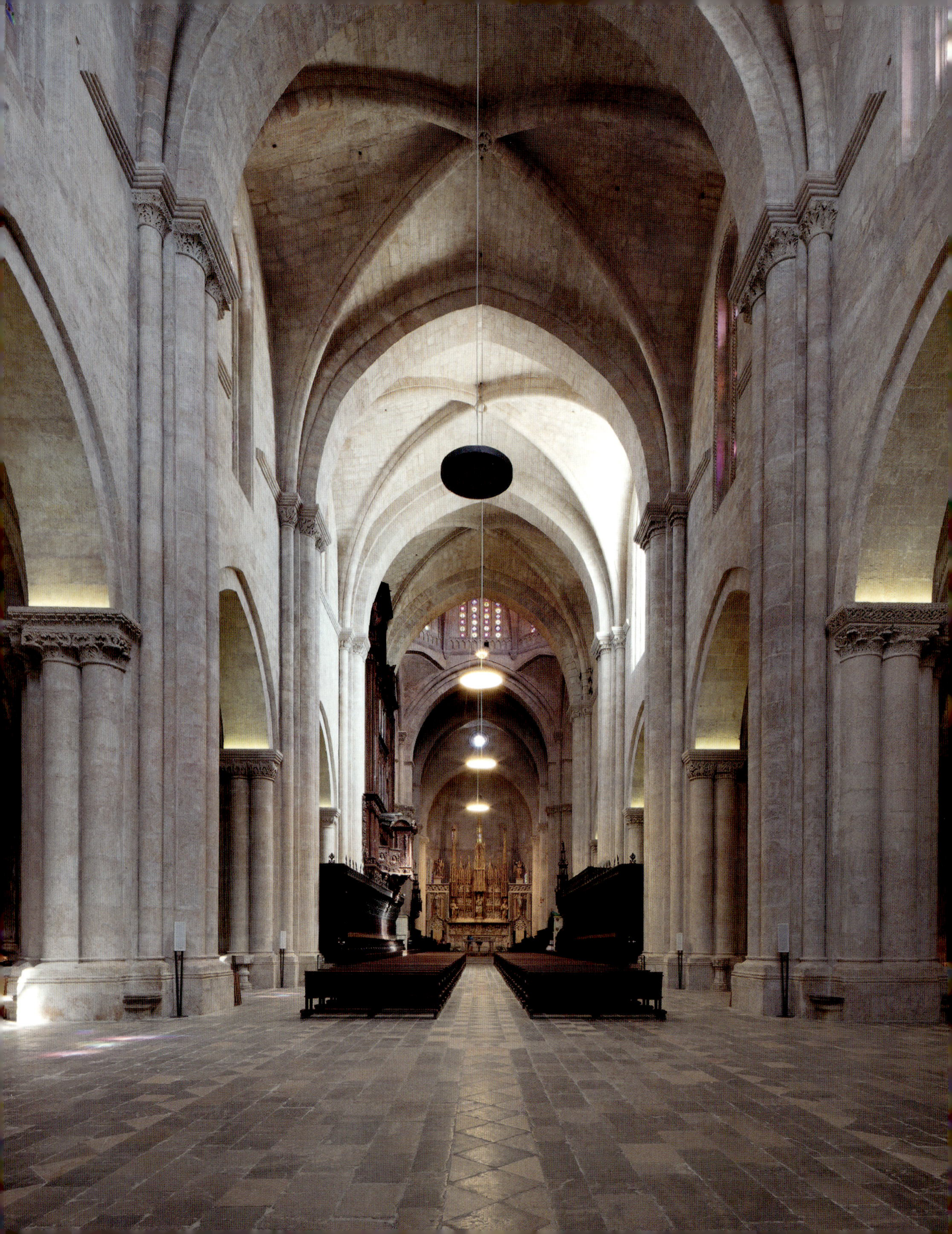

Central nave

The wide, light-filled central nave is 100 metres long, more than 25 metres high — 37 metres if we count the 13th century octagonal dome — and more than 16 metres wide. The bell tower stands on the right-hand side. The three naves are covered by cross vaults underpinned by cruciform pilasters attached to columns arranged in twos. The windows date from the Romanesque and Gothic periods. The stained glass windows with their openwork tracery date from the latter period and are a wonderful example of this art form. The nave also contains windows made at a later date.

Gothic reredos of Santa Tecla

This is one of the Cathedral's most important artworks and is dedicated to the patron saint of Tarragona. It was begun in 1426 by the sculptor Pere Joan, who also made the reredos in Zaragoza Cathedral, and is a Gothic masterpiece made of polychrome alabaster. The central figure of the Virgin and Child is flanked by Saint Paul and Saint Tecla. The reredos is carved with scenes from the life and martyrdom of the saint as well as the life of Christ.

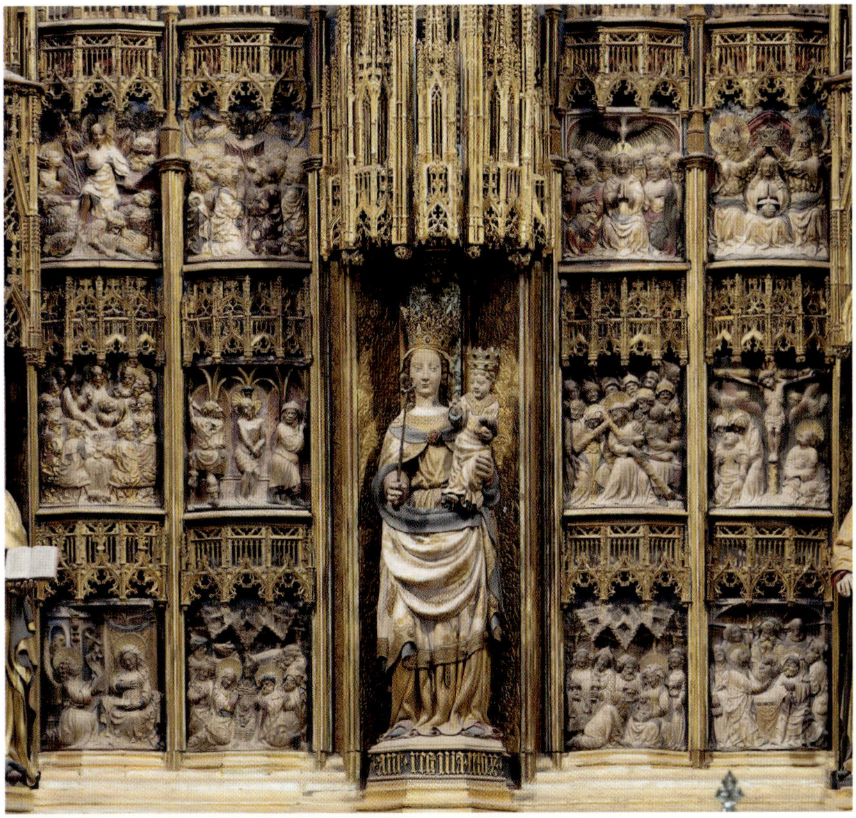

Detail of the reredos of Santa Tecla

Gothic and Renaissance chapels

The oldest chapel is dedicated to Saint Oleguer and dates from the 12th century. The chapels of Santa Maria (predating 1350) and Corpus Christi (1330, the former chapter house of the Romanesque canonry), Sant Miquel (middle of the 14th century), Santa Llúcia (14th century) and the Onze Mil Verges (between 1340 and 1344, now the chapel of the Baptistery) date from the Gothic period. The Renaissance is represented by the chapel of the Holiest, designed by Jaume Amigó and Pere Blai. The latter also designed the chapels of Sant Fructuós and Sant Joan, as well as the tomb of Archbishop Terés, which stands between the two chapels.

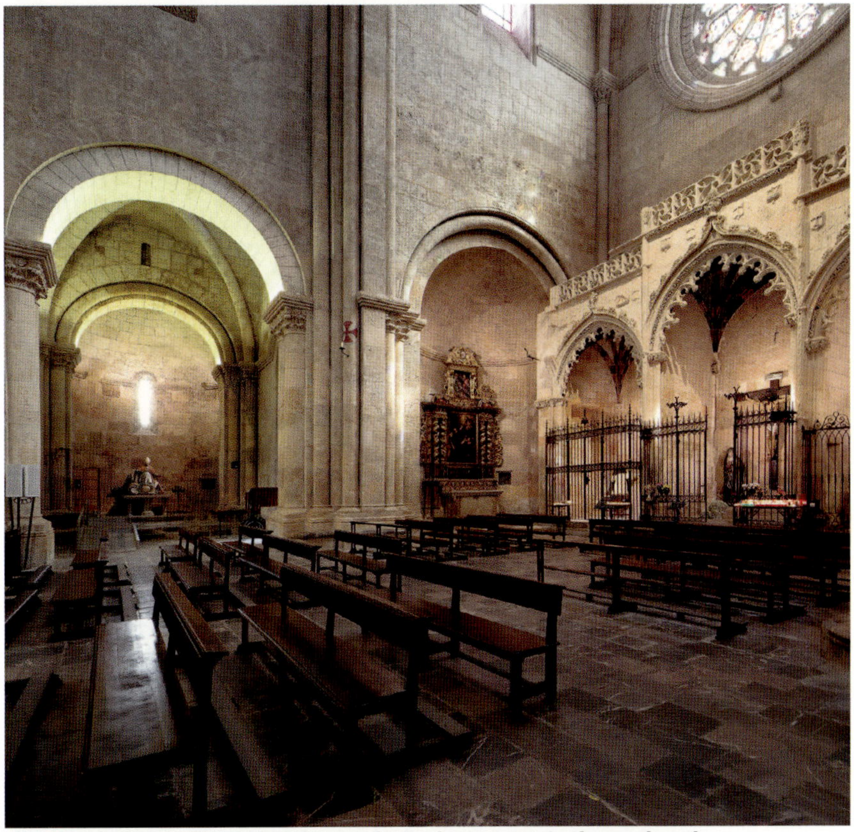

The chapel of Sant Crist de la Salut overlooks the transept in the north end

← Central nave

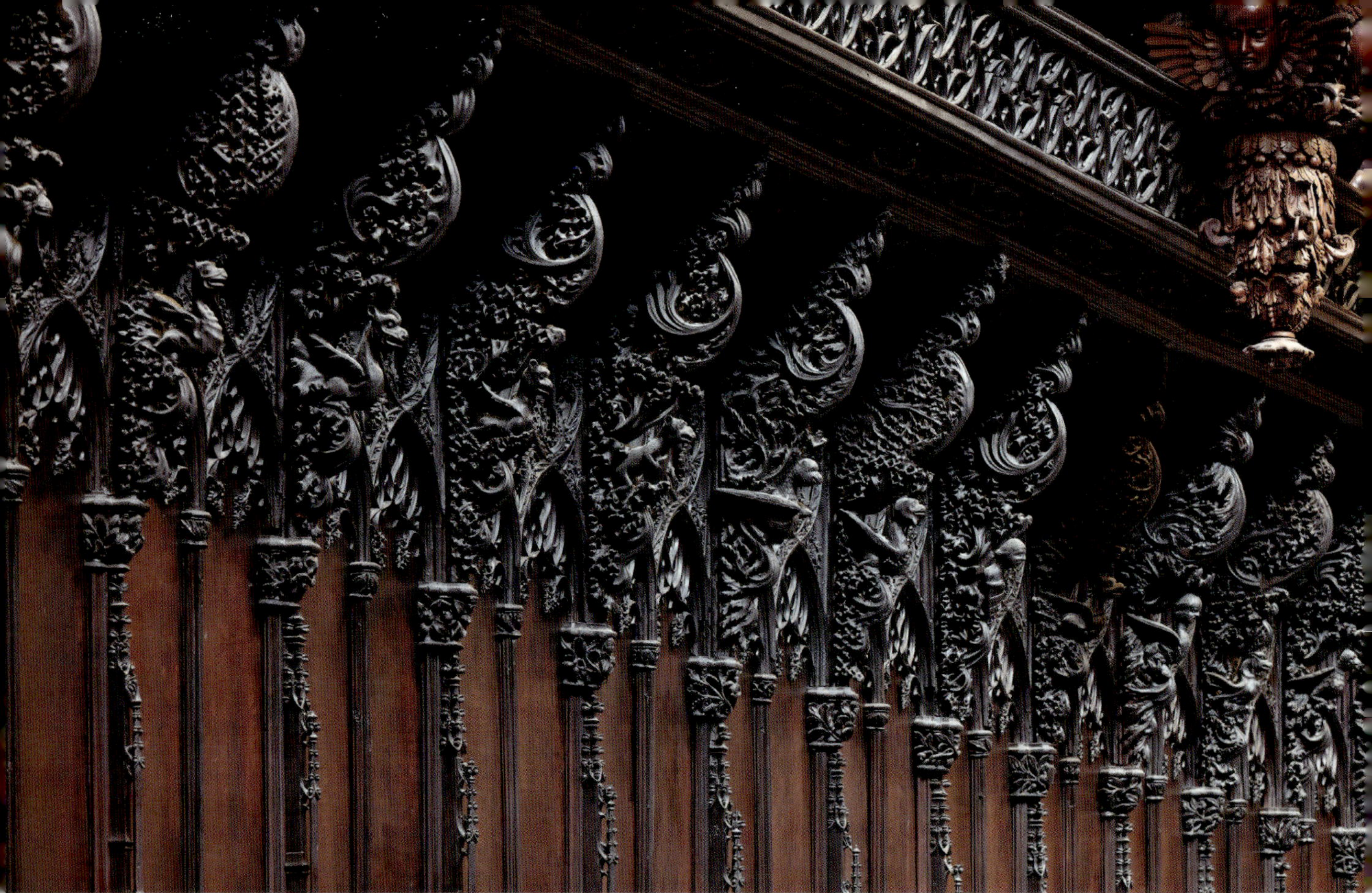
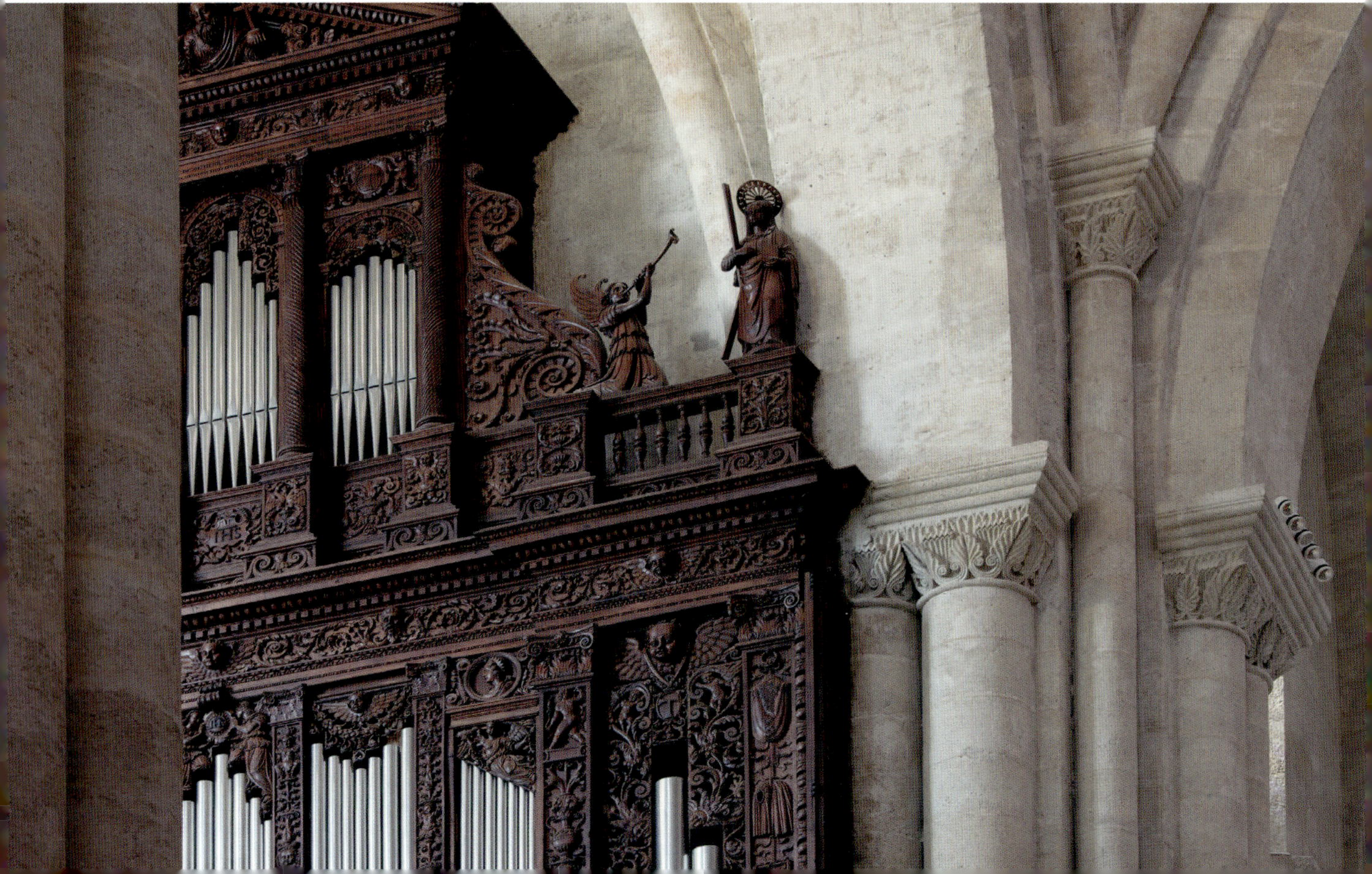

Choir

The choir stalls were made from Flanders oak by the carpenter Francesc Gomar between 1478 and 1488. He was commissioned by Archbishop Pedro de Urrea, who had made his solemn entrance into the city through the gate of Sant Antoni on 19th May 1446. Ten years later he captained the ship sent by Pope Callixtus III to fight the Turks. Urrea was born in Zaragoza and began his ecclesiastical career in Tarragona as a canon and treasurer at the Cathedral. He was also president of the Catalan Government, the Generalitat de Catalunya (1446). The pontifical seats date from 1534, and were carved by the sculptors Jean of Tours and Henri of Burgundy.

Organ

The organ is one of the most important in Europe and was designed in 1560 by the priest and architect Jaume Amigó, one of the leading exponents of the Camp de Tarragona school. He was self-taught and one of the first people to introduce Renaissance architecture to Catalonia. The sculptures and reliefs by Jeroni Xanxo and the Austrian, Perris Austris, were made between 1562 and 1566. The paintings on the door are by the Italian, Pietro Paolo de Montalbergo and the Greek, Pere Serafí. They were begun in 1563 and, when open, show the scene of the Annunciation, and when closed, the Adoration of the Shepherds and the Resurrection. The restored organ was reopened in 2013.

Tomb of Archbishop Joan of Aragon

Joan of Aragon and Anjou was the patriarch of Alexandria, and the archbishop who consecrated the Cathedral. He was the son of Jaume II, the king who found the relics of Saint Tecla in Armenia. Joan of Aragon died at the age of 30 in 1334. The white marble mausoleum is in the Italianate-Gothic style. The sarcophagus bears the recumbent effigy of the archbishop. He looks youthful and is smiling.

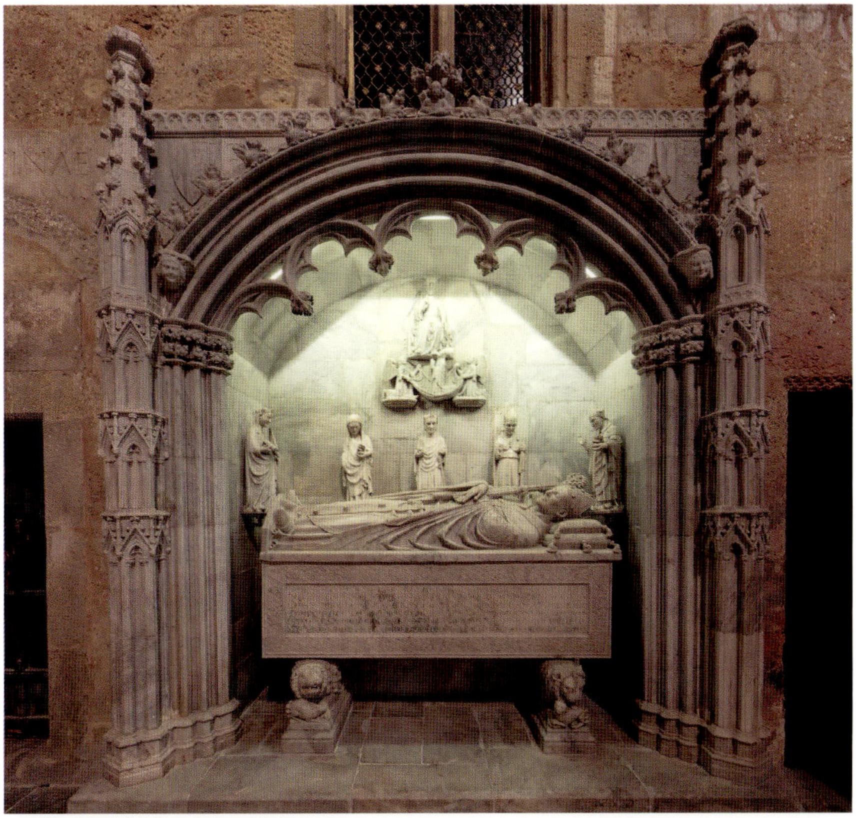

Tomb of Archbishop Joan of Aragon

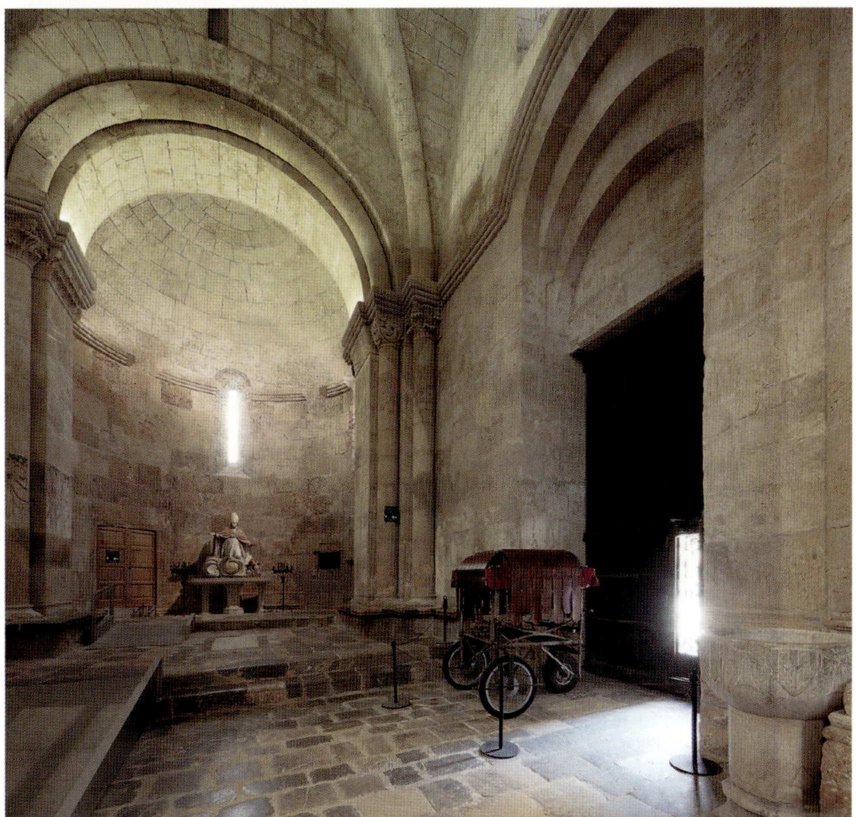

Chapel of Sant Oleguer

← Detail of the choir stalls and organ

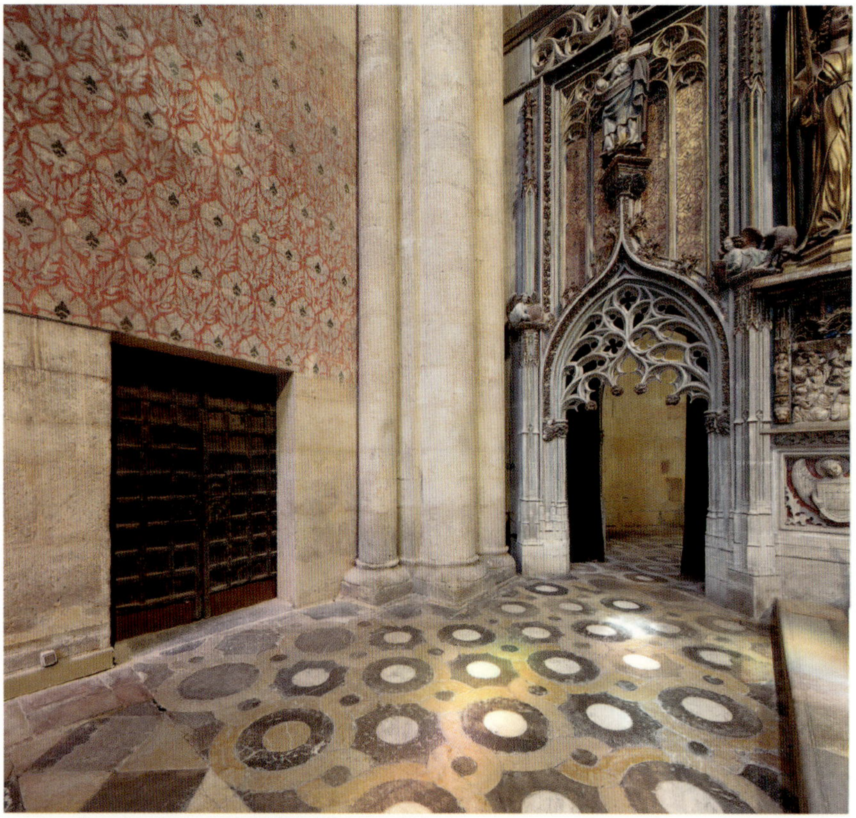

Roman floor in the *opus sectile* of the presbytery

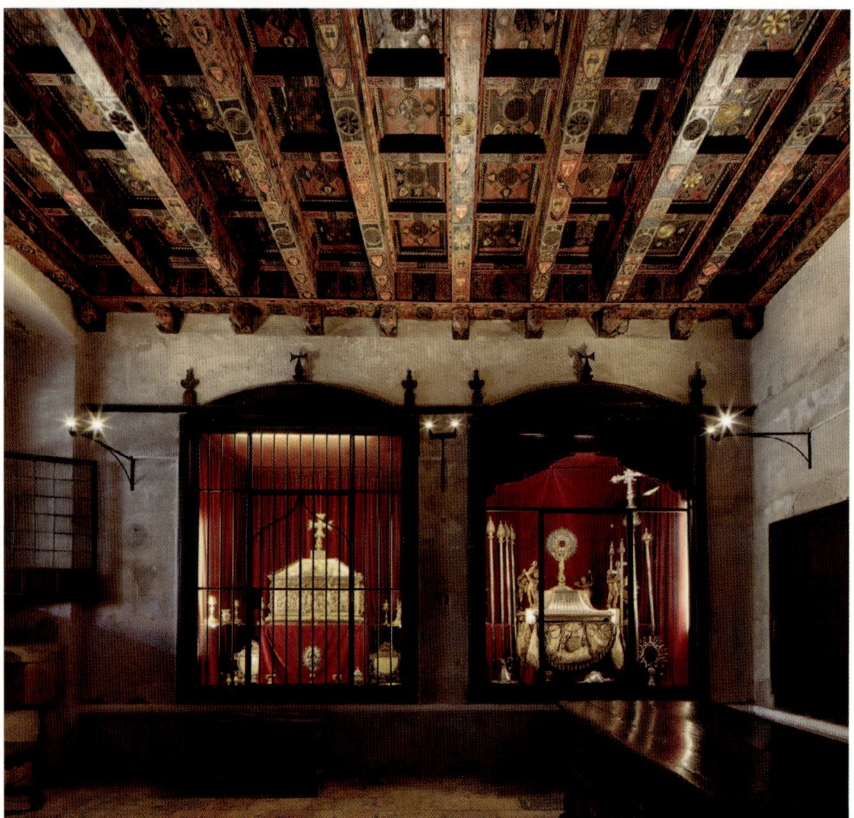

The treasury has a wonderful Gothic-Mudejar polychrome coffered ceiling

Sacristy

The sacristy has a rectangular floor plan and is covered by a pointed barrel vault. It was built in the 13th century in part of the Cathedral associated with the 12th century chapter house. Restoration work carried out between 1999 and 2004 removed obsolete structures and the row of Romanesque windows was restored. A wall with a Gothic portal separates the sacristy from the treasury, which has a wonderful Gothic-Mudejar coffered ceiling.

Baroque

The chapel of the Conception, was designed in 1674 in the classic baroque style. Some of the leading Catalan artists of the day worked on the project, including the architect Fra Josep de la Concepció and the sculptors Domènec Rovira II and Francesc Grau. The chapel is a wonderful example of the way architecture and the visual arts can be integrated. The chapel of Santa Tecla is mainly classical-baroque in style. It was begun in 1760 to house the reliquary of the saint. The altarpieces in the chapels of Santa Bàrbara, Sant Francesc and Sant Fructuós, and the marble tabernacle on the great altar, are baroque.

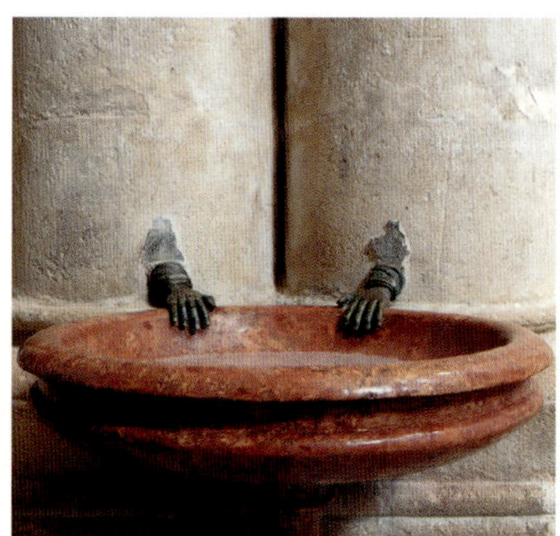

Baroque stoup

Chapel of the Immaculada Concepció →

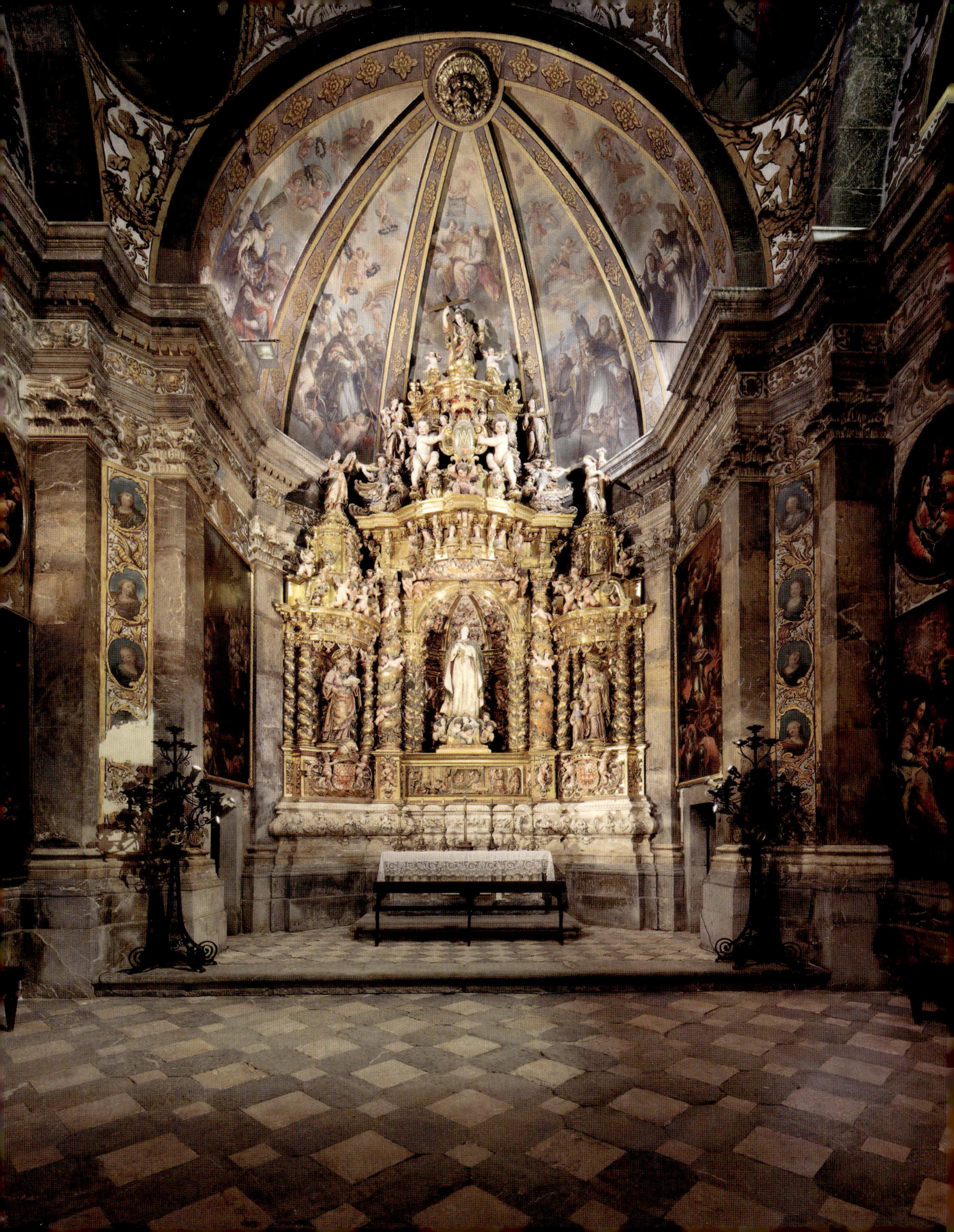

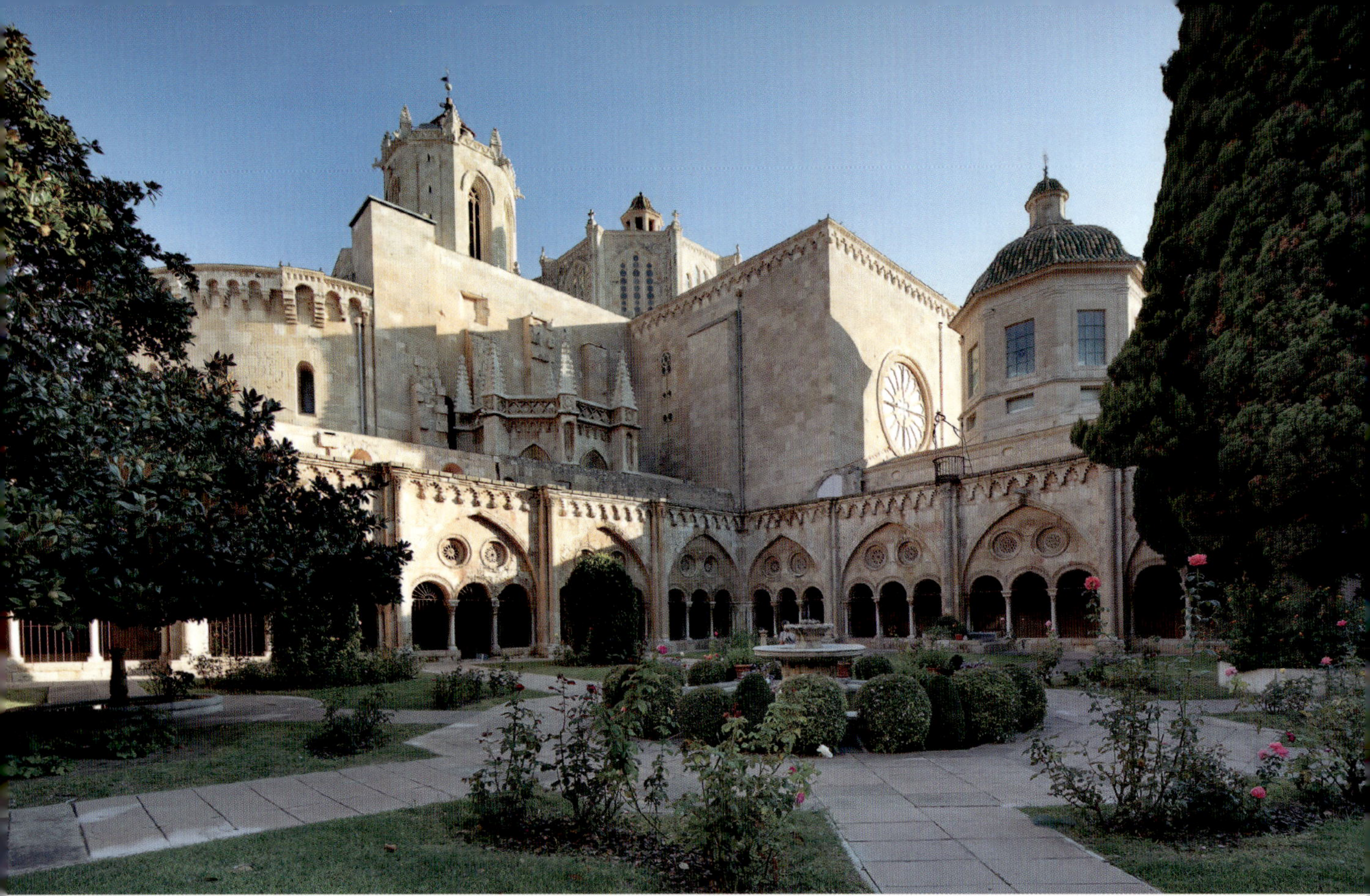

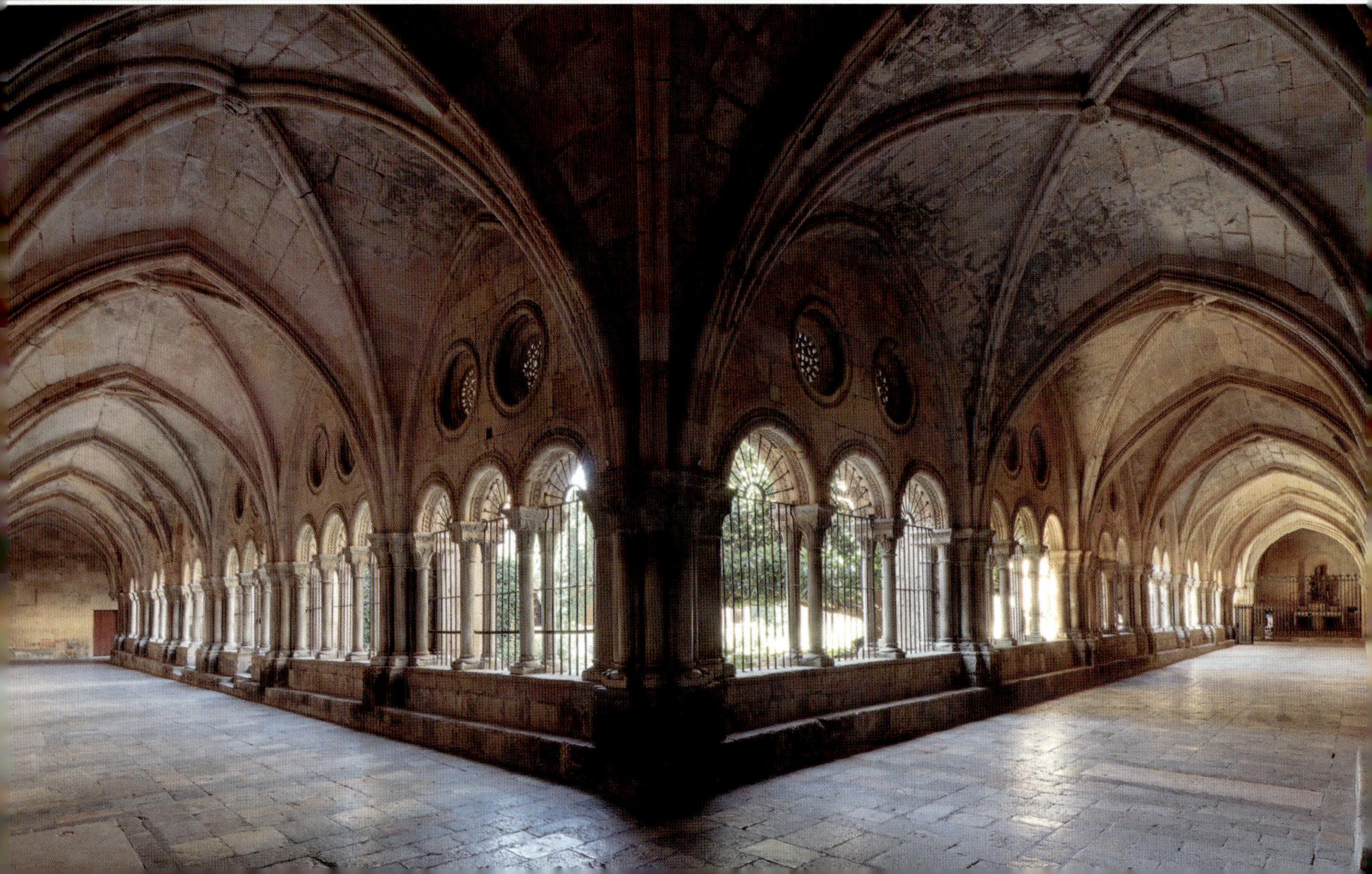

Romanesque gate

The majestic Romanesque gate dates from the 13th century and leads into the cloisters. It is made of white marble and the tympanum depicts Christ surrounded by the symbols of the four Evangelists. Its capitals feature naturalistic decorations of foliage inspired by Roman monuments, and scenes from the visit of the three Marys to the Holy Sepulchre. The single column is carved from one piece of stone. Its capital depicts scenes from the birth of Christ, the adoration of the Kings and their visit to Herod. The capitals at the sides feature scenes from the Resurrection. There is a chrismon above the door bearing the symbols of alpha and omega.

Cloisters

The cloisters are almost square and measure just over 45 metres by 45 metres. They were begun in the middle of the 12th century and consist of four galleries, each one with six pointed arches, subdivided into three semi-circular arches. The sculptural decorations are Romanesque and the ribbed vaults date from the early Gothic period. The capitals and cornices feature scenes from the Bible and other profane subjects, plant motifs, the yearly cycle... Highlights include the cornice showing the procession of the rats, showing that cunning can outdo strength: a cat that wants to catch some rats plays dead and when the rats take him for burial he “comes back to life” to catch them.

You can see the remains of the Temple of Augustus below ground level at one end of the cloisters. They were discovered during excavation work and include the 1st-century exedra and the monumental gate measuring 7 metres.

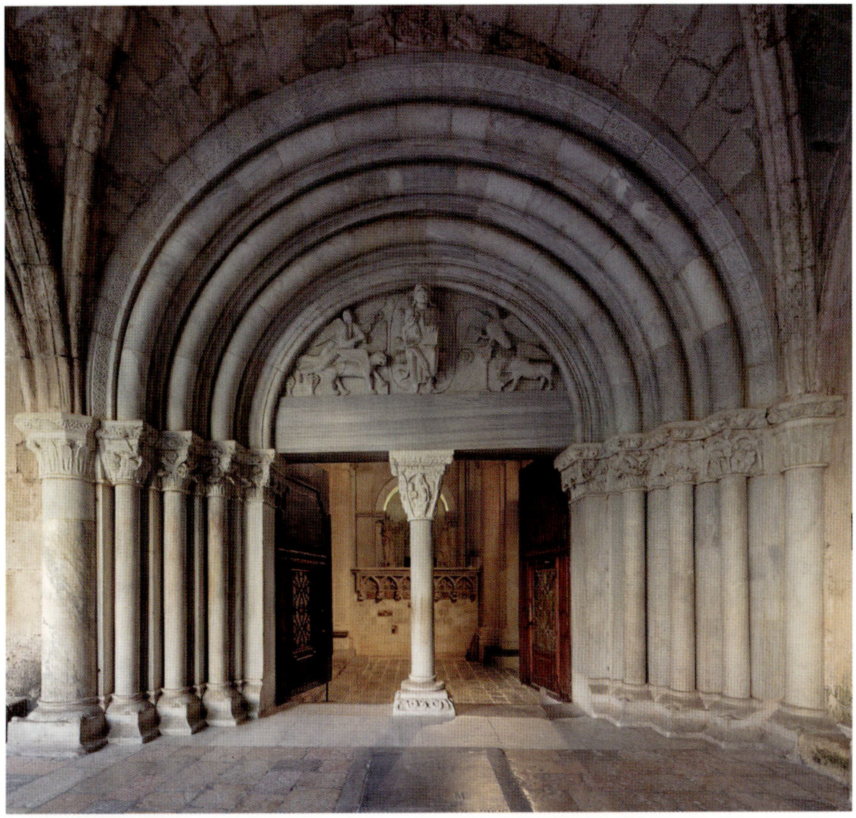

Romanesque gate

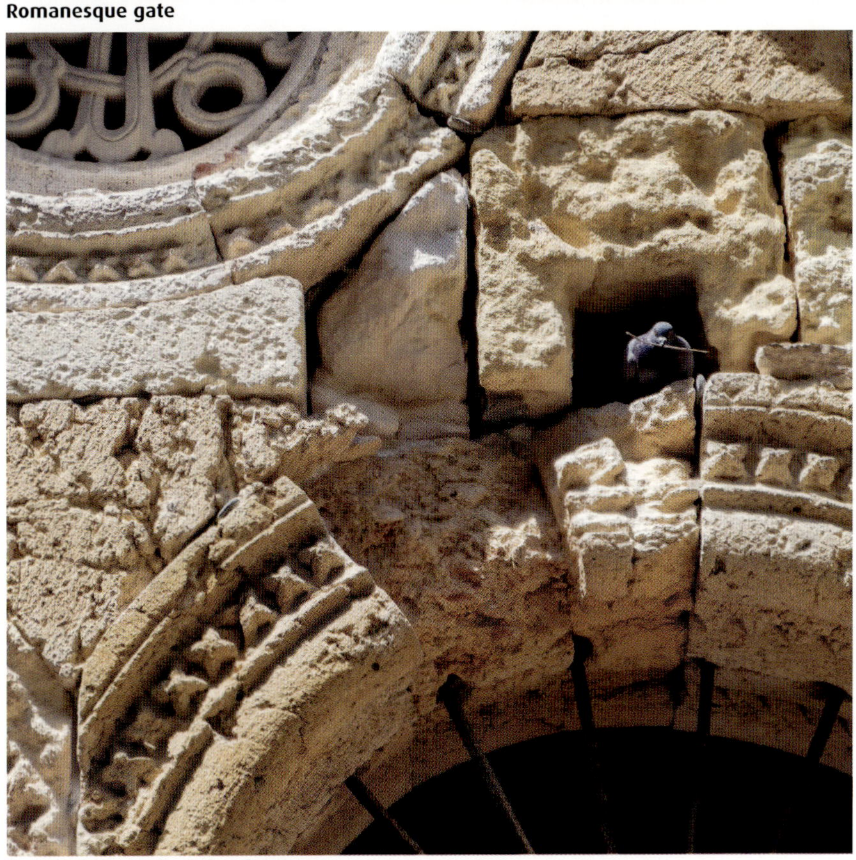

Detail of the wall of the cloisters

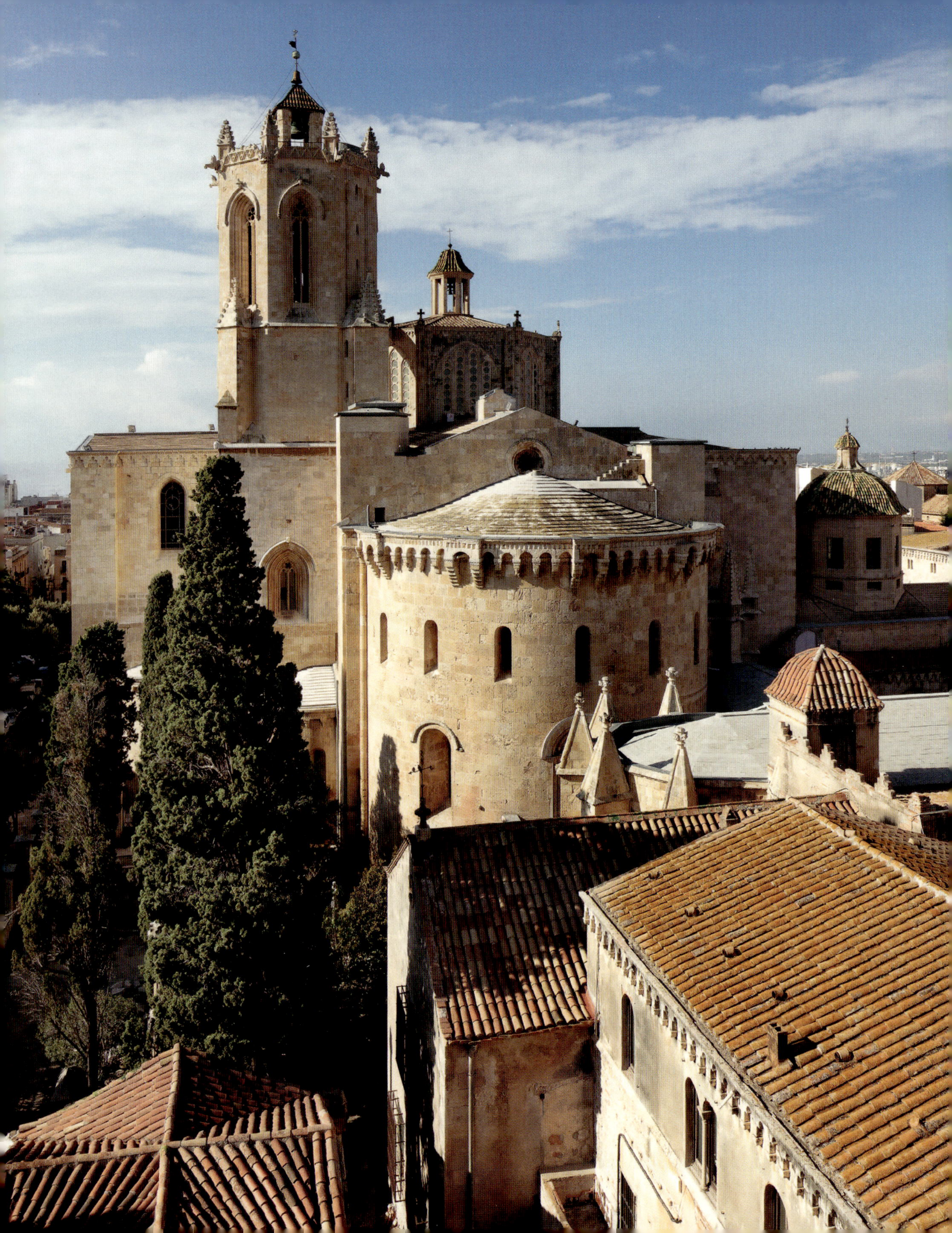

Bell tower

It contains some of Europe's oldest working bells dating from 1313 and 1314. They are called Fructuosa, Assumpta and Clàssica Rocabertina. The bell tower stands 70 metres high and was built in several different phases from the 14th century. It is surmounted by an early 16th-century small temple containing the famous hour bell Capona. You can climb to the top using the staircase that passes through the Sala dels Monjos (Hall of the Monks), the Sala dels Rellotges (Hall of the Clocks) and the Sala de les Campanes (Hall of the Bells). Some of the bells are rung using the Catalan full-circle method, meaning the bell rotates 360 degrees and is stopped by the bell-ringer when it is balanced mouth upwards.

Museu Diocesà

The museum opened in 1914 and showcases some 400 objects from its flagship collection of more than 10,000 items. The periods represented span the Roman era to the 18th century. Highlights include the funeral stele of Eutyches; the sarcophagus of Apollo and the Nine Muses; the Islamic arch dated 960 AD; six Romanesque images of the Blessed Virgin; the collection of Gothic painting, sculpture and silverwork by artists including Bernat Martorell, Jaume Ferrer II and Lluís Borrassà; an important collection of tapestries, including *The Good Life*, woven in the 15th century in Arras, France; and an impressive baroque carving of Christ.

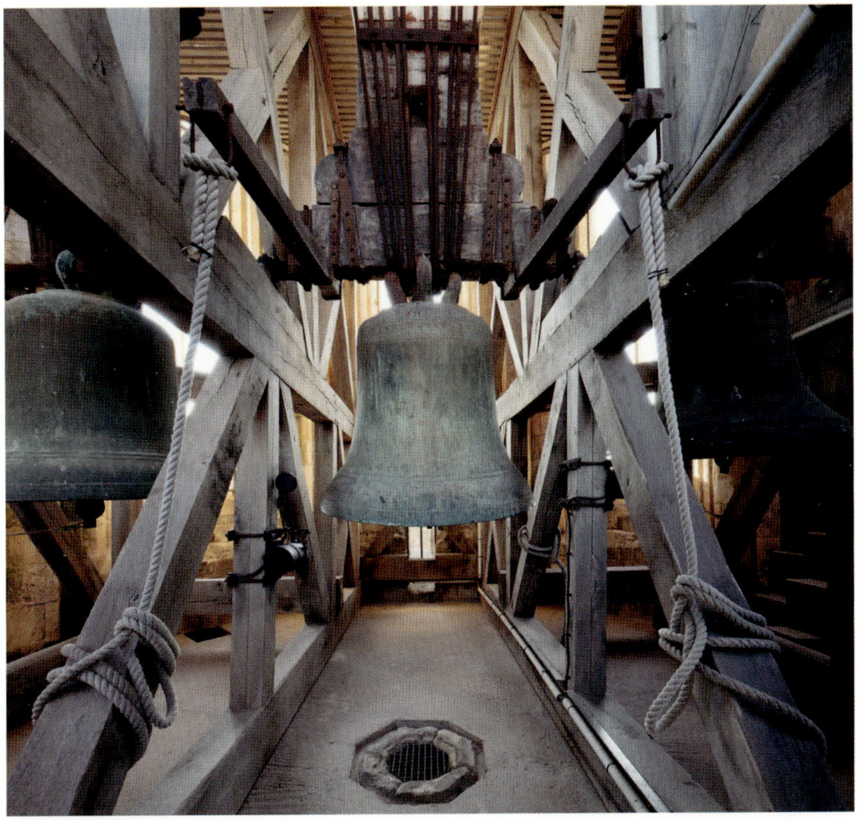

The Cathedral bells

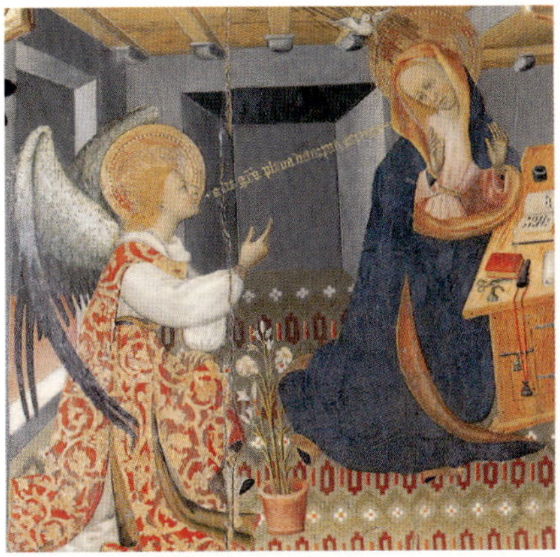

Altarpiece of the Annunciation, by Jaume Huguet

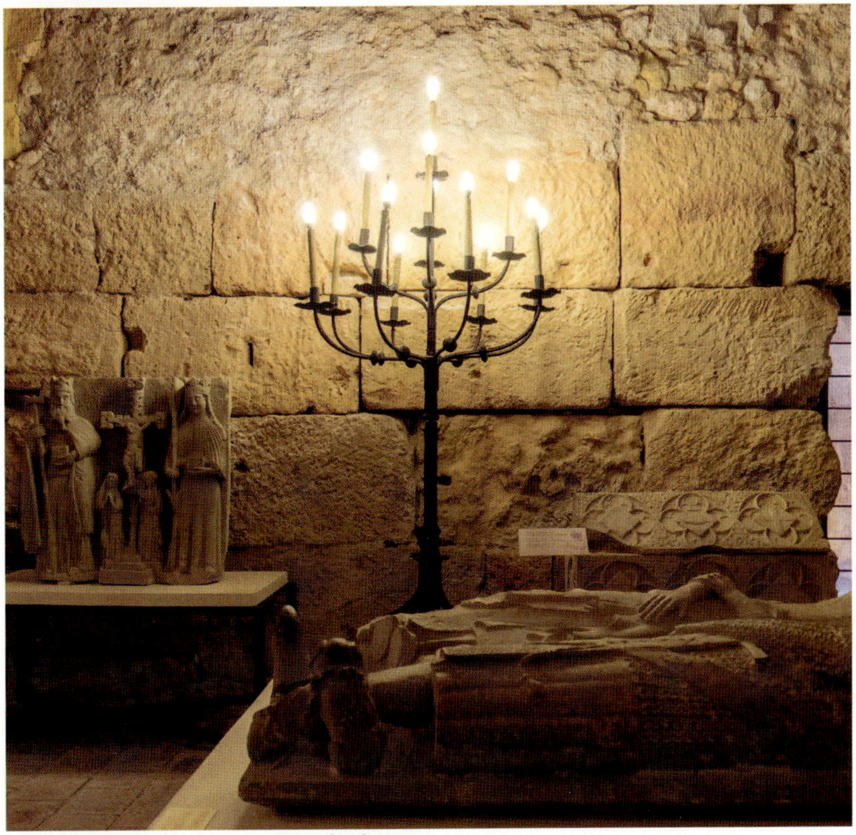

Museu Diocesà, the former canons' refectory

The modern and contemporary city

From the 16th to 21st centuries

The city was fortified with a new wall, the Muralla de Sant Joan, in the 16th century. During the Reapers' War, which began in 1640, it came under siege on two occasions. This was the first of the conflicts that hampered the city's growth during the modern era.

Tarragona's economy experienced a severe downturn and didn't recover until the end of the 18th century, with the rebuilding of the port from 1790 onwards. But it wasn't all doom and gloom. The archbishops who held office in the 16th century, Gaspar Cervantes de Gaeta (1568-75) and Antoni Agustí i Albanell (1577-86), founded the university, known as the Reial Estudi Literari, and made the city a cultural hub. It was the age of the humanists and a time when the modern city was at the height of its splendour, matched only perhaps by the Enlightenment in the late 18th century.

The second conflict was the War of the Spanish Succession in the early 18th century. At the end of that century, in 1798, the city received its eagerly awaited water supply. In the early 19th century a number of exiles from the French Revolution sought refuge in the city, among them the former Parisian prefect of police, Antoine de Sartine, who had been born in Barcelona and died in Tarragona in 1801. Another conflict, the Peninsular War, had devastating consequences. On 28th June 1811, the assault by Napoleon's army, following a siege, ushered in two years of poverty, hunger and destruction.

The economy recovered slowly, spurred on by the emergence of a middle class of shopkeepers. The demolition of the Muralla de Sant Joan began in 1854, making way for an expansion project, the Eixample, and a new street, Carrer de la Unió, which brought the Part Alta and the district of La Marina, in the Part Baixa, closer together. El Serrallo was added to these in 1865.

During the Spanish Civil War, the city was heavily bombed from the air. After the war, the city grew in a haphazard fashion and its population rose from 39,000 inhabitants in 1950 to 102,000 in 1975. In the 1950s a number of chemical works were set up in the city and the oil refinery was built in 1975. Neighbourhoods such as Bonavista, Torreforta — named after a fortified farmhouse —, Campclar, Icomar, Riuclar, Sant Salvador, and Sant Pere and Sant Pau grew. They have all developed their own unique personalities, attractions and central areas. In the case of Bonavista, this personality has been captured by the photographer David Mocha.

In the 21st century (its 23rd century in existence) Tarragona remains one of the poles of the second-largest metropolitan area in Catalonia and the Camp de Tarragona, the land where artists of the calibre of Antoni Gaudí and Joan Miró, and the photographer Francesc Català-Roca were born and lived.

Modern and contemporary route

→ Appendix p. 4

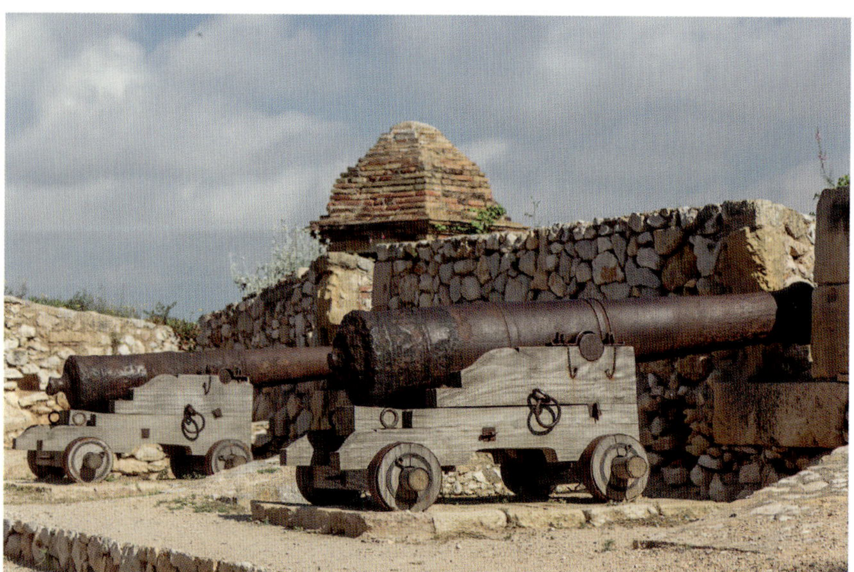

Walls of the Falsa Braga on the Passeig Arqueològic

Courtyard of Casa-Museu Castellarnau →

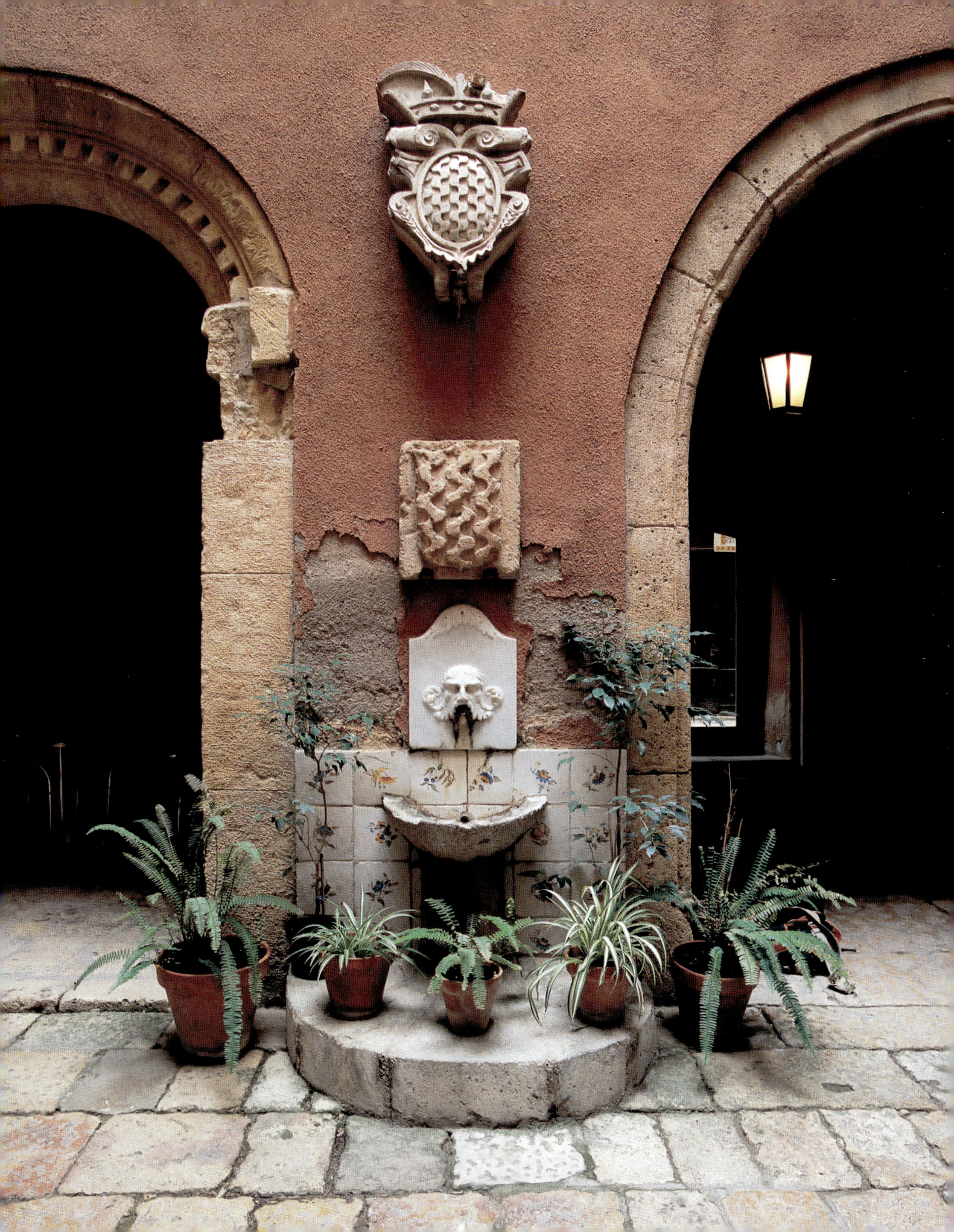

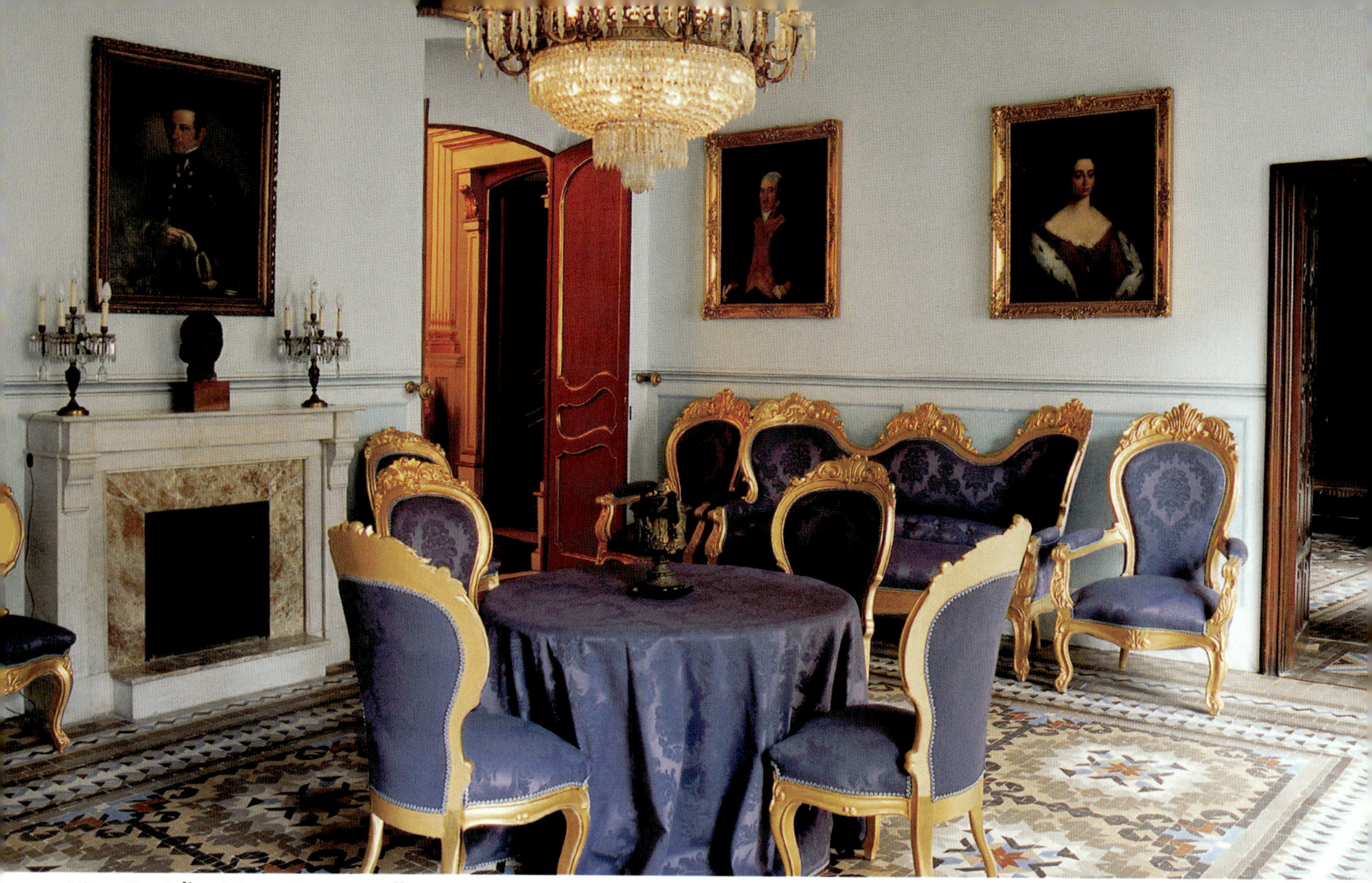

↑ Casa Montoliu ↓ Casa-Museu Castellarnau

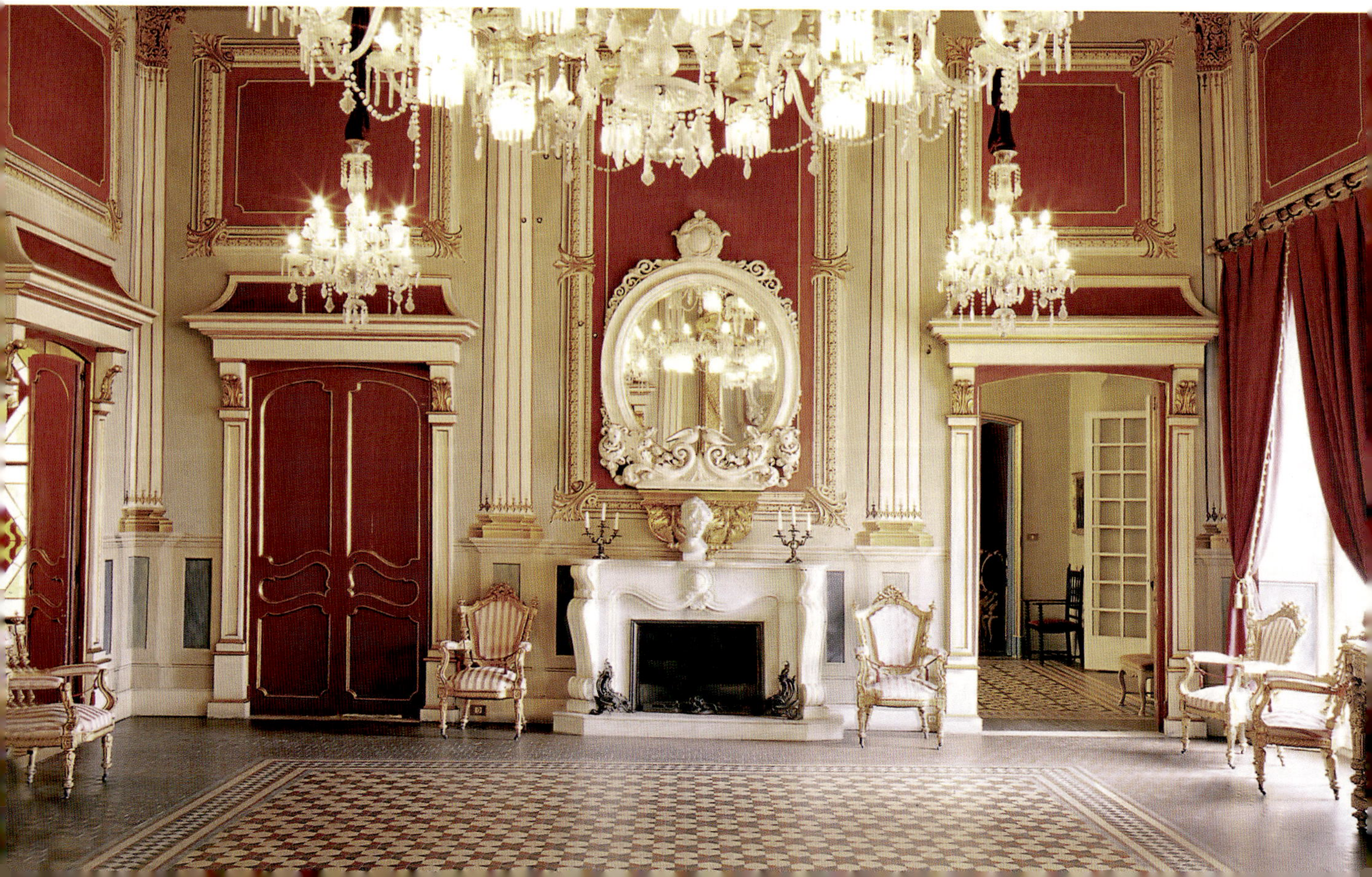

Gate and cross of Sant Antoni

In 1737 a new gate in the city wall was commissioned to replace the medieval one. It was also known as the gate of the Mal Consell, or Bad Advice. It has stone ashlars decorated with white marble almost certainly obtained from Roman monuments. In front of the gate of Sant Antoni, near the Palau de la Diputació — a 14th century former convent which is now the administrative building of the Provincial Council — we find the cross of the same name, built in 1604.

Carrer Cavallers

This street was the home of knights and noblemen from the 12th century onwards, and has been the setting for processions and the arrival of illustrious figures in the city. It had two arches marking the entrance located just off Plaça del Pallol, but they were demolished in the 18th century. Many of the houses had a door coming out onto Carrer dels Ferrers, which was nicknamed Carrer de les Portes Falses, or Street of the False Doors, for this very reason.

Casa Montoliu

Since 1983 it has been the home of the music school, the Conservatori i Escola de Música de la Diputació. This 14th century mansion was built in the late-Gothic style but archaeological excavations found a section of a wall from the Roman administrative building. The Marquises of Montoliu lived here until the end of the 19th century and a neoclassical-style façade was added in the 18th century. The stone doorway from the façade survives today.

Casa-Museu Castellarnau

The main exhibition centre of the Museu d'Història de Tarragona (MHT). Roman and medieval structures have been found on the site but the vaults on the ground floor date from the 14th and 15th centuries. The Emperor Charles V lived here while he was staying in the city in 1542. The Castellarnau family bought the property in 1764 and renovated the façade. The ballroom has a ceiling decorated by the Provençal painter Josep Bernat Flaugier dating from the late 18th century.

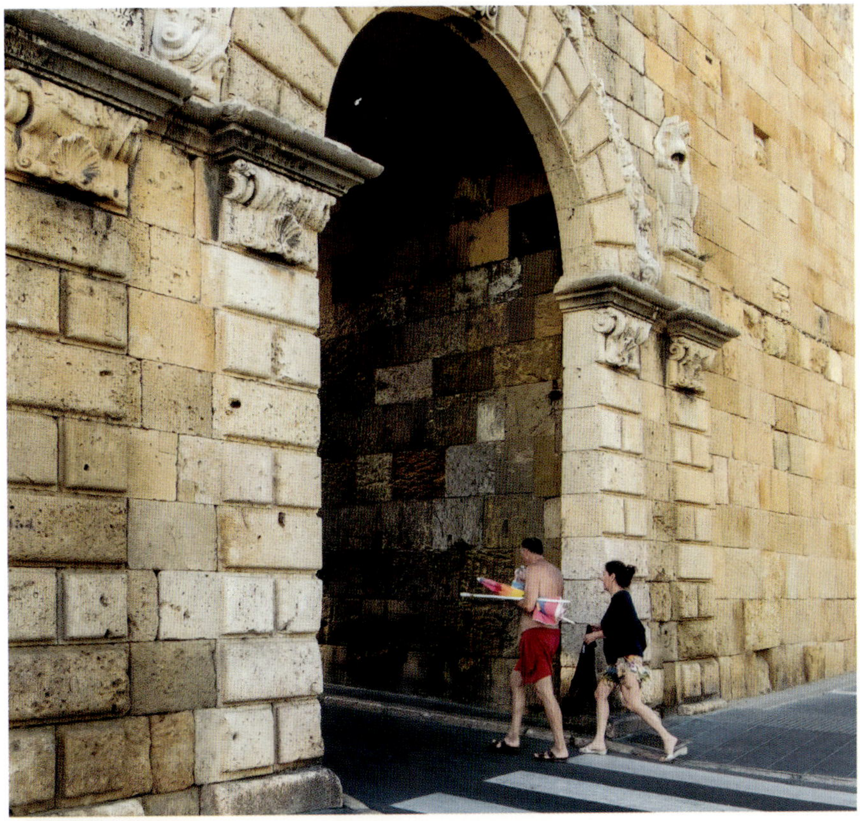

Gate of Sant Antoni

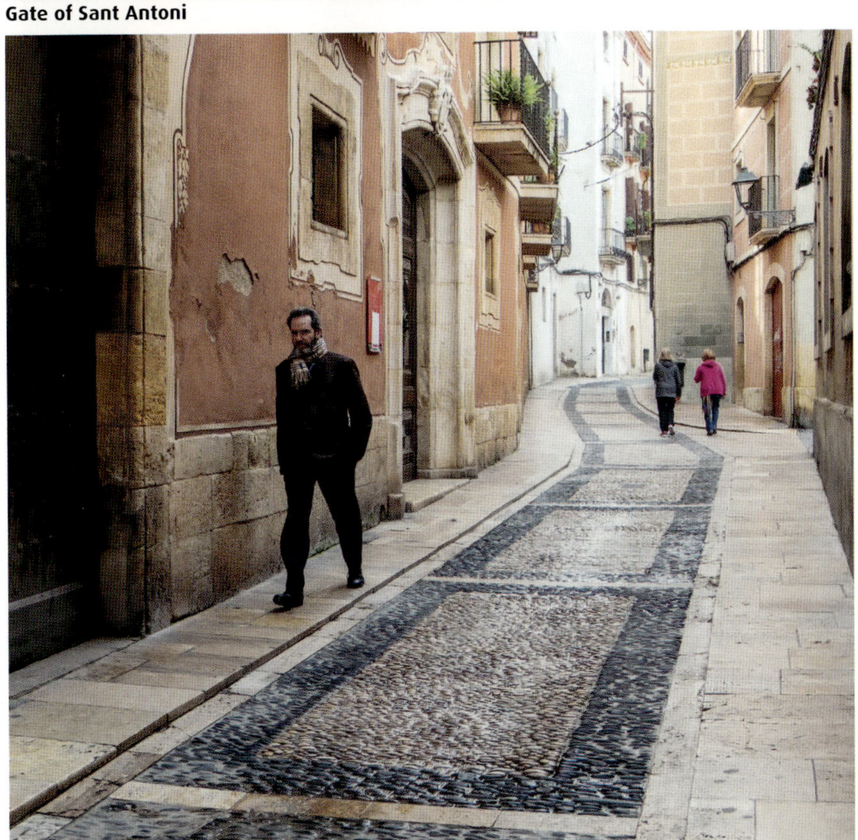

Carrer Cavallers

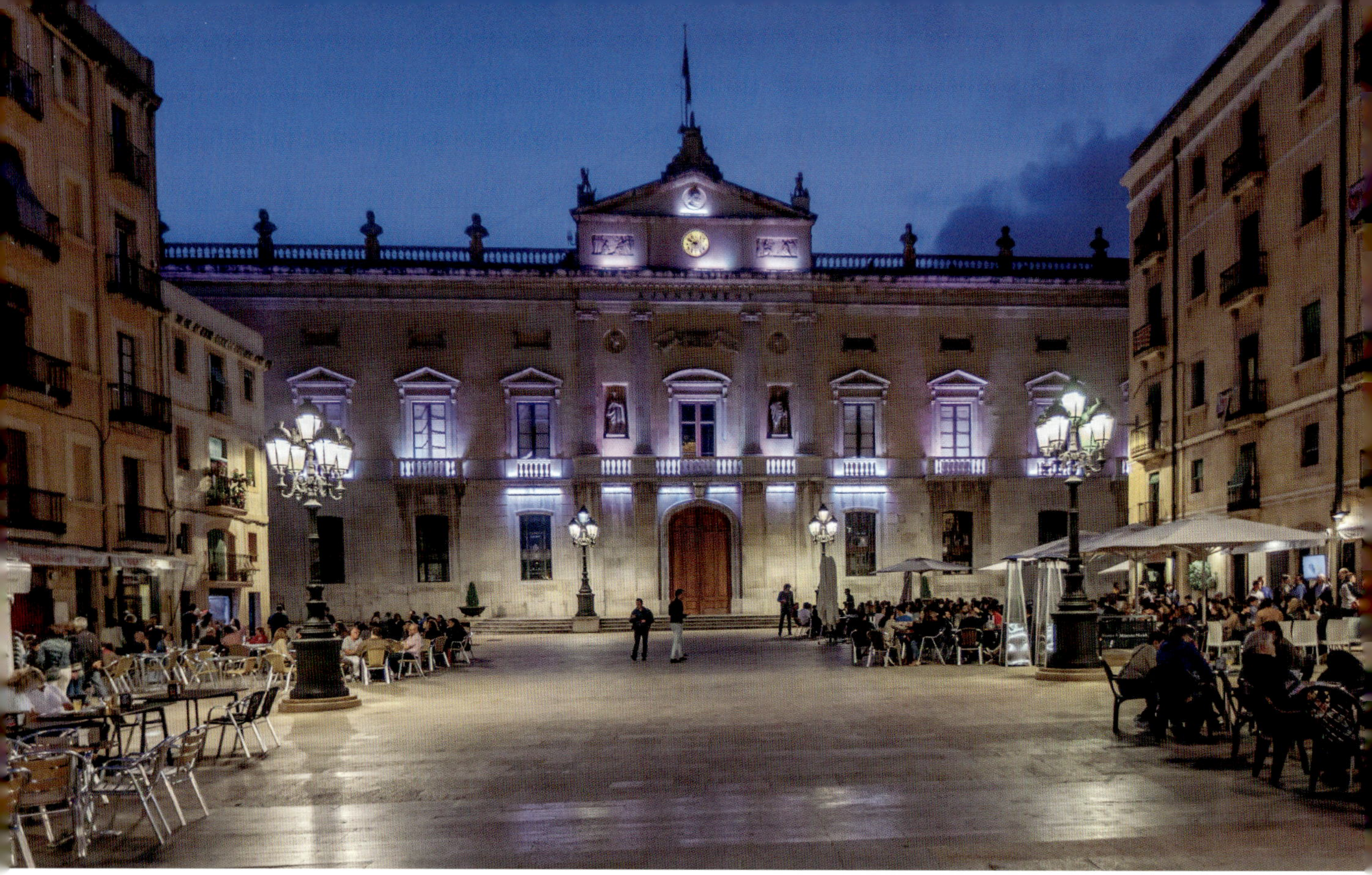

↑ Plaça de la Font and Tarragona City Hall ↓ The packed square during a human tower display

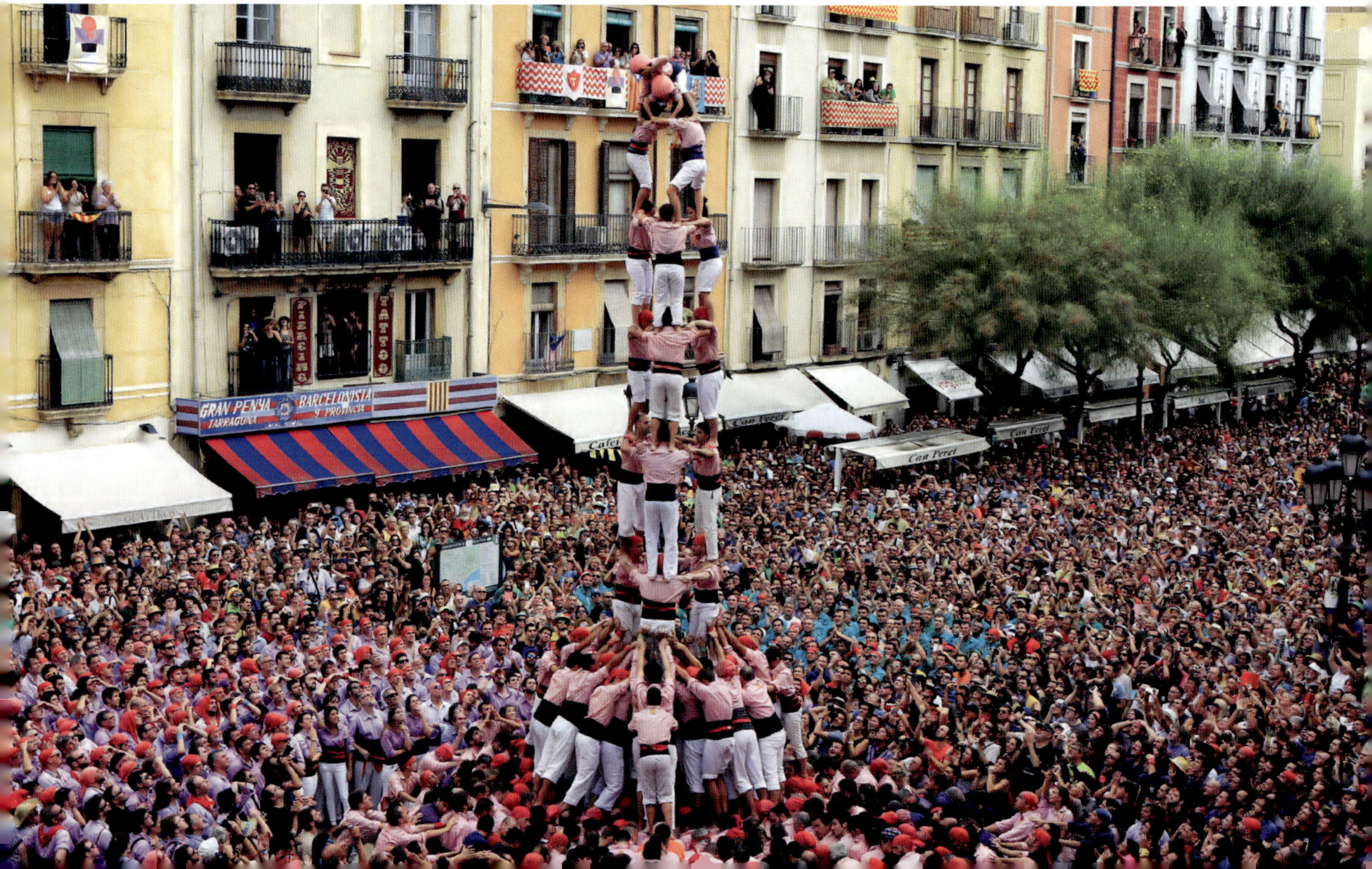

Plaça de la Font

Just like the Piazza Navona in Rome, which was built on the site of the Stadium of Domitian, or the Piazza dell'Anfiteatro in Lucca, this square stands on a Roman building, the Circus. It occupies a quarter of the surface area of the arena and has retained some of the original structures. The houses on the side closest to the Rambla Vella are of equal width, and stand on the same spot as the vaults of the Circus. The square hosts human tower displays and local festivals. It also has a wide range of restaurants and bars.

City Hall

The Palau Municipal housed the convent of Sant Domènec until 1835. The neoclassical façade was completed in the 1860s and features sculptures of the city's resettlers, Saint Oleguer and Robert Bordet, medallions with the heads the city's founders, the Scipio brothers, and the emperors Augustus and Hadrian, who lived in the city, and the busts of illustrious figures from Tarragona. The monumental staircase is particularly noteworthy.

Casa Canals

Part of the MHT like the Casa-Museu Castellarnau. It is also an ideal place to see how the noble families lived between the 18th and 19th centuries. The current house has sea views from the balconies in the city wall and dates from the late 1700s, replacing one that was destroyed during the Reapers' War (1640-52). There is a charming romantic garden on the mezzanine floor.

Museu d'Art Modern

Tarragona Provincial Council, the Diputació de Tarragona, set up this museum in 1976 to bring modern and contemporary art to a wider audience and showcase its collections which began with works by the sculptor Julio Antonio (1889-1919). Joan Miró's *Tarragona Tapestry* is also on display.

The museum is located in the former home of Antoni de Martí i Franquès (1750-1832), the first scientist to accurately establish the composition of air.

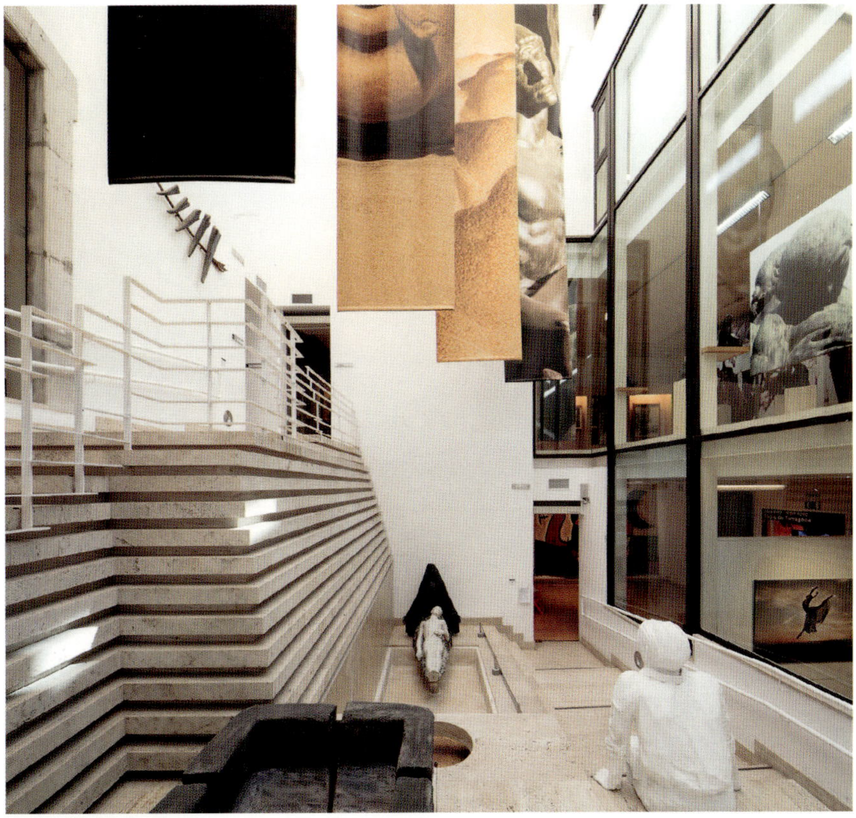

Museu d'Art Modern

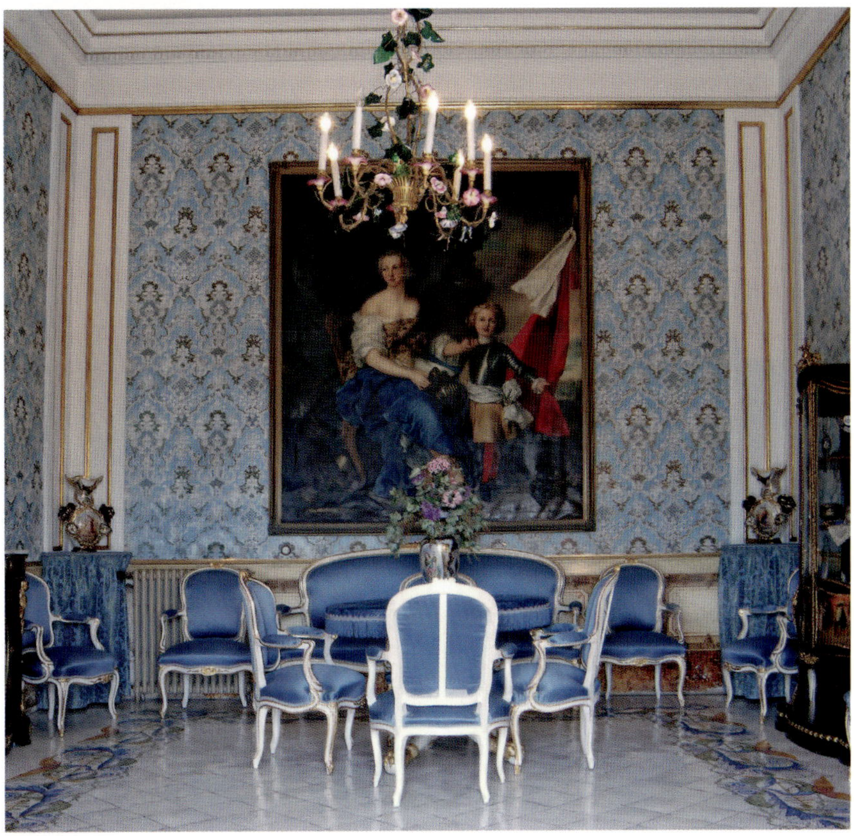

Casa Canals

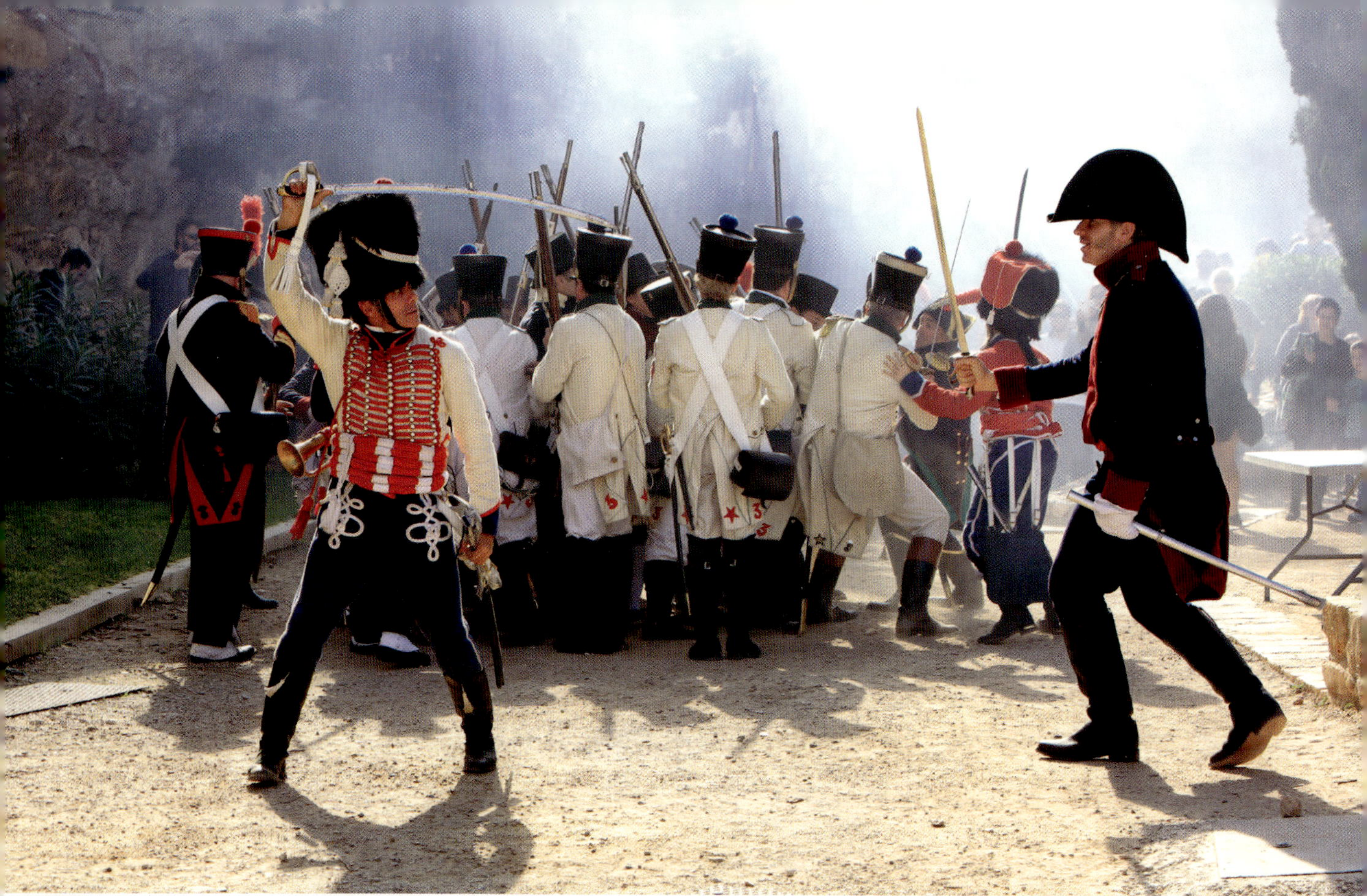

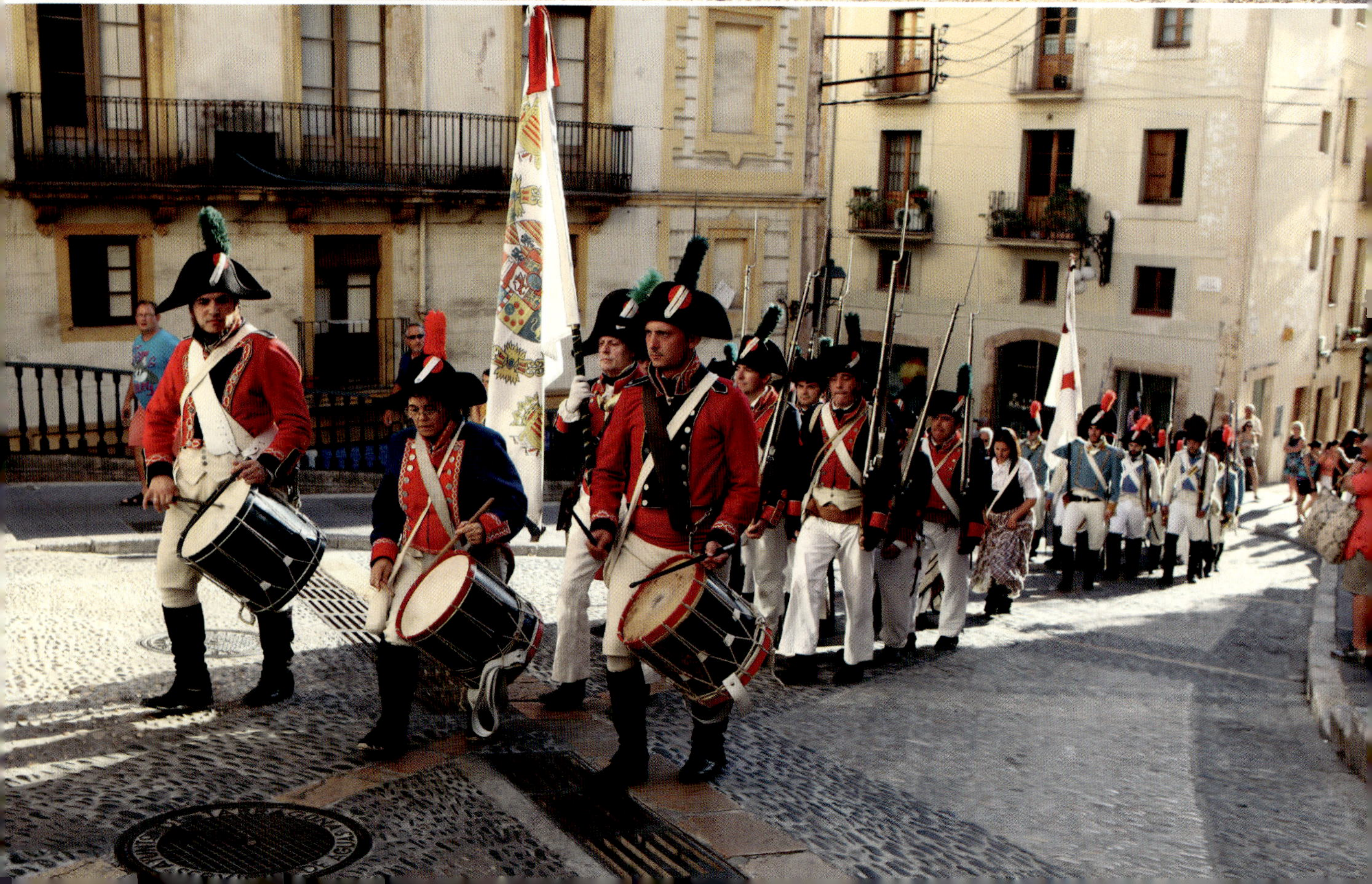

Fortí de la Reina and Fortí de Sant Jordi

The two forts were built by the British during the War of the Spanish Succession and are named after Queen Anne and the patron saint of Catalonia respectively. Nearby stands the Jans cemetery, where British citizens have been buried since 1849. The cemetery replaced a common grave for British soldiers located in the quarry inside the port.

Tarragona 1800 Historical re-enactment

Tarragona 1800 is an event designed to bring the city's history to a wider audience. Held every October, it commemorates the bloody siege by the Napoleonic troops in 1811. The aim is to show people what the city was like in the late 18th and early 19th centuries, the way the local population lived and discover the characters who made history at that time. The event features displays by the Tarragona Urban Militia, historical re-enactments, military camps, parades, educational workshops, talks, exhibitions... in the actual period settings, such as the bulwark known as the Falsa Braga.

Plaça de Braus, Tarraco Arena Plaça

The former bullring, now known as the Tarraco Arena Plaça (TAP), is the second largest indoor arena in Catalonia and holds more than 10,000 spectators. The original building dates from 1883 and was designed by the architect Ramon Salas i Ricomà. The redevelopment was carried out by Xavier Romaní and is surmounted by a spectacular dome measuring 92 metres across.

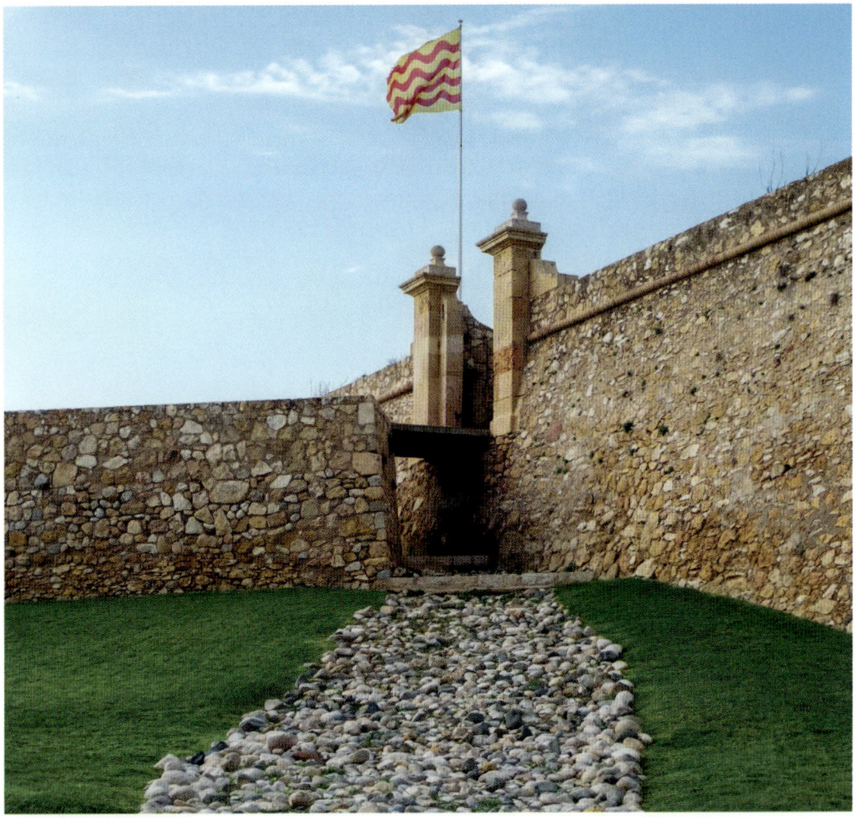

Fortí de Sant Jordi

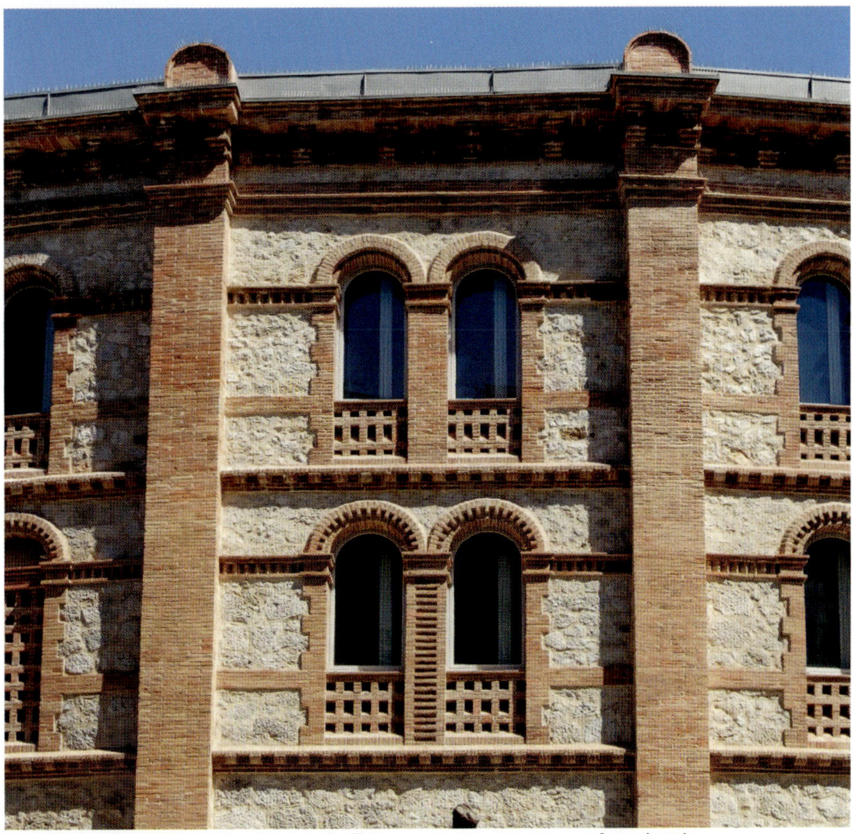

Detail of the façade of the former bullring, now Tarraco Arena Plaça (TAP)

← Historical re-enactment during Tarragona 1800

Modernista Tarragona

The Eixample

Tarragona also showcases wonderful examples of Catalonia's home-grown art nouveau, *modernisme*. The city's *modernista* heritage was undervalued until relatively recently but it has undergone a reappraisal and is now featured on one of Tarragona's city routes. According to the inventory, there are some 50 *modernista* landmarks in the city: more than 30 noteworthy buildings, many of them on the Rambla Nova, as well as *modernista* elements that have been incorporated into other architectural styles, such as, for instance, *noucentista*, and a number of landmarks, including the Balcó del Mediterrani and the Mausoleum of Jaume I.

Tarragona is a treasure trove of buildings designed by great architects, some of them world famous, such as Antoni Gaudí — who designed an altar and monstrance in the chapel of Nostra Senyora del Sagrat Cor, on Carrer de Méndez Núñez —, Domènech i Montaner and Josep Maria Jujol. Many of them were born in Tarragona itself, such as Jujol (1879-1949), Ramon Salas i Ricomà (1848-1926), Josep Maria Pujol de Barberà (1871-1949), Pau Monguió (1865-1956) and Francesc de Paula Morera (1869-1951).

Art nouveau was a worldwide cultural movement that spanned the late 19th and early 20th centuries and went by different names: *modernisme* in Catalonia, *Jugendstil* in Germany; and *Liberty* and *Stile Floreale* in Italy. It encompassed a wide range of disciplines, from the arts to thinking, but was particularly outstanding in the field of architecture and the applied arts. In Catalonia, it is particularly broad in scope and is considered a political and social movement that came into being with the aim of modernising society and the country as a whole.

In Tarragona, *modernisme* must be viewed in the context of the growth of the city, with the expansion project, the Eixample, and the building boom this brought about. After the Peninsular War, the city had some 6,500 inhabitants and by 1887 the population had risen to more than 27,000. The demolition of the city wall, the Muralla de Sant Joan, which began after the progressive state revolution of 1854, and was partly carried out by prisoners, was completed in 1856, and the city ceased to be a military stronghold in 1868. The engineer Josep Criviller won the competition to design the city expansion plan, but he died prematurely and the final project was carried out by the military engineer Àngel de Romero. The project was built on land between Carrer de Pons d'Icart and Carrer d'August, with a broad avenue, the Rambla Nova, as its central point, which started on the uneven terrain left by the quarry inside the port.

Modernista route

→ Appendix p. 5

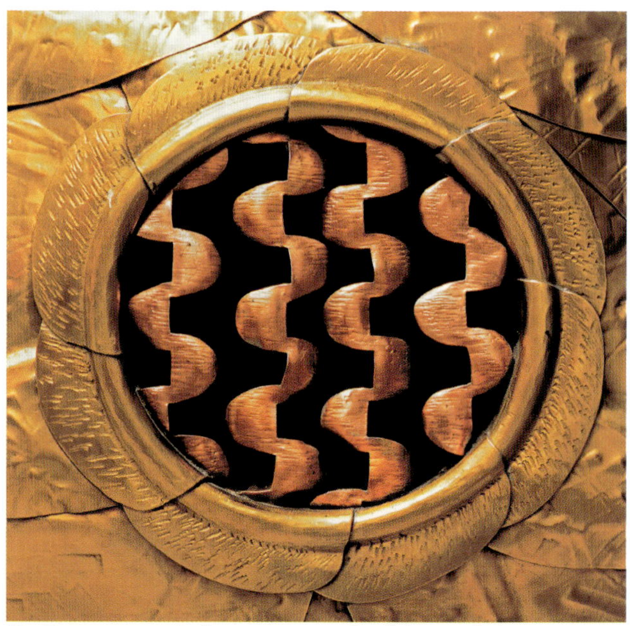

The Tarragona coat of arms on a *modernista* peephole

Teatre Metropol, vestibule →

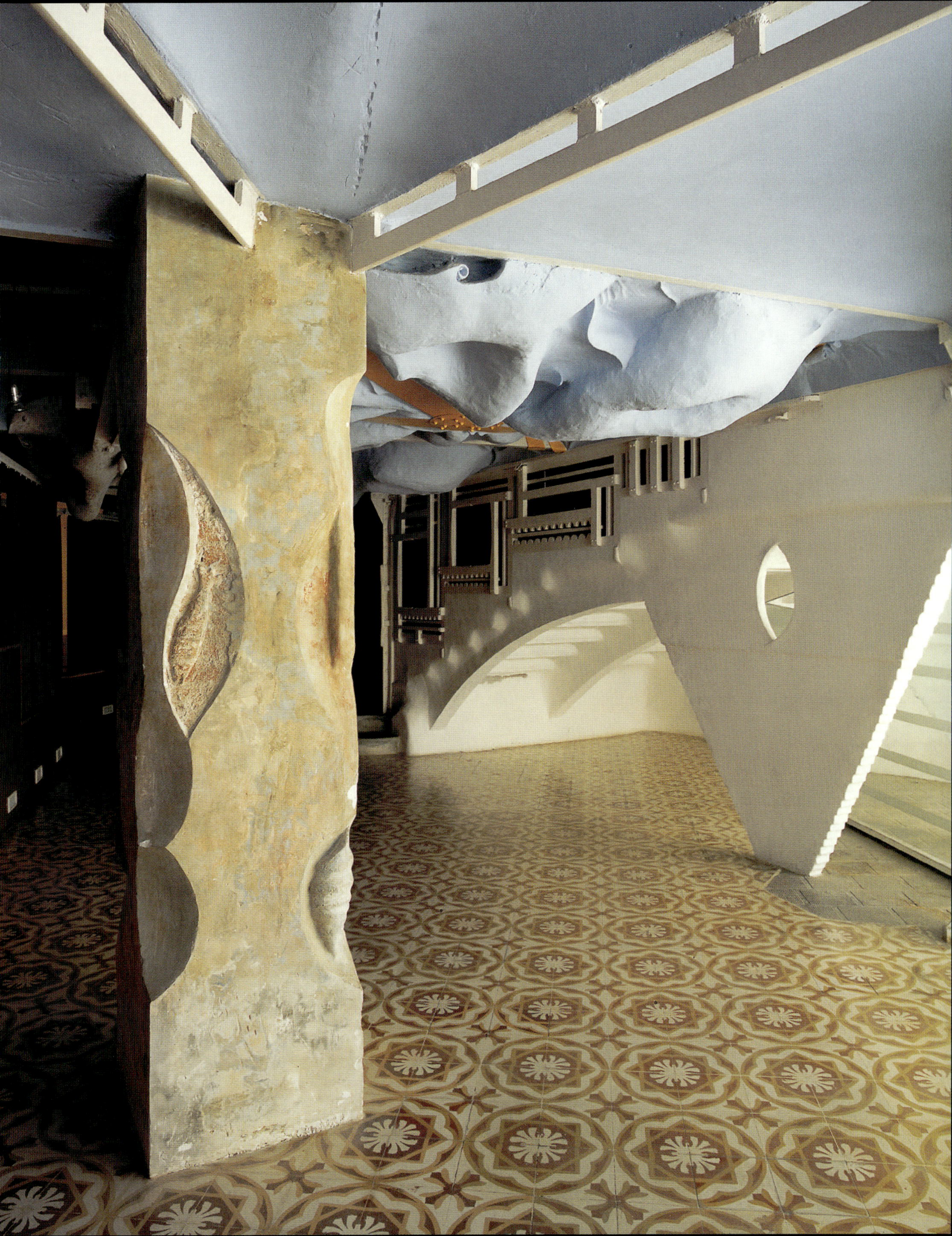

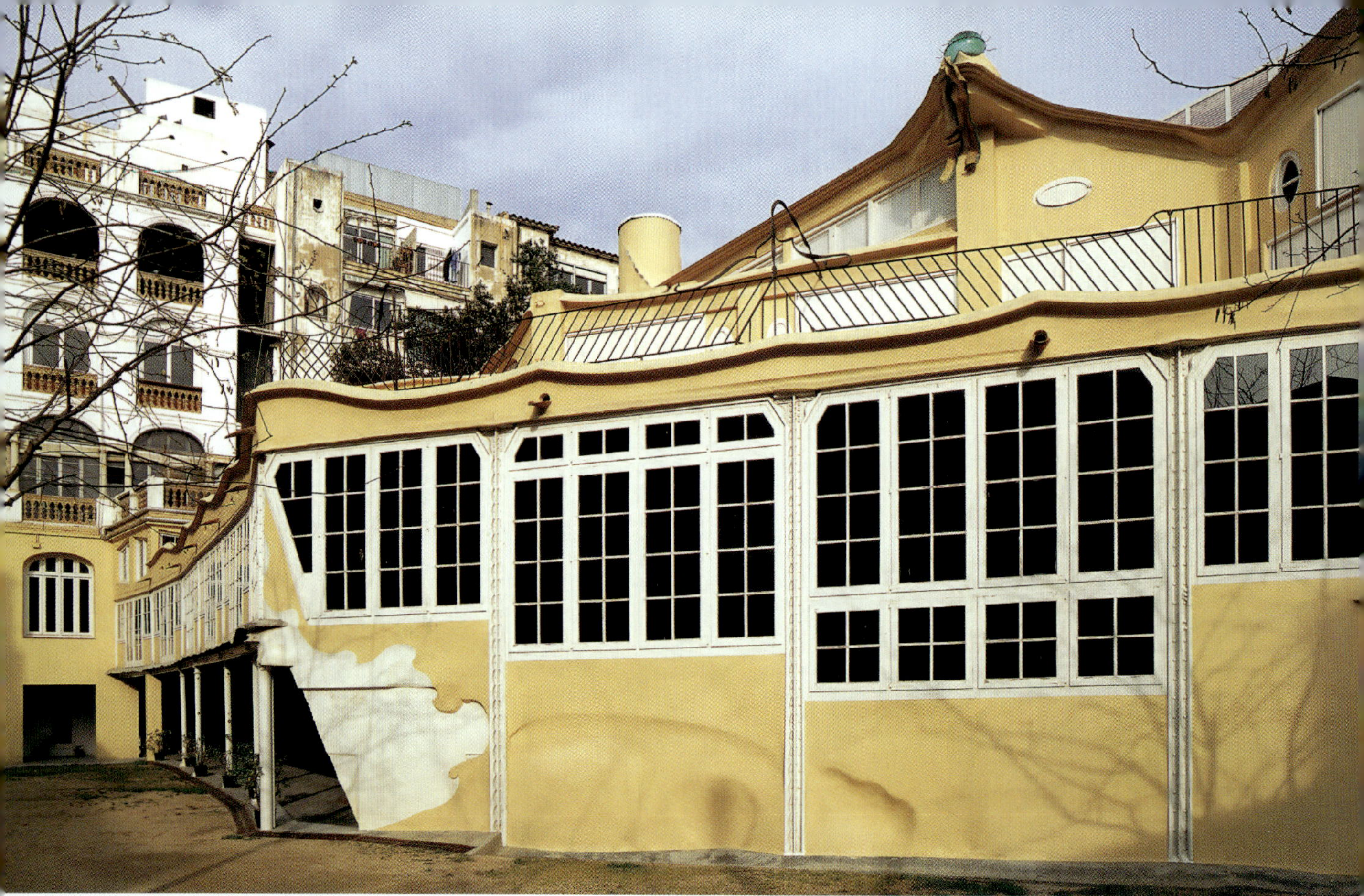

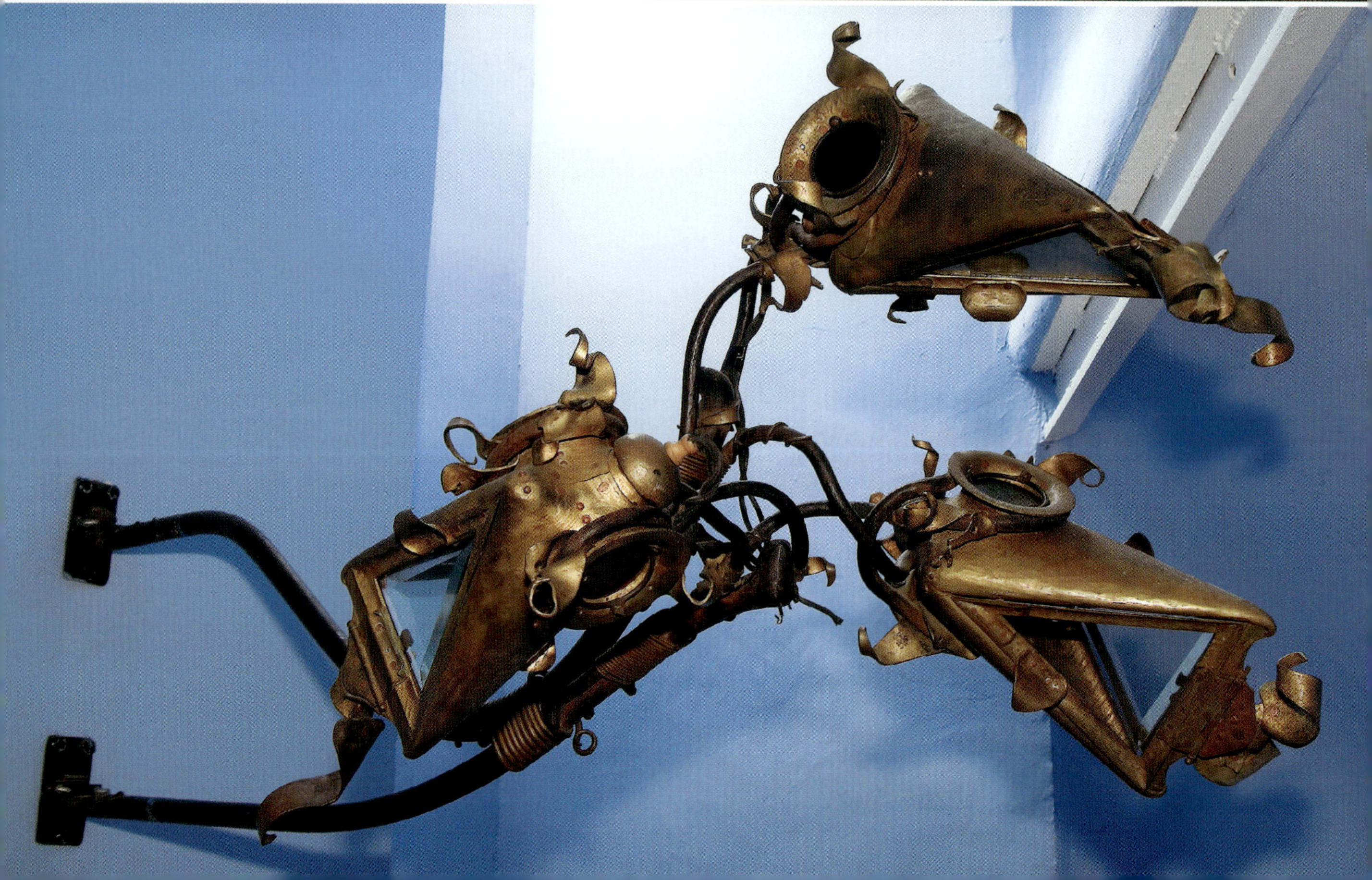

Teatre Metropol
Josep Maria Jujol

Born in Tarragona in 1879, Josep Maria Jujol is one of the great Catalan architects. He was ahead of his time aesthetically and technically. The American actor John Malkovich is a huge fan of Jujol's work which can be seen on the fountain in Plaça d'Espanya in Barcelona or, nearer Tarragona, in the church of the Sagrat Cor in Vistabella or the shrine of Montserrat, in Montferri. Although Jujol worked with Gaudí — on La Pedrera, Casa Batlló and Park Güell — he had his own distinctive style. The Teatre Metropol, refurbished by Josep Llinàs in 1995, is one of the most outstanding buildings he left to his home town. The decorative elements are an allegory of the sea with waves, fishes and shapes depicting a ship's keel, and also include religious symbols, with the letter M for Mary the Mother of God, whom Jujol worshipped. The workers' association, the Patronat de l'Obrer, commissioned the theatre in the gardens of its headquarters and it opened in 1910. The refurbishment of the auditorium and building on the Rambla Nova where it stands seek to pay tribute to and preserve the legacy of this unique architect.

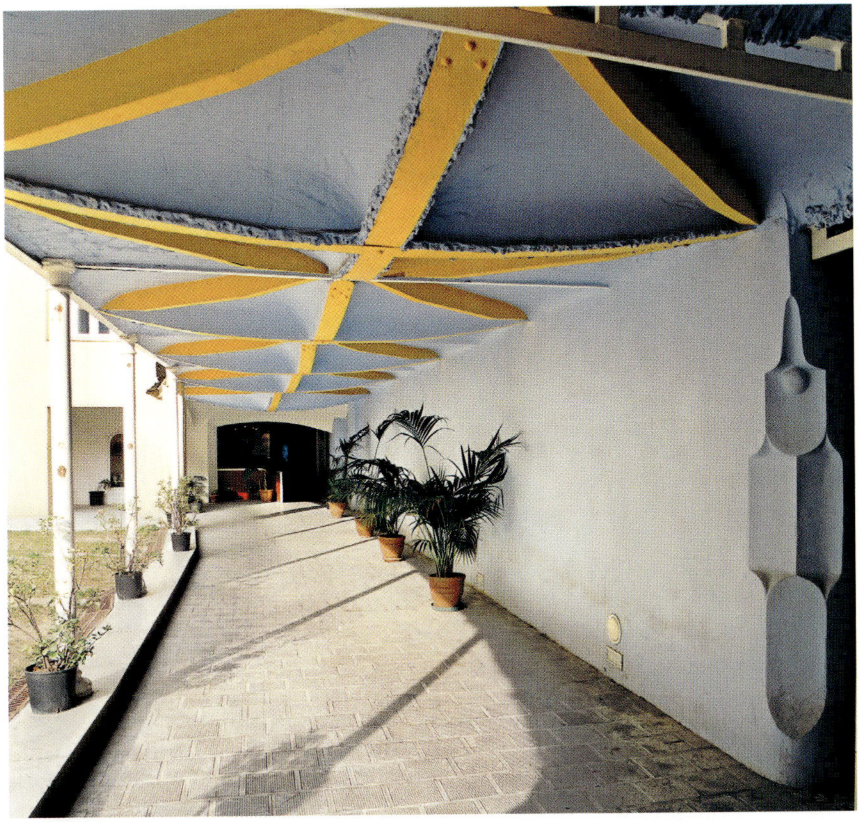

Courtyard corridor

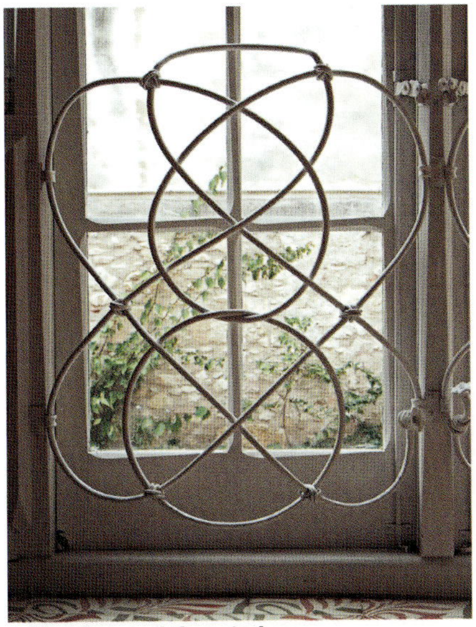

Grille of one of the windows

← Wall light

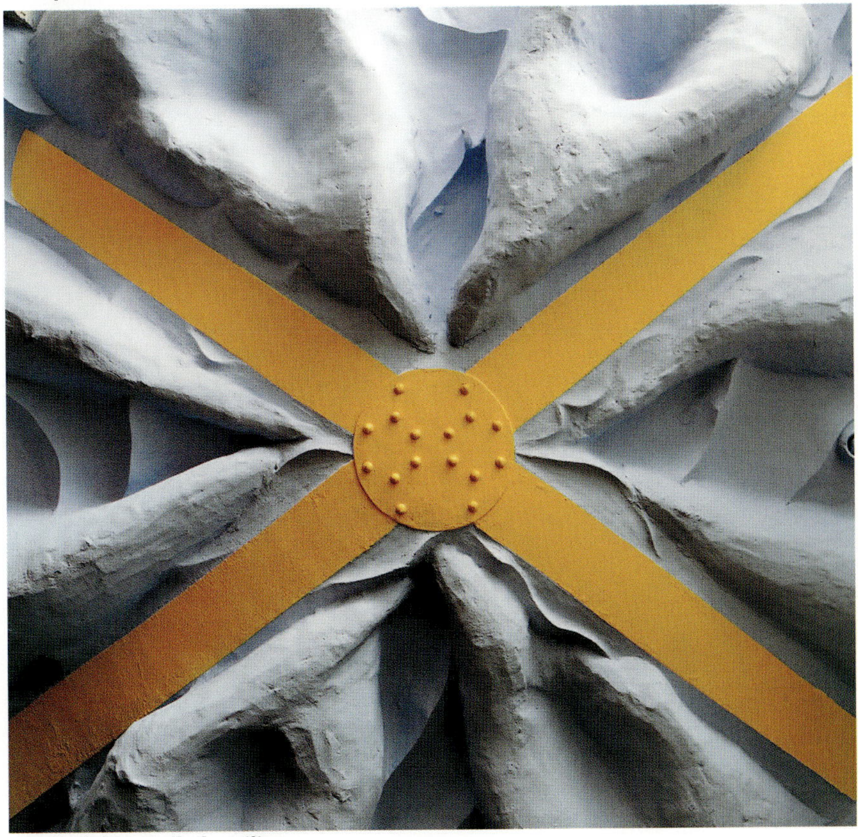

Detail of the vestibule ceiling

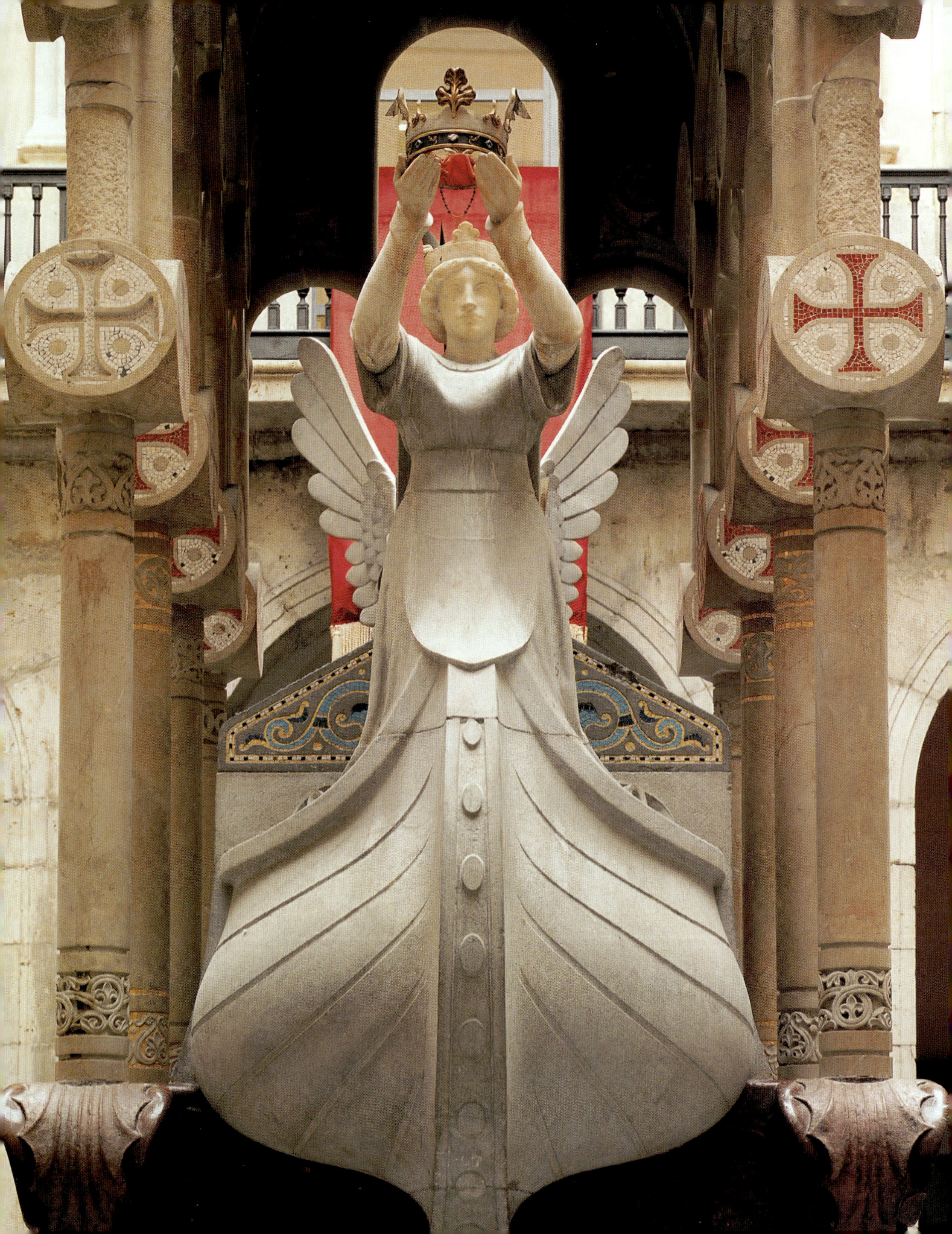

Mausoleum of Jaume I

At the beginning of the 20th century, Lluís Domènech i Montaner was commissioned to design this boat-shaped mausoleum to house the remains of King Jaume I (1208-1276), one of the greatest monarchs from the Crown of Aragon, which had been interred in Tarragona Cathedral and moved to Poblet Monastery in 1952. Domènech i Montaner was responsible for landmark buildings such as the Palau de la Música Catalana and the Hospital de Sant Pau in Barcelona and the Casa Navàs in Reus. He died in 1923 before work on the mausoleum could be completed but his son Pere Domènech i Roura took over the project. The mausoleum has stood in the courtyard of City Hall since 1992.

Casa Ximenis
Josep Maria Jujol

In 1914 Josep Maria Jujol was commissioned by the canon Pau Ximenis to design a building that would be attached to the city walls. The project was not only respectful of history but a wonderful showcase for wrought iron and sgraffiti work, with geometrical forms and plant motifs which were restored when the building was refurbished in 1989. The balconies have seats in the style of old courting chairs.

Chartreuse Factory

The liqueur Chartreuse was made at this distillery in Plaça dels Infants from 1904 to 1989. The brick clock tower is one of its most outstanding architectural features. It was originally a textile mill but was extended when the community of Carthusian monks moved into the building. It was refurbished in 2013 to house the language school, the Escola Oficial d'Idiomes.

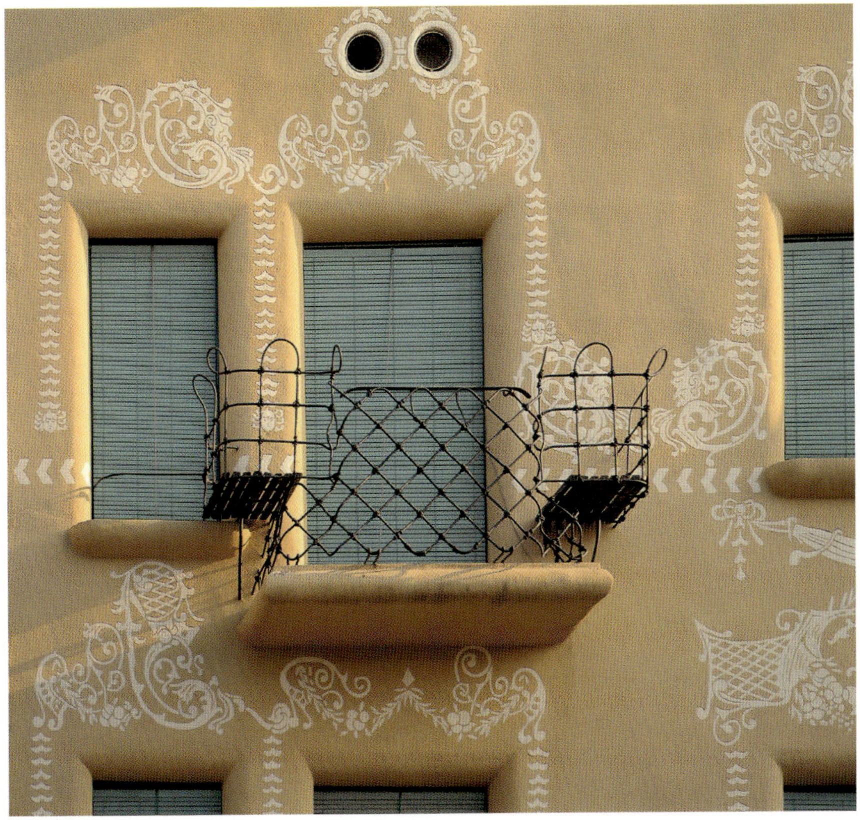

Casa Ximenis

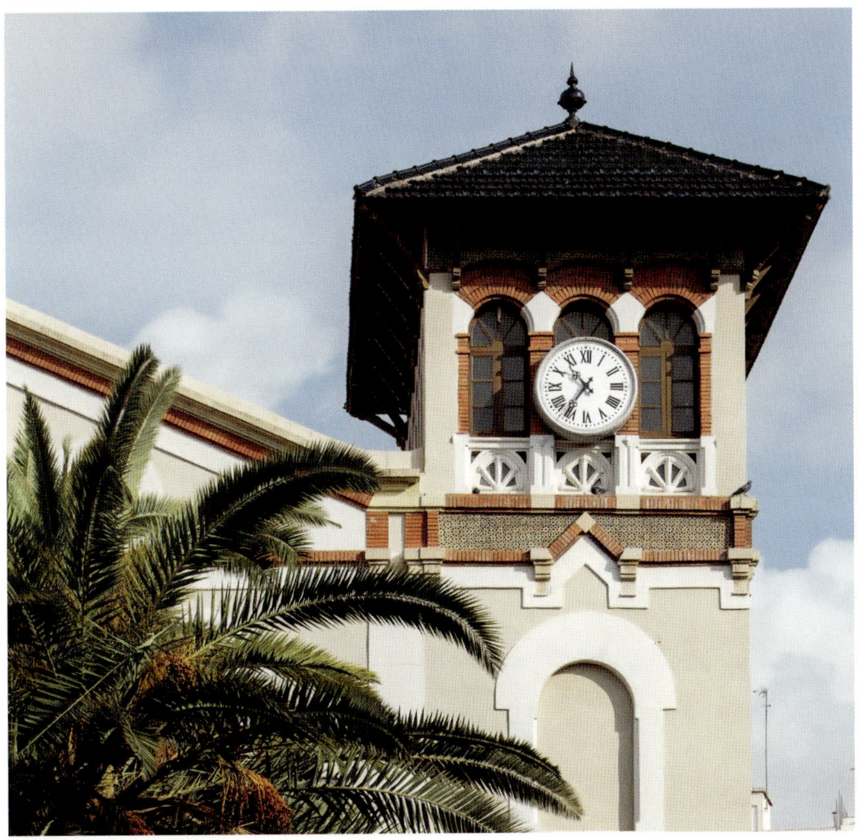

Old Chartreuse Factory

← Mausoleum of Jaume I

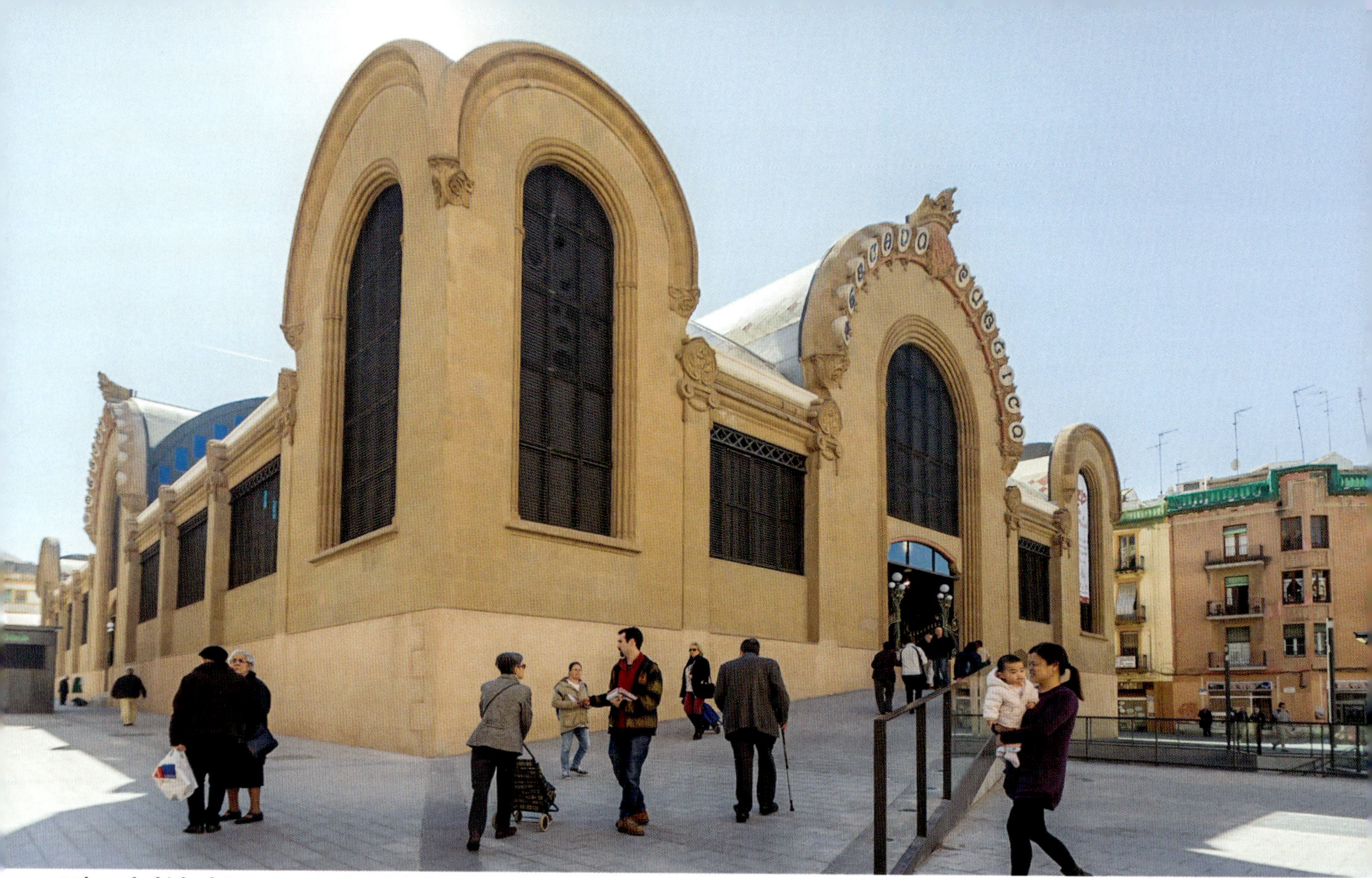

↑ The refurbished Mercat Central ↓ Old Abattoir, today the dean's office of the Rovira i Virgili University

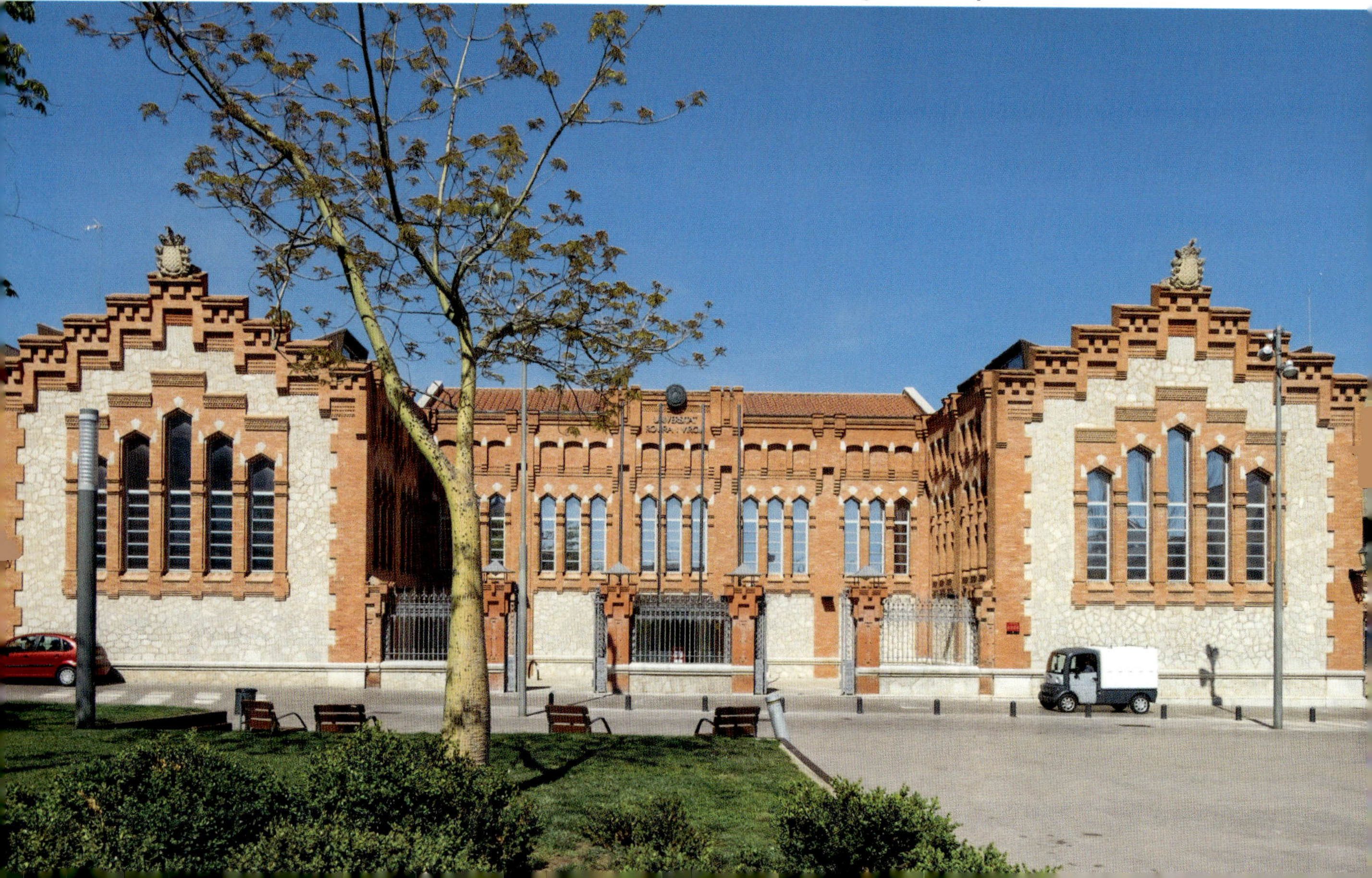

Mercat Central

The main food market, the Mercat Central, is always a hive of activity. It stands in Plaça Corsini and you'll find stalls selling fish, vegetables, meat and all kinds of produce. To a certain extent it is the heir to the local Roman Forum which stands close to the market. It was built in 1915 to a design by Josep Maria Pujol, an architect responsible for many other buildings around the city. An imposing, elegant building, it is reminiscent of the Karlplatz metro station in Vienna by the Austrian architect Otto Wagner. It is rectangular with a Latin-cross floor plan and decorated with *modernista* elements and wrought ironwork. It has four façades with pilasters joined together by Ionic columns.

The Mercat Central is one of the city's main retail hubs and a bustling area of shops, businesses and restaurants.

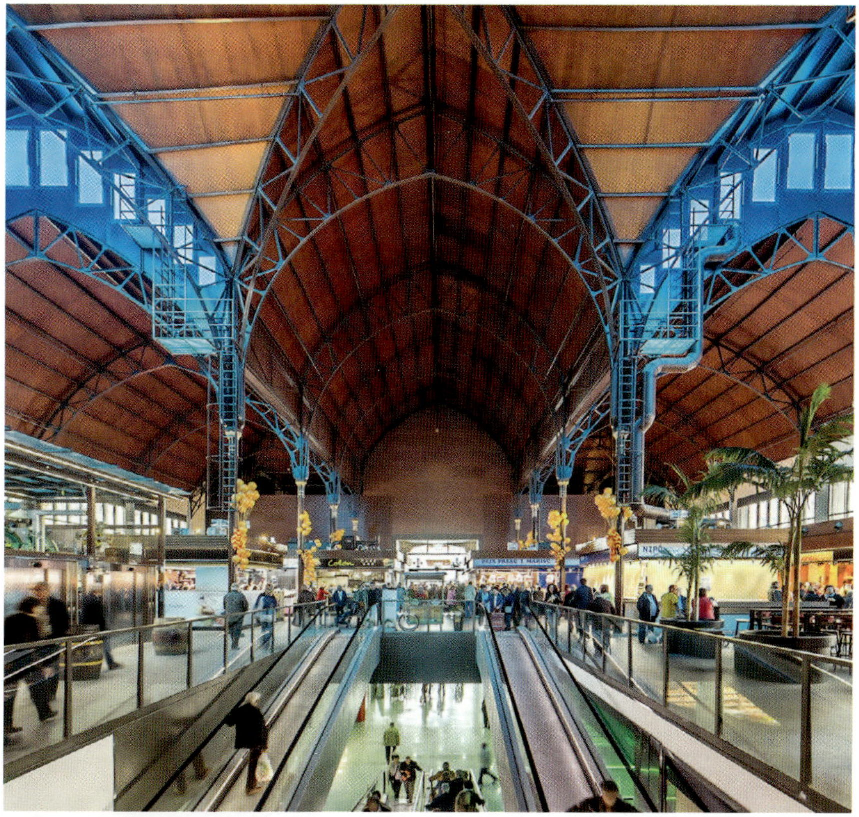

Ceiling of the Mercat Central

Antic Escorxador

Completed in 1902, this building, with its exposed brickwork, masonry and stone, and wrought iron railings, was designed by the architect Josep M. Pujol de Barberà. It was the municipal slaughterhouse until the 1970s. Refurbished by the architect Xavier Romaní in 1992, it is currently home to the dean's office of the Rovira i Virgili University, named after the journalist and politician who was born in Tarragona in 1882.

Quinta de Sant Rafael

A *modernista* mansion designed by the architect Juli M. Fossas and built in 1913. It stands in the middle of the Parc Rafael Puig i Valls, named after the great environmentalist who built the house and garden.

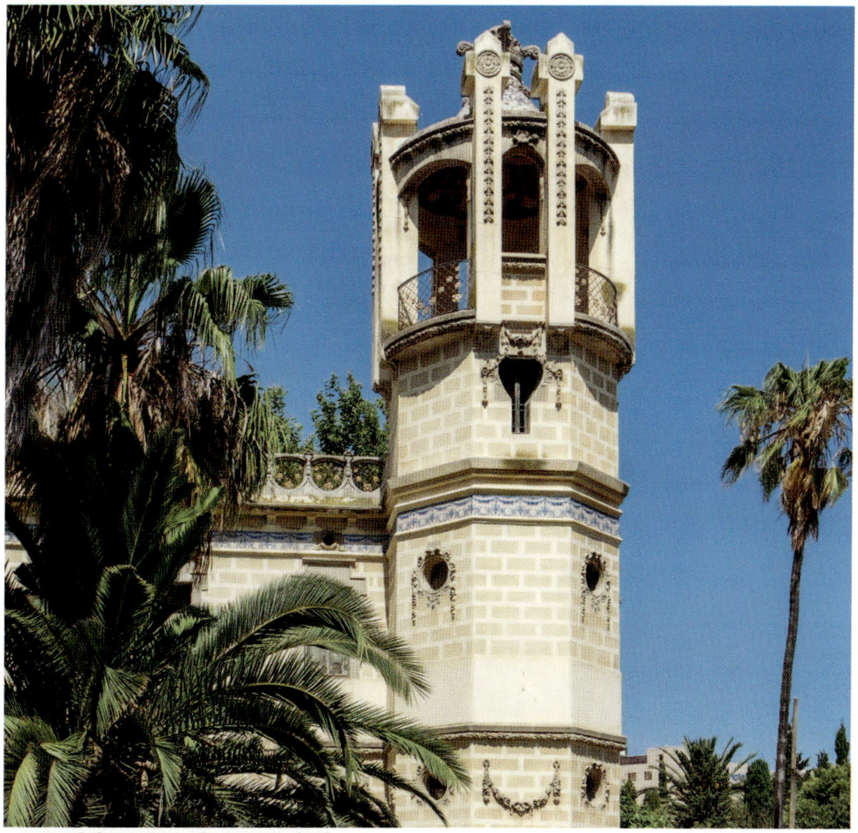

Tower of the Quinta de Sant Rafael

Modernista houses

Work on the city's expansion project began at the end of the 19th century and brought with it a great many new houses, from mansions and detached dwellings to apartment blocks. They were built in the prevalent architectural styles of the day — historicism and eclecticism — shifting to *modernisme* in the early 20th century. Although there are *modernista* houses in other parts of the city, we only have to walk along the Rambla Nova and look at the façades to realise the importance of this architectural style in Tarragona's history. Some of the houses have been listed as *modernista* heritage landmarks, among them the Casa Salas, by the architect Ramon Salas i Ricomà, the Casa Josep Mas, the Casa Bofarull, the Casa Musolas and the Casa del Doctor Aleu, all four of them designed by Josep M. Pujol de Barberà, the Casa Rabadà by Alfons Barba or la Casa Rosell de Francesc de Paula Morera. Away from the Rambla Nova you'll find other interesting *modernista* buildings, including the Casa Ripoll and the Casa Porta Mercadé, both of them by the prolific Pujol de Barberà.

Cooperativa Obrera Tarraconense

A sign on the façade reads "fundada en 1904" (founded in 1904), and refers to the workers' cooperative that set up a general store, café and bakery in the building and also hosted cultural events. The building was designed by Pujol de Barberà in 1917 but wasn't completed until 1932. The ground floor houses the Teatre El Magatzem.

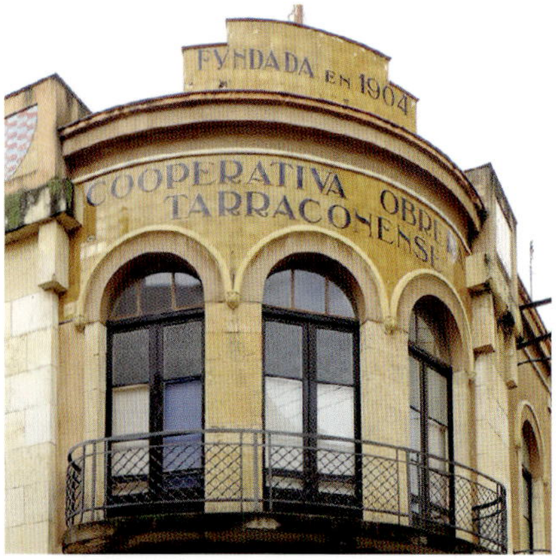

Cooperativa Obrera Tarraconense

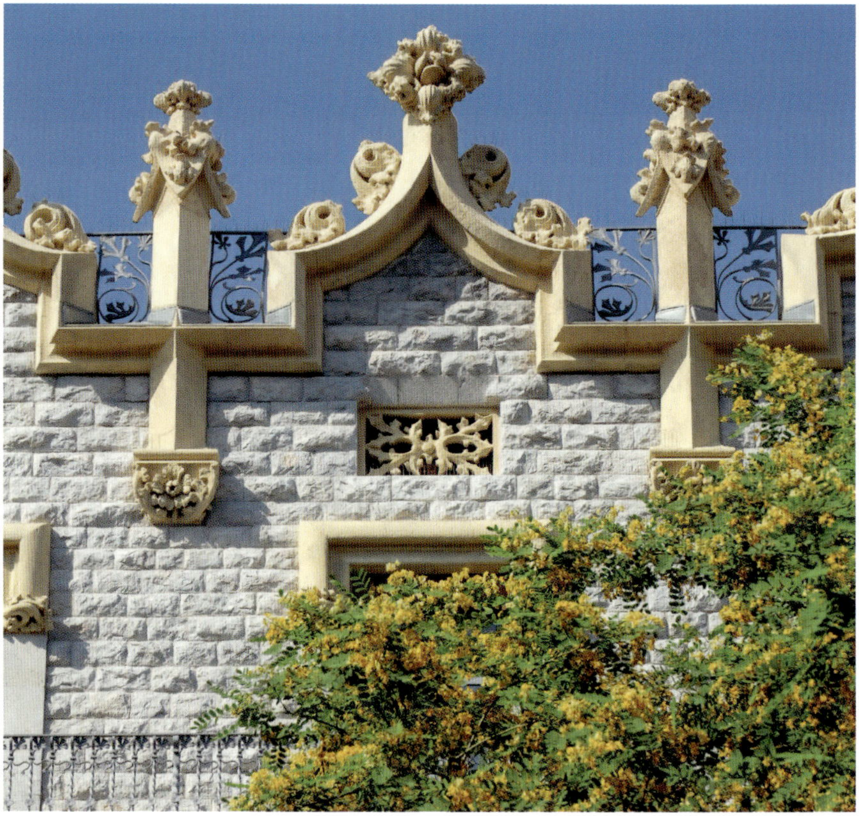
Casa Salas

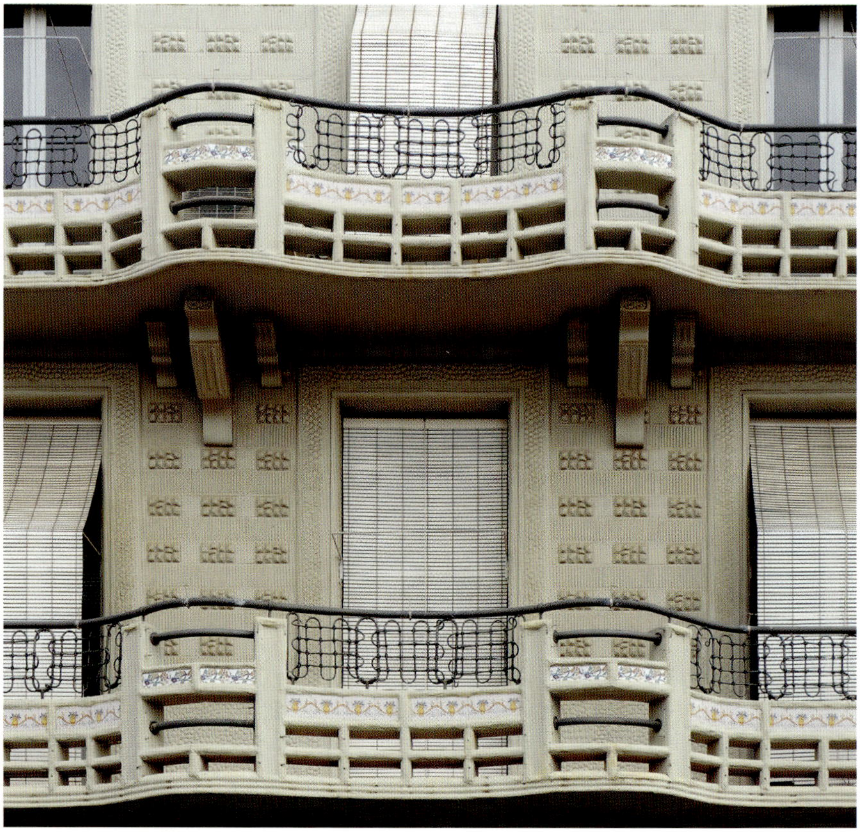
Casa Porta Mercadé

Col·legi de les Teresianes

Bernardí Martorell, a follower of Gaudí's, started work on this school and convent in 1922. The project was completed by Josep M. Pujol de Barberà and Antoni Pujol Sevil. Highlights include details such as the parabolic arches at the entrance. It was heavily bombed during the Spanish Civil War and had to be rebuilt almost from scratch.

Altar in the Chapel of Nostra Senyora del Sagrat Cor

Antoni Gaudí

The altar in the chapel of Nostra Senyora del Sagrat Cor, is the only work by Antoni Gaudí in the Camp de Tarragona. Gaudí oversaw the project around 1880 and also designed the monks' choir stalls, which were destroyed in 1936, and the manifestor, which was rebuilt.

Niche of the Church of the Pares Carmelites Descalços

Josep Maria Jujol

This neo-Gothic-style convent was designed by Pau Monguió in 1897. It is known locally as La Punxa — the Catalan for "spike" — due to the shape of the bell tower and spire that resembles a needle. In 1918, Josep Maria Jujol designed a niche dedicated to Our Lady of Carmel. Only the octagonal lantern survives.

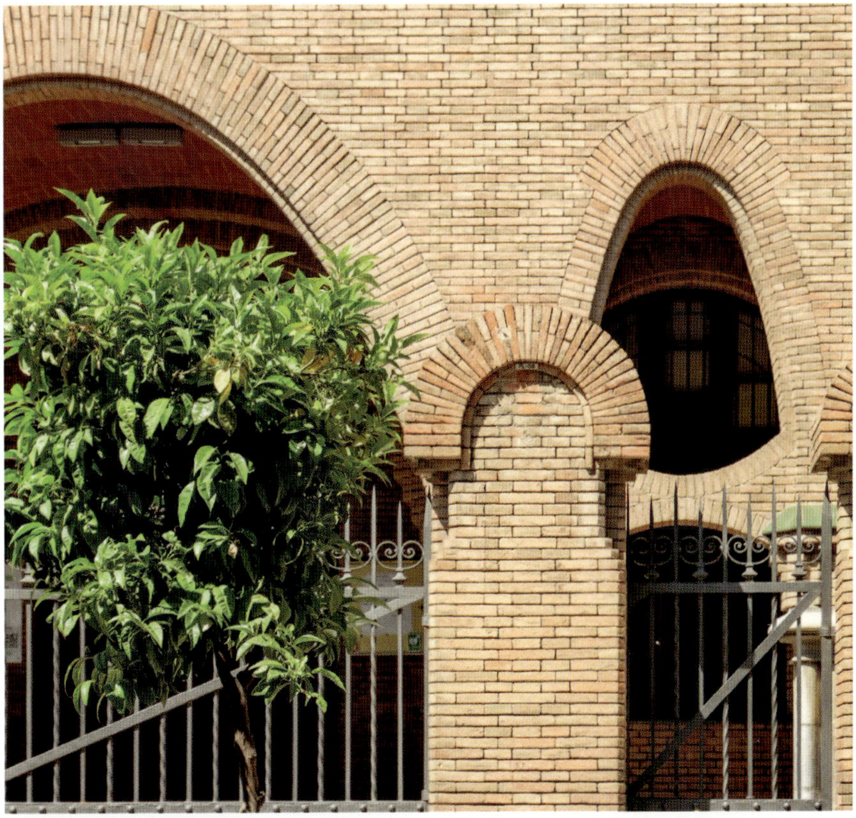

Col·legi de les Teresianes

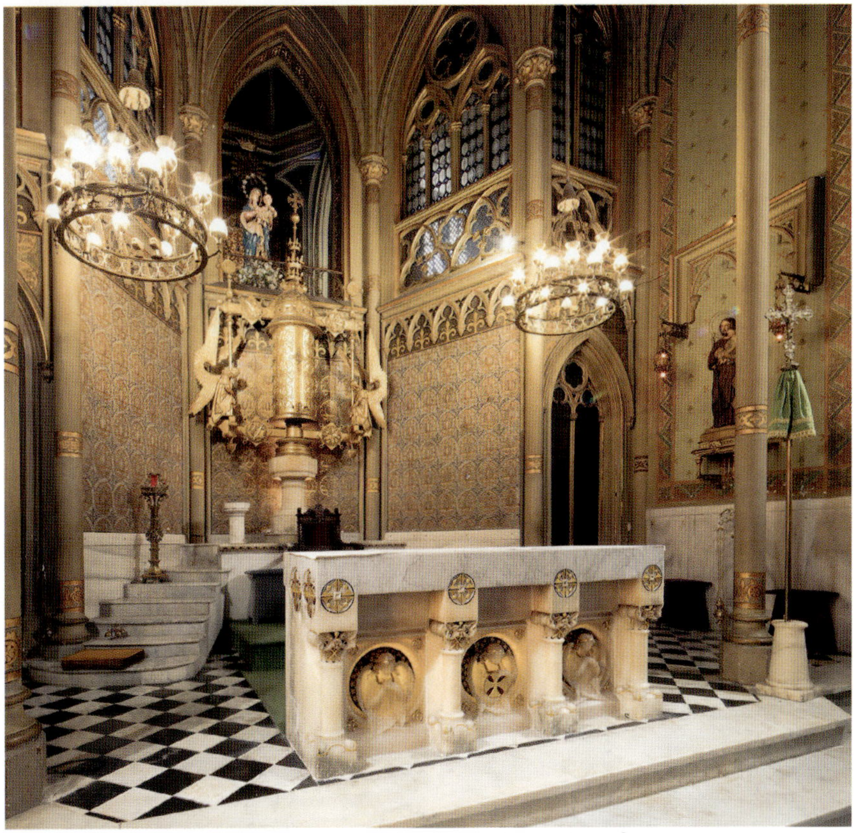

Altar in the chapel of Nostra Senyora del Sagrat Cor of Antoni Gaudí

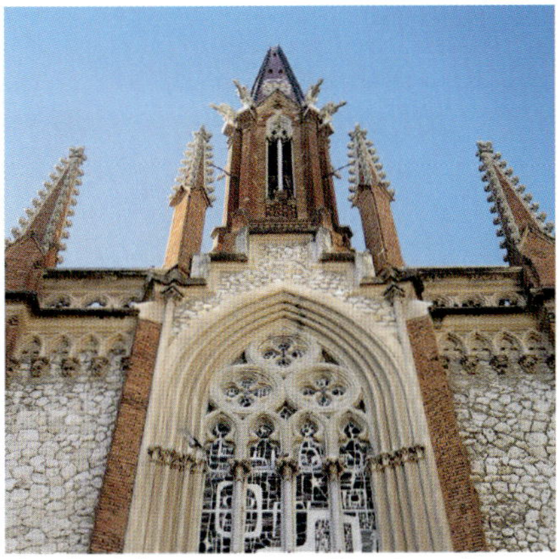

Church of the Pares Carmelites Descalços

The Rambla Nova

The Balcó del Mediterrani

One of the most popular traditions among Tarragona locals is to go and "tocar ferro" (touch iron), which involves going for a stroll along the Rambla Nova as far as the iron railings of the Balcó del Mediterrani, with its spectacular sea views. This sweeping promenade, which is one of the city's most iconic sights, is 45 metres wide and stretches for almost 2 kilometres as far as the banks of the river Francolí. It isn't just a meeting point or place for strollers; it also hosts all kinds of community events, from festivals to processions and fairs. The development of the site began in the middle of the 19th century when it was known as the Esplanada. The first building went up in 1859 on the corner of Carrer de la Unió. The Rambla Nova only stretched as far as Carrer de l'Assalt until the end of the 19th century when it was extended as far as the junction where the fountain, the Font del Centenari, now stands. In the 1920s, it was developed as far as Plaça Imperial Tàrraco. In the 1950s, the promenade was extended along the stretch known today as the Rambla President Lluís Companys, and, by the end of the century, it attained its current proportions when it was extended as far as the Rambla President Francesc Macià. The different periods of its growth can be seen in the buildings and landmarks in each section.

In addition to the *modernista* buildings described above, and the monuments and statues, which we will look at in a separate section of the book, the Rambla Nova has many unique buildings from different eras. The Teatre Tarragona, the city's main theatre, which opened in late 2012, in a brand-new building designed by the architect Xavier Climent on the site of a cinema and theatre of the same name dating from 1924; the building that was once the headquarters of the bank "La Caixa", with its trademark towers surmounted by domes, designed by the renowned Barcelona architect, Enric Sagnier, which was home to the station Ràdio Tarragona for many years; the former Banco de España, a neo-classical building dating from 1928. Other outstanding buildings include the Seguredad Social, home of the social security office; the tax office, the Delegación de Hacienda; and the Banco Atlántico, the city's tallest building.

In Plaça Imperial Tàrraco, we find one of the most noteworthy examples of rationalist architecture in Spain, the central government office, the Subdelegación del Govierno Central (1963), by Alejandro de la Sota.

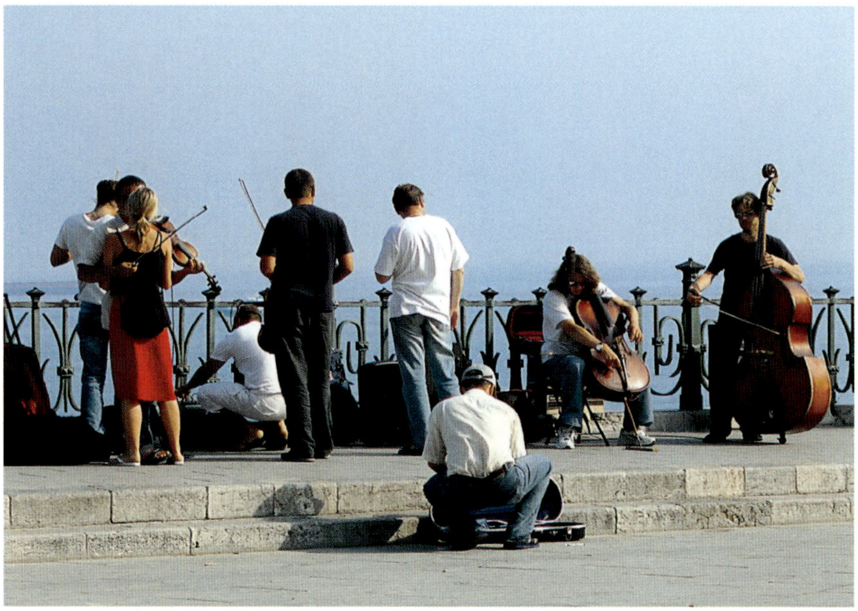

Musicians on the Balcó del Mediterrani

The Rambla Nova, at the end of September →

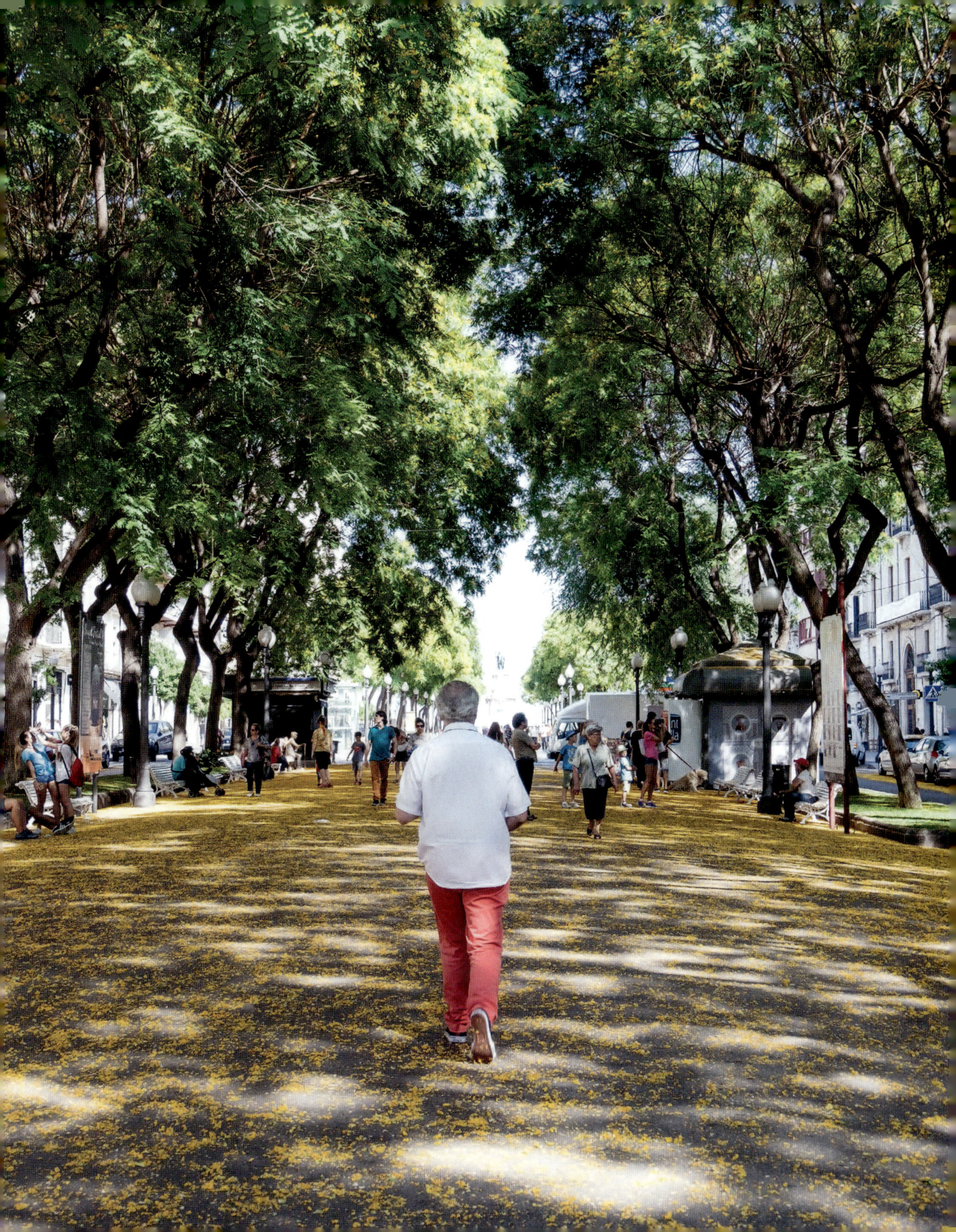

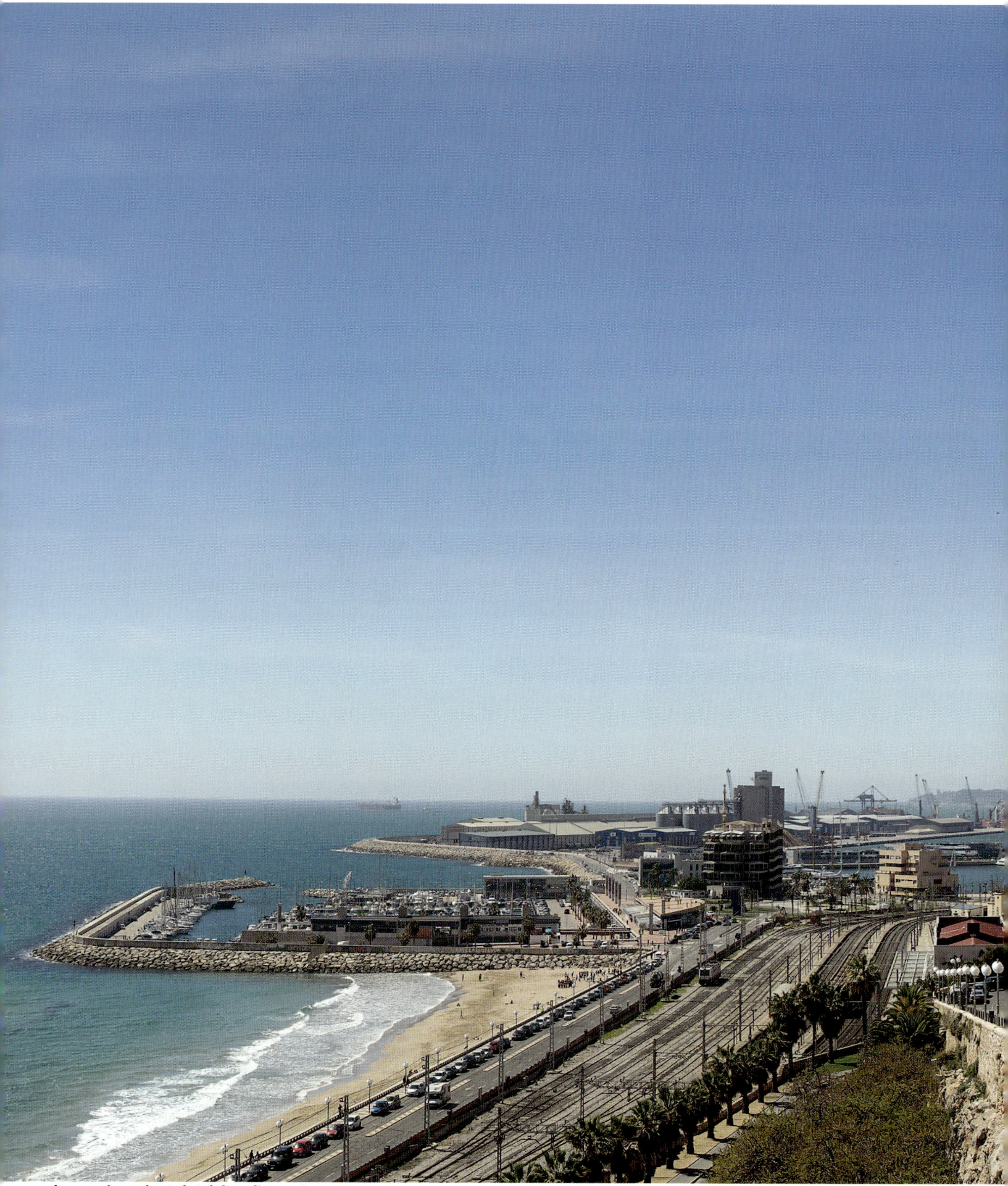

The port from the Balcó del Mediterrani

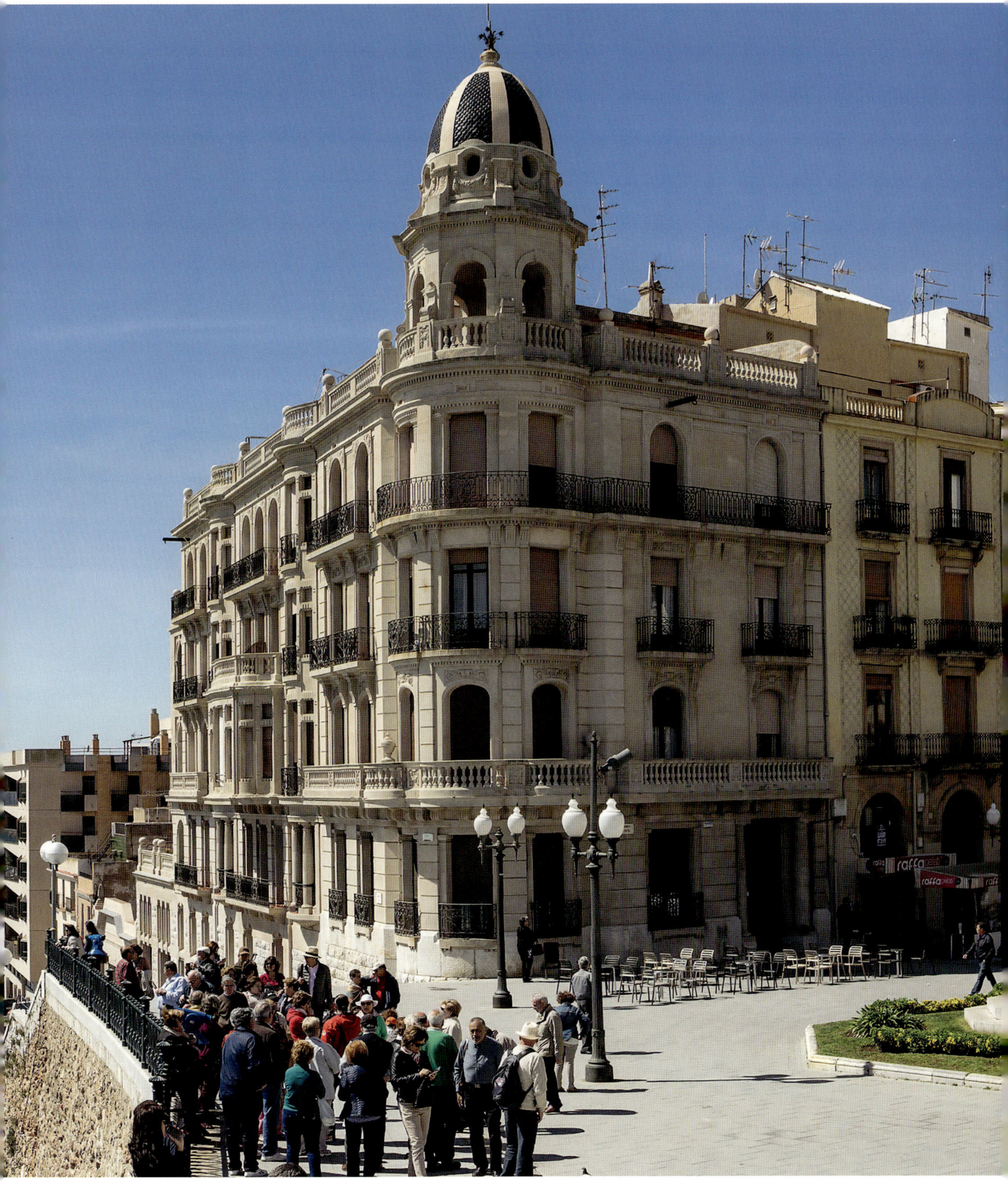
raffa
raffa

The Balcó del Mediterrani

The iron railings along the Balcó del Mediterrani were designed by the architect Ramon Salas i Ricomà in 1889, and have become one of Tarragona's iconic symbols. The vistas from this viewing point that overlooks the sea, the Amphitheatre, the promontory, the Punta del Miracle, and kilometres of coastline, are one of the most popular attractions for locals and visitors alike. The name Balcó del Mediterrani was suggested by Emilio Castelar, the man who went on to become president of the First Spanish Republic. A 300 metre-long promenade covers the sheer drop beneath the Balcó del Mediterrani and seafront, and was built over the railway lines.

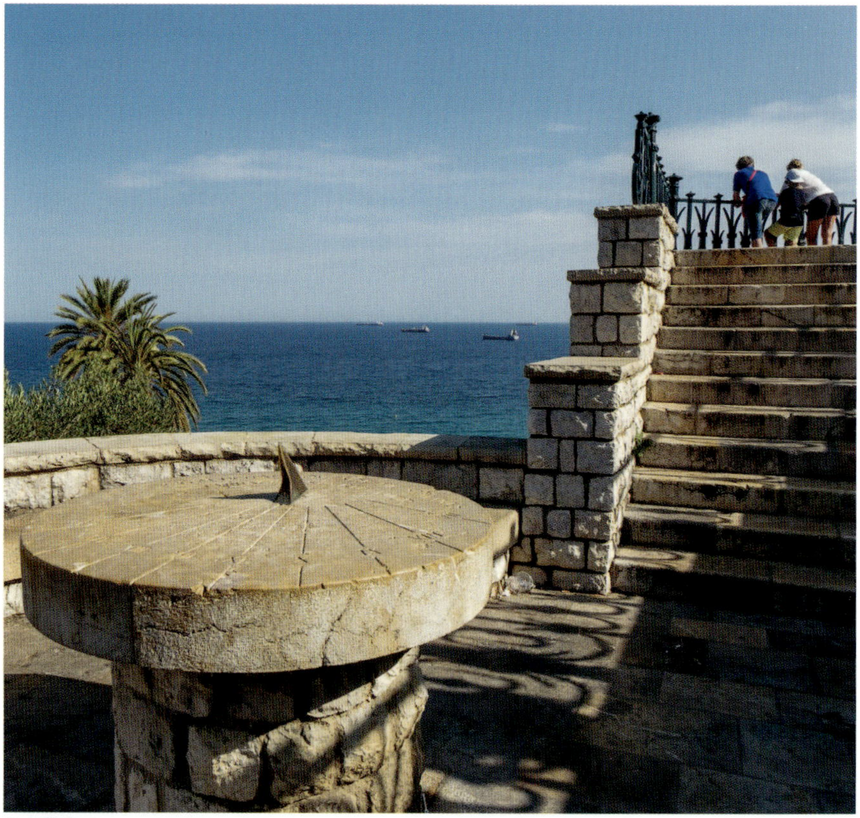

Sundial

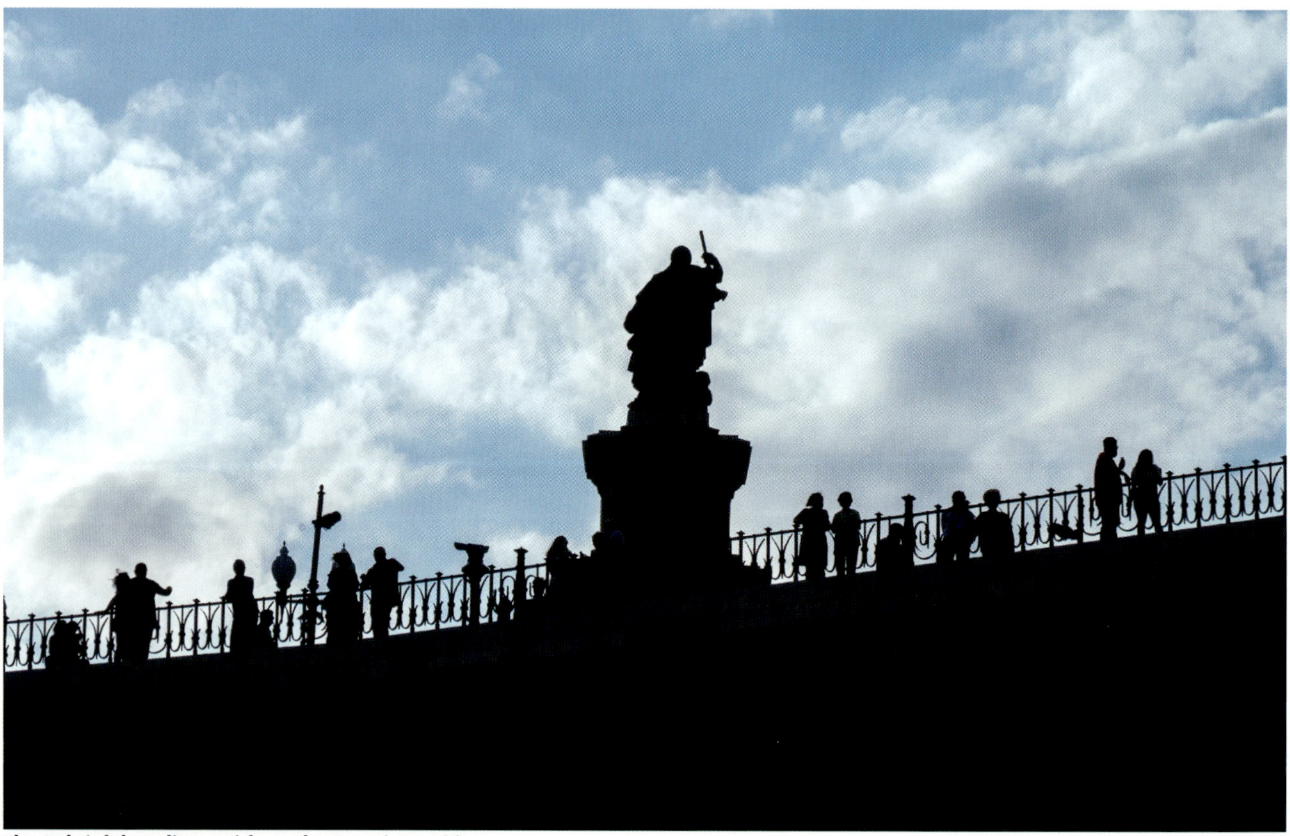

The Balcó del Mediterrani from the Passeig Marítim

Cambra de Comerç
Known as the 'Casa de la Punxa de la Rambla' (house of spikes on the Rambla) to distinguish it from the church of the Pares Carmelites Descalços, it was designed by Antoni Pujol Sevil in 1929 and called the Casa Escorsa. Until 1954, its outline was a major reference point at the entrance the city, but after years of building it has become a central landmark.

CaixaForum Tarragona
The architect Pujol Sevil designed this building in 1950 for the bank, the Caixa de Pensions de Catalunya i Balears (now CaixaBank), which has its headquarters in the city. The bank's community projects department opened a cultural activities centre in the section of the building on Carrer Colom in 2001. It houses a world-class exhibition gallery.

Shopping while you wander
The Rambla Nova and the streets in the centre make up the Via T, one of the city's main retail quarters. This is a veritable open-air shopping centre where you can shop as you wander. It continues on the other side of Plaça Imperial Tàrraco, where you'll find a famous department store. This isn't the city's only shopping area. There are traditional shops in the Part Alta, as well as the Parc Central shopping centre, the Les Gavarres leisure and retail complex and shops in every neighbourhood.

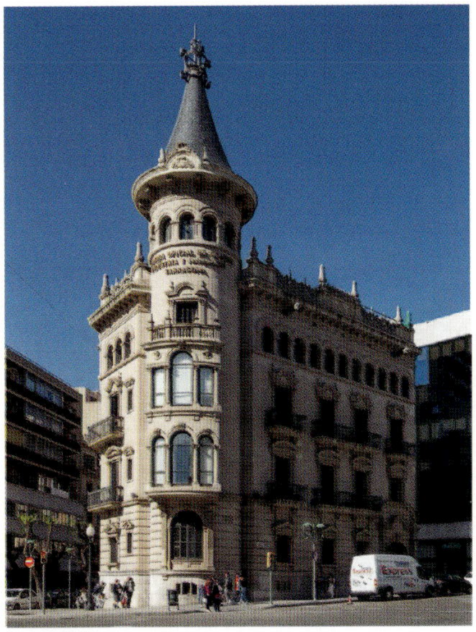

Casa de la Punxa

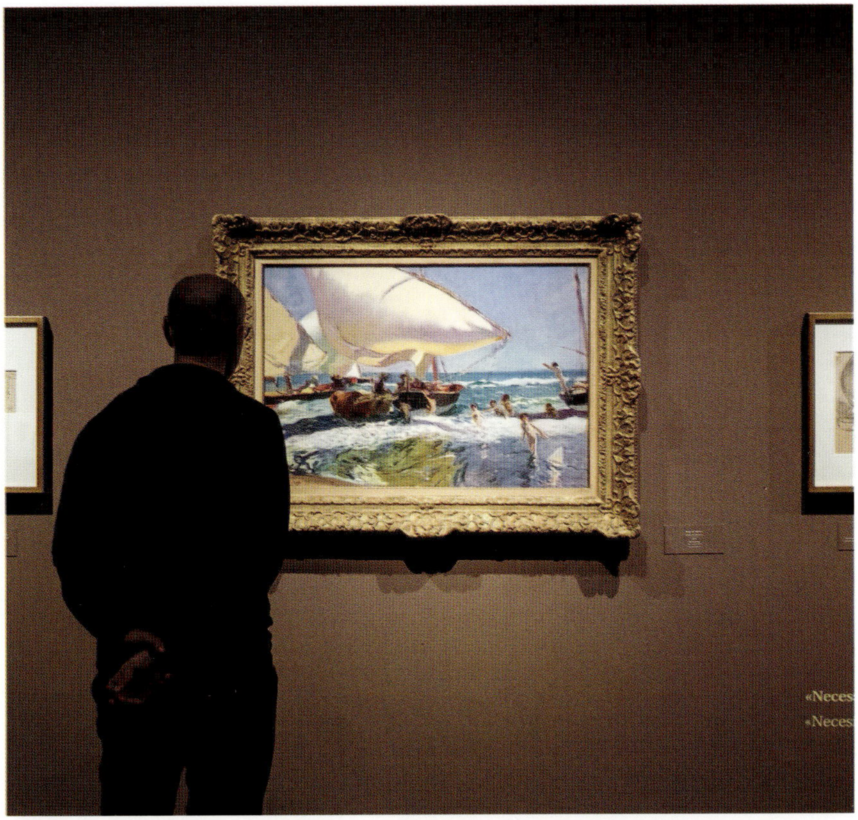

CaixaForum Tarragona

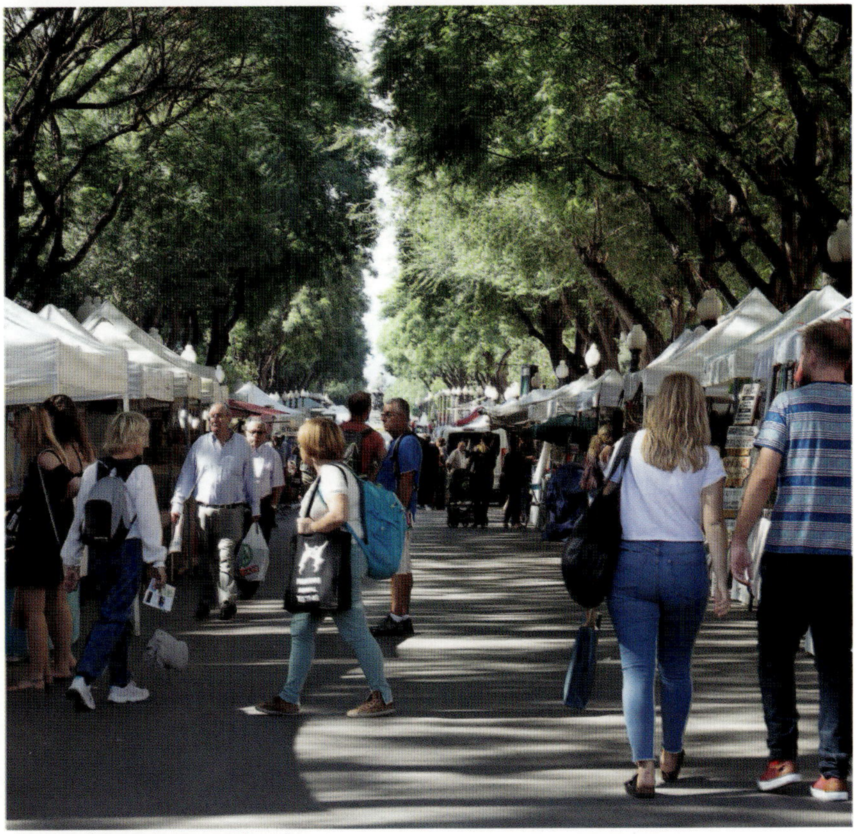

The Rambla Nova on market day

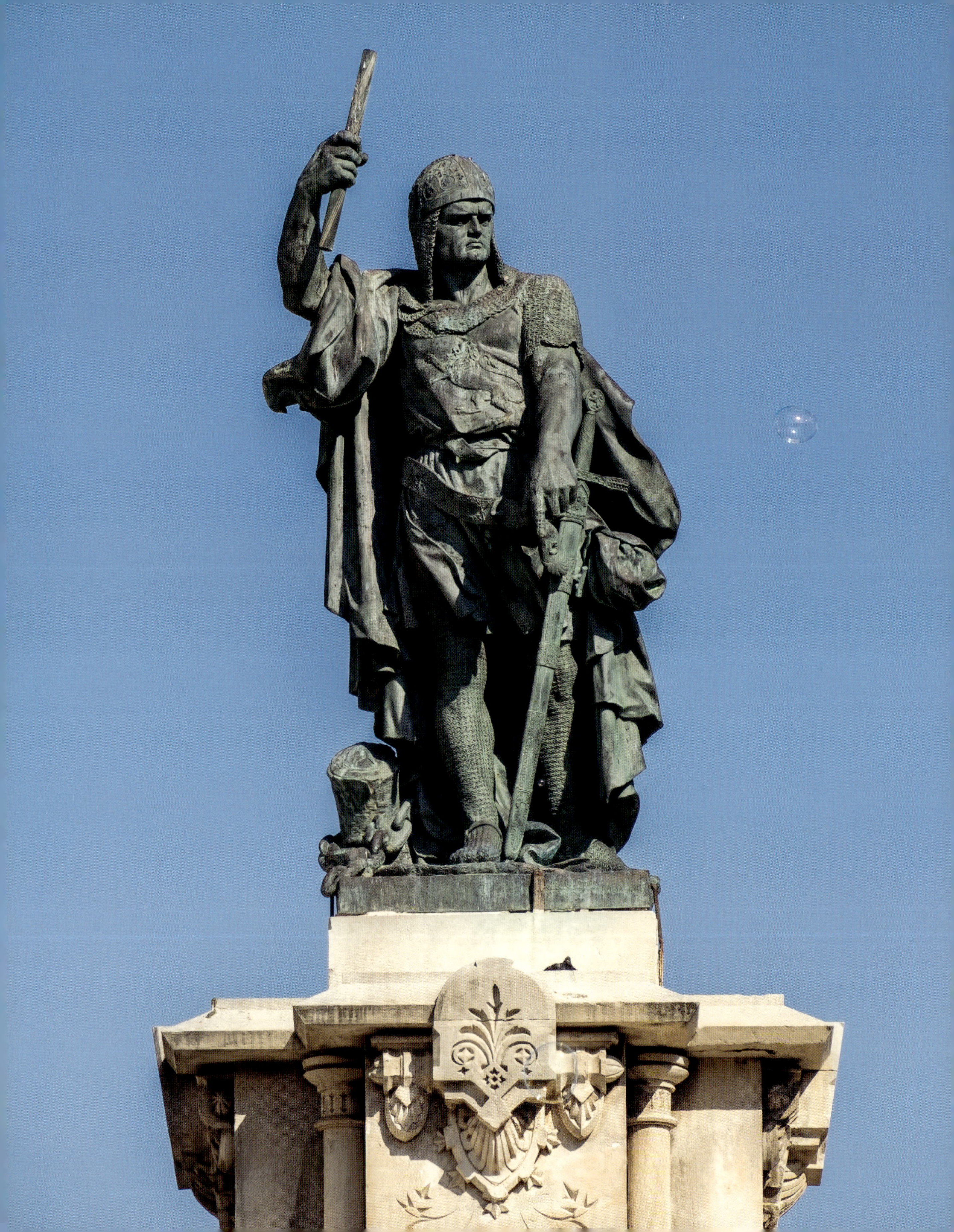

Statues and monuments

From the Balcó del Mediterrani to the river Francolí, you'll come across sculptures that tell the history of the city and country, such as the monument to admiral *Roger de Llúria* (1889) by the sculptor Fèlix Ferrer, with its plinth by Salas i Ricomà; *Old Virgili* (1995), a sculpture by Josep Agustí depicting the Tarragona-born printer Josep Virgili sitting on a bench; *The Monument to the Heroes of 1811* by the sculptor Julio Antonio (erected in 1931), which is also known as *The Naked*; the *Centenary Fountain* (1954) by Josep Viladomat, which commemorates the centenary of the demolition of the city walls; the *Monument to Human Towers* (1999) by Francesc Anglès; Bruno Gallart's statue of the president of the Catalan Government *Lluís Companys* (2005), who was executed by firing squad in 1940; and the *Wind Tower* (2006) by the ironsmith and sculptor Antoni Mas.

← ***Roger de Llúria***

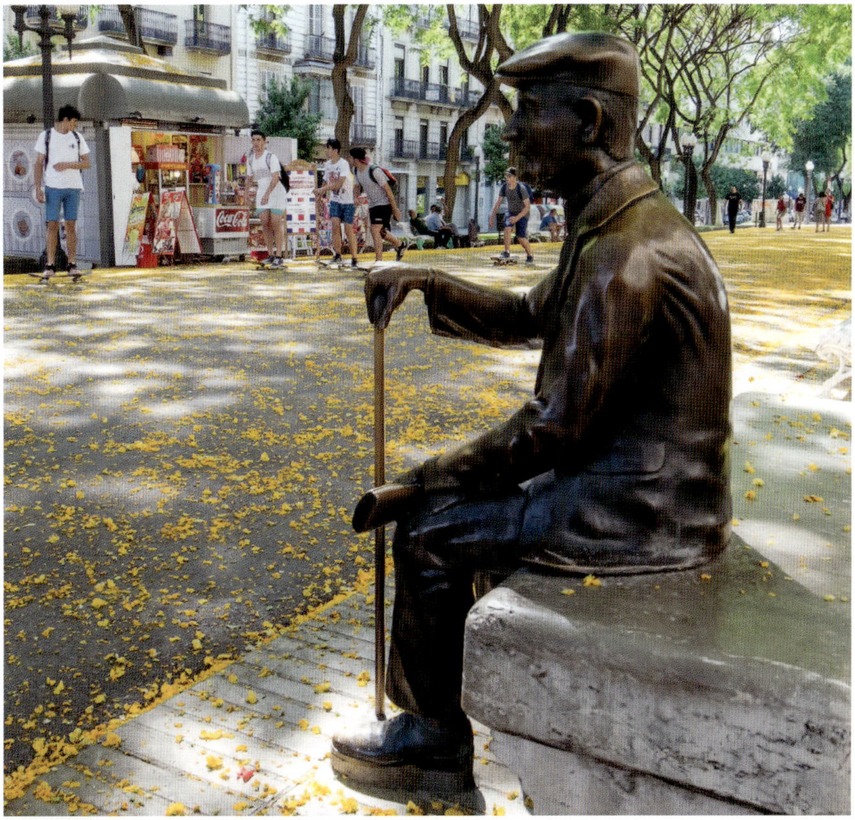

Old Virgili

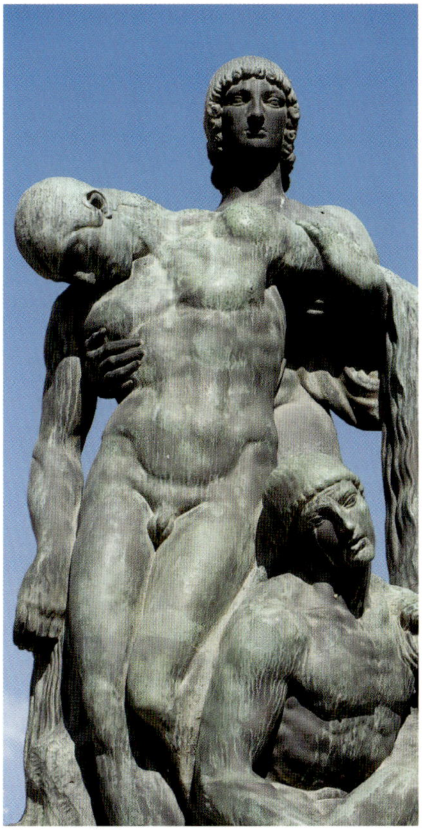

Els Despullats

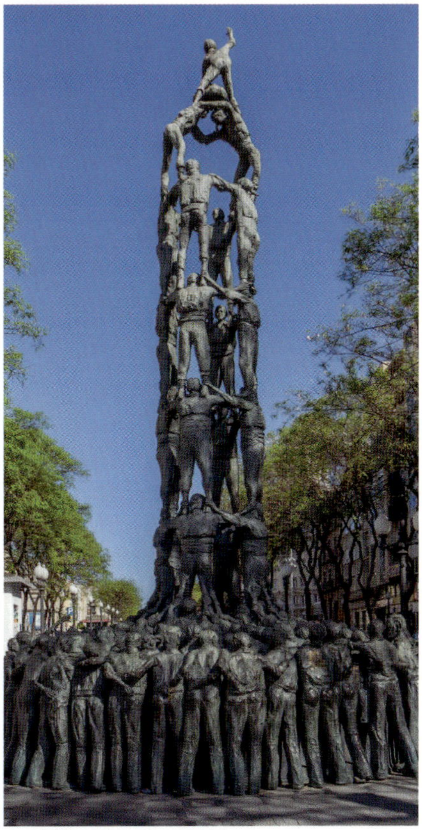

***Castellers*, human towers**

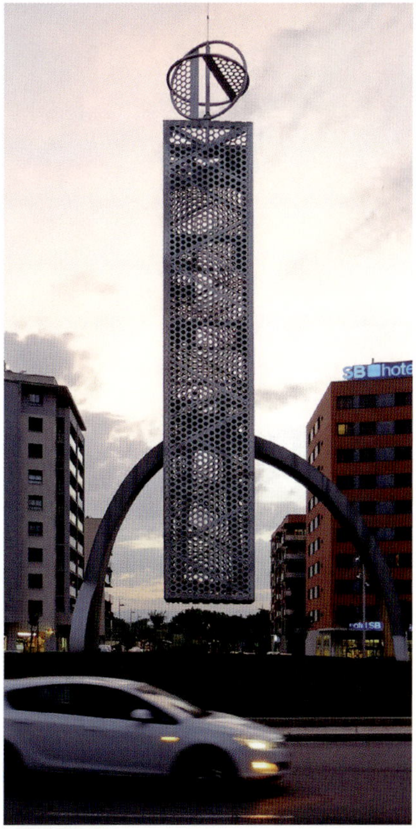

Wind Tower

Tarragona and the sea

El Serrallo, the port and beaches

The trading and industrial port of Tarragona was originally the gateway to the Iberian Peninsula in classical times. Today it also a favourite port of call for yachts and has a well-equipped marina.

Tarragona's symbiotic relationship with the sea dates back to ancient times. Even before the Romans arrived during the 2nd Punic War, which resulted in the city of Tarraco, Greek historians already knew about an anchorage and bay at the mouth of the river Tulis. Exposed to the winds, a dock was built to protect it, meaning that many of the ships involved in the war and conquest of Hispania Citerior stopped off there.

The port and its activities were the drivers of Tarraco's history. It was used by the traders who were involved in the import and export business between the Italian and Iberian peninsulas, and with the other ports in the Mediterranean. The remains of a large dock with arches underpinned by pillars could still be seen in the 19th century. The most widespread hypothesis suggests that, at the height of its success, the port extended as far as Carrer Real and Carrer Smith.

The port was abandoned from the time of the Visigothic occupation until it was resettled by the Christians, and obstructed by the ruins from the buildings. Land encroached on the sea and, although the port was back in use by the 12th century, a section of the dry dock was converted to land for growing crops. Nonetheless, in the 13th century, it was an export base for many products, including wine, olives, walnuts, honey, saffron and tar, destined for the ports on the Languedoc coast, Andalusia and North Africa.

The Reapers' War, in the middle of the 17th century, caused serious damage and diverted trade to the neighbouring port of Salou. The port of Tarragona was completely sidelined in 1717, after the War of the Spanish Succession, when a ban was placed on offloading foreign goods, and the beaches at Salou, Torredembarra and Altafulla were used instead. The ban was lifted in 1761 and a customs post built, but this was not enough. A new wharf had to be built for berthing ships and loading goods.

In 1790, a royal decree gave permission for the port to be repaired based on a project by the ship's captain Juan Ruiz de Apodaca. From 1800 onwards, Juan Smith took over from Apodaca to oversee the project. Smith considered it necessary to expand on Apodaca's design and build the district known as La Marina.

Port Heritage route

→ Appendix p. 6

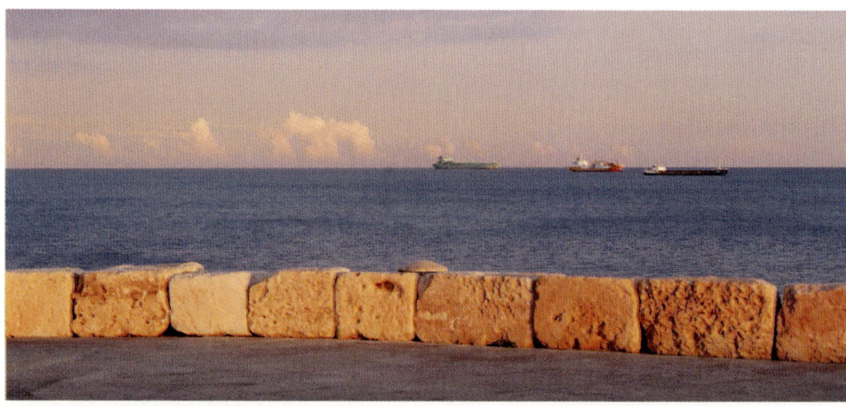

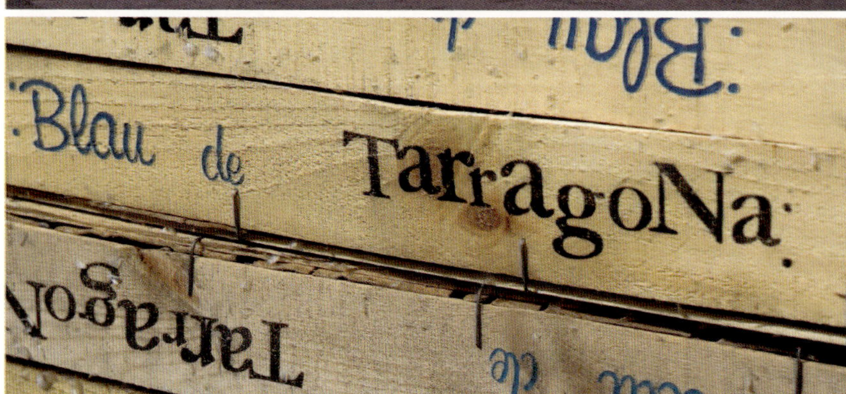

Boxes of fish and the breakwater

Fishermen's wharf, Moll de Pescadors →

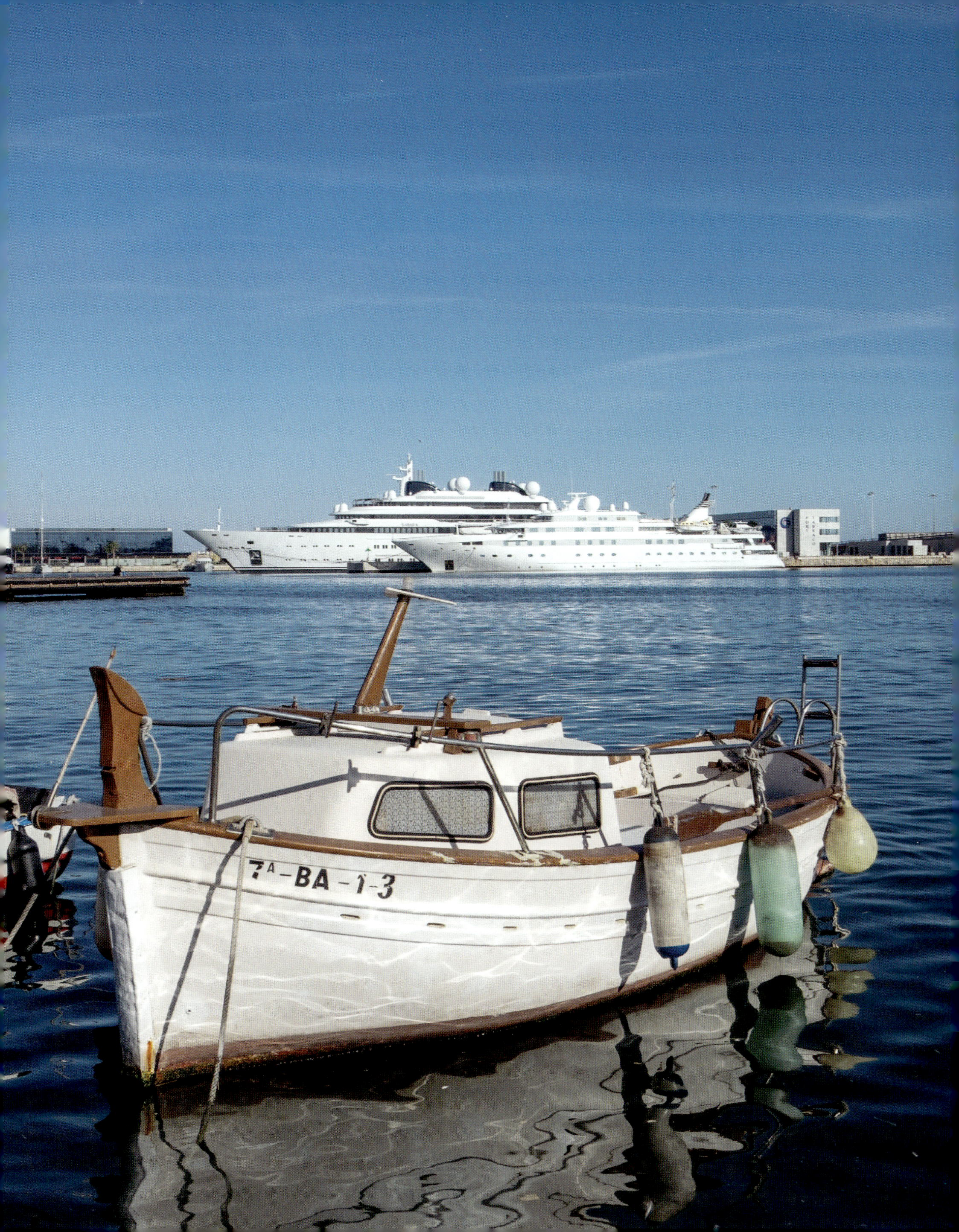
7A-BA-1-3

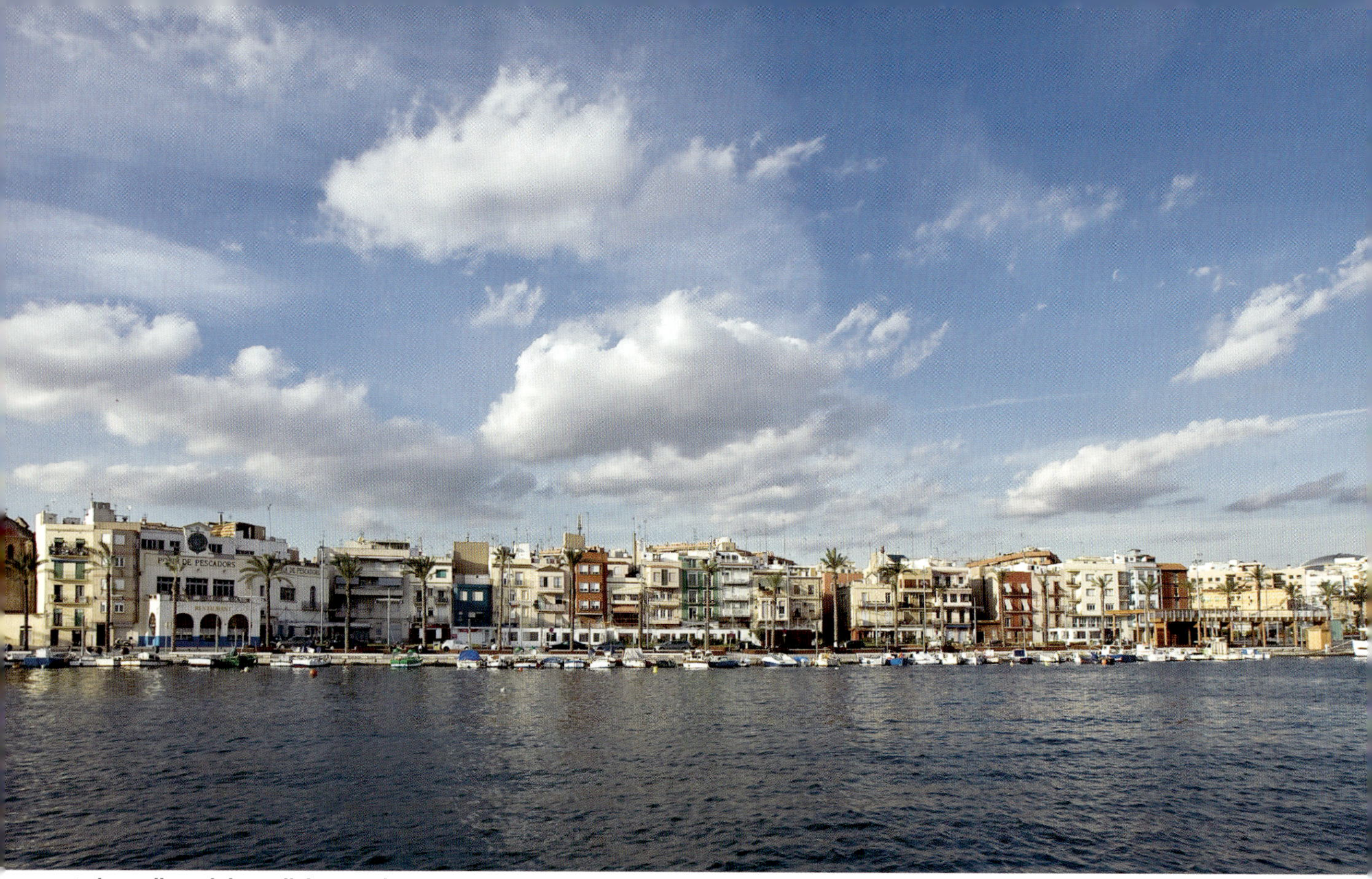

↑↓ **El Serrallo and the Moll de Pescadors**

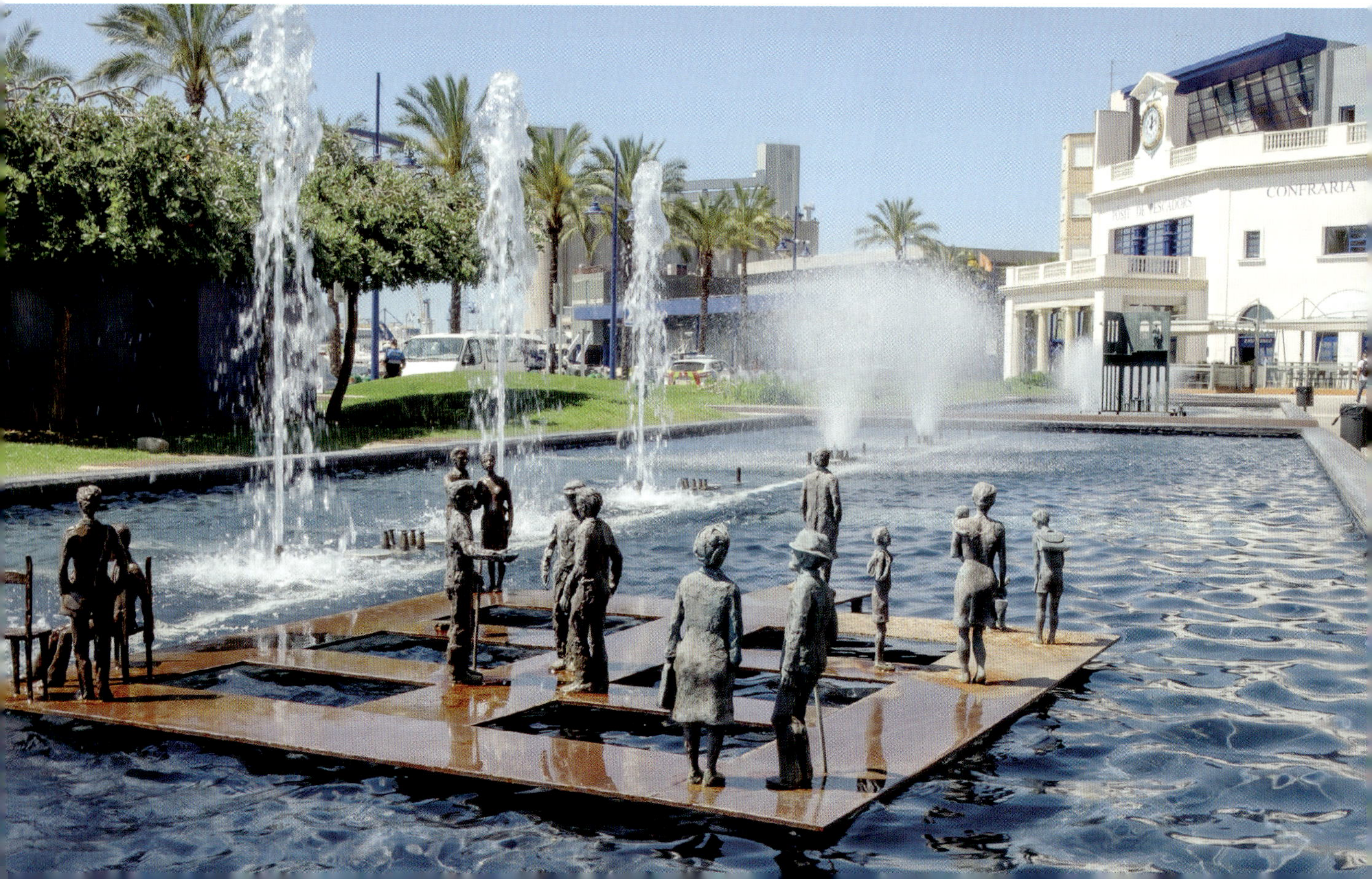

El Serrallo

The fishing quarter with its narrow streets was originally a cluster of fishermen's huts that were moved to Llatzaret beach in 1865 when the railway line was built and the port expanded. Their approximate location was the site where the Moll de Costa dock now stands. In 1811, it had a population of about 1,000. The huts had to be made of wood and on wheels so they could be moved if the military authorities ordered them to do so. After the Revolution of 1868, permission was granted to build permanent homes and the government of the First Republic allotted them plots of land at a low rent. The neogothic church of Sant Pere, by the architect Ramon Salas i Ricomà, was built in 1878 on the remains of the fortress, the Fortí del Francolí.

El Serrallo is also home to the city's fish restaurants, the wholesale fish market and auction rooms. It is a constantly changing neighbourhood, recent examples being the promenade that has linked it to the Moll de Costa since 2007, or the more recent refurbishment of the old fishermen's guild building, the Pòsit de Pescadors, which includes new amenities such as a theatre.

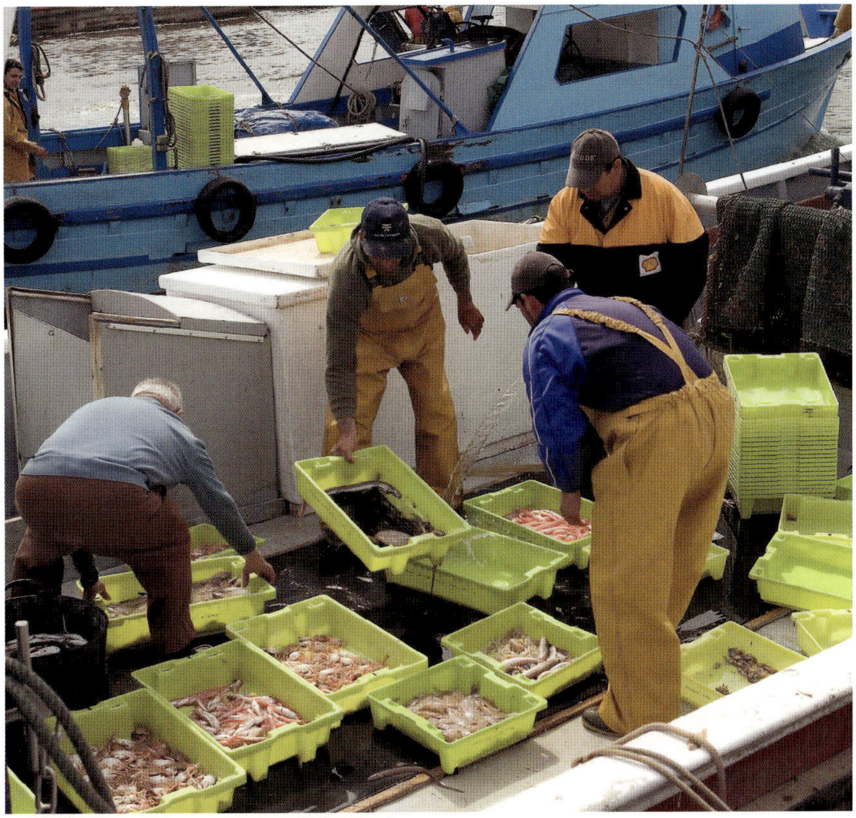

Unloading the fish into the reception tank

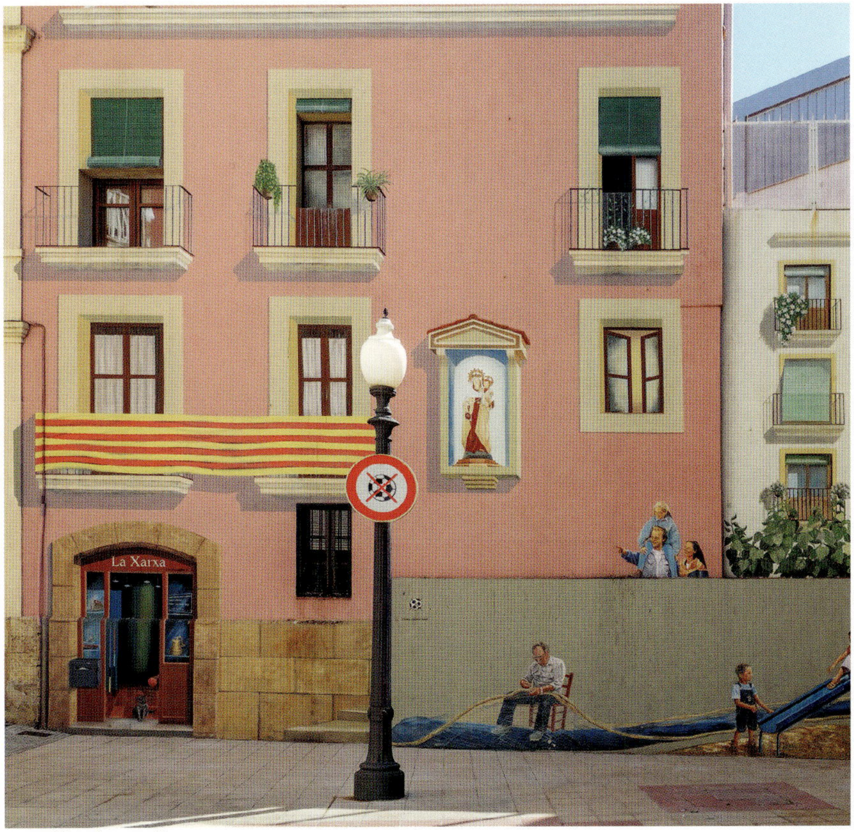

Mural in El Serrallo

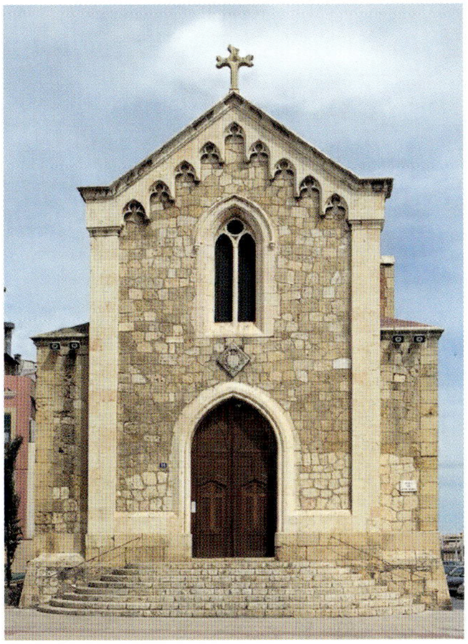

Church of Sant Pere

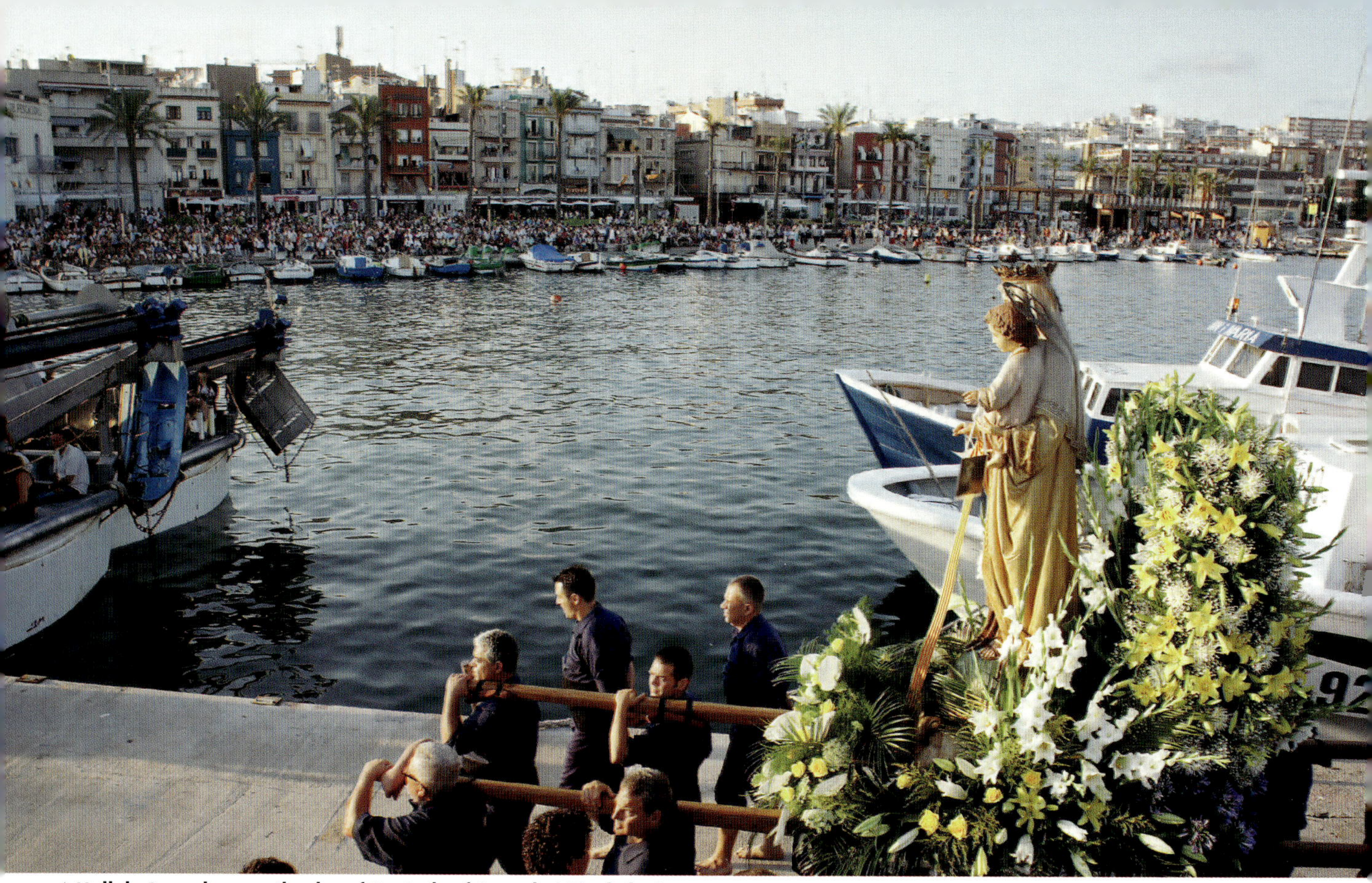

↑ Moll de Pescadors, on the day of Our Lady of Carmel ↓ Tinglado 4

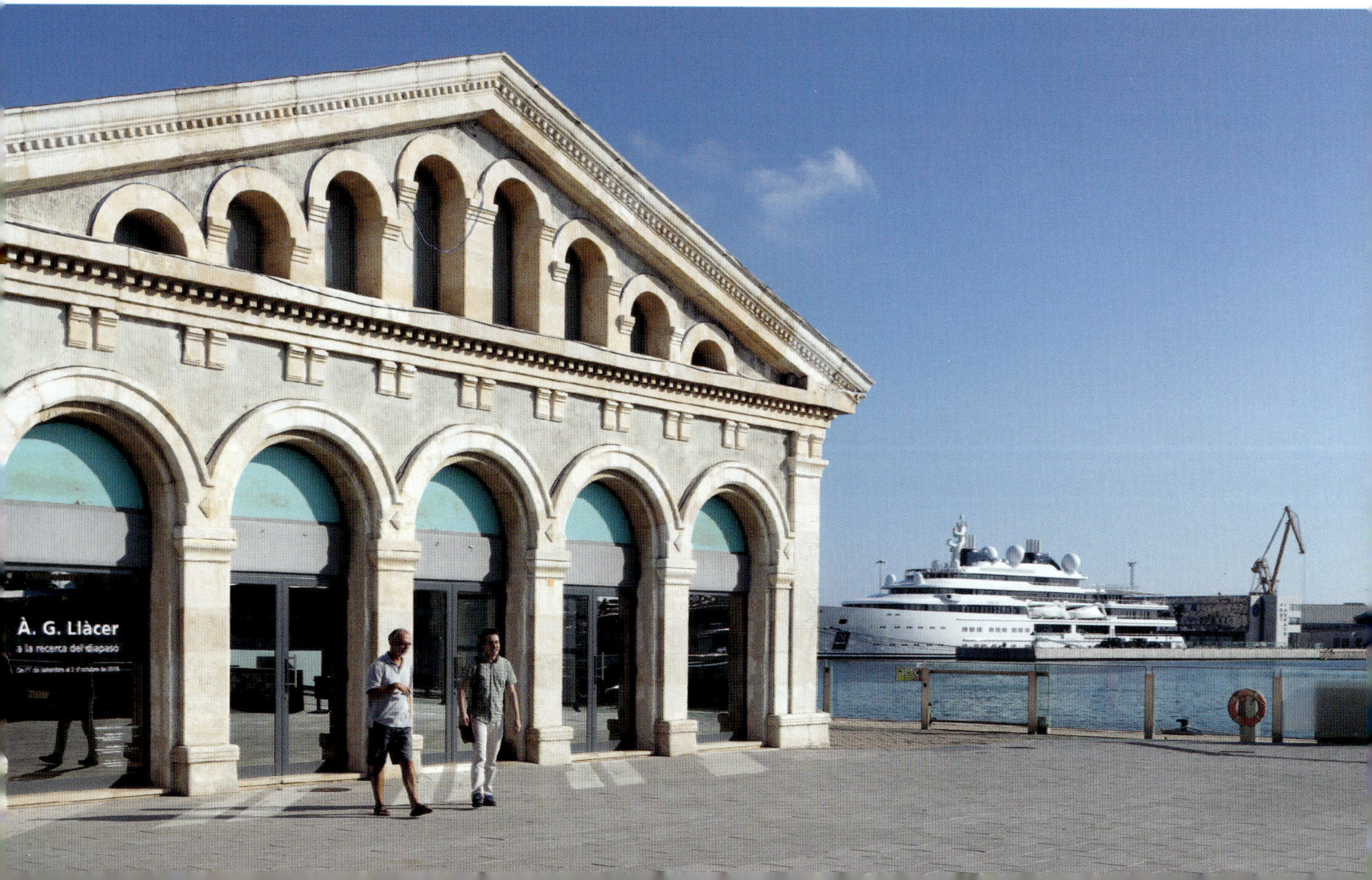

The Port

Tarragona has one of the most important ports on the Mediterranean coast. Most of its activities are associated with the petrochemical industry, but a large area is still used for fishing and sailing. It has also established its position as a cruise terminal, with thousands of passengers passing through every year. The fishing harbour was planned during the Second Republic and built in 1942. It is one of the main harbours in Catalonia in terms of the volume of fish caught by trawling and night-time seine fishing. Prawns and oily fish, hake, octopus, monkfish, cuttlefish and gilthead bream are particularly prevalent. The marina has more than 400 moorings and a dedicated area for yachts: Port Tarraco.

Moll de Costa

This promenade opened in 1986 and is one of the sunniest spots in Tarragona with some of the best views. Stretching along the seafront, it is a truly beautiful place, popular with walkers and joggers, set against the backdrop of the city skyline and the azure waters of the Mediterranean. "Moll de Costa" is also the cultural brand name of the port and is a vibrant hub of community, social and cultural life, hosting exhibitions, concerts and other activities

Tinglados and *refugis*

Building work on the Moll de la Costa began in 1884. In 1893, four giant warehouses, known as *tinglados*, were built to protect goods from the elements and theft. The first of these were numbers 2 and 3. Initially they were simple platforms with iron columns and roofs, but numbers 1 and 4, begun in 1908, were made of brick and masonry. Between 1922 and 1924, the two oldest warehouses were moved and placed alongside the newest ones. Two hangar-like sheds, known as *refugis*, were also built one row back from the warehouses. Today, clearly signed in large letters, the warehouses and sheds are used for different purposes. For instance, Tinglado 2 is a contemporary art centre.

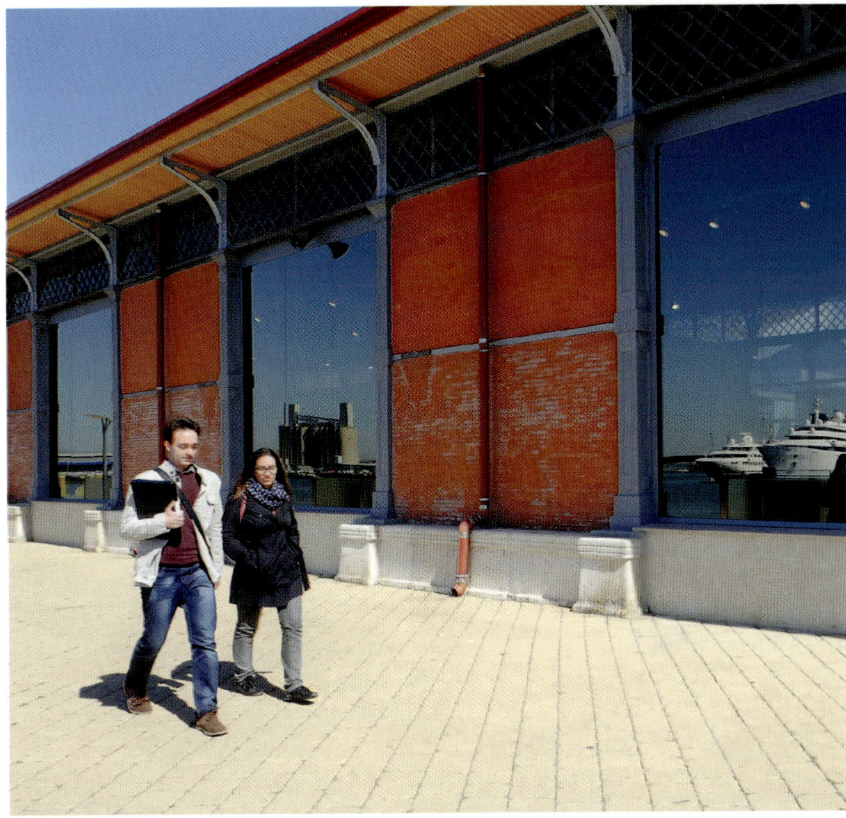

Moll de Costa

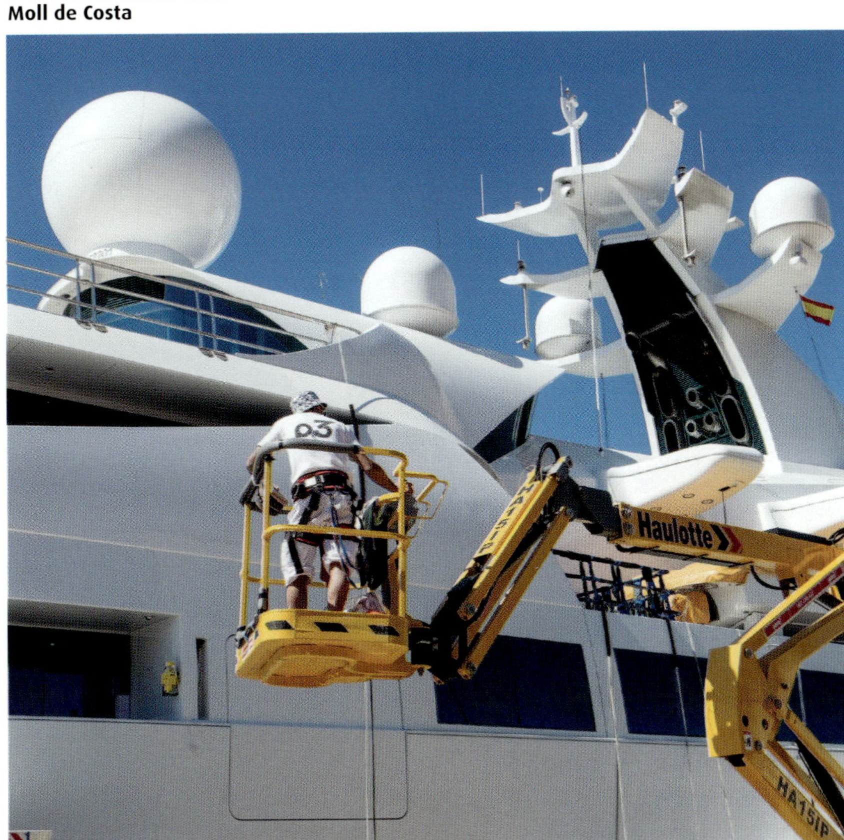

Imposing yachts in Port Tarraco

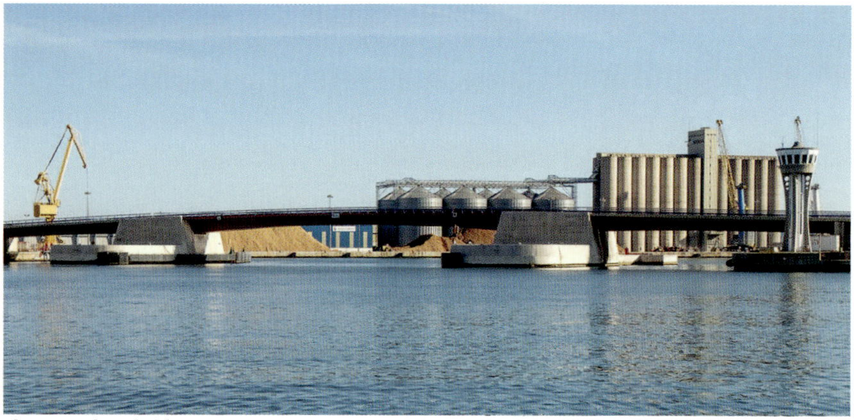

The port drawbridge

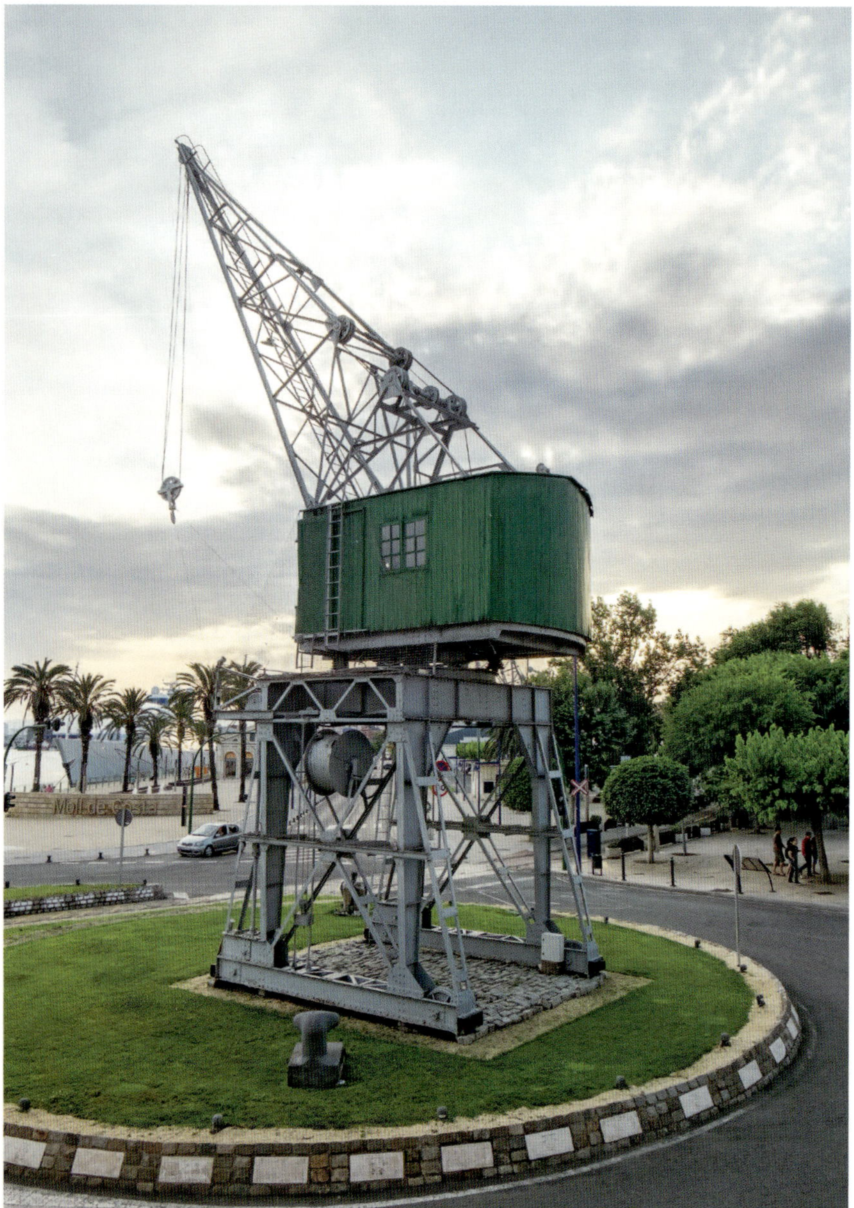

First electric crane in the port of Tarragona

Industrial Port

If you're sailing inside the port on a pleasure boat, or *golondrina*, you'll be amazed at its size. Covering a surface area of almost 4 square kilometres, including storage facilities, it is a city within a city with a huge turnover. It is one of Spain's foremost ports in terms of traffic, moving more than 30 tonnes a year, and a leading port in the transportation of cereals and agrifoods.

Museu del Port

Opened in 2000, the museum traces the history of the Roman port through different types of vessels, fishing gear... It also explores life on the docks, sporting activities and the goods transported by sea, and there is a large section devoted to the fishing quarter. The museum is particularly popular with schools and hosts a wide range of activities, such as guided and dramatised tours.

Plaça dels Carros

When it was first built, this square, in the centre of La Marina, had strong connections with the port and the ambiance of a bustling working harbour district. The carts used for transporting goods would congregate here and it was renowned for its wineries. Now, the Part Baixa, which centres on this square and Carrer Apodaca and Carrer Reial, is a bustling, lively place that simply has to be explored, with its shops, cultural attractions and restaurants serving classic local fare. A Tarragona waiting to be discovered.

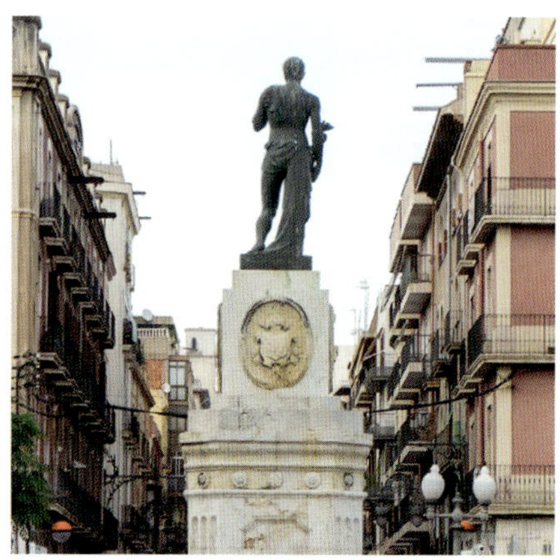

Mercury, in the Plaça dels Carros

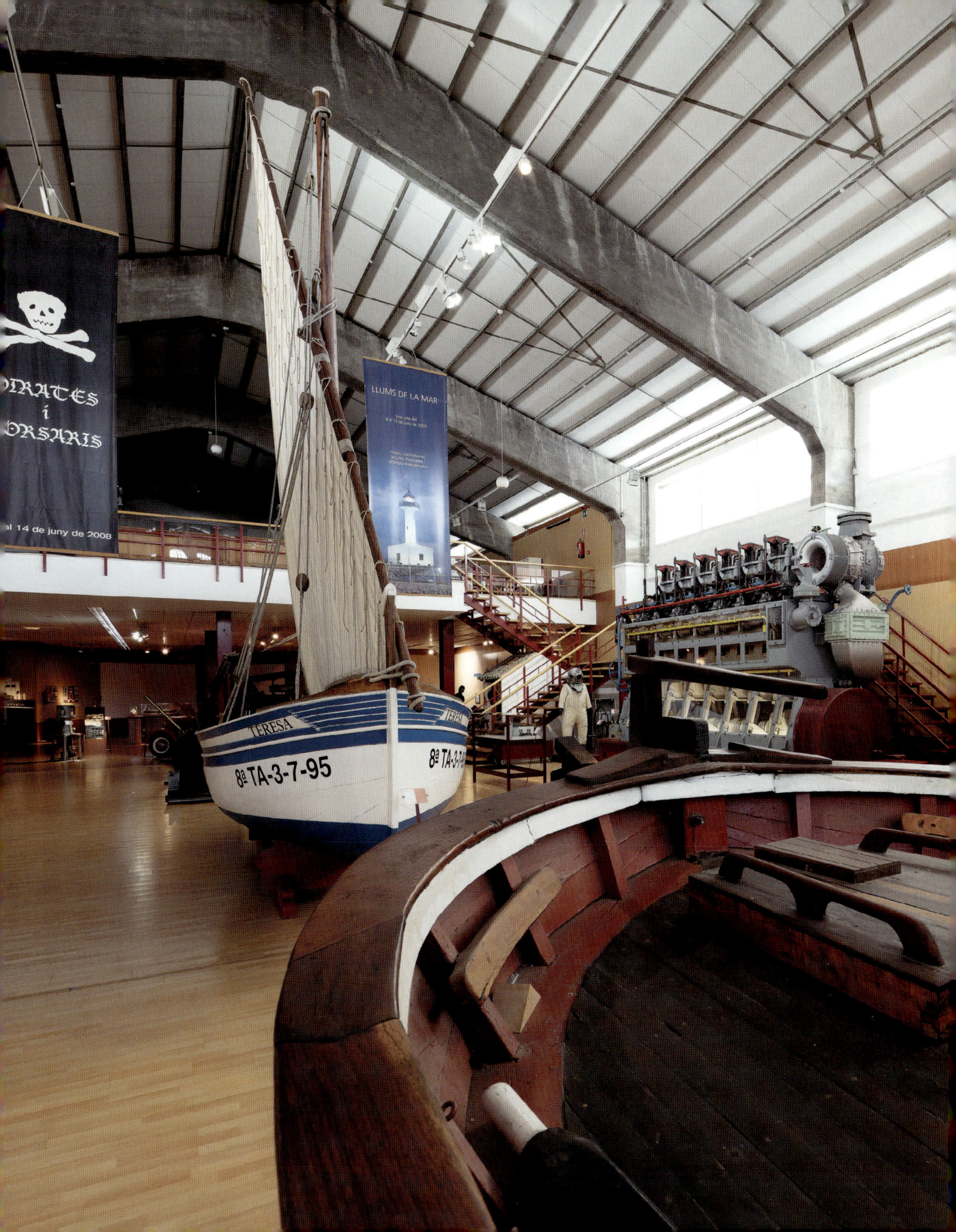
LLUMS DE LA MAR
TERESA
8ª TA-3-7-95

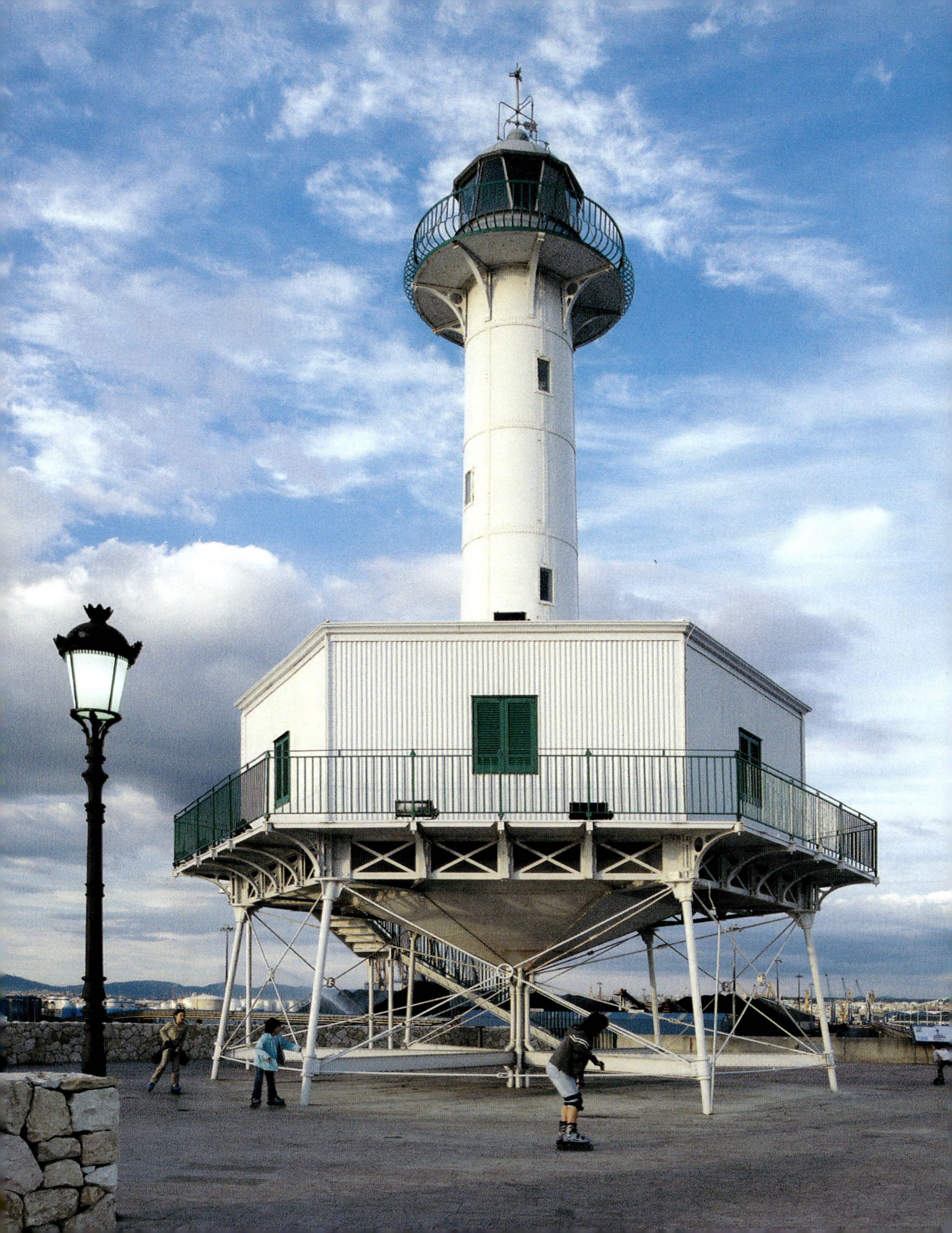

La Banya lighthouse

This lighthouse opened on 1st November 1864 on the headland, the Punta de la Banya, in the Ebro Delta and remained in use until 1978. In the middle of the 1980s it was restored and relocated at the end of the Llevant dock. You can get there on foot or by bike as part of the circuit known as Quilòmetre Zero.

Torre del Rellotge

Since midnight on 31st December 1922, the clock tower has let the harbour workers know when it's time to clock on and clock off. It was designed by the port manager and placed on the Moll de Llevant, in line with Carrer Apodaca, so people could see the time from the Part Baixa. It is shaped like a small temple with four Ionic columns underpinning a three-sided clock. The side facing the sea was enamelled on copper to prevent it from dazzling the ships.

Palau Firal i de Congressos

Tarragona's trade fair and congress complex is one of its key facilities. It comprises two auditoriums, one of them seating more than 1,100 people, and ten meeting rooms, most of them for congresses, but some used for concerts and large-scale entertainments. The trade fair site has an indoor area of 2,000 square metres and an outdoor esplanade of 3,000 square metres. It hosts cultural and tourism events.

La Banya lighthouse

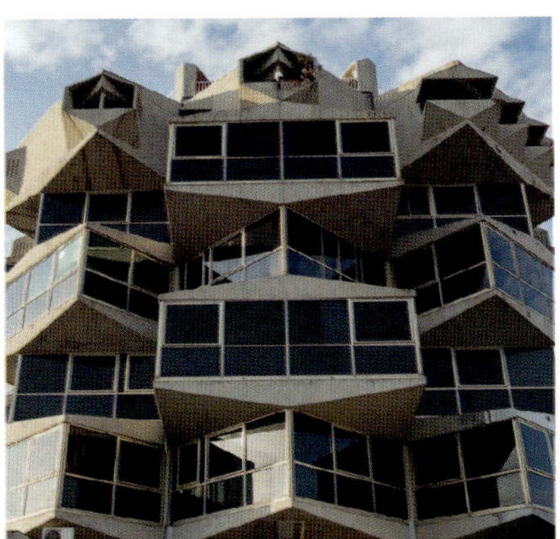

Old Port Authority building

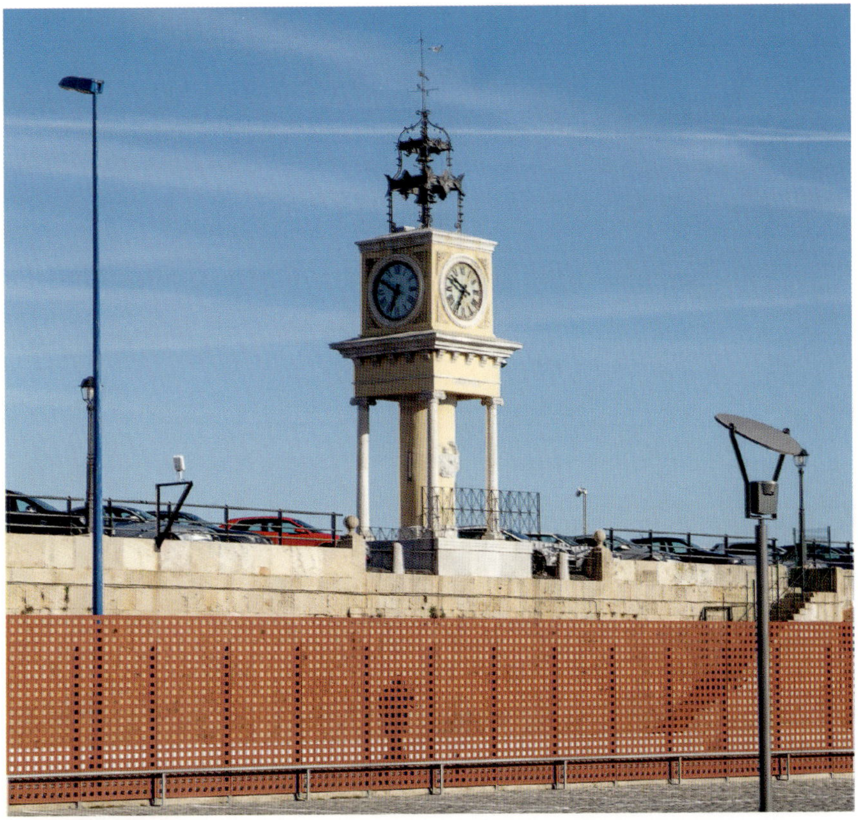

Torre del Rellotge

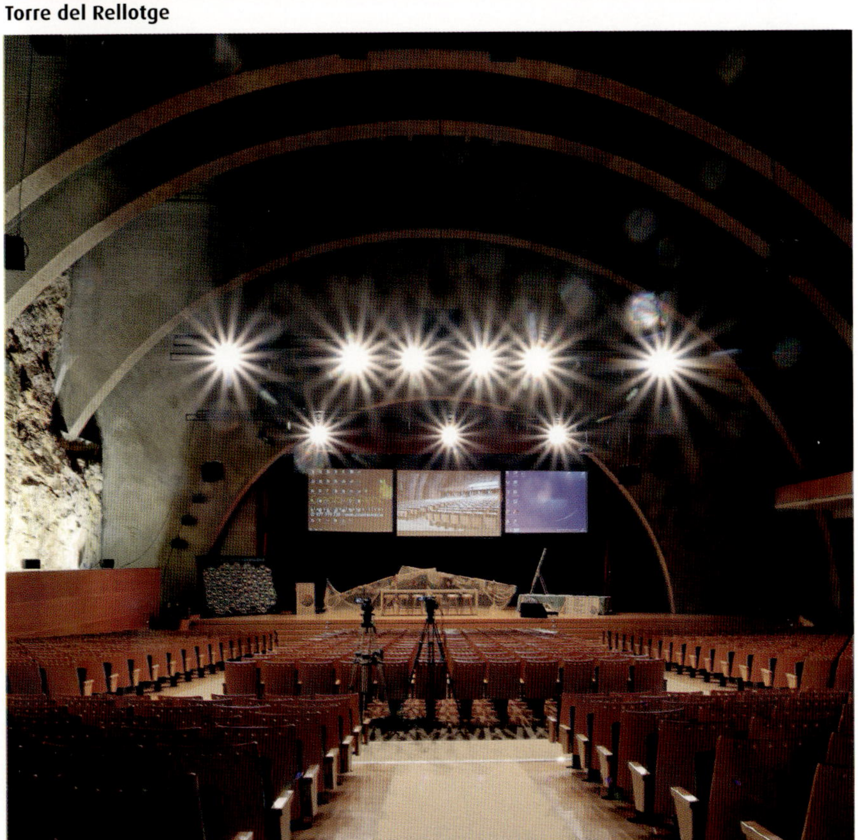

Palau Firal i de Congressos

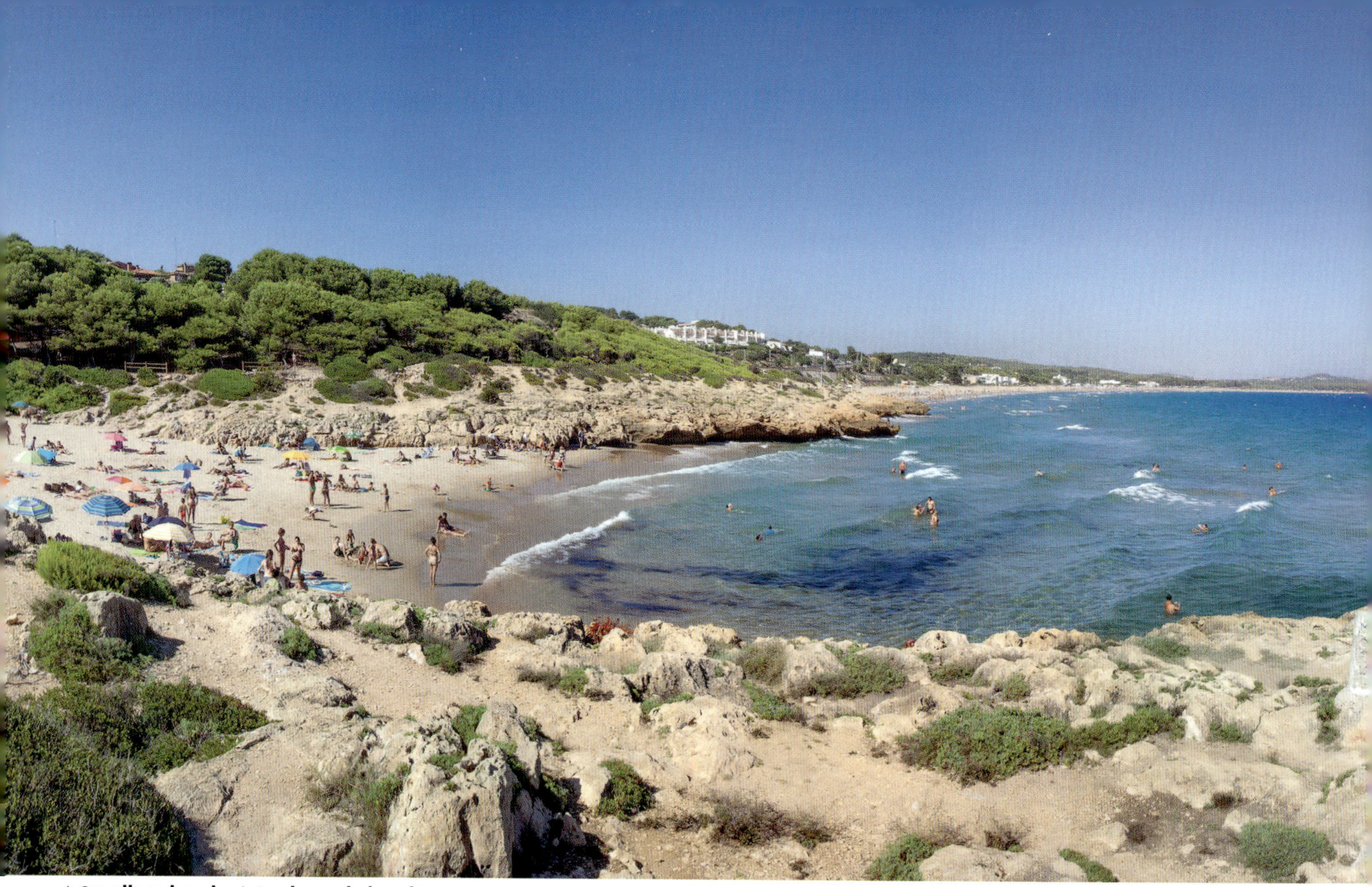

↑ Capellans beach ↓ Arrabassada beach

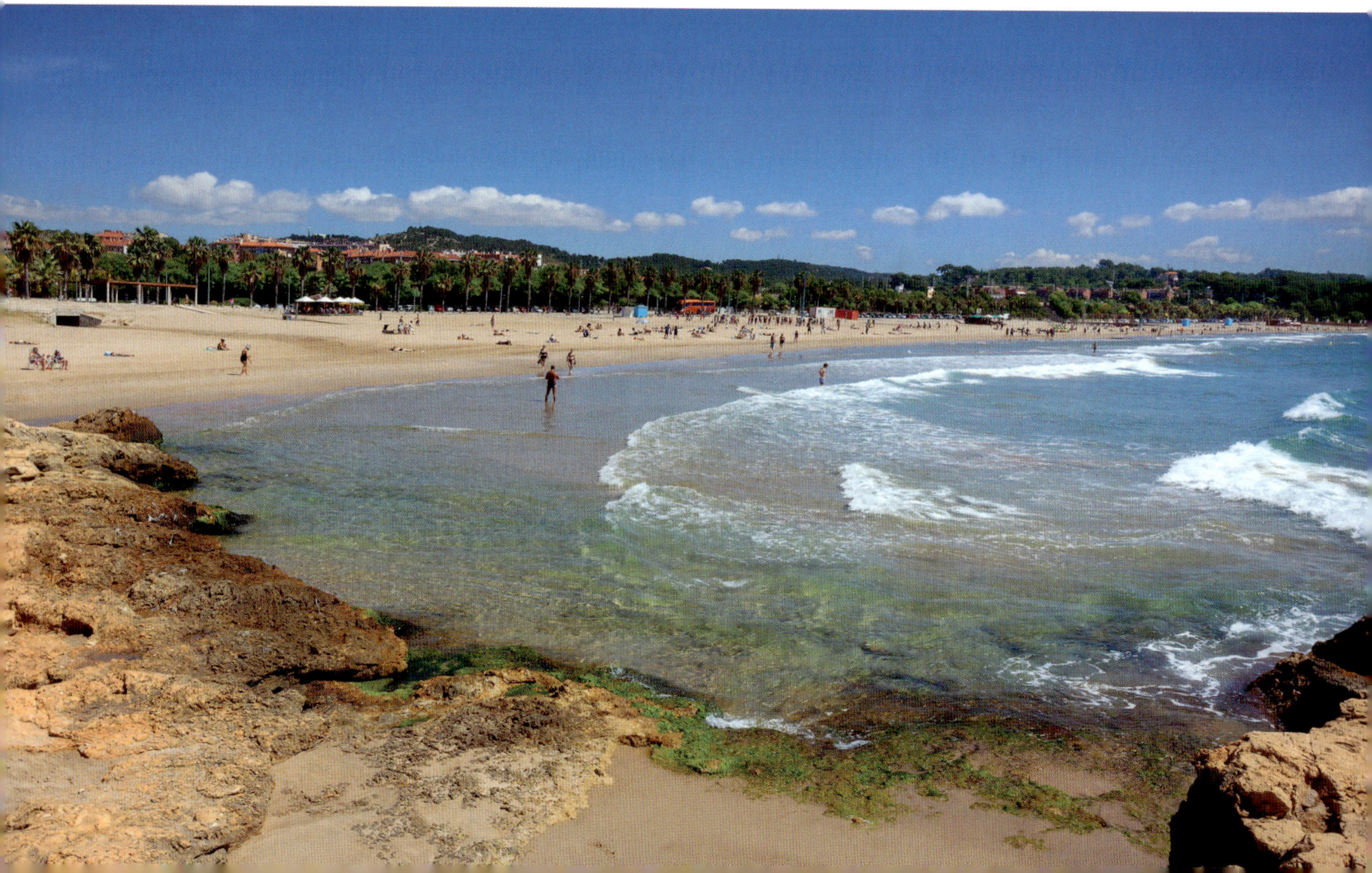

Tarragona's beaches

The long coastline and large number of beaches where you can swim and walk, in winter and summer, are the luxuries of a seaside town that everyone can afford. Tarragona has 15 kilometres of coastline, seven beaches and three coves. They are all within easy reach, either by public transport or on foot.

Miracle beach

This is the closest beach to the city centre and, as a result, offers a front-row seat for the firework competition and the celebrations on Midsummer's Night, the *revetlla de Sant Joan*. It is 500 metres long and is easily accessible on foot from the side of the Amphitheatre. It is also wheelchair accessible, has a car park, amphibious chairs, showers and toilets. Drinks, ice cream and food are also available.

Arrabassada beach

Stretching for more than half a kilometre, this beach, with its fine sand and crystal-clear waters, is popular with families. Located just 1 kilometre outside the city, you can get there on foot, by bus or car. There is a car park and the beach is wheelchair accessible. Services include amphibious chairs, showers and toilets. Drinks, ice cream and food are available. It is a favourite spot for water sports.

Savinosa beach

This popular beach never gets crowded. It is located 3 kilometres from the city centre and is 350 metres long. Half of the beach is nudist friendly. You can get there by bus or car. Car park, wheelchair accessible, amphibious chairs, showers and toilets. Drinks, ice cream and food are also available.

Capellans beach

This is a tiny cove measuring 60 metres across, which is also known as Cala Romana, named after the neighbouring housing development. You can get there on foot from the housing development, by bus or car. A little road leads to the beach where you can park and turn round to go back to Tarragona. There are showers and toilets.

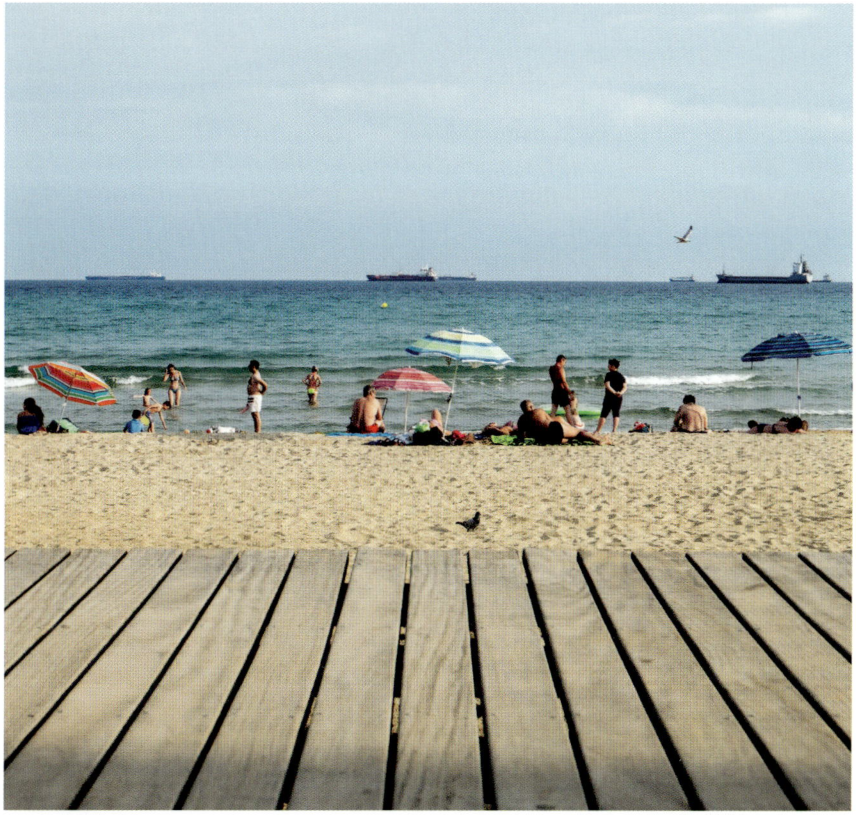

Miracle beach

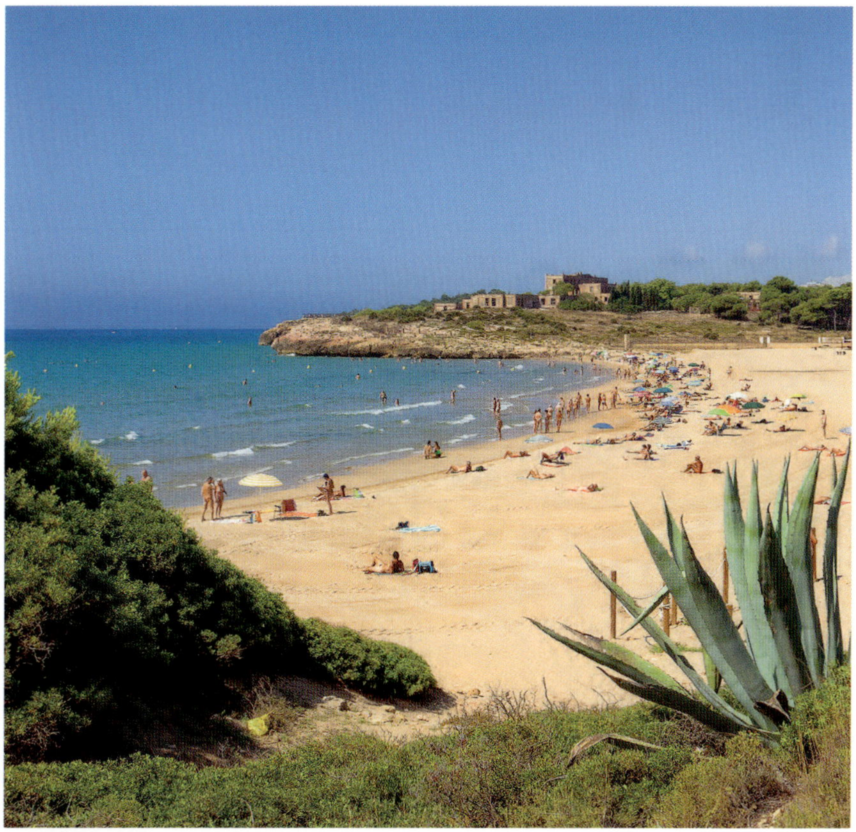

Savinosa beach

Platja Llarga

This beach stretches for 3 kilometres among beautiful scenery. It is wheelchair accessible and has showers and toilets as well as kiosks selling food and drinks. This beach, the ones mentioned above, and La Móra and Tamarit have lifeguards patrolling in summer. The rest of the year, you can contact the lifeguards on the emergency number 112.

Platja de l'Arboçar
(the old Cala Fonda)

This secluded beach is only accessible on foot. To get there you need to go along the paths through the Marquesa woods, among the pines, and down a steep slope. Locals refer to Cala Fonda by the Hawaiian name Waikiki and it is popular with nudists. The beach is only 200 metres long and is protected by yellow limestone cliffs. The limestone is said to have natural properties.

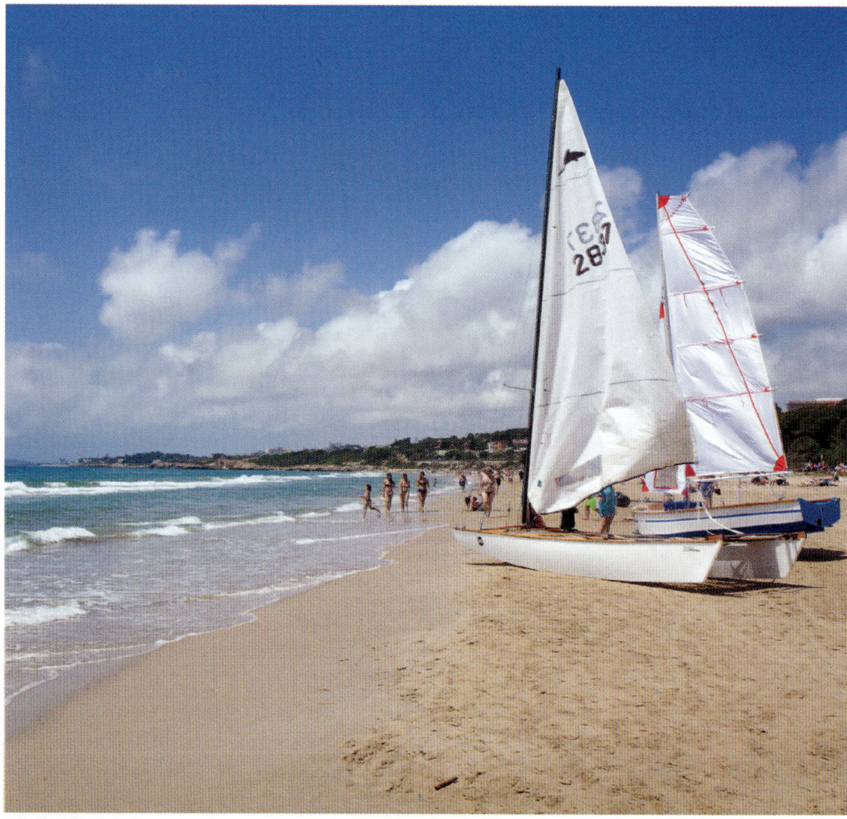

Platja Llarga

Cala dels Becs

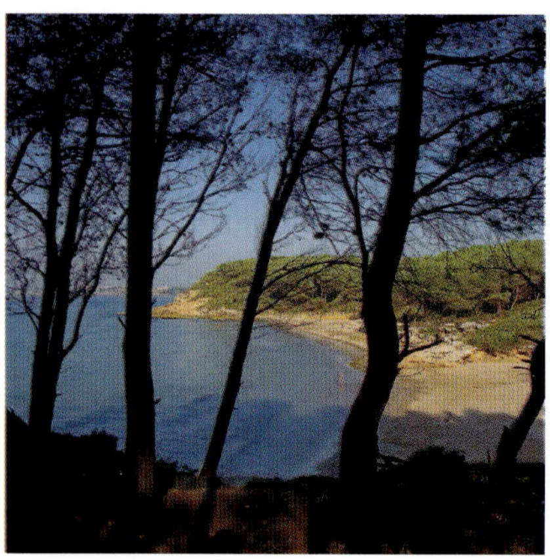

Cala dels Becs
(the old Cala de la Roca Plana)

Stretching for 200 metres, this beach goes by several names — Roca Plana, Calabecs or Cala dels Becs, or L'Arboçar — and is only accessible on foot through the Marquesa woods, from Platja Llarga or La Móra, along signposted paths. It is a nudist beach.

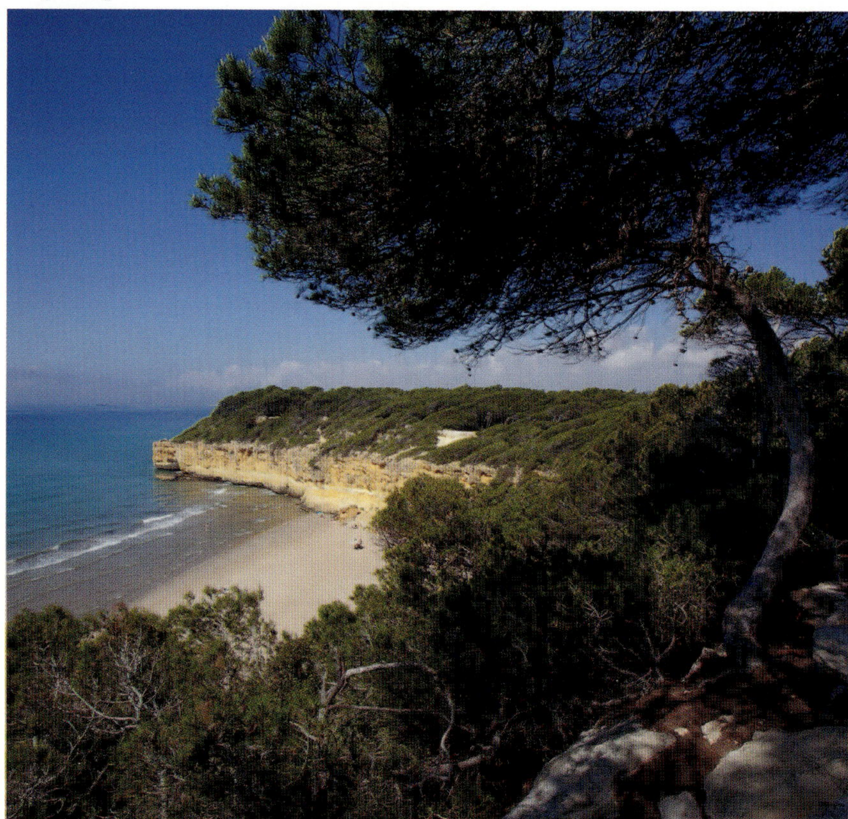

Platja de l'Arboçar

La Móra beach

Between the Punta de la Móra and Tamarit, set among beautiful scenery, this beach is popular with families. It is half a kilometre long and easy to reach. It is wheelchair accessible and has a car park. Services include amphibian seats, showers, toilets and kiosks selling drinks, ice creams and food. A popular spot for water sports.

Cala Jovera

This beach, with its small island, is located below the walled medieval village of Tamarit. It is 90 metres long and you can get near to the beach by bus or car and walk the rest of the way. You can also get there from the Tamarit and La Móra beaches. Nearby, are the remains of houses from the medieval village of Tamarit.

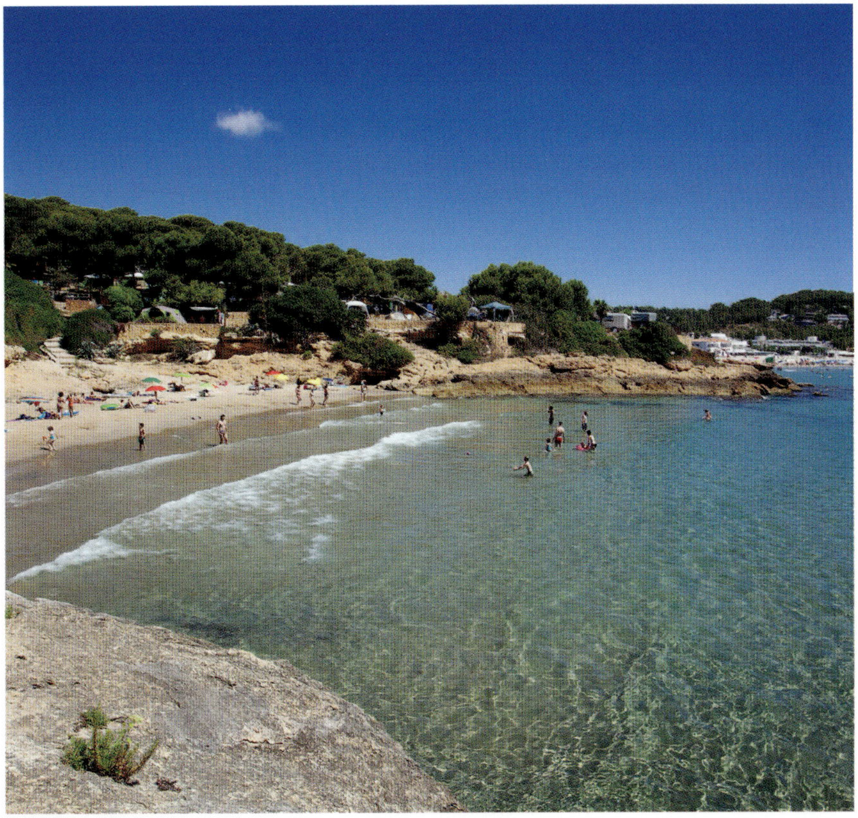

La Móra beach

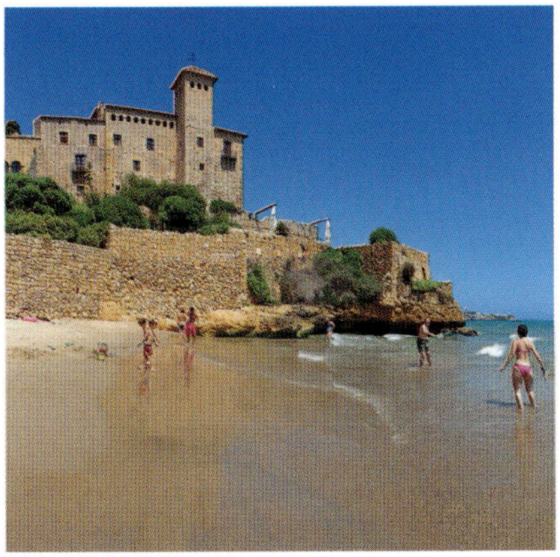

Cala Jovera

Tamarit beach

Tamarit is the continuation of Altafulla beach and includes the natural area at the mouth of the river Gaià. You can get there easily by bus, car or on foot from Tamarit and Altafulla. It is also wheelchair accessible. Services include bike hire and boat trips. It is a popular place for water sports.

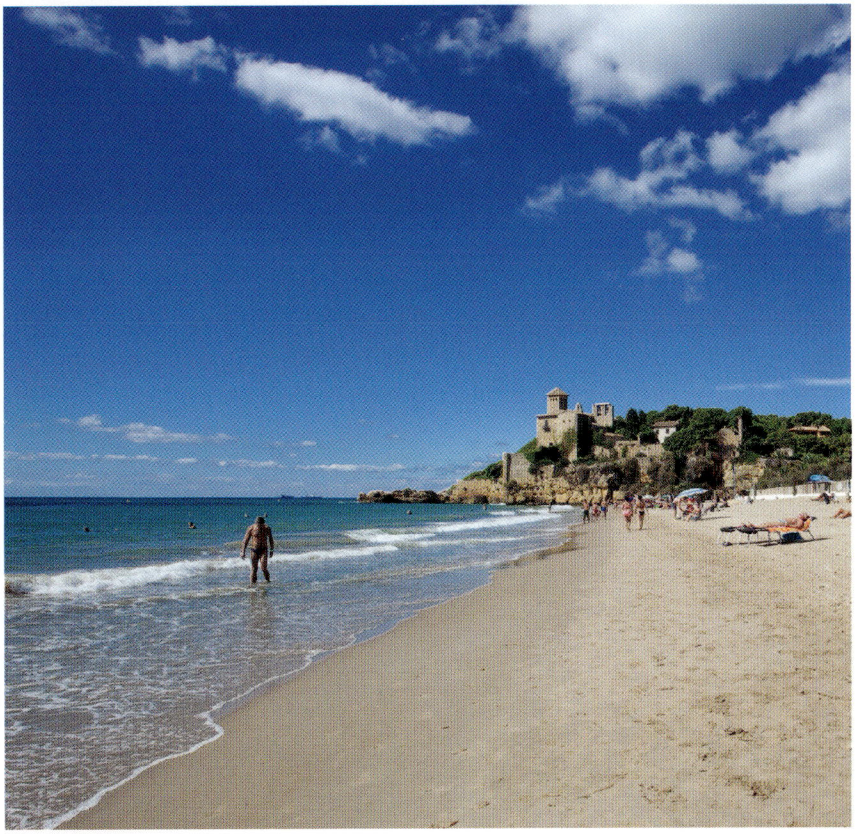

Tamarit beach

The Anella Verda

Natural areas and the footpath network

Natural scenery forms a ring — "anella" in Catalan — around the city. Just a short distance from the centre you'll find areas of vegetation of high ecological value, such as the Marquesa woods and the mouth of the river Gaià, on the eastern side. The name Anella Verda refers to land that can't be built on, and covers almost half — 44% — of the municipal area. It isn't a vast public park, but a grouping of plots of woodland and farmland, most of it privately owned, which is criss-crossed by a network of public footpaths.

More than 75 kilometres of signposted paths, some of them Roman in origin, connect the city centre with the countryside and coast among breathtaking landscapes. The network has been designed for walking, running, cycling and doing exercise, while enjoying the wonderful scenery and landmarks that encircle the city: woodland, farmhouses, drystone walls... Many locals are unaware that they exist.

In the words of the Tarragona-born geographer and photographer Rafael López-Monné, the creation of the Anella Verda, a number of years ago, "represented the first serious attempt at a political debate about the land around the city, its values, functions and future". A new network of footpaths crossing the county of the Tarragonès — which Tarragona is the capital of — was added in 2016 to the 100 kilometres or more of signposted paths that form the city network. This means that the Camp de Tarragona region now has its own extensive footpath network.

These footpaths are home to a number of World Heritage Sites, including the Pont del Diable, the Torre dels Escipions and the Mèdol quarry, as well as others that are Roman in origin and less well known, such as the Punta de la Creueta quarry and the fascinating Llorito caves. There are also farmhouses that were fortified in the Middle Ages and later in the 16th and 17th centuries, to prevent robberies and pirate attacks. Farmhouses like Mas de Sorder, which is a superb example of *modernista*-style architecture with its splendid mosaic dome, and the Mas dels Arcs. In addition to the agricultural drystone heritage — huts and walls — the network of paths brings us closer to protected natural areas, such as the mouth of the river Gaià, which has been designated a Special Protection Area, where you can see species of local fauna, like the Spanish pond turtle. Or the Marquesa woods where the species *Juniperum lyciae* — which is unique to Catalonia — has been reintroduced. And others including the Parc Ecohistòric del Pont del Diable, with its native Mediterranean plant species.

A number of green areas in the guise of city parks can be found in the different neighbourhoods of the city. They include the Parc de les Granotes, next to the Amphitheatre, the Parc de Bonavista, Parc del Camí de la Coma, Parc del Camp de Mart, Parc la Col·lectiva, Parc Saavedra, Parc de Sant Antoni, Parc de Sant Pere i Sant Pau, Parc Rodríguez de la Fuente, and an unusual one: Europe's largest vertical garden attached to the Espai Tabacalera building.

The Anella Verda circuit

→ Appendix p. 7

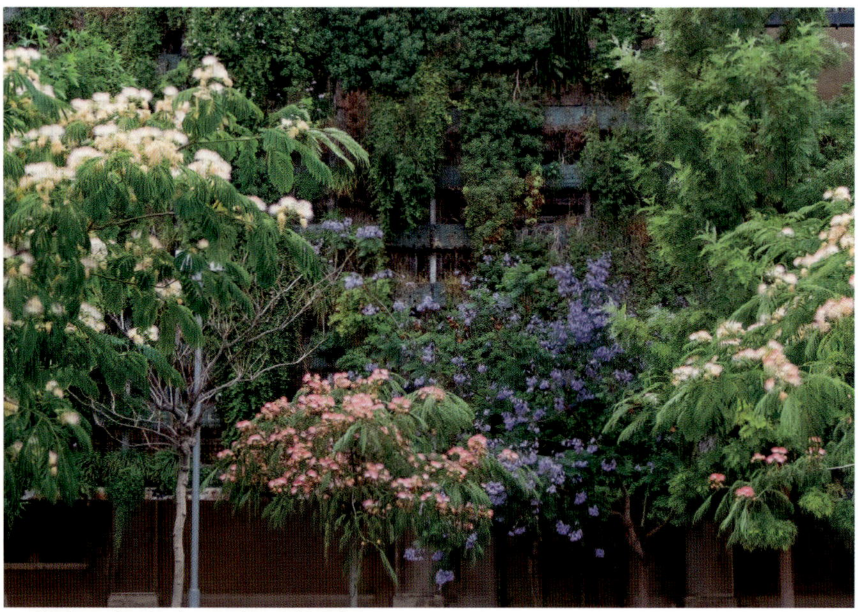

Vertical garden in the Antiga Tabacalera

The Camí de la Costa, coastal path →

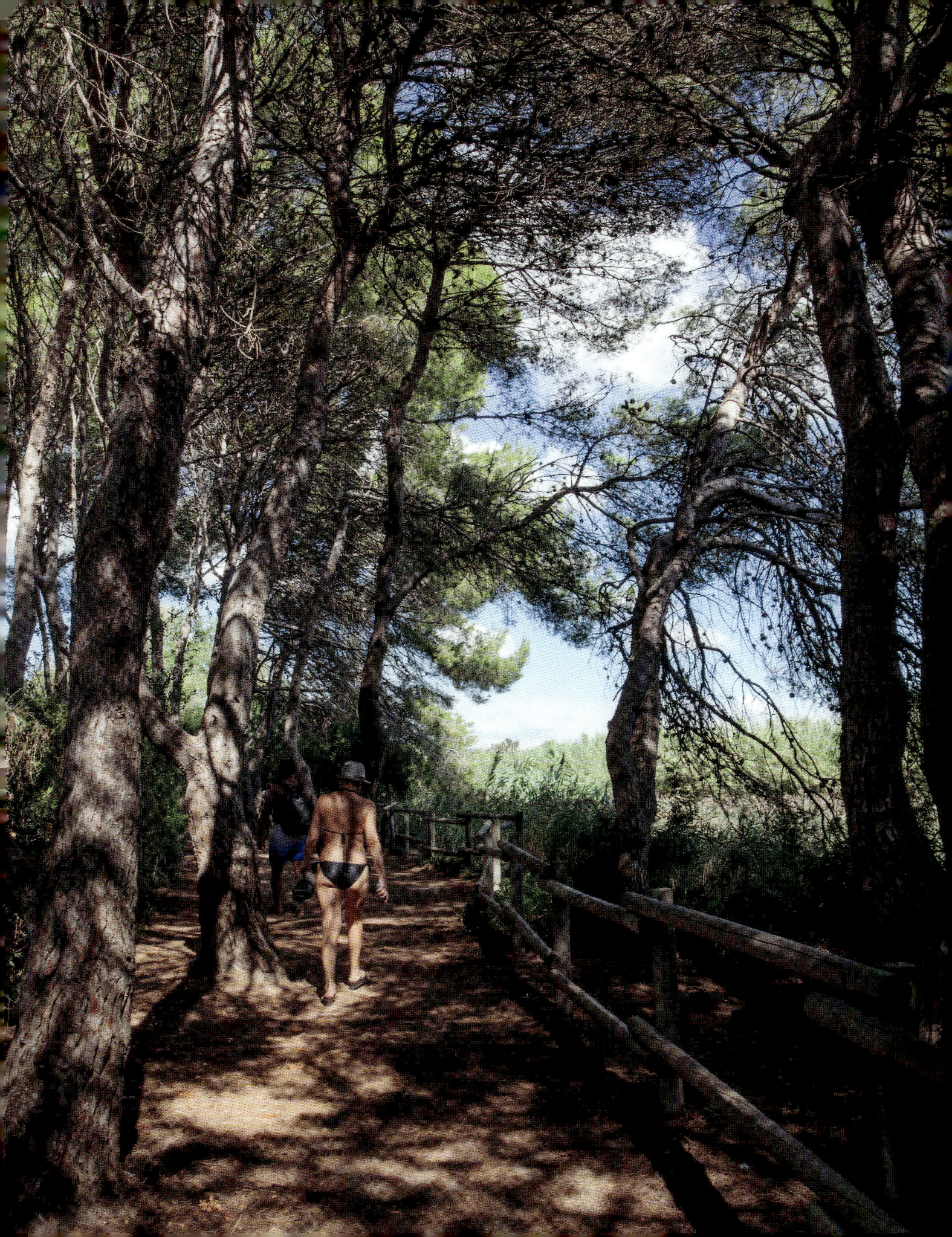

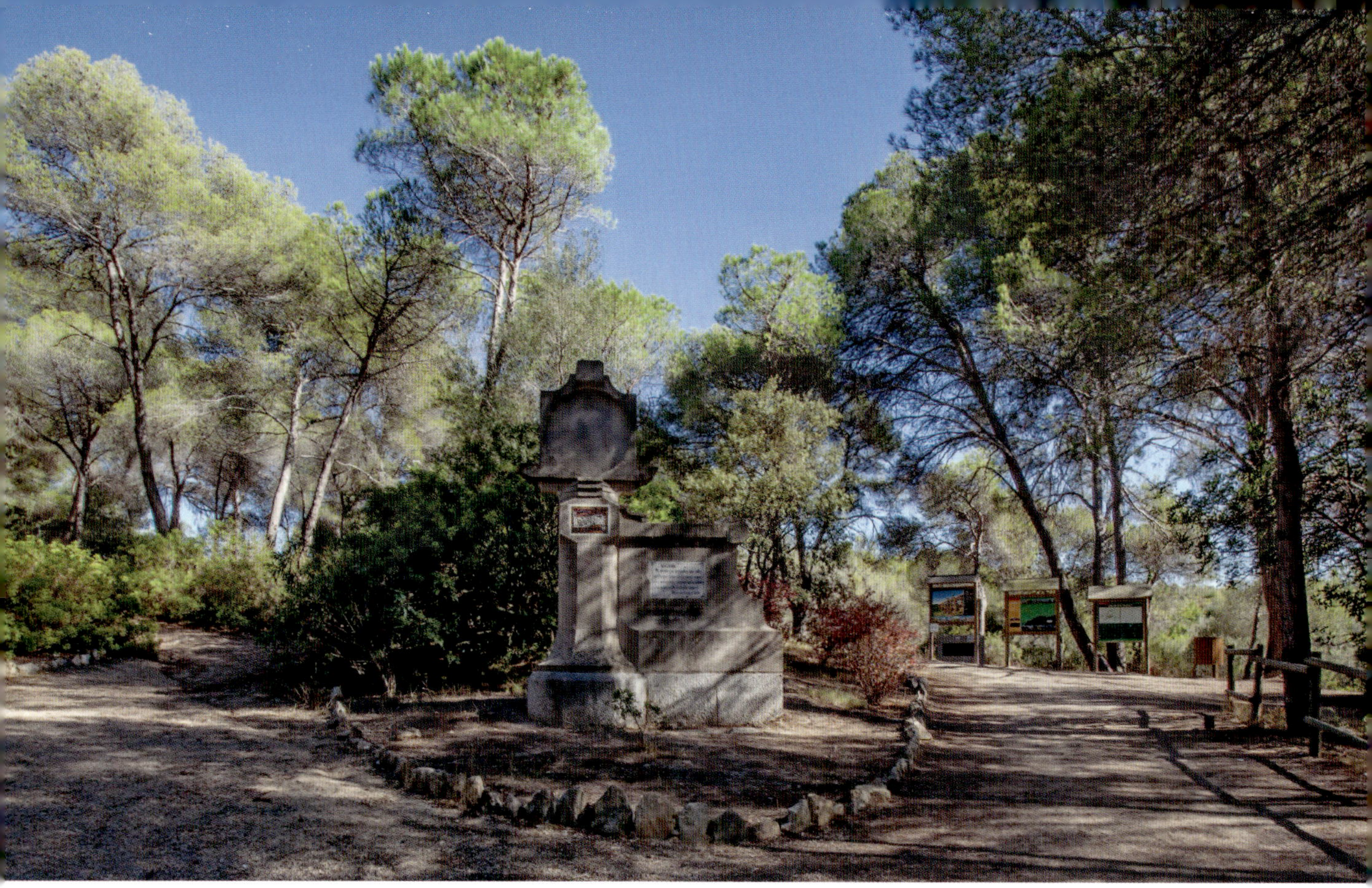

↑ Parc Ecohistòric del Pont del Diable ↓ Ferran Castle

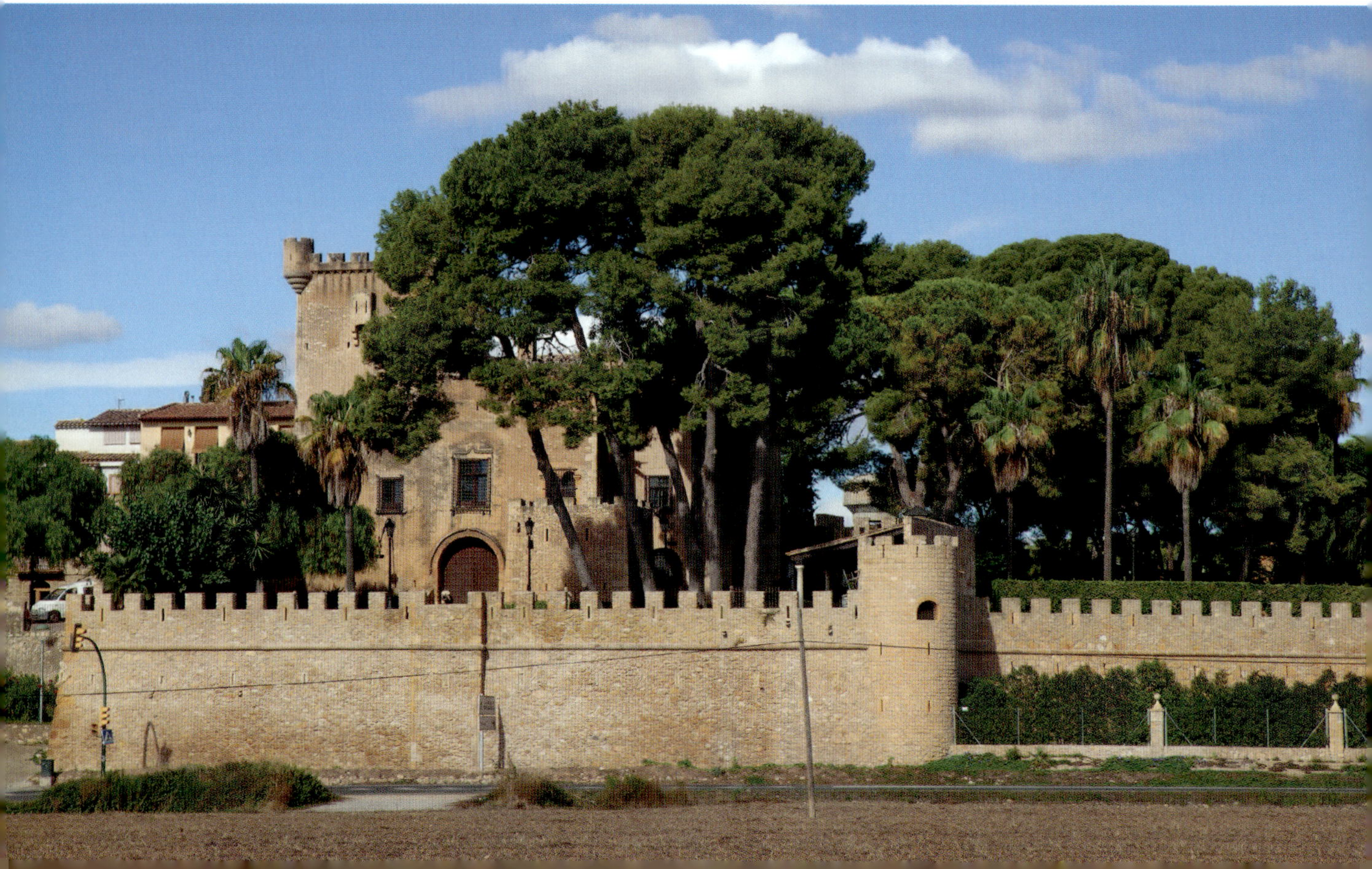

The inland path

The paths on the Tarragona Footpath Network are signposted in yellow. The Anella Verda is part of the network and consists of two sections, the inland path, which you can explore on foot or by bike, and a coastal path for walkers. The entire route covers a distance of 34 kilometres and is featured on a map at the end of the book. The inland path begins in the Parc del Francolí, continues through the Parc del Pont del Diable and ends in Ferran and the mouth of the river Gaià.

Parc del Francolí

Standing on the banks of the river Francolí, this is the city's biggest park, covering almost 13 hectares and more than 16,000 square metres of grass, 2 kilometres of tarmacked paths and 3 kilometres of dirt paths. It is popular with walkers and keep-fit enthusiasts. As you follow the river, you come to the Parc del Pont del Diable.

Parc Ecohistòric del Pont del Diable

This park opened in 2005 and houses the remains of a garden designed in the early 20th century by the Puig i Valls brothers — a poet and a forest engineer — to make people more environmentally aware. Today it is a hive of activity and a wonderful example of Mediterranean biodiversity with scrubland, pine glades and evergreen oaks.

Ferran Castle

The origins of the castle date back to the 11th century when a watchtower stood on the site. It was located in the small village of Ferran, which was part of the ancient municipality of Tamarit. From the 17th century onwards it became a residential palace that underwent many alterations in the romantic and historicist style.

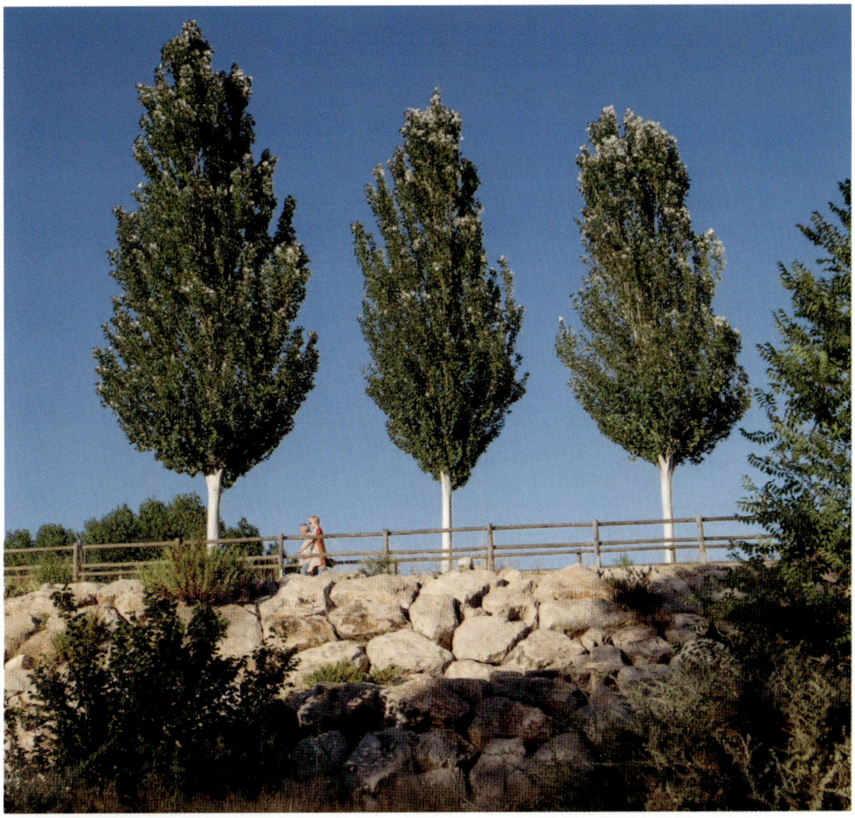

Parc del Francolí

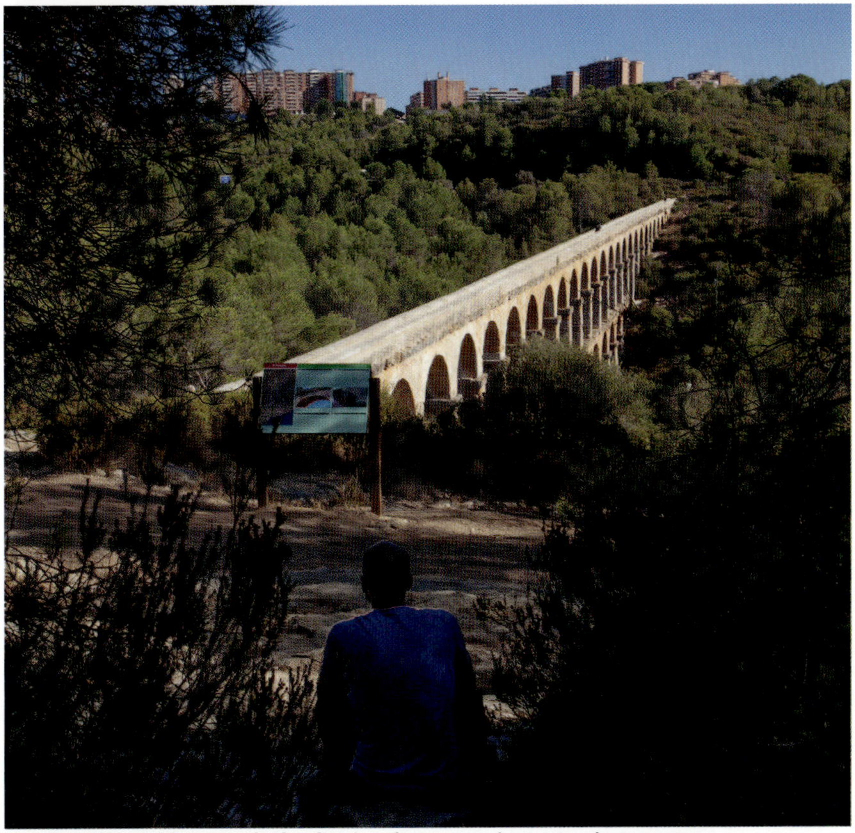

The Pont del Diable towards the district of Sant Pere i Sant Pau in Tarragona

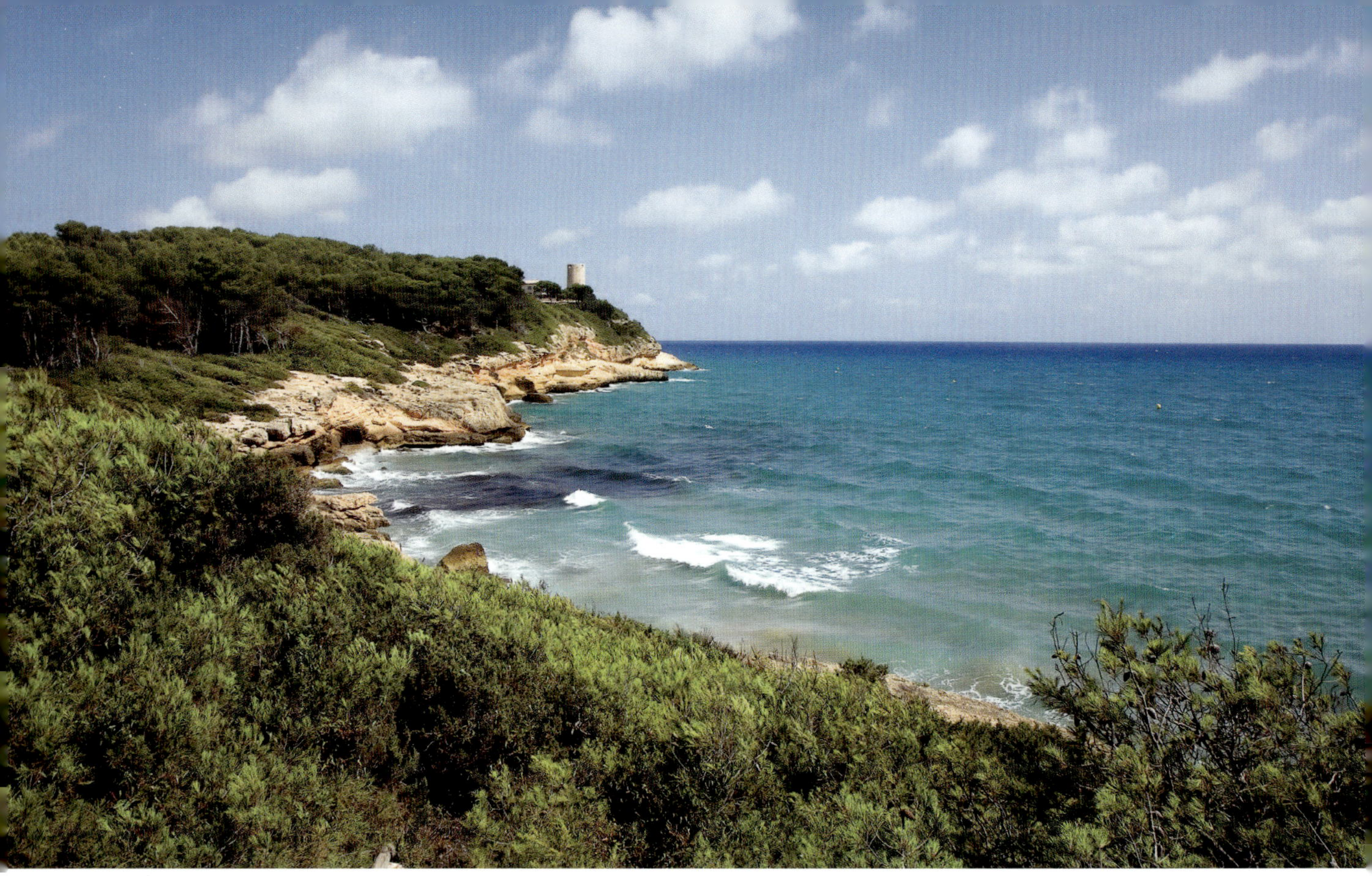

↑ Punta de la Móra ↓ Walled village of Tamarit

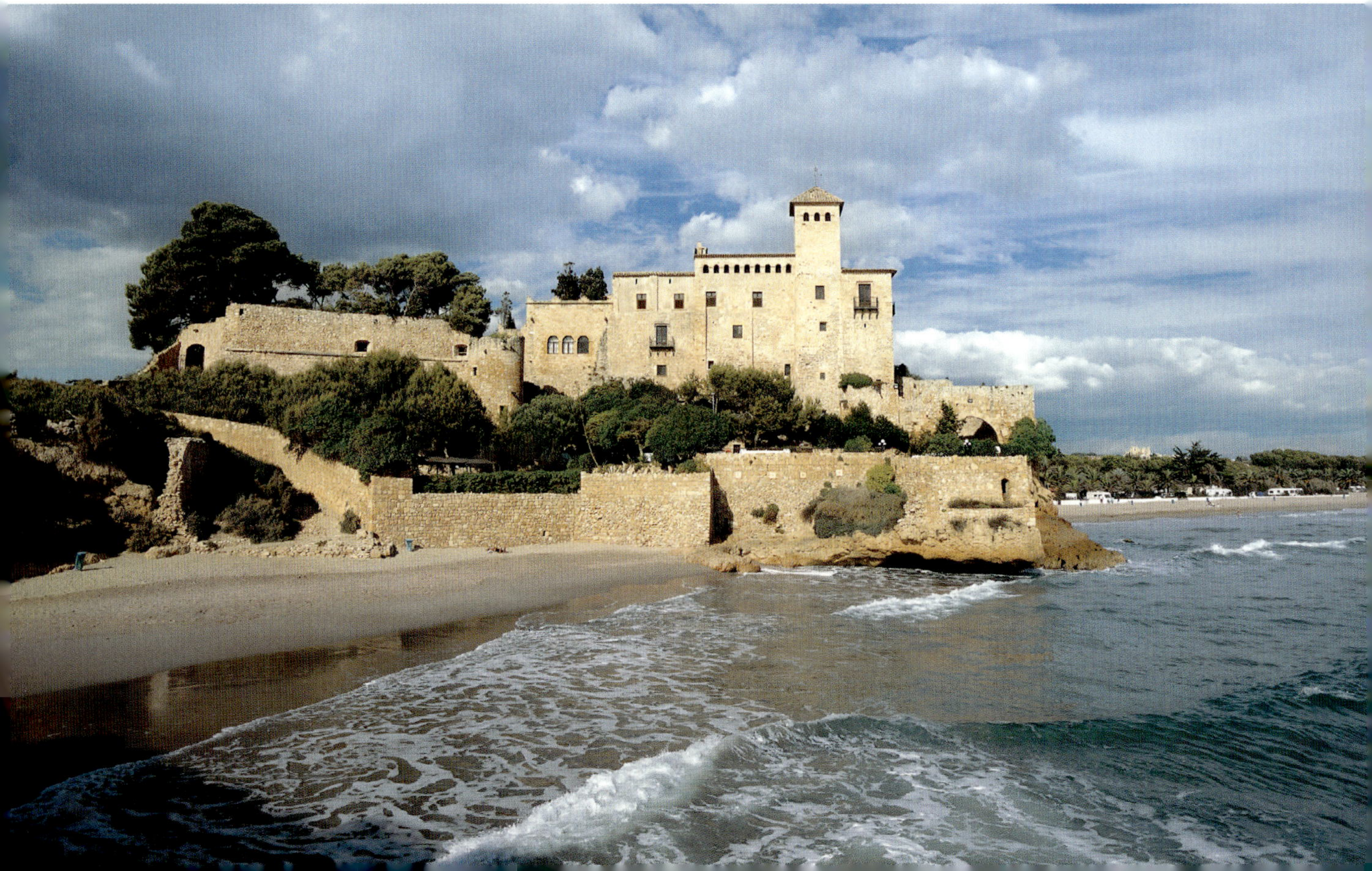

The coastal path

As you leave the city, continue along the Punta del Miracle, the Arrabassada, Savinosa and Capellans beaches, the Els Morrots rocks and Platja Llarga, through the Marquesa woods, past the Punta de la Móra and Tamarit to the river Gaià. You can go back round the other way to complete the Anella Verda circuit.

Els Morrots

Despite human pressure, the natural area of Els Morrots, between the headland of the same name and Savinosa beach, is home to some of the most diverse and best-preserved plant communities found among the rock formations along the Tarragona coast. It has been protected as a result of an escrow agreement with an environmental association.

Punta de la Móra

This promontory has a tower built in 1562 to protect it from pirate attacks. It is part of the Espai Natural Protegit Tamarit-Punta de la Móra, which protects and preserves coastal species that have almost vanished. Across the road you can climb Sant Simplici hill which boasts some of the finest views in the area.

Walled village of Tamarit

Tamarit isn't a castle: its walls enclosed an 11th-century fortified village that marked the southern boundary of the county of Barcelona. It is the centre of the municipality of Tamarit de Mar, which covers an area of more than 1,800 hectares. It became part of Tarragona in 1950 and included the villages of Monnars and Ferran.

Mouth of the river Gaià

It forms a small lagoon separated from the sea by a spit of sand. It is a designated wild fauna natural reserve and is one of the few coastal wetland areas in Catalonia. You can reach it from a well-signposted path. The environmental association that takes care of the site also runs an education and information centre close by.

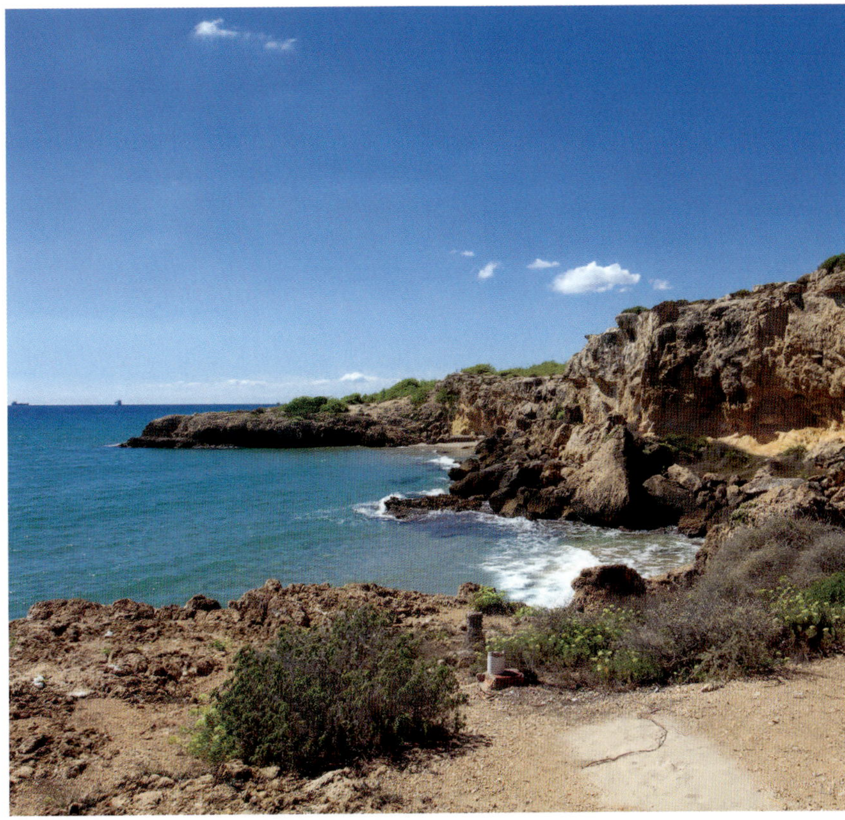

Els Morrots

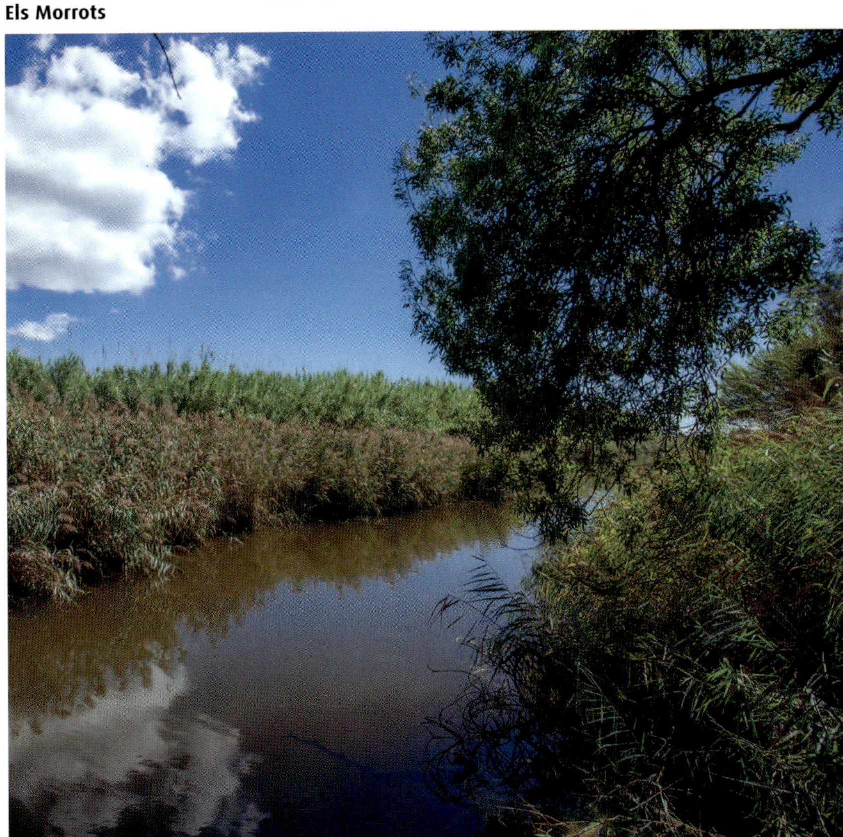

The river Gaià close to its estuary

Festivals and traditions

Tarragona, all year round

The city's calendar of festivals features all kinds of events, from the most entertaining to the most solemn, and includes music and film as well as historic recreations.

The year's festival calendar begins on the eve of 5th January with the arrival of the Three Kings, and on 6th January, Epiphany; it continues with *Carnaval*, in February or March, and the Tres Tombs procession with the blessing of the animals. The International Dixieland Festival is held the week before Easter, which falls in March or April and is one of the milestone events of the year. In April, books and roses take centre stage for the Feast of Sant Jordi, the patron saint of Catalonia, a day when locals congregate on the Rambla Nova.

In May it's time for Tàrraco Viva, el Festival roman de Tarragona and Tàrraco a Taula and the same month, or in June, it's Corpus Christi, with the traditional cherry brioches, *coques amb cireres*, and the tradition of the *Ou com balla*, or "dancing egg". In May or June the city also hosts the wine festival dedicated to local Designation of Origin wines, the Fira del vi de la Denominació d'Orígen Tarragona, on the Rambla Nova. June ushers in 30 days packed with musical and cultural events for all the family, including the Festival Minipop, Midsummer's Eve — the *Nit de Sant Joan* — on 23rd June, with its bonfires and street parties, and Sant Pere, the main festival in El Serrallo and another neighbourhood, Sant Pere i Sant Pau. From this month until September (October in even-numbered years), Tarragona becomes a 'City of Human Towers'. The International Fireworks competition takes place from the end of June until the beginning of July, and in summer it's time for the Festival Internacional de Teatre, Tarragona Història Viva, of the Bouquet Festival, a combination of historic heritage, music and vermouth, and the entertainments in the Tàrraco Arena Plaça (TAP). In July, El Serrallo hosts the procession of the Mare de Déu del Carme, or Our Lady of Mount Carmel.

On 16th and 19th August it's time for the festivals of Sant Roc and Sant Magí, which take place on 19th. The National Day of Catalonia, the Diada Nacional de Catalunya, falls on 11th September and a few days before 23rd September, the city erupts into one giant celebration, the Feast of Santa Tecla. Every other year, on the first weekend in October, it's time for the human-tower competition, the Concurs Biennal de Castells. Autumn is time for the historical and cultural event, Tarragona 1800, the medieval market, the Mercat Medieval, the SCAN (biennial) Photography Festival, the REC Film Festival, and Teatre Màgic festivals; and on the eve of 31st October and 1st November, All Saints. From November to December the new olive oil is presented. And, in December, it's Christmas time again with its traditional markets and craft fairs, and the character known as the *Home dels Nassos*, or Man with the Noses, who makes an appearance on the last day of the year.

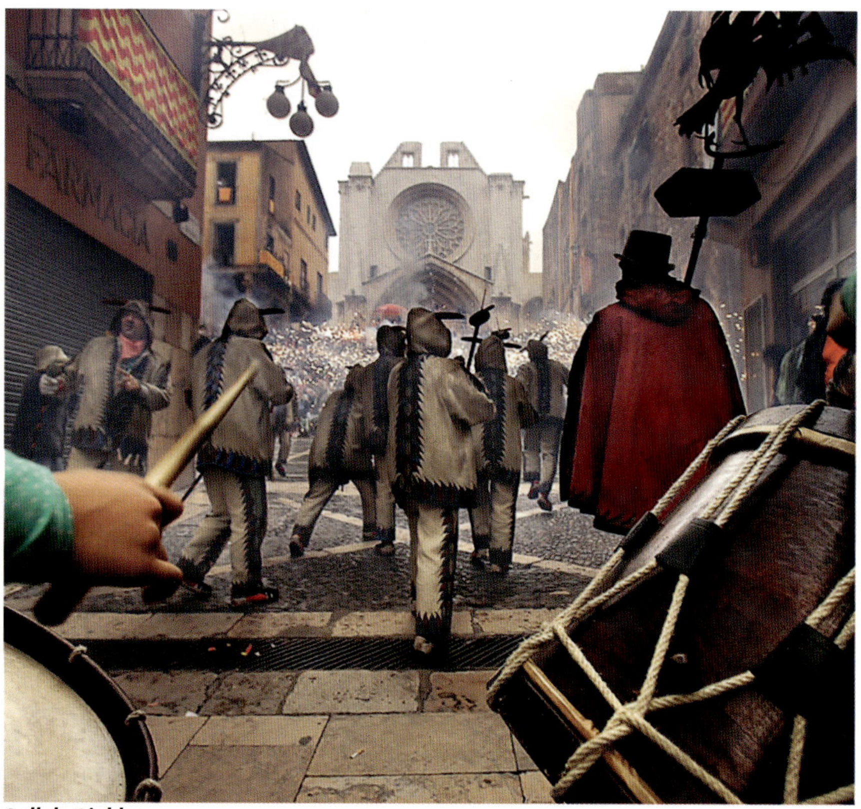

Ball de Diables

Colla Jove Xiquets de Tarragona →

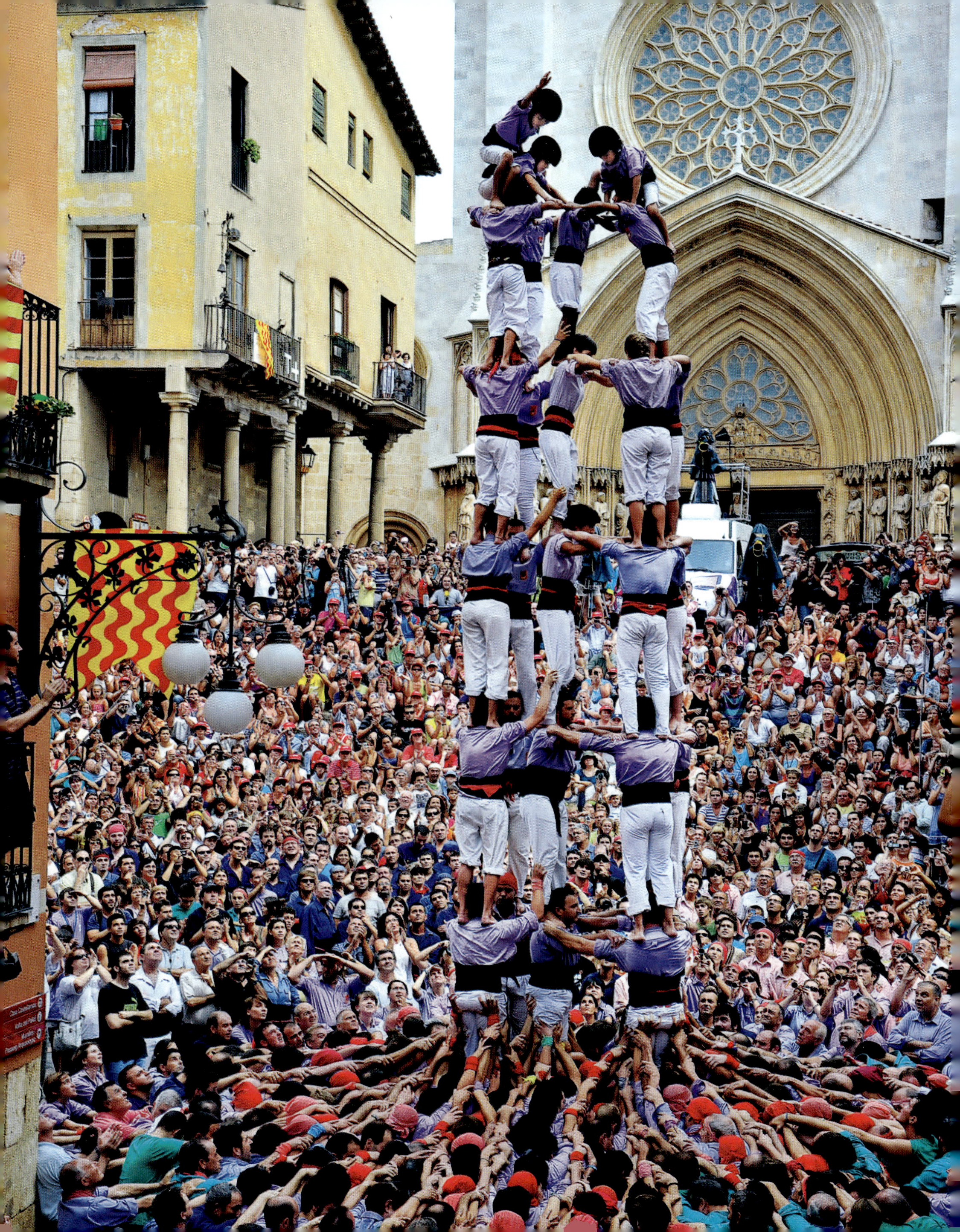

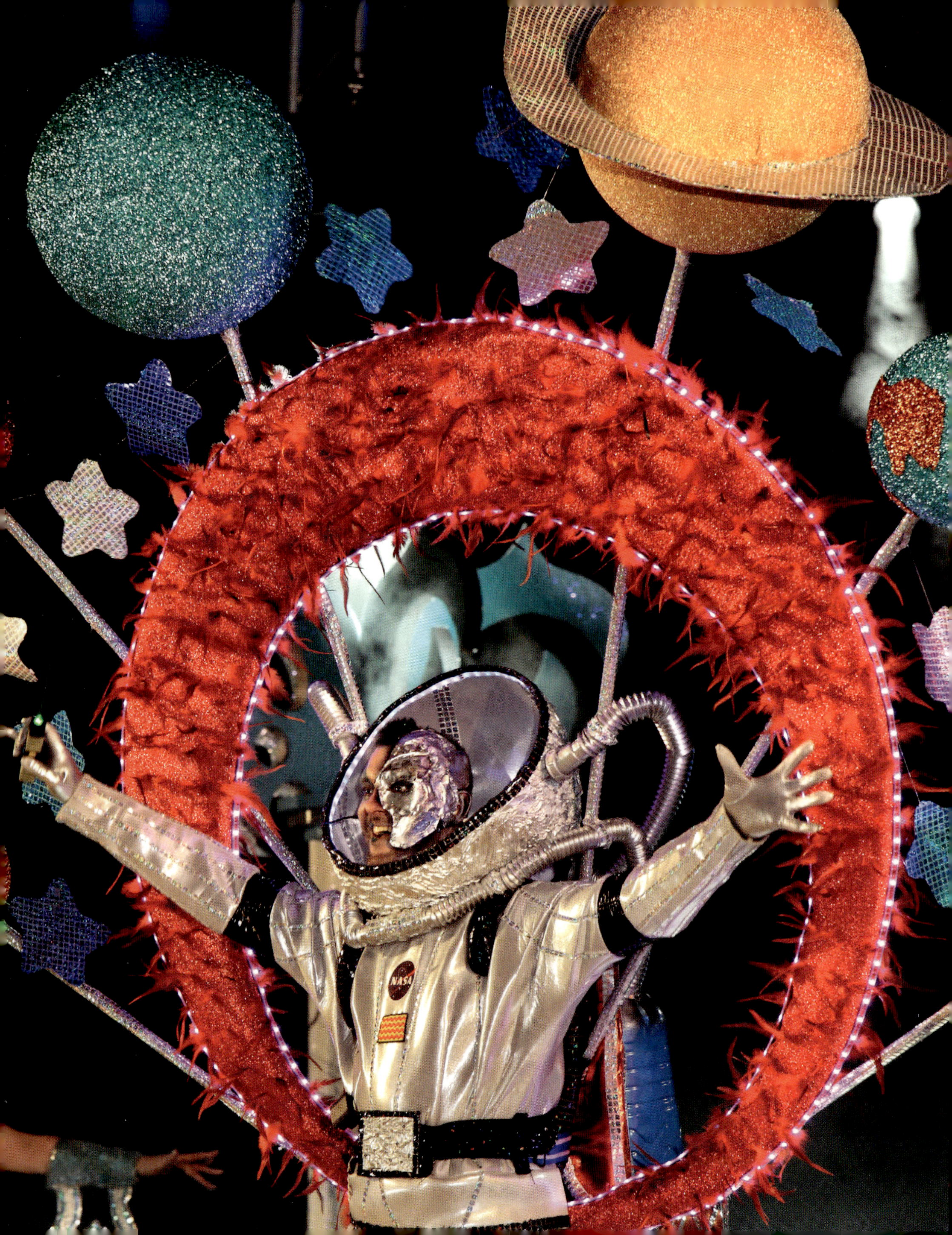
NASA

A year of celebrations

Tarragona's mild climate means that most of the festivals held throughout the year are in the open air. Life al fresco, food and traditions embody the very essence of the Mediterranean. The wide range of events fill streets and squares with people, music, light and colour.

Carnaval

Tarragona's carnival celebrations attract huge crowds who dress up in homemade fancy-dress costumes. It has established itself as one of the biggest carnivals in the country, attracting thousands of people from every neighbourhood. The celebrations reach their climax with two parades, the Rua de l'Artesania, held on Saturday evening, and the Rua de Lluïment, on Sunday. The carnival maintains its own unique sequence of secular rituals, beginning with the placing of a giant barrel, or *bòta*, in Plaça de la Font, which marks the beginning of the celebrations, and its end, on Dimarts de Dol, or Tuesday of Sorrows, when it is set alight and burnt, along with the effigies of the Carnival King, Rei Carnestoltes, and his concubine.

Diables

You'll see these figures in devil's costumes taking part in the carnival celebrations and at other times of the year, particularly during the Feast of Santa Tecla when they are an integral part of the *Seguici Popular*, a procession of mythical beasts and allegorical figures. During the *Seguici Popular* the devils take part in a dance, the *Ball de Diables*, which has its roots in medieval street entertainment. In Tarragona, the dance was first documented in 1426 but by the late 19th century it had largely died out. The dance was revived in the 1920s as part of the festival of the chapel of La Salut. On the eve of the Feast of Santa Tecla, the *diables* take part in the *Ball de Sant Miquel i Diables,* when they recite satirical verses, known as *Versots*. They are one of the main attractions of the Feast of La Mercè, when they take part in the *correfoc*, a fast-moving procession of fire, flames and sparks.

← *Carnaval*

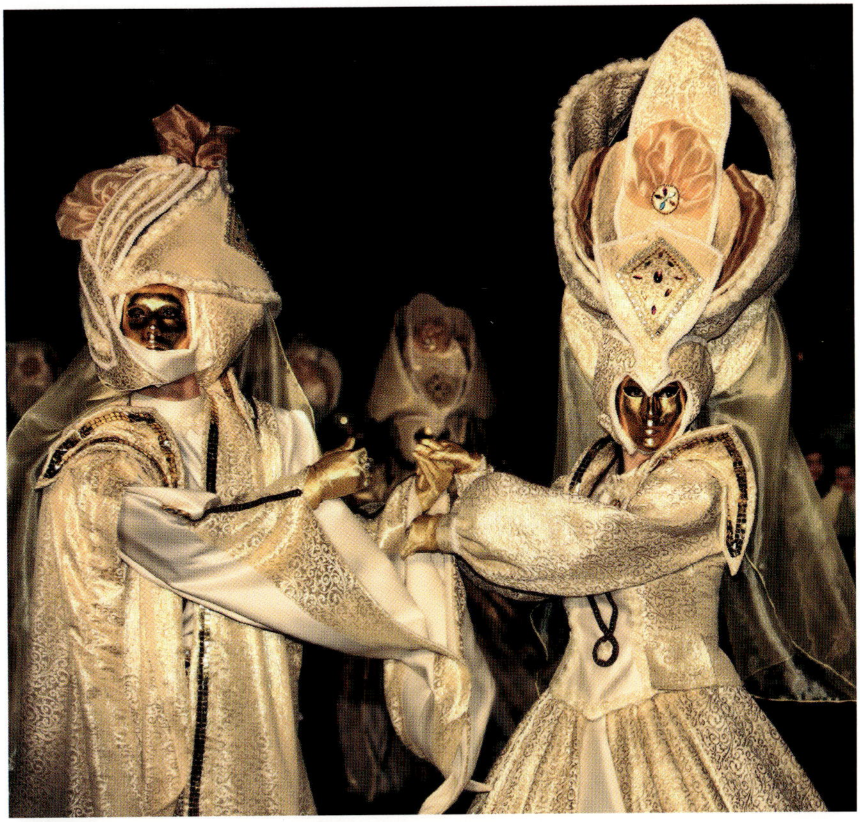

Carnaval

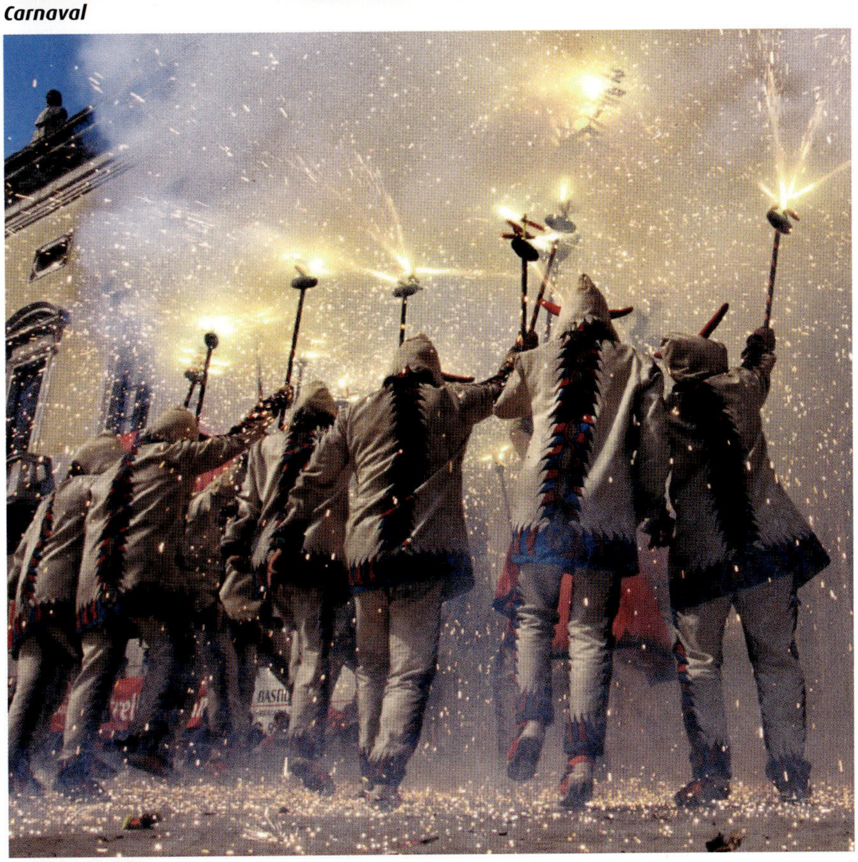

Ball de Diables

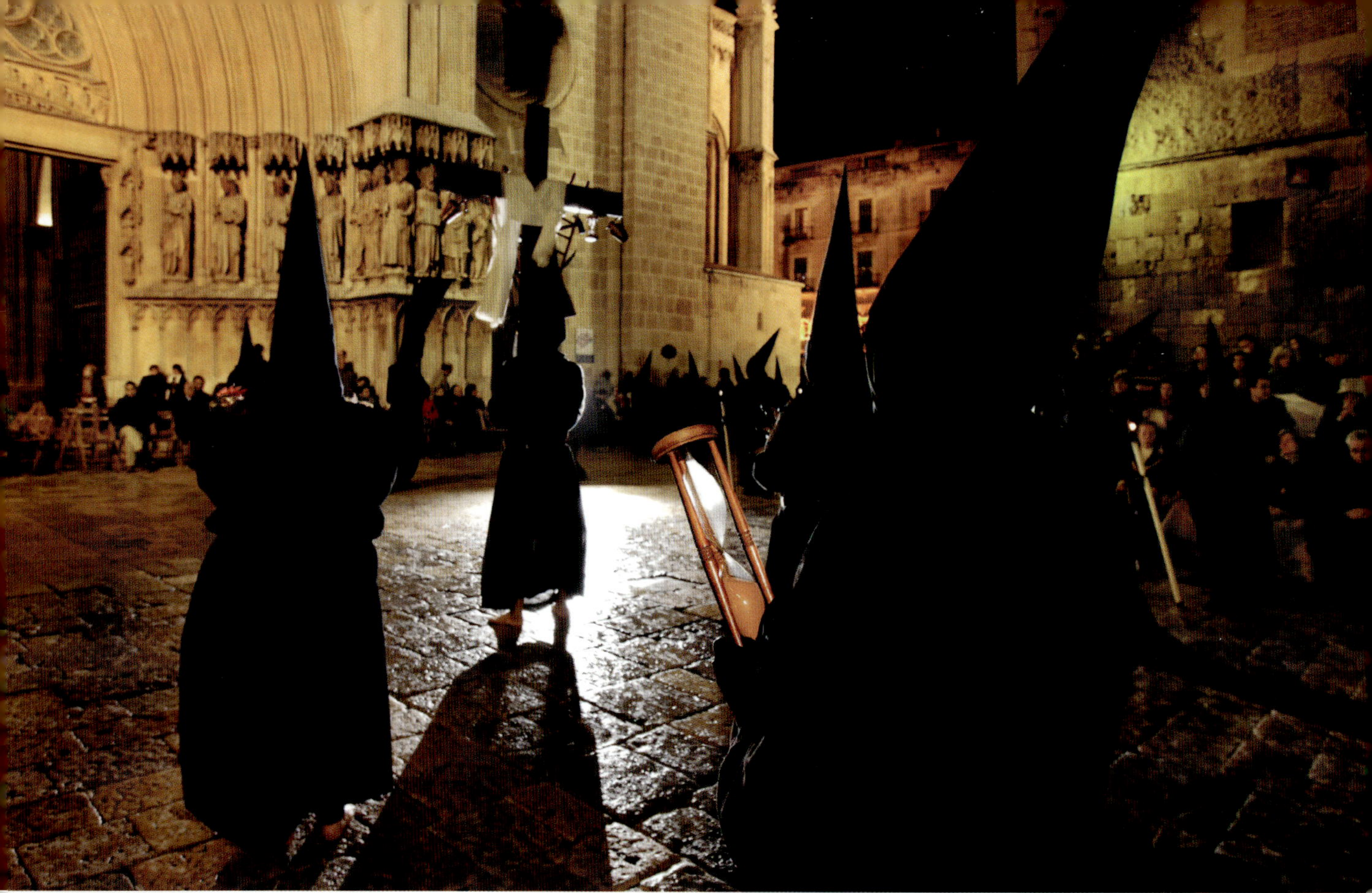

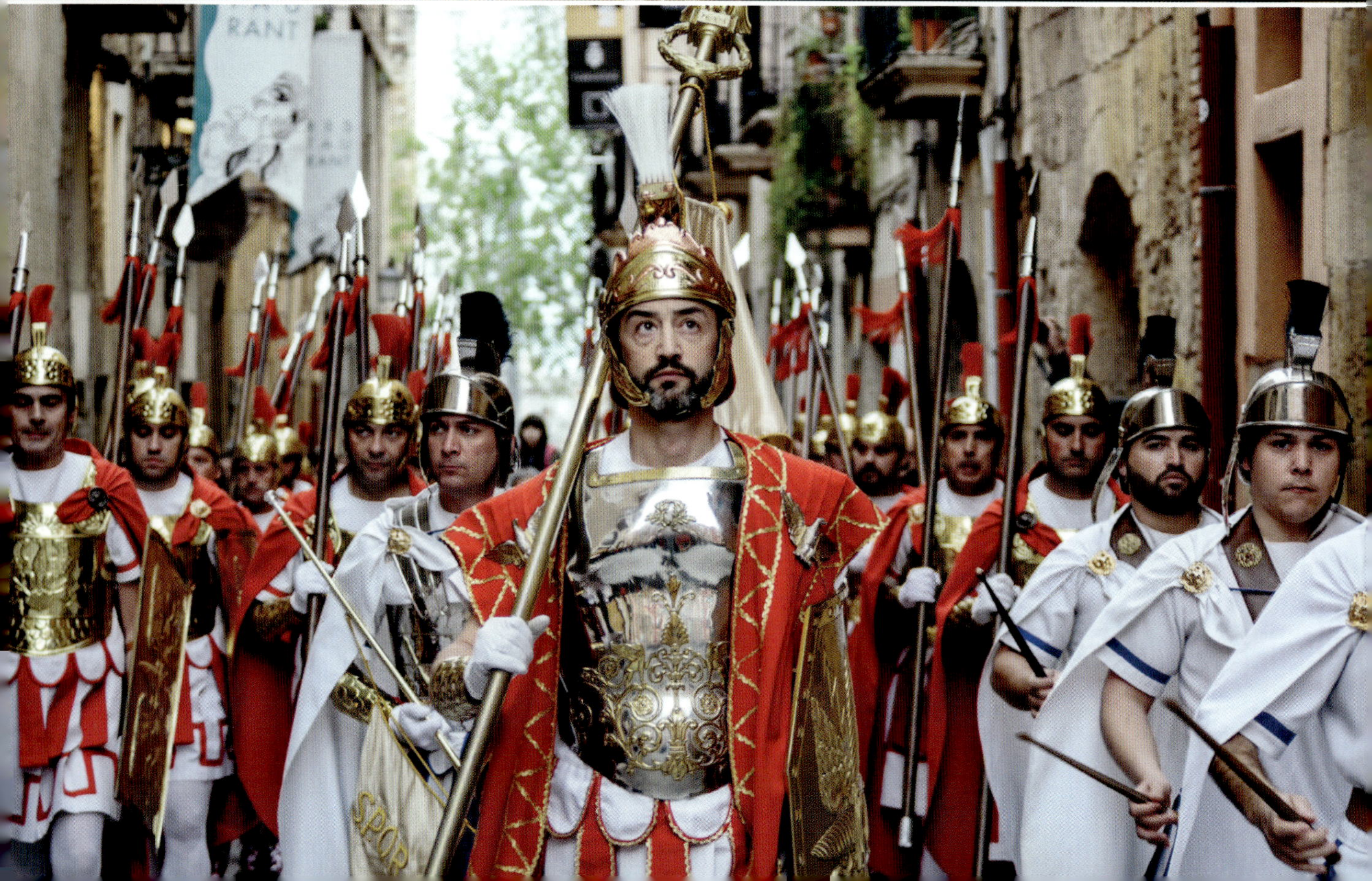

RANT

Holy Week

On Good Friday, huge crowds throng the narrow streets of the Part Alta to witness the solemn procession of the Holy Burial, the climax of Tarragona's Easter celebrations. This is one of the most impressive processions in the Mediterranean and has been declared a Heritage Festival of National Interest by the Catalan Government. The procession has taken place almost every year since 1550. Initially, it took place on Maundy Thursday but it has been held on Good Friday since 1859. Some 5,000 people are currently members of the 12 associations, brotherhoods, congregations, brotherhoods and guilds from the Holy Week association, the Agrupació d'Associacions de la Setmana Santa, who carry the 20 mysteries in the procession. The Roman soldiers, or armed guards, lead the procession.

In 2009, the Catalan Government declared Tarragona's Holy Week celebrations a Traditional Festival of National Interest . The procession has been organised since its inception by the Reial i Venerable Congregació de la Puríssima Sang de Nostre Senyor Jesucrist, founded in 1545 by the guilds of espadrille-makers and esparto-weavers. The only mystery to survive intact from before the Spanish Civil War is the effigy of Simon the Cyrenian, *El Cirineu*, dating from 1930, which belongs to the brotherhood, the Reial Germandat de Jesús Natzarè, who also saved a section of the mystery of Jesus the Nazarene, *El Natzarè*, dated 1907. A 17th-century baroque sculpture of Christ in the Holy Sepulchre is the earliest surviving image. The plinth and urn were designed by the architect Josep Maria Jujol.

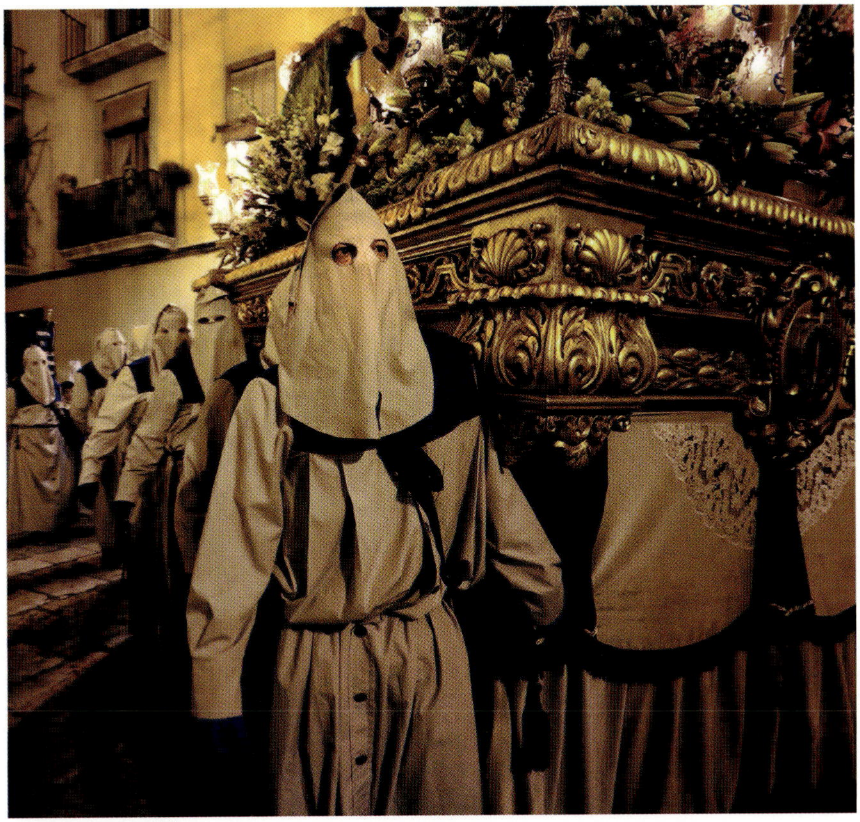

Fishermen's Guild

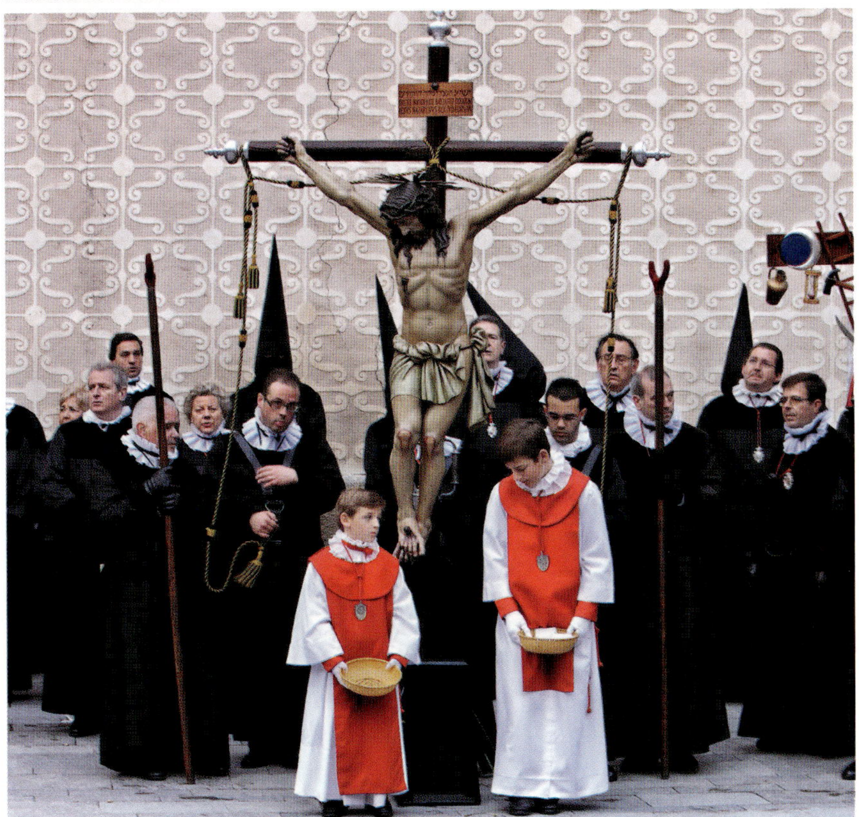

Sant Crist de la Congregació de la Sang

← Armats de la Sang

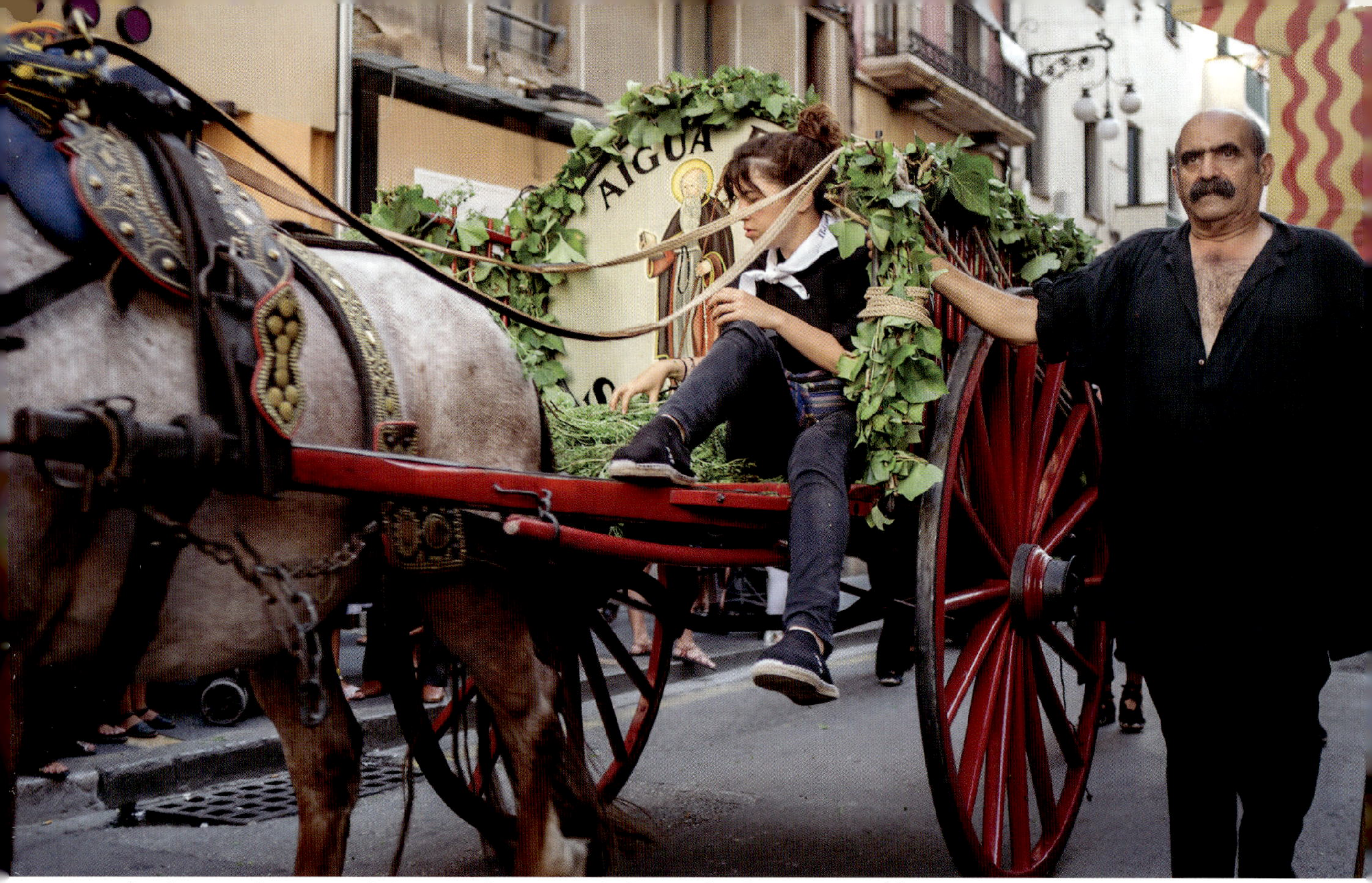

↑ Carrying the water for Sant Magí ↓ Sant Magí, a very convincing angel and two Roman soldiers

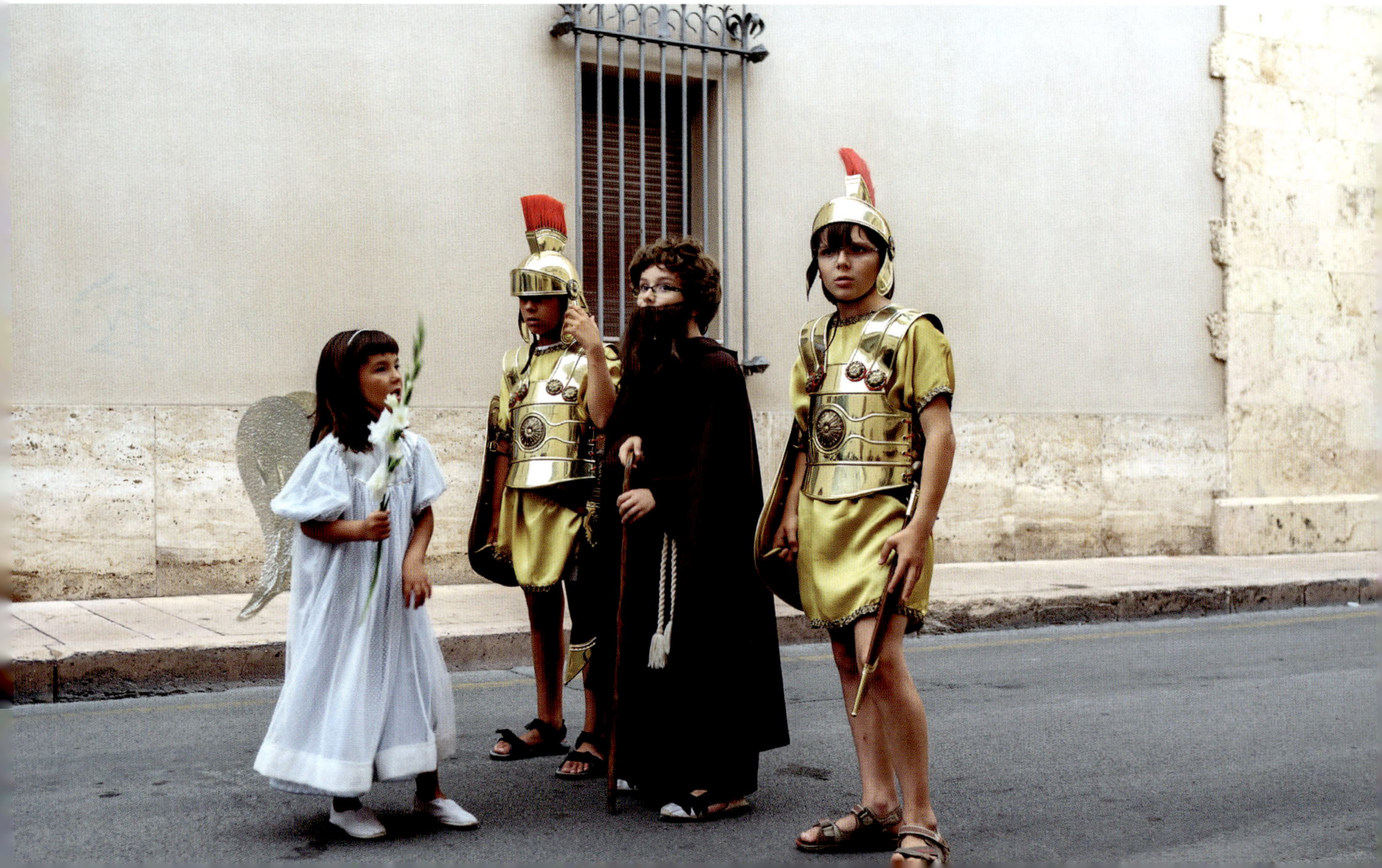

Dixieland and Minipop Festivals

Two different, equally unmissable musical events. The week-long Dixieland Festival transports you to the birthplace of jazz and the style that originated in the city of New Orleans.

In June, the Passeig de les Palmeres is the main venue for Minipop, the pop music festival for all the family.

International Fireworks Competition

This is one of the most important festivals of its kind in the Mediterranean and attracts pyrotechnicians from all over the world. The winner is responsible for staging the firework display on the night of 23rd September, the Feast of Santa Tecla. One of the best ways to enjoy the display is to have dinner on the beach or the Passeig de les Palmeres.

Sant Magí

Water is a central element of the Festivities of Sant Magí, which reaches its climax on 19th August, the anniversary of the death of Emperor Augustus. Figures from the *Seguici Popular* welcome carts laden with barrels of water brought from the shrine of Sant Magí de la Brufaganya to be blessed.

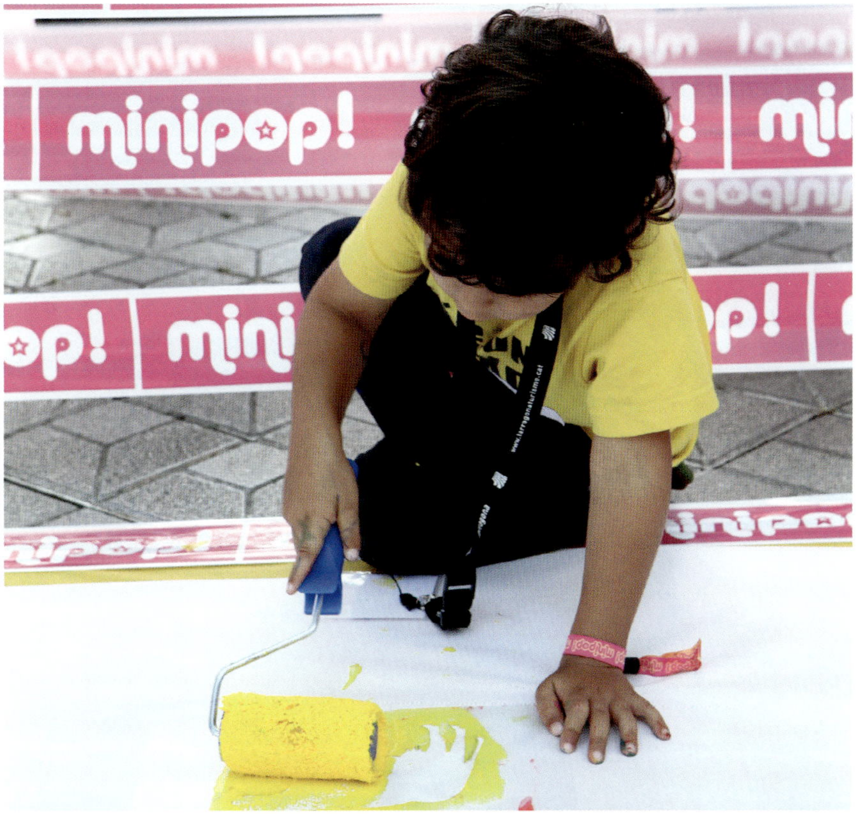

Minipop Festival

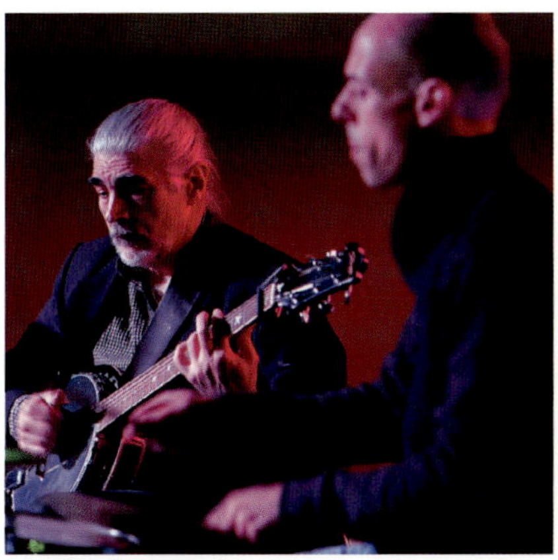

Dixieland Festival

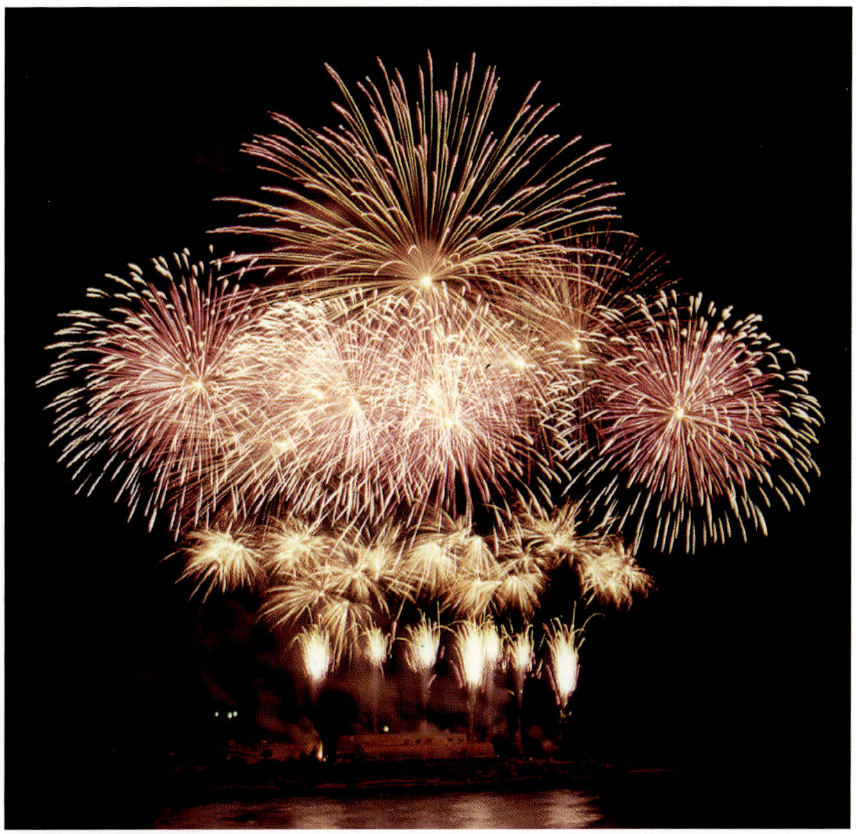

Spectacular fireworks

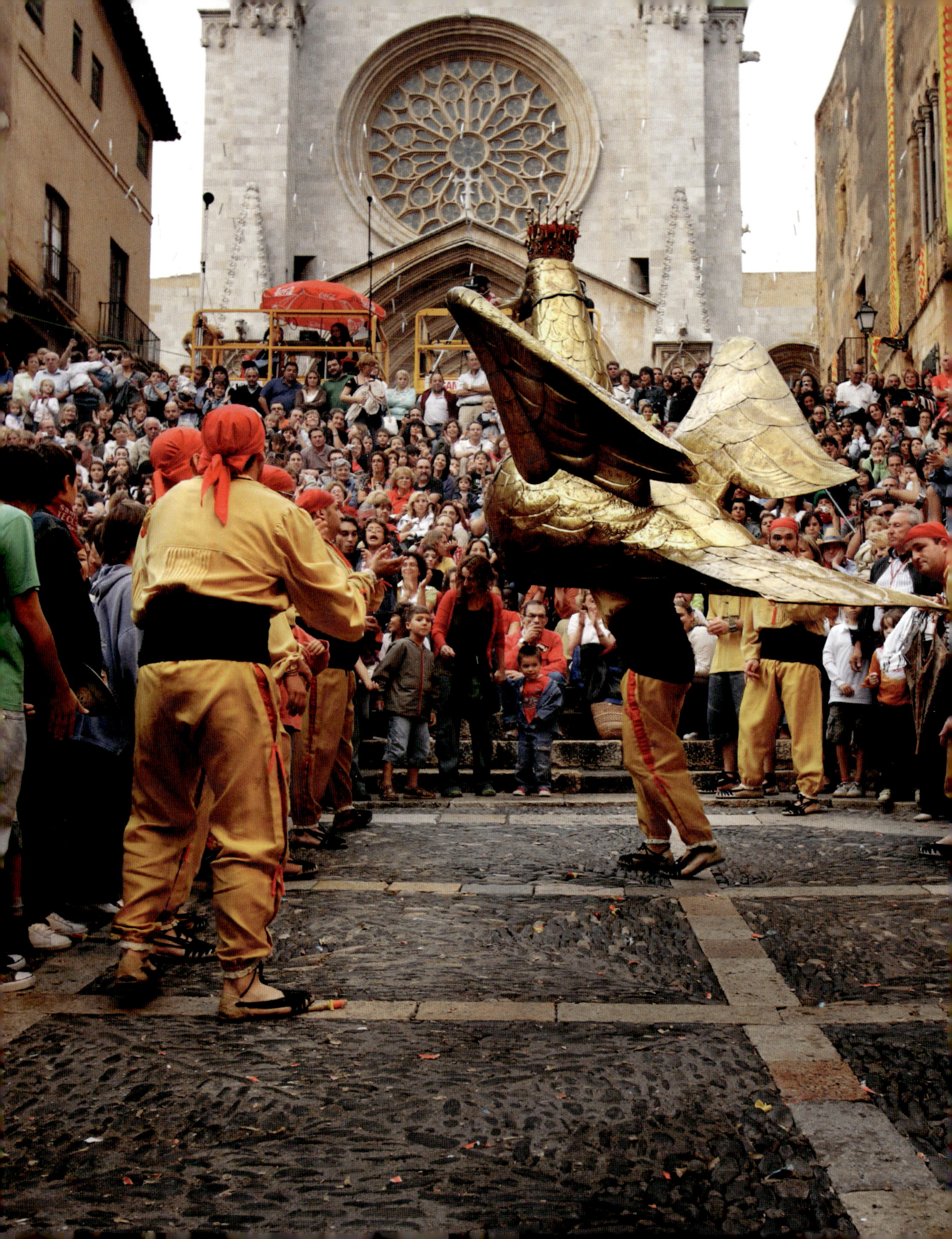

Santa Tecla

Steeped in tradition, Santa Tecla is Tarragona's big festival and one of the most important in Catalonia. It falls on 23rd September, the day Emperor Augustus was born. The festivities last 11 days: ten days and one night, from 22nd to 23rd. In 2002 it was declared a Festival of Tourist Interest and in 2010 a Heritage Festival of National Interest.

On the first day of the festival, the mayor gives the opening address urging people to take part in the celebrations; afterwards, the Cobla de Ministrers, one of Europe's first early music groups perform the *Toc de Crida*, a musical piece announcing the start of the festival, and then 11 mortars are set off in Plaça de la Font, one for each day of the festivities, and the first *Tronada*, a firework display first recorded in 1550.

On the Saturday, the city hosts the Mostra de Folklore Viu, a festival involving folk groups who usually only perform in their own towns and villages and travel to Tarragona specially for the event. On the following day, the city plays host to one of the most important displays of human towers of the season. It features two of Catalonia's most important teams of *castellers* and the two local teams who built the best human towers the previous year.

The grand entrance of the musicians, the *Entradeta de Músics*, takes place on 18th September, through the Portal del Roser. Little boys and girls join in the children's procession, and in the evening, at the Baixadeta, some of its members make their way down the Cathedral steps to Plaça de la Font. Another children's procession, the Santa Tecla Petita, is also held 19th September. It is an exact replica of the adult *Seguici Popular.*

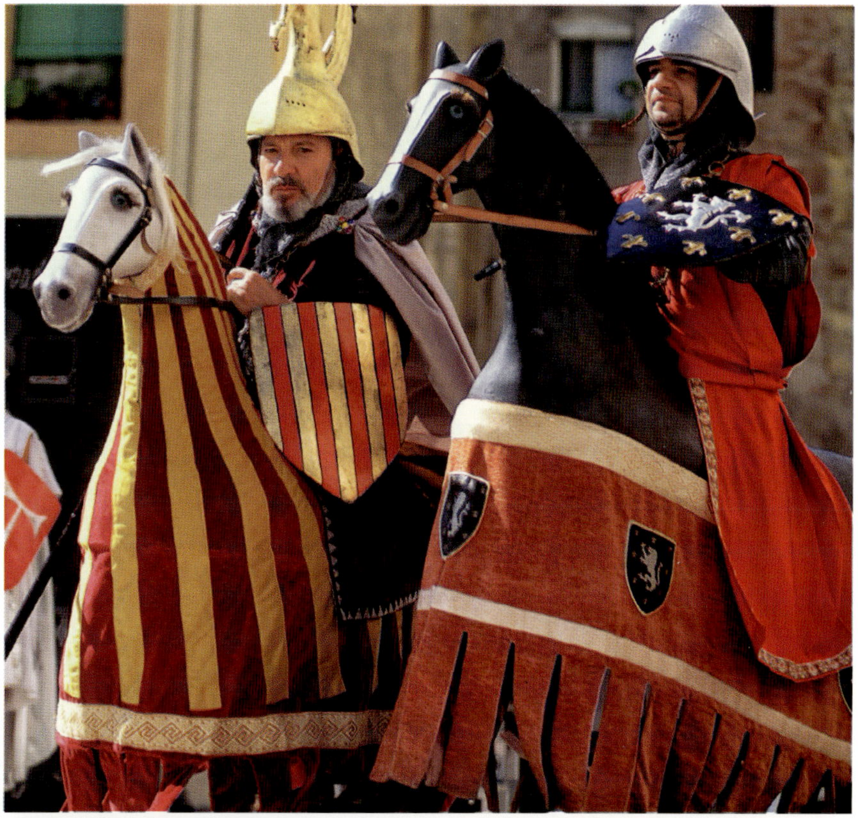

Dance of the Turks and Horses

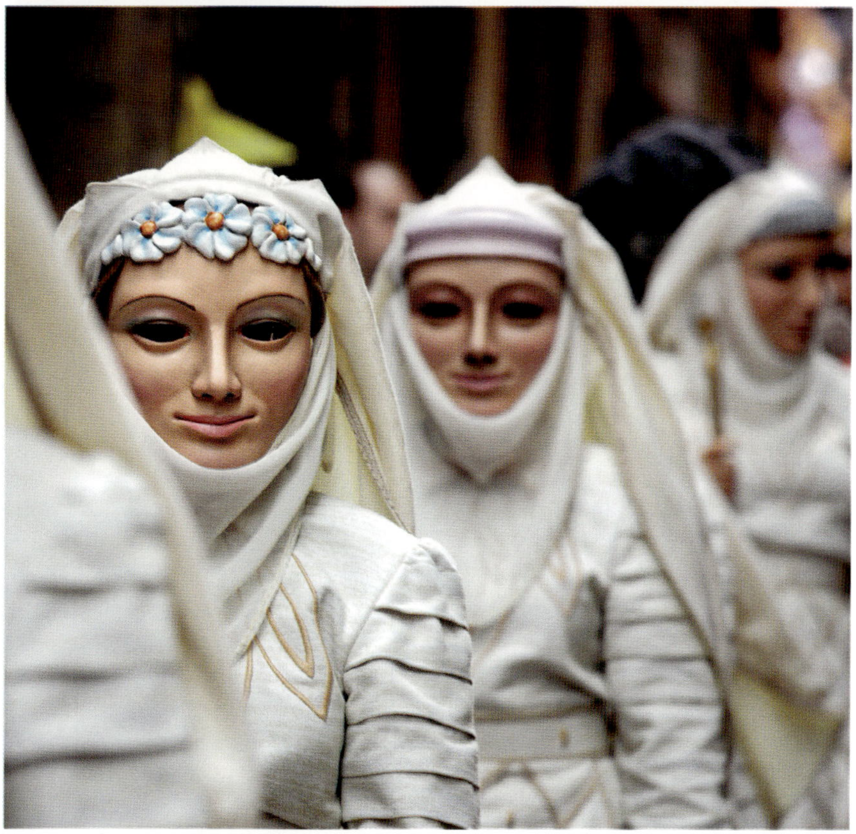

Dance of the Seven Deadly Sins

← The Eagle of Tarragona

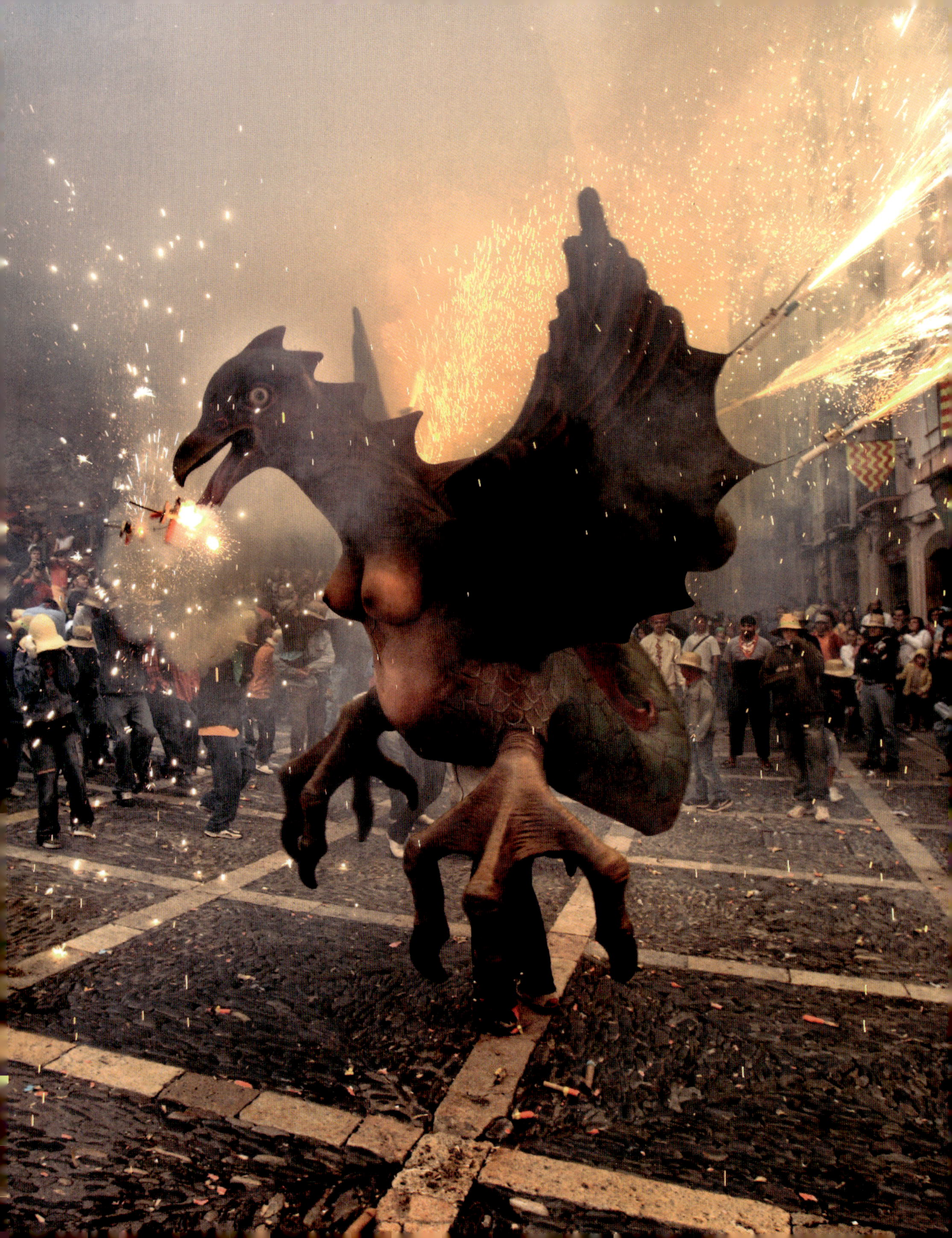

The Santa Tecla tableau has been one of the focal points of the celebrations of 20th September since 1991. It is a dance piece based on the life of the saint. The kids' *correfoc* also takes place on 20th. The 21st starts with the opportunity to have a coffee, drink and a cigar for 5 cents. It's a hectic day featuring the opening address, the *Pregó*, the *Arrencada*, or procession of giant figures — *gegants* — around the city, and, at midnight, one of the festival's most spectacular moments, the *Baixada de l'Àliga*, when the golden eagle from the *Seguici Popular* descends the Cathedral steps with other figures from the procession, to the rhythm of the paso doble *Amparito Roca*.

On 22nd September, the eve of the festival, traditional musicians make their entrance and the *Seguici Popular* parades with its full retinue. The first of the spoken dances, or *balls parlats*, is performed with verses criticising certain aspects of life in the city. It is also the day of the *Moixiganga*, which represents the mysteries of the Passion of Christ through human tower displays. People stay up all night partying and dancing until the great day, 23rd September, arrives.

Santa Tecla begins with the *Toc de Matinades*, the musical piece played at daybreak by musicians on a reed instrument known as a *gralla*. Later, the official procession, the *Seguici Popular*, accompanies the municipal authorities to the square in front of the Cathedral. Afterwards, the main figures from the procession dance and there are human tower displays by four local groups of *castellers*. In the evening, it's time for the procession and perhaps the most powerful and emotive moment of the festival: the holy relic, the arm of Santa Tecla, is carried through the streets to the Cathedral, accompanied by all the figures from the *Seguici Popular* who dance around and set off fireworks. The day concludes with the firework display on the Punta del Miracle.

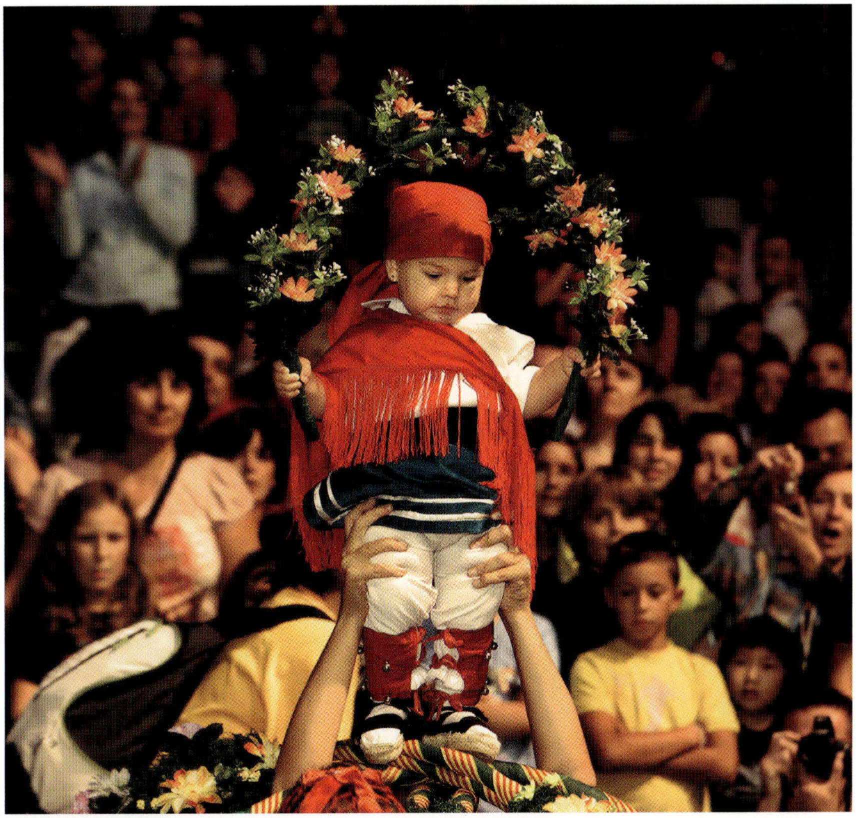

Dance of Cercolets

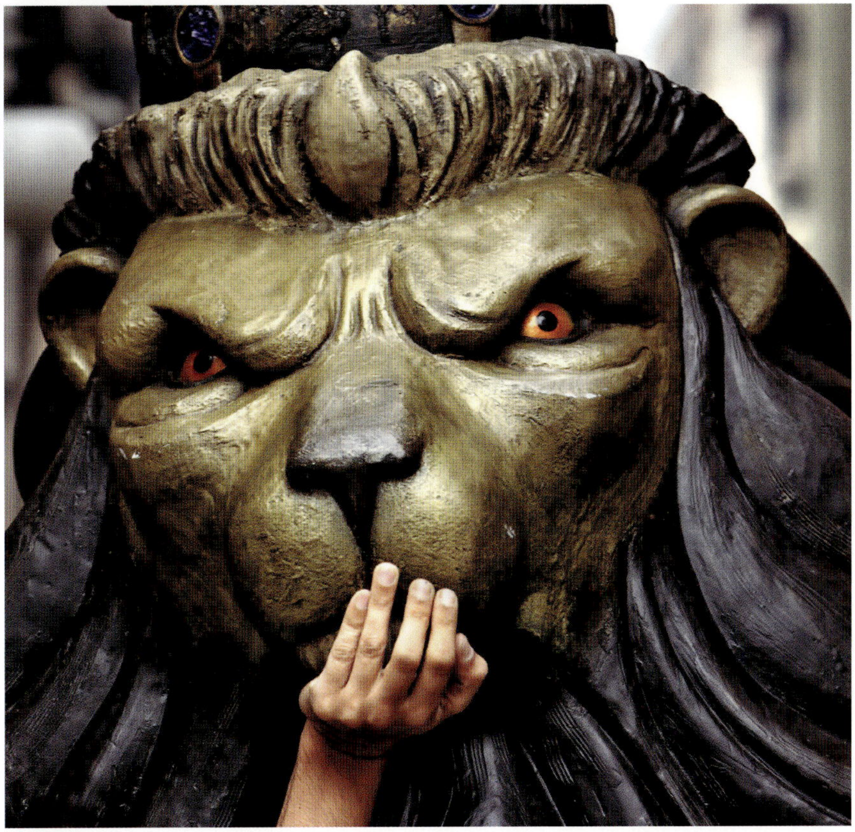

The Lion

← The Wyvern

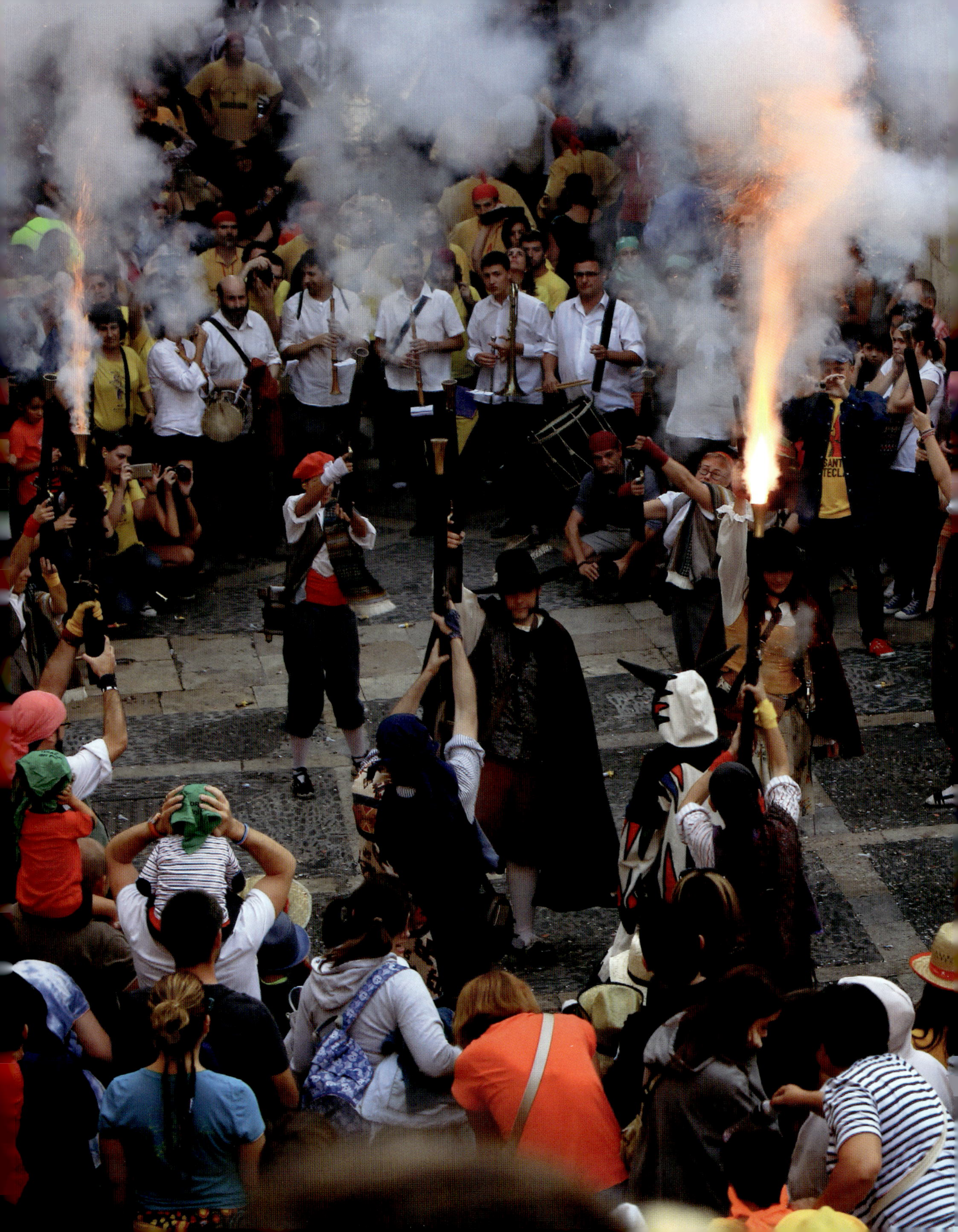

One of the real highlights of the festivities takes place at mid-day on 24th September, the day of La Mercè, when local teams of *castellers* build a four-tier *pilar*, or pillar — a human tower with one person per tier —, that goes up and down the Cathedral steps and makes its way to City Hall along Carrer Major, down the Baixada de la Misericòrdia and through Plaça de la Font. At night, the *correfoc* procession, when people dressed as devils and fearsome beasts run among the crowds throwing firecrackers, is one of the most important ones in Catalonia, and has an explosive ending, the *Traca*, when rows of firecrackers placed overhead on strings are set off in sequence.

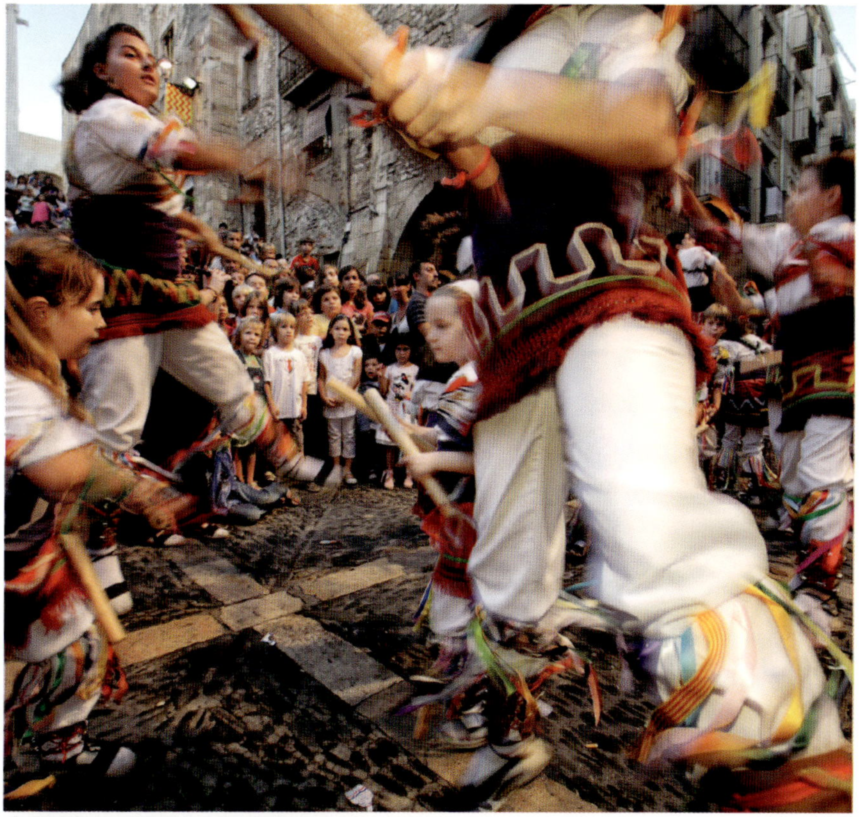

The Stick Dance

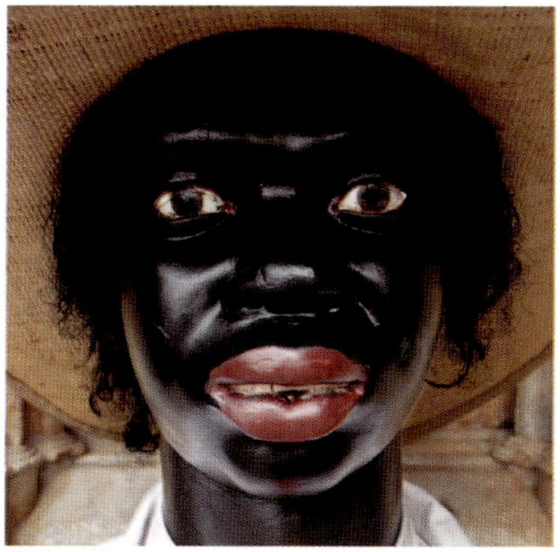

El Negrito

Casa de la Festa

This building houses the main figures from the *Seguici Popular* that take part in the festival of Santa Tecla, some of them heritage elements. It has been open to visitors since 2008 and features an exhibition that explains the ritual sequence of the festival. A ritual sequence that is one of the most important examples of intangible cultural heritage in Catalonia and the Mediterranean. The community plays a major role in the event which dates back to 1321 and has its origins in medieval European street theatre.

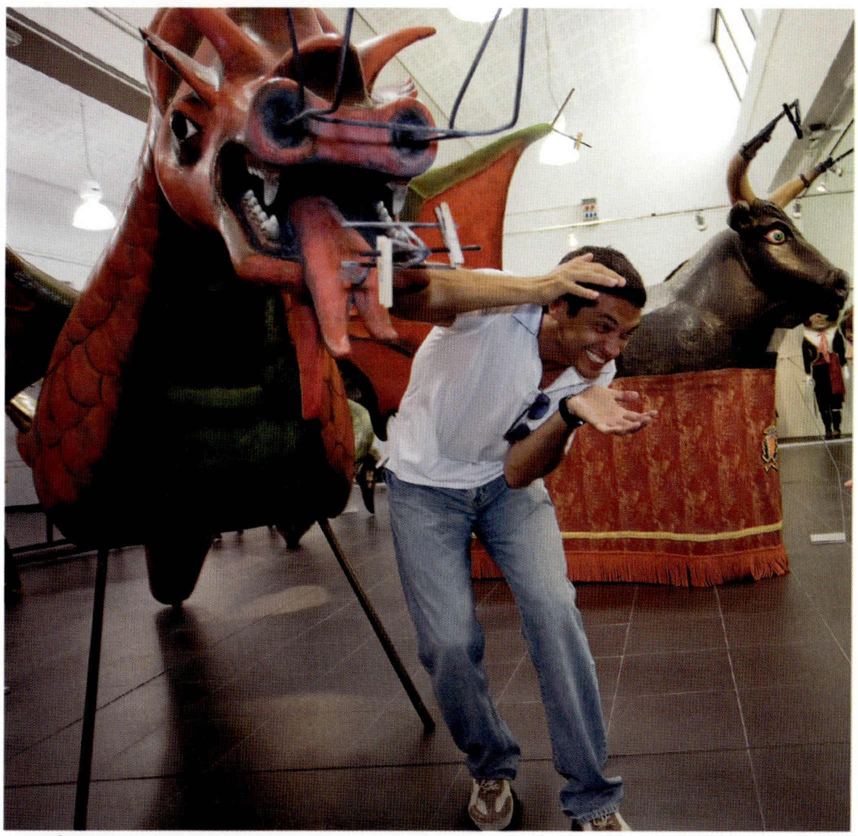

Casa de Festa, Via Augusta, 4

← Dance of Serrallonga

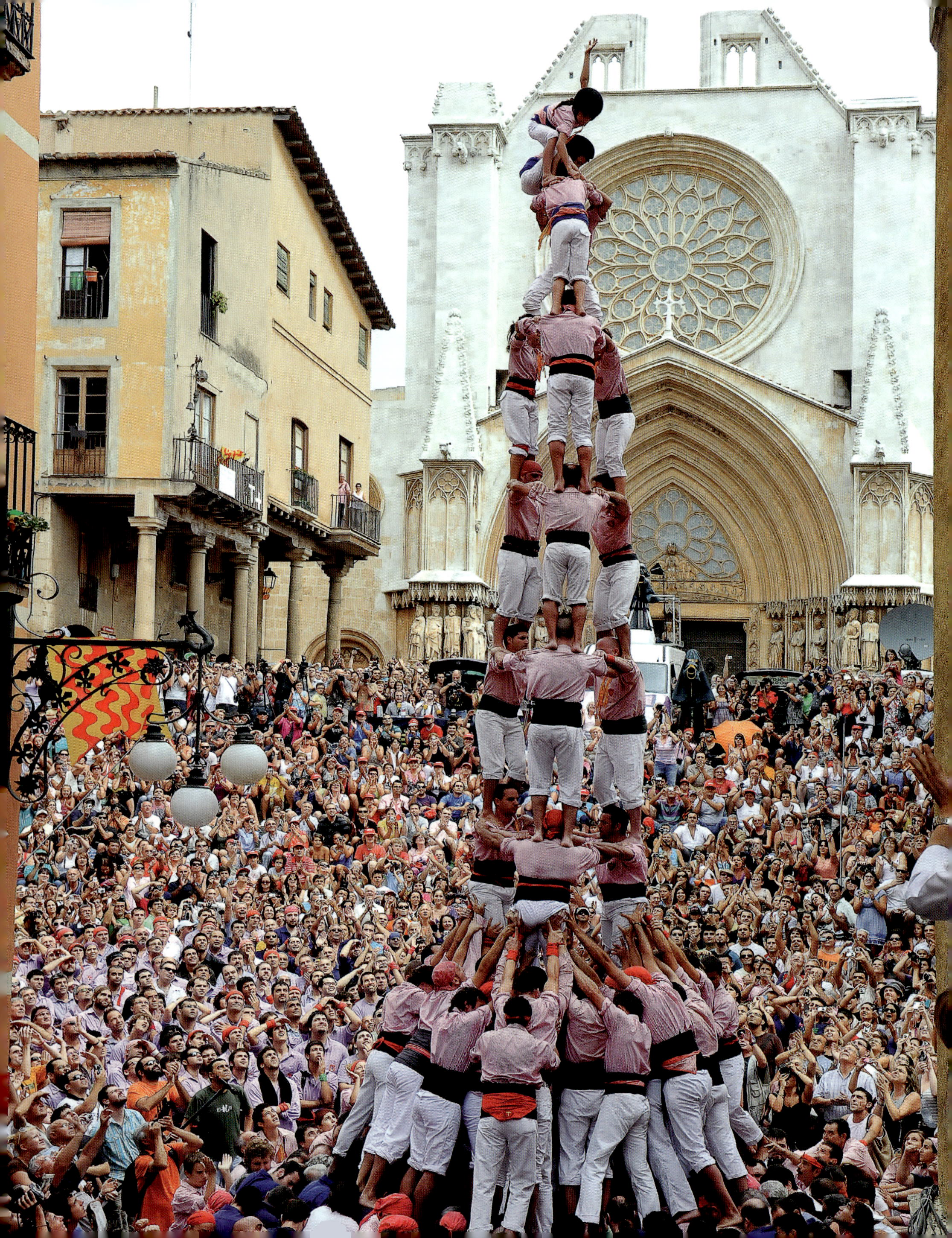

Tarragona, City of Castells

The *casteller* season in Tarragona features a plethora of spectacular human-tower displays held on feast days, such as Sant Joan, Sant Magí, Santa Tecla… in the city's squares including Plaça de la Font and Plaça de les Cols (officially Plaça Santiago Rusiñol). The city has four teams, or *colles* (Xiquets de Tarragona, with their white- and red-striped shirts; the Colla Jove Xiquets de Tarragona, with their purple shirts; Xiquets del Serrallo, in navy blue shirts; and the Colla Castellera Sant Pere i Sant Pau, who wear green shirts) and they all take part in the competitions, along with other noteworthy teams of *castellers*. Tarragona is one of the strongholds of this thrilling tradition, which has spread from its birthplace in the Camp de Tarragona, Penedès and Alt Camp throughout Catalonia and beyond: the Balearic Islands, Occitanie, Andorra and other countries. Associations of *castellers* have been founded by the many Catalans who live in cities such as Paris, London, Copenhagen, Santiago de Chile, Montreal… and Tarragona's human-tower competition has even attracted a team of *castelles* from China, the Xiquets de Hangzhou. In 2010, *castells* were awarded Intangible Cultural Heritage of Humanity status by UNESCO.

One of the high points of the season, in Tarragona and in the world of *castellers*, is the competition, which gives human towers the chance to take a break from the usual routine of staging displays at home and visiting other towns. During the competition, three or four *colles* stage displays in the traditional format of *tres rondes*, or three rounds, meaning they have three attempts to complete a *castell*. The display concludes with a formation known as a *pilar*, or pillar, consisting of one person per tier.

Concurs de Castells

The human tower competition, the Concurs de Castells, is a biennial event held in early autumn in even-numbered years. Spread over three days, it is the most spectacular human tower championship of them all and brings Tarragona widespread coverage from the world's media. The first day of the competition takes place in

← **Xiquets de Tarragona**

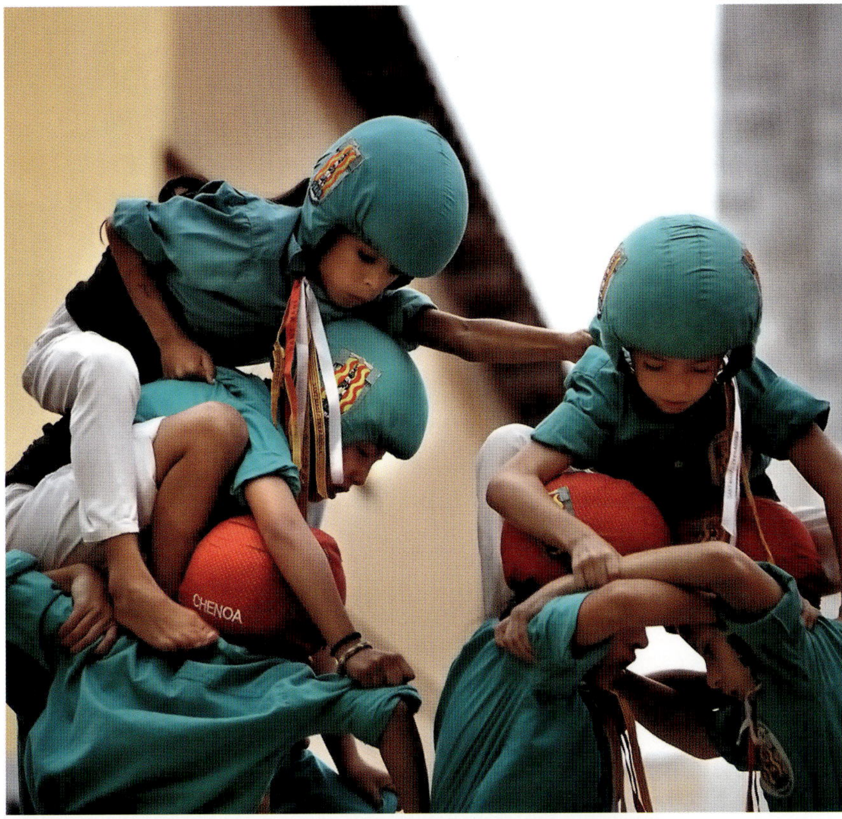

The *pom de dalt*, the summit of the Colla Castellera Sant Pere i Sant Pau

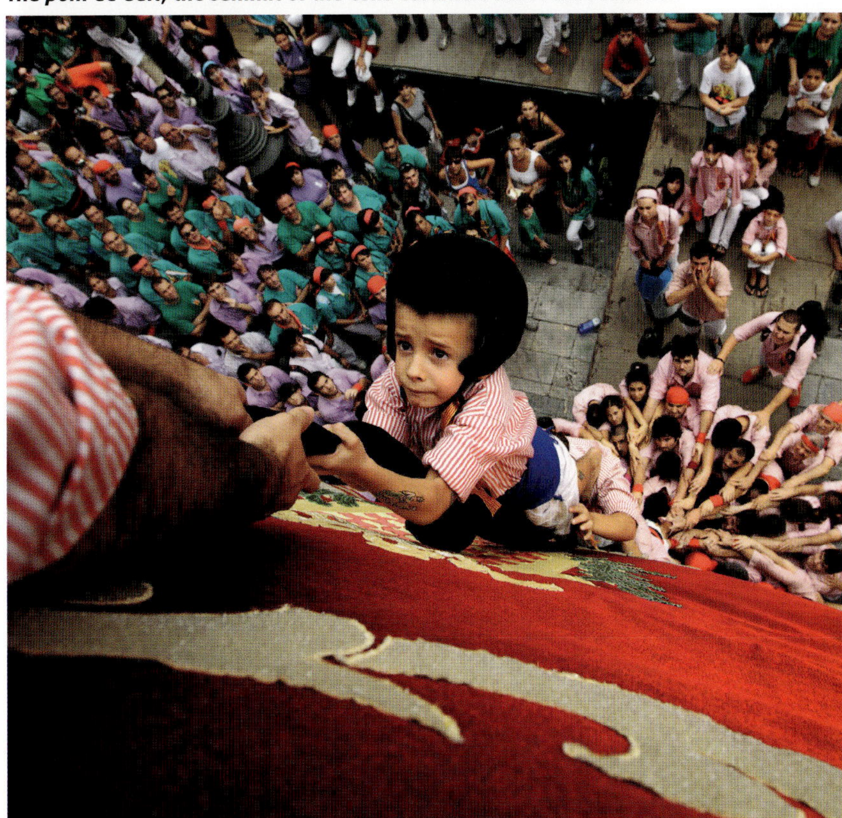

The *enxaneta* from the Xiquets de Tarragona

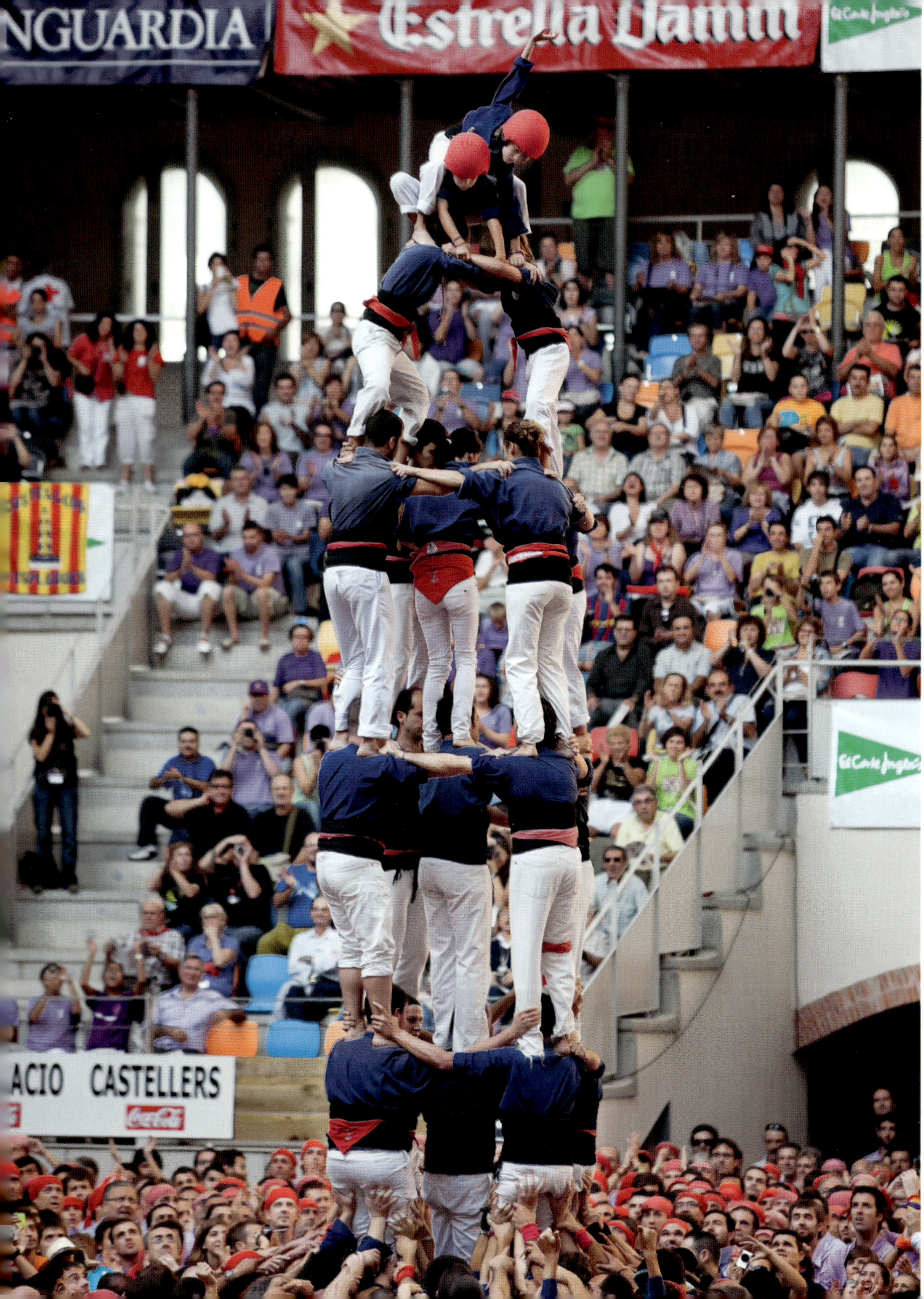
NGUARDIA
Estrella Damm
El Corte Inglés
ACIO CASTELLERS
Coca-Cola

the seaside town of Torredembarra, and moves on to Tarragona, which hosts the last two days of the event in the former bullring where it first took place in 1932, now the TAP. The skill of the *colles* and the level of difficulty increase as the competition progresses. The last day of the competition takes place on the first Sunday in October. Among a sea of colours, emotions run high as the *colles* attempt to build the highest and most complex towers. There can only be one winner, but each colour, each shirt, battles to build their own ceiling, their own sky.

Rehearsal spaces

In summer, as part of the programme of Tarragona visitors can spend the day with a team of castellers and experience what it's like to build one of these intricate human towers. From June to September, visitors can enjoy human-tower displays, guided tours of the rehearsals among other opportunities to experience this tradition. It's a great chance to get to know the places where the colles rehearse, such as the Xiquets, in Carrer Santa Anna, and La Jove, in Carrer Cós del Bou. The Xiquets del Serrallo is based in the Moll de Costa and Colla Castellera Sant Pere i Sant Pau in Carrer A of this neighbourhood.

SCAN and REC Festivals

The SCAN International Photography Festival was first held in 2008 and, since then, has promoted creativity in the field of photography, particularly from up-and-coming new talents. SCAN is run by the Fundació Forvm per a la Fotografia, and brings together public and private initiatives from different cultural agents. It holds exhibitions, talks, film screenings and workshops.

The REC is the international film festival which mainly focuses on new talents and includes sections such as Òpera Prima, which screens some of the world's best film debuts; and My First Time, which seeks to bring to a wider audience the first films shot by filmmakers who are now well established. REC also hosts thematic strands of films by young directors that are distributed at other festivals in Europe and America.

← Xiquets del Serrallo

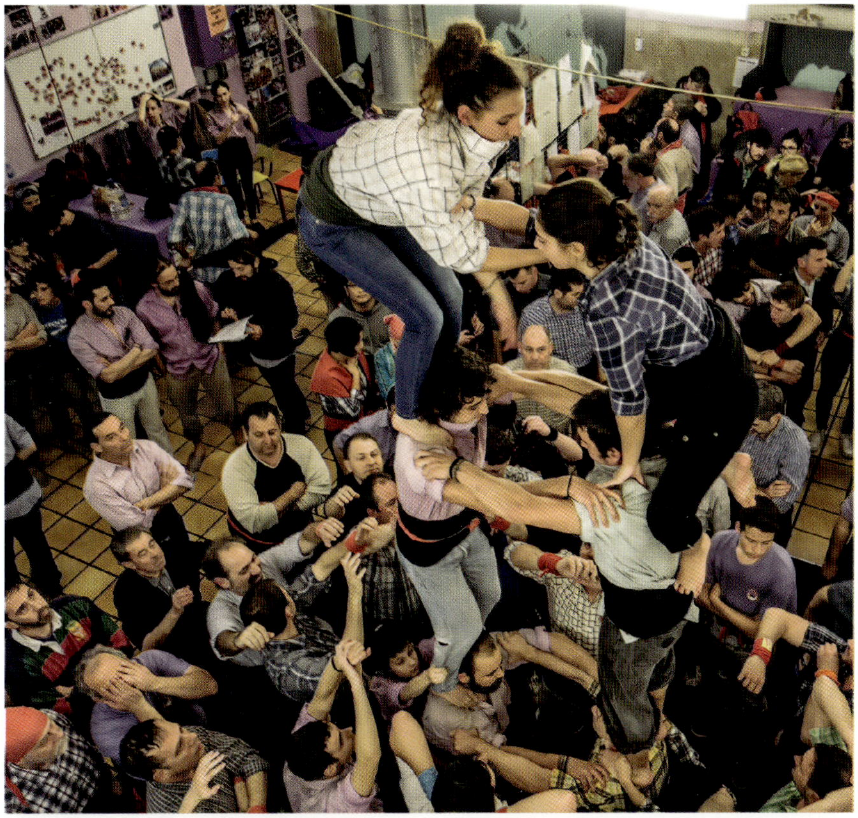

The Colla Jove rehearsal centre

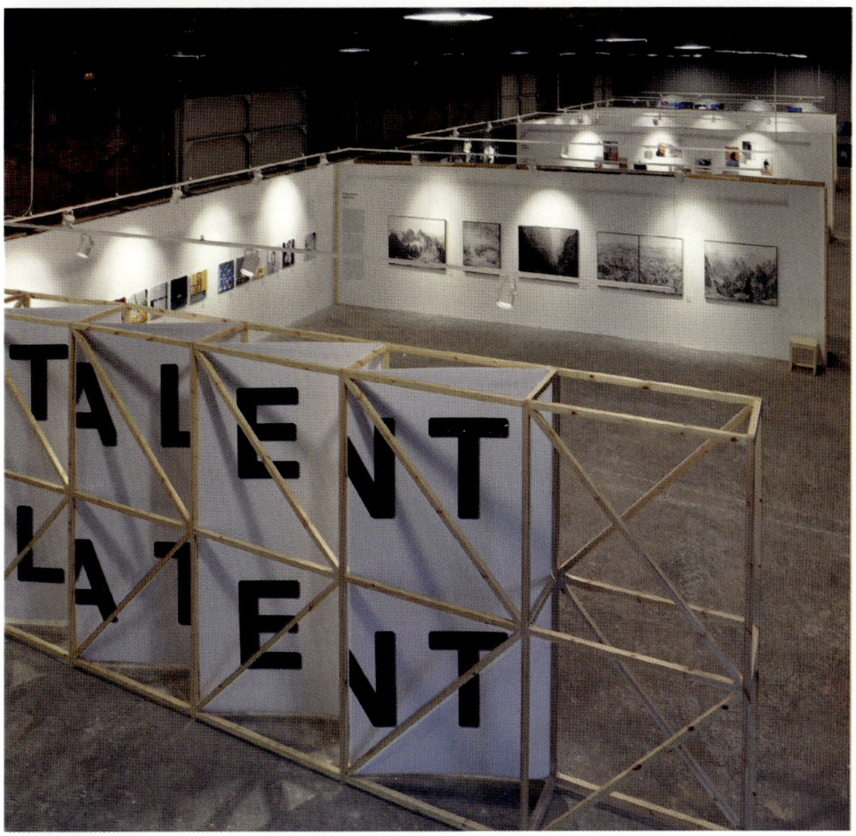

www.scan.cat

With the flavours of Tarragona

Food and wine

Throughout the year, in addition to the wonderful local food you can sample every day at the city's many restaurants, Tarragona hosts special events showcasing its cuisine and unique flavours, as well as wines and olive oils with their own Designations of Origin. Tarragona's cuisine reflects its distinctive landscape and close links to the sea and the land: fish, vegetables, olive oil, hazelnuts and almonds.

The land is rich in produce and, in late autumn and in winter, it's *calçot* season throughout the Camp de Tarragona. *Calçots* are a type of onion, larger than a spring onion and smaller than a leek, which are eaten chargrilled at *calçotades*, communal barbecues that originated in the town of Valls. And by the sea, throughout the year, the Fishermen's Guild and the city's restaurateurs serve up the Tarragona prawn, the ***gamba de Tarragona***, on their menus.

In February, the old town hosts the gastronomic event, La Part Alta Somriu a la Crisi (The Part Alta keeps smiling during the crisis) with menus to suit all pockets; and from April to May the city becomes the tapas capital of Catalonia during Tarraco Tapes, a gastronomic festival during which many of the city's restaurateurs serve up tapas made from locally sourced ingredients. In May, tying in with Tàrraco Viva, you'll be able to sample dishes inspired by Roman recipes at the food fair Tàrraco a Taula.

And in May or June — you can check the exact dates on the Tarragona Turisme website — the Rambla Nova hosts the wine fair, the Fira del vi de la Denominació d'Orígen Tarragona, which gives visitors the chance to discover the wide variety of wines from this Designation of Origin, and the new wines of the year.

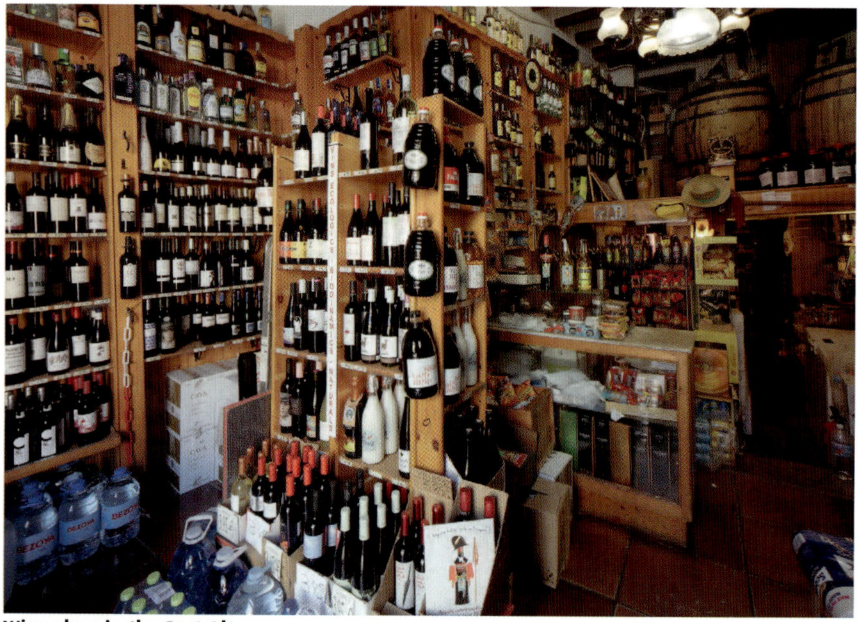

Wine shop in the Part Alta

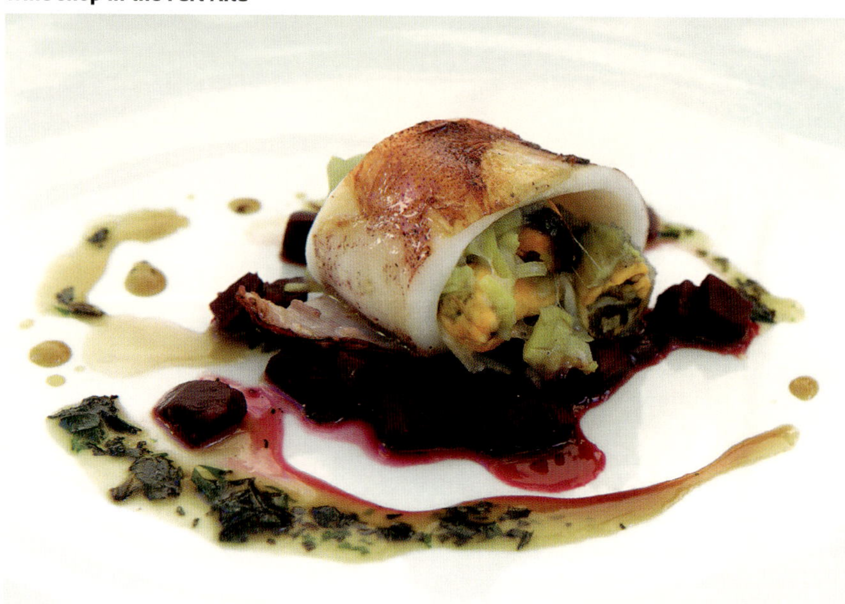

Tàrraco a Taula

Show cooking with the *gamba de Tarragona* →

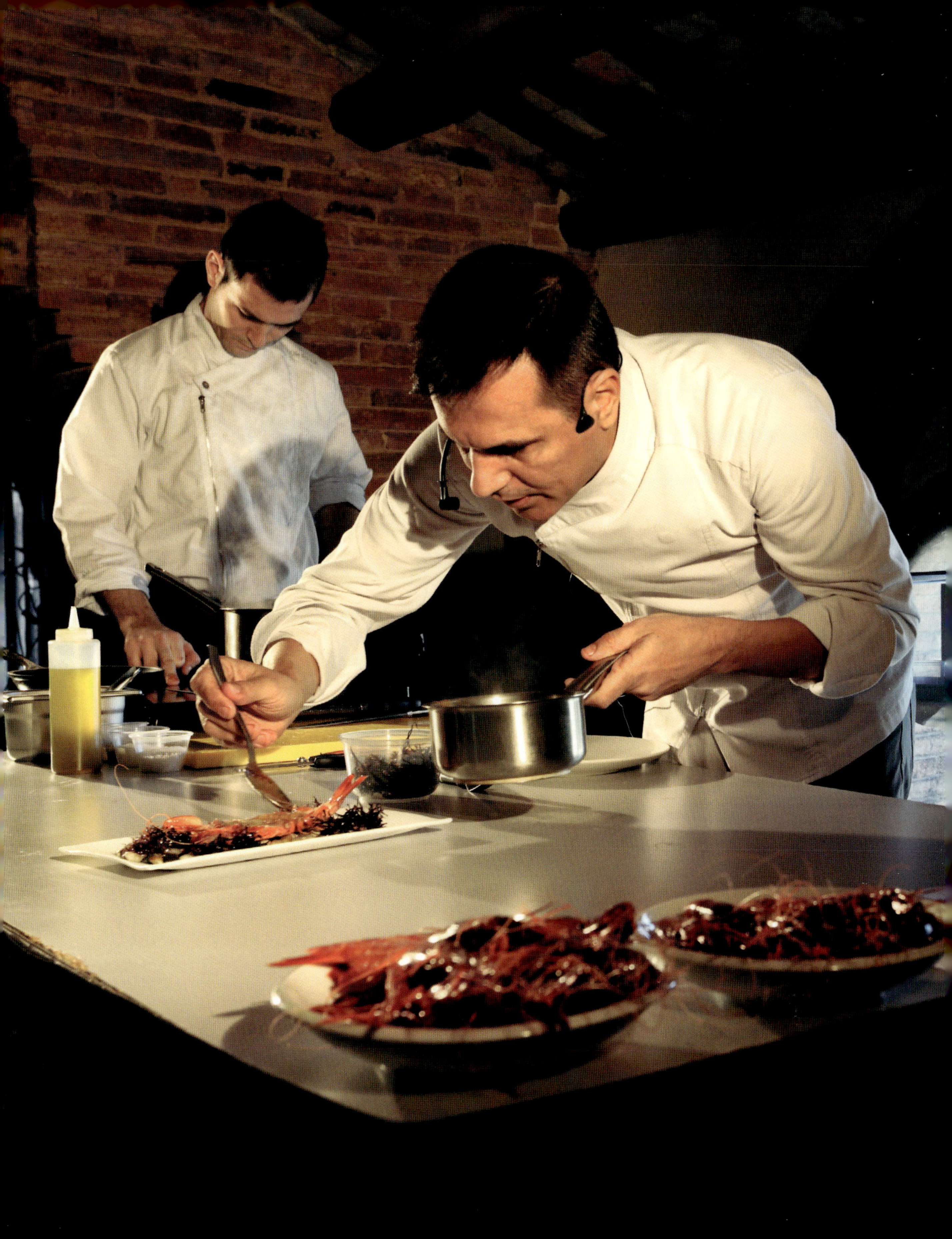

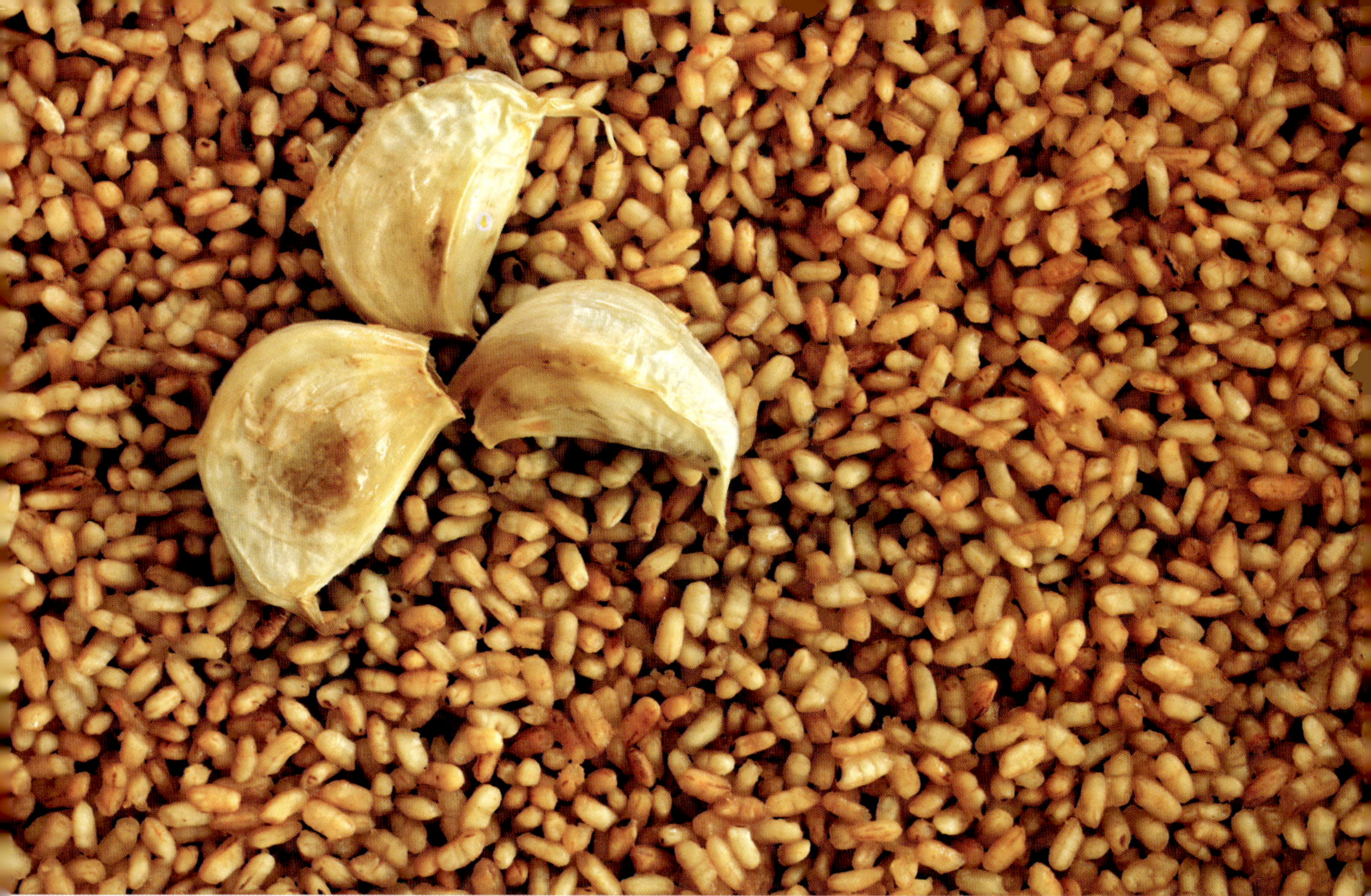

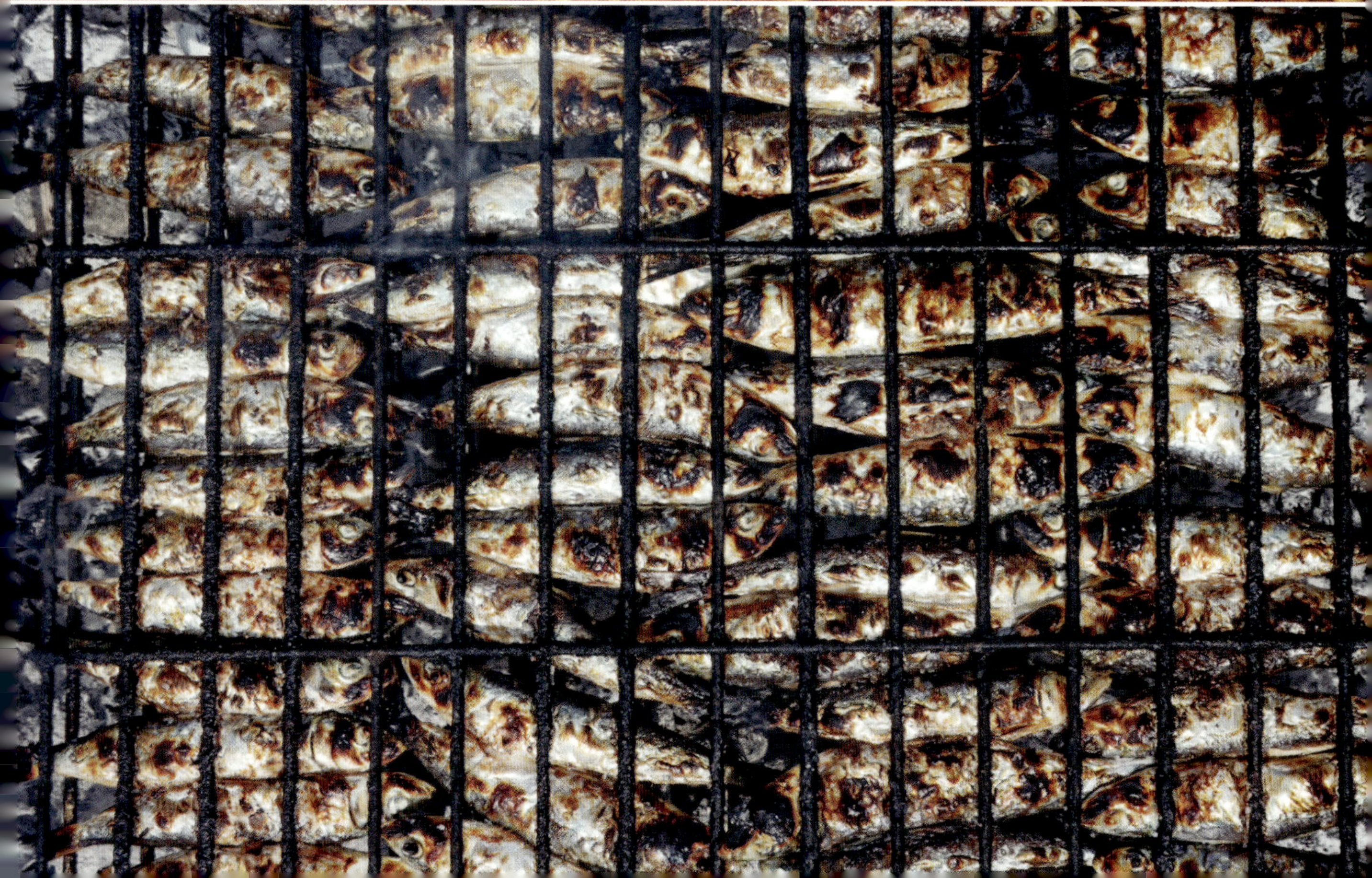

Romesco

This is the most typical dish, the true star of Tarragona's cuisine. The name refers to the sauce served as an accompaniment to fish, meat and vegetables, or as the dish made when all the ingredients are combined in an earthenware casserole as a base to cook with: that's when we talk about a *romesco* of... and the name of the fish that goes with it. The recipe varies depending on the cook, but the base is usually made from mild and sweet dried peppers, garlic, tomato, fried bread, almonds, hazelnuts and olive oil.

Rice and noodle dishes

Other dishes that take pride of place on the table have rice or noodles as their basic ingredients. Rice from the Ebro Delta, which has been awarded Protected Designation of Origin status, is particularly popular. Recipes include the simple but tasty one-pot dishes fishermen used to cook on their boats, and other more time-consuming ones that were cooked at home. These include *rossejat d'arròs*, rice cooked in fish stock until it is golden and crunchy, and its noodle variant, *fideus rossejats*; rice cooked in a stock with squid ink, *arròs negre*; seafood rice, *arròs a la marinera*.

Oily fish and the *gamba de Tarragona*

The sardine is one of the species of oily fish which is highly valued in the prevention of cardiovascular diseases. It is caught off the coast of Tarragona and has been awarded Protected Designation of Origin status. Other species of oily fish include anchovies, mackerel, bogue, chub and horse mackerel.

Tarragona's succulent red prawn, the *gamba de Tarragona* is one of the tastiest on the Iberian Peninsula and is served at some of Spain's finest restaurants. Here you can eat it with a zero-carbon footprint, cooked on the griddle, with rice and *romesco* sauce...

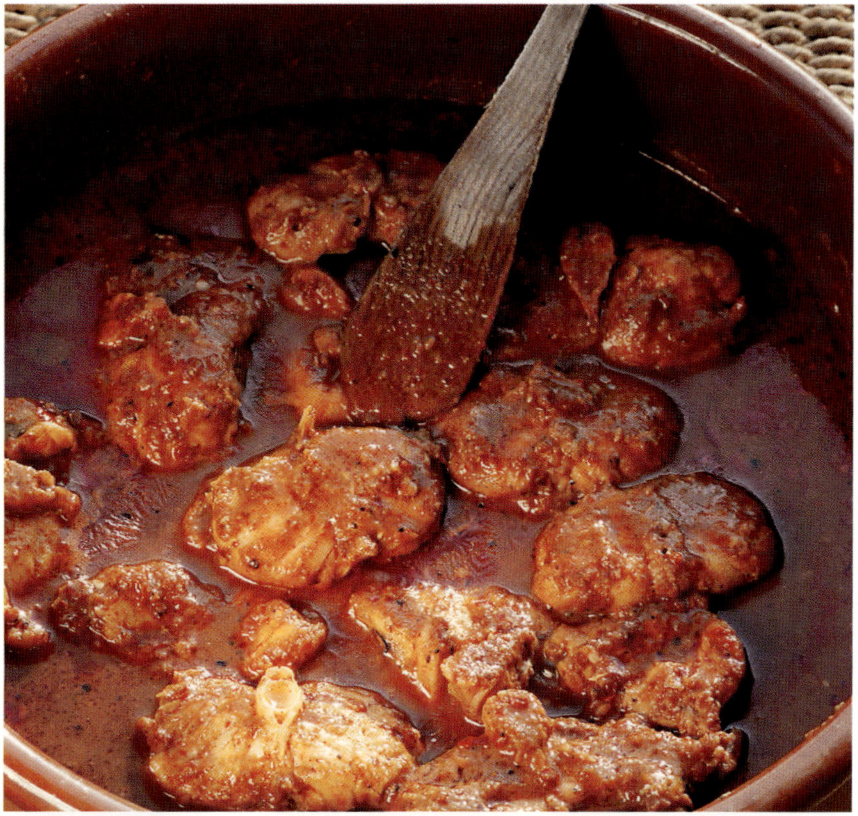

Monkfish romesco

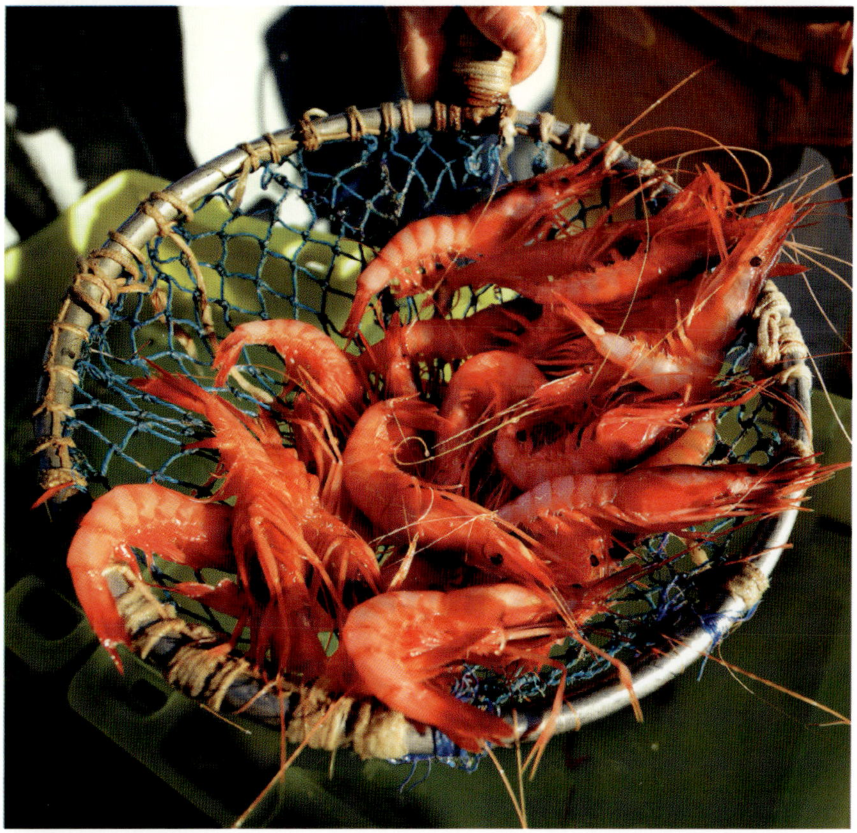

Gamba de Tarragona

← **Browned rice and grilled sardines**

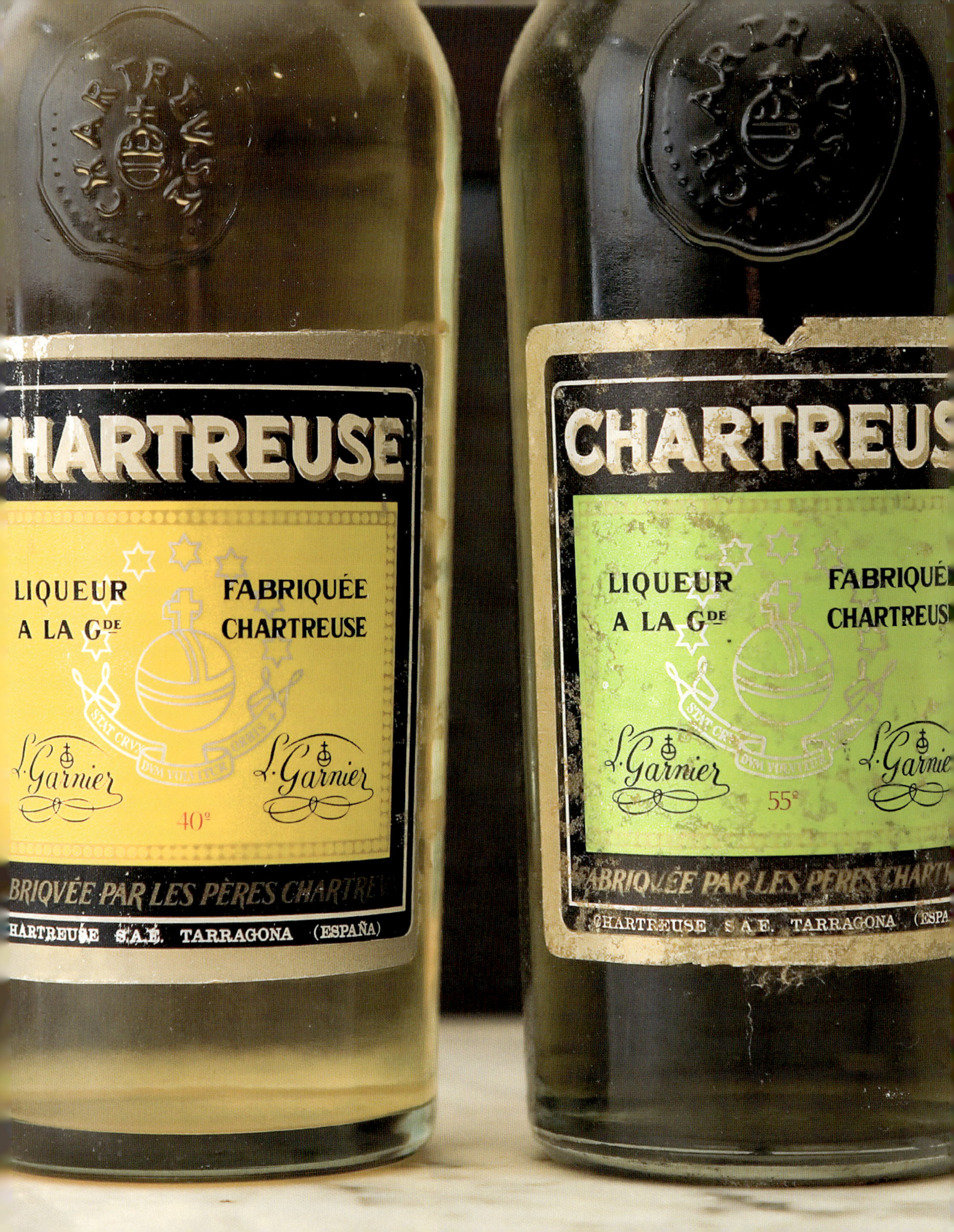

HARTREUSE
LIQUEUR A LA Gde
FABRIQUÉE CHARTREUSE
L. Garnier
L. Garnier
40º
BRIQVÉE PAR LES PÈRES CHARTRE
HARTREUSE S.A.E. TARRAGONA (ESPAÑA)
CHARTREUS
LIQUEUR A LA Gde
FABRIQUÉE CHARTREUS
L. Garnier
L. Garnie
55º
ABRIQVÉE PAR LES PÈRES CHART
CHARTREUSE S.A.E. TARRAGONA (ESPA

Chartreuse

Chartreuse is currently produced by Carthusian monks in Voiron, France. Until 1989 is was also made at a factory in Tarragona. The liqueur dates back to 1605 when the monks received an ancient manuscript containing the formula for an "Elixir for long life". There are two types: yellow Chartreuse, which is 40° proof, and green, 55° proof. It has become one of the locals' favourite tipples and the key ingredient in the traditional drink of the Feast of Santa Tecla, known as *mamadeta*: green and yellow Chartreuse served with lemon granita.

Vermouth

Having a pre-lunch glass of vermouth and a snack on the terrace at the weekend, when the sun is out, is one of Tarragona's most enjoyable customs. Reus and different towns in the Camp de Tarragona and Priorat produce half a dozen great brands of this fortified aperitif wine, flavoured with wormwood and other bitter herbs. It's the perfect drink to enjoy with hand-made crisps, olives and cockles served with a piquant sauce and brings together friends and families before lunch on Saturday and especially Sunday.

Designation of Origin (DO) wine and olive oil

The wines made in more than 70 municipalities in the Camp de Tarragona and the Ribera d'Ebre belong to the Designation of Origin Tarragona. The whites are smooth and fruity, the rosés fresh and cherry coloured, and the reds full bodied and fragrant. You can visit the *modernista* cooperative wineries in this DO region, and ones in the counties of the Conca de Barberà, Terra Alta and Priorat. They are known as the "Cathedrals of wine".

The seven counties around Tarragona produce high-quality olive oils that have been awarded Siurana Protected Designation of Origin (PDO) status.

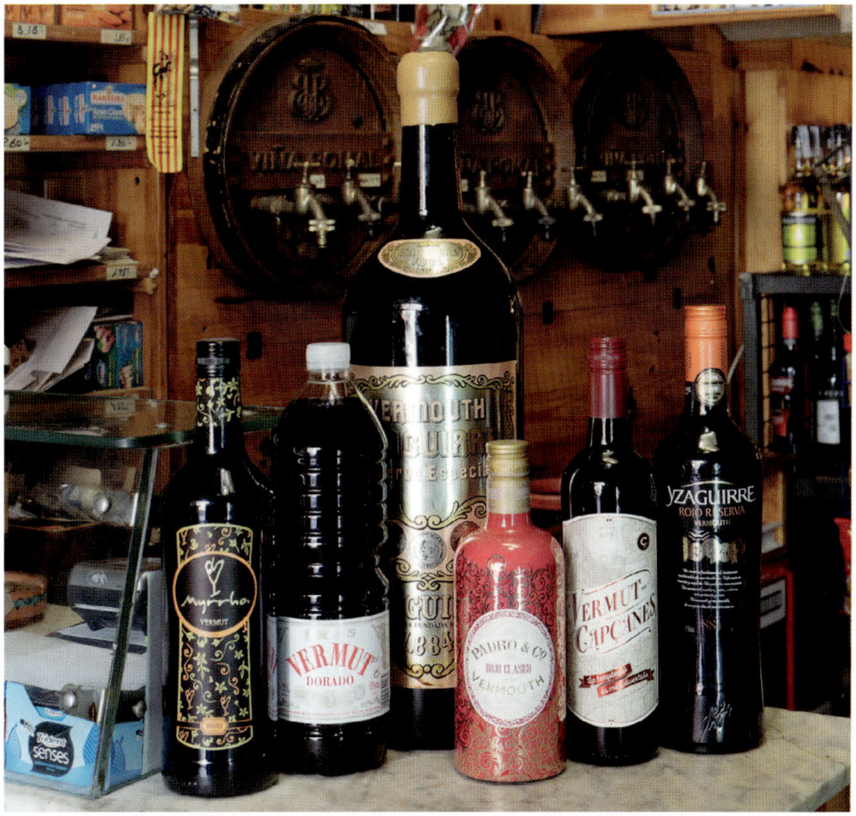

Vermouth

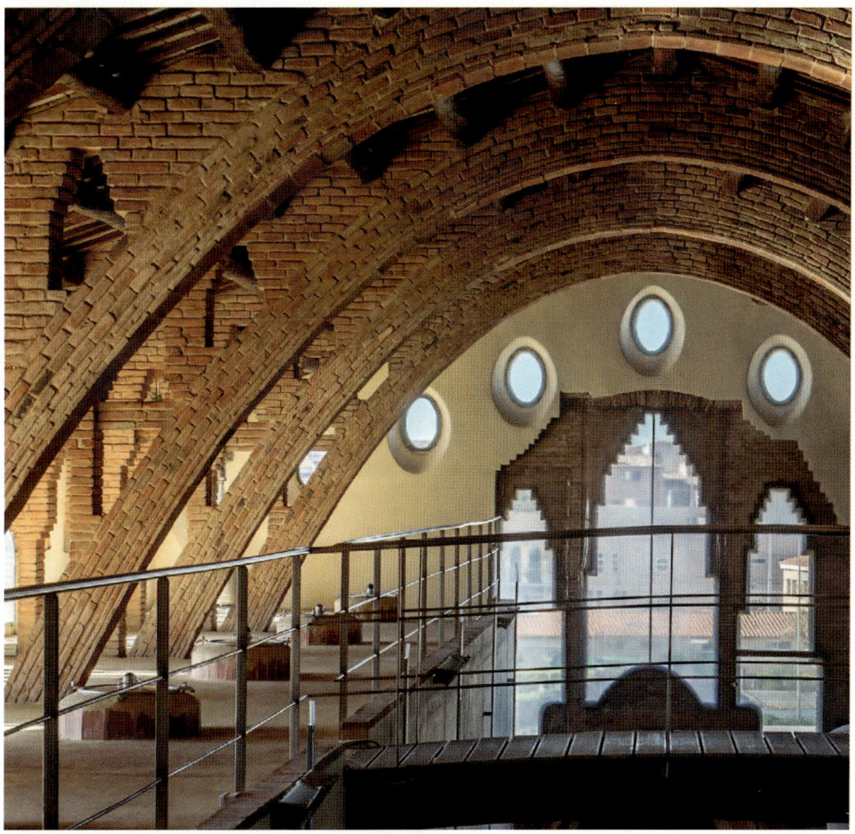

Nulles *modernista* winery, by Cèsar Martinell

← **Old bottles of Chartreuse**

Published by
© Triangle Postals, 2017

Text
© Carles Marquès i Virgili

Photographs
© Joan Colomer 2, 9, 12a, 13b, 14a, 14b, 15a, 24b, 26a, 26b, 27b, 27c, 34, 35a, 36, 37a, 37b, 38a, 38b, 39a, 39c, 39d, 41a, 41b, 41c, 43b, 43c, 44a, 44b, 45a, 46, 55b, 61a, 61b, 65a, 65b, 71b, 72b, 73b, 74a, 74b, 74c, 75b, 77, 80a, 80b, 81a, 81b, 82, 83a, 83d, 85, 86b, 87c, 89a, 89b, 90a, 90b, 90c, 93a, 93b, 95a, 98, 101a, 129b **© Joan Colomer | Arquebisbat de Tarragona** 55b **© Jordi Puig** 5, 8, 16, 17a, 17b, 17c, 18, 21, 24, 27, 28, 30a, 30b, 35, 39, 40a, 40b, 44, 45, 47, 56, 59, 60a, 60b, 63, 66, 70, 71, 75, 81, 88, 91, 122, 124, 125, 126, 127, 129, solapa **© Jordi Puig | Arquebisbat de Tarragona** 48, 49a, 49b, 50a, 50b, 51a, 51b, 52a, 52b, 52c, 53, 54a, 54b, 55a, 57b **© Jordi Puig | Museu Diocesà de Tarragona** 57a, 57c **© Rafael López-Monné** portada, solapa, 12b, 22a, 23b, 23c, 24a, 29a, 29b, 104, 106, 107a, 107b, 108a, 109a, 109b, 112, 113a, 113b, 114, 115a, 115b, 117a, 117b, 119a, 119b, 121a, 123, 124a, 125b **© Laia Moreno** 18b, 18c, 31a, 31b, 94a, 94b, 95b, 96a, 96b, 96c, 97a, 97b, 97c, 99, 100a, 100b, 101b, 102a, 103a, 103b **© Hans Hansen** 4, 8b, 10, 13c, 15c, 22b, 23a, 28c, 32, 33, 42, 58, 62a, 72a, 73a, 83c, 120, 127b **© Ricard Pla** 6, 7, 13a, 15b, 19, 20, 28a, 43a, 75a, 83b, 84a, 84b, 87a, 87b, 92, 102b **© Manel R. Granell** 62b, 63b, 64a, 64b, 93c, 111a, 111b, 111c, 116, 122b **© Jordi Puig | Pere Vivas** 67, 68a, 68b, 69a, 69b, 69c **© Pere Vivas** 21b, 76, 78 **© Pep Escoda** 108b, 110a, 110b **© Fèlix Miró** 105, 118 **© Iván Sánchez** 117c **© Joan Capdevila Vallve** 86a **© Margarita Alberich** 25 **© Pep Rigol | SCAN Tarragona** 121b **© Patronat de Turisme de Tarragona** 88a

Art director
Ricard Pla

Design
Joan Colomer

Translation
Mark Waudby

Cartography
© Joan Esteve | Triangle Postals

Coordination
Paz Marrodán

Printed by
Tallers gràfics Soler

Legal deposit
Me 306-2017

ISBN
978-84-8478-761-7

Printed in Barcelona

Acknowledgements
Ajuntament de Tarragona
www.tarragona.cat
Arquebisbat de Tarragona
www.catedraldetarragona.com
CaixaForum Tarragona
Centre Tarraconense El Seminari
www.ctarraconense.cat
Museu d'Art Modern de Tarragona
www.diputaciodetarragona.cat/mamt
Museu Bíblic Tarraconense
http://museu.biblic.arqtgn.cat
Museu Diocesà de Tarragona
http://museu.diocesa.arqtgn.cat
Museu d'Història de Tarragona
www.tarragona.cat/patrimoni/museu-historia
Museu Nacional Arqueològic de Tarragona
www.mnat.cat
Museu del Port de Tarragona
www.porttarragona.cat/ca/port-i-ciutat/museu-port
Palau Firal i de Congressos
www.palautarragona.com
Tarragona turisme
www.tarragonaturisme.cat

www.ssantatarragona.org
www.tarracoviva.com
www.minipop.cat
www.concursdecastells.cat
www.dotarragona.cat

TRIANGLE BOOKS

TRIANGLE POSTALS, SL
Carrer Pere Tudurí, 8
07710 Sant Lluís, Menorca
Tel. +34 971 15 04 51
Fax +34 971 15 18 36
www.triangle.cat

Tarragona turisme

Carrer Major, 39
43003 Tarragona - Spain
Tel. +34 977 25 07 95
www.tarragonaturisme.cat

Tarragona

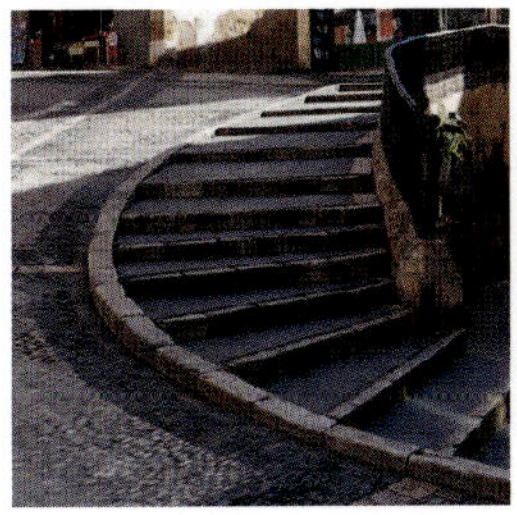

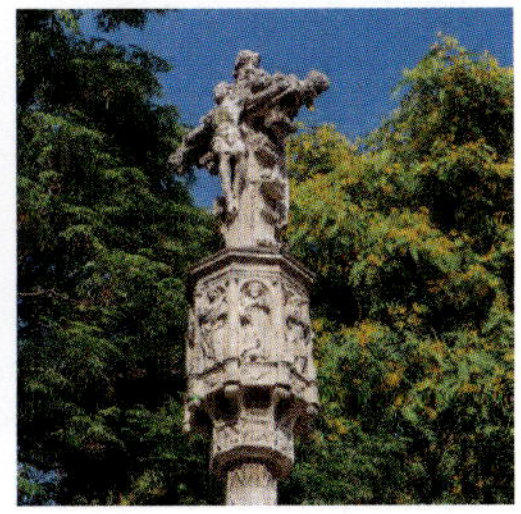

Roman route I

This route takes you through the Roman colony of Tarraco and the monuments in the archaeological complex that has been declared a World Heritage Site. It can be divided into two parts: the first can be done on foot in one day, or two, if you want to enjoy it at a more leisurely pace. After you've had a look at the model of the Roman city, you'll go through the Part Alta, the monumental and administrative centre of Tarraco, as well as a place of worship, to the Amphitheatre, next to Miracle beach, as far as the shores of the river Francolí.

1 Model of Roman Tarraco (Old Court Building) **2** City wall - Passeig Arqueològic **3** Temple. Place of worship (Cathedral cloisters) **4** Provincial Forum - Plaça del Pallol **5** Provincial Forum - Plaça del Fòrum **6** Provincial Forum - Plaça del Rei. Praetorium **7** Museu Nacional Arqueològic de Tarragona **8** Circus **9** Amphitheatre **10** Museun and Early-Christian Necropolis. Early-Christian complex of the river Francolí

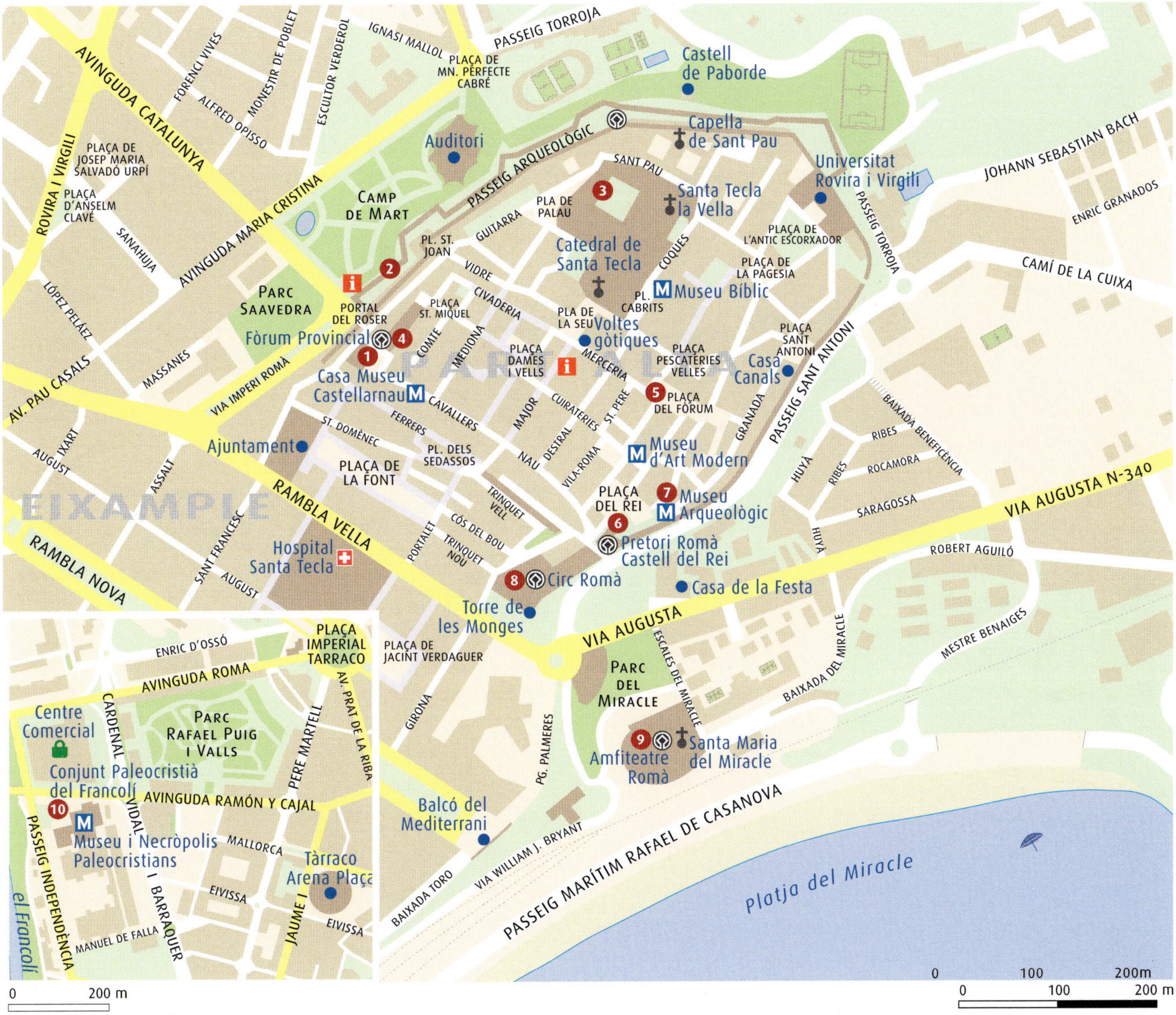

Roman route II

The second section of the Roman route requires transport and more time, at least two or three days, and maybe even more depending on how curious you are. The first sights on the route can be visited on foot in the Part Baixa, which was the residential and harbour area and the most vibrant in the Roman city. You'll need a vehicle for the next stage of the route to get to the outskirts of town and head east to west to discover the area around Tarraco, known as *ager tarraconensis.*

1 Local Forum or Colony Forum **2** Theatre **3** Archaeological landmarks in the Part Baixa: Jardins del Vapor **4** Aqueduct-Pont del Diable **5** Villa of Centcelles (Constantí) **6** Torre dels Escipions **7** El Mèdol quarry **8** Villa of Els Munts (Altafulla) **9** Arc de Berà (Roda de Berà) **10** Other villas and sites: villas of Paret Delgada (Selva del Camp), La Llosa (Cambrils), La Pineda (Vila-seca), El Moro (Torredembarra)...

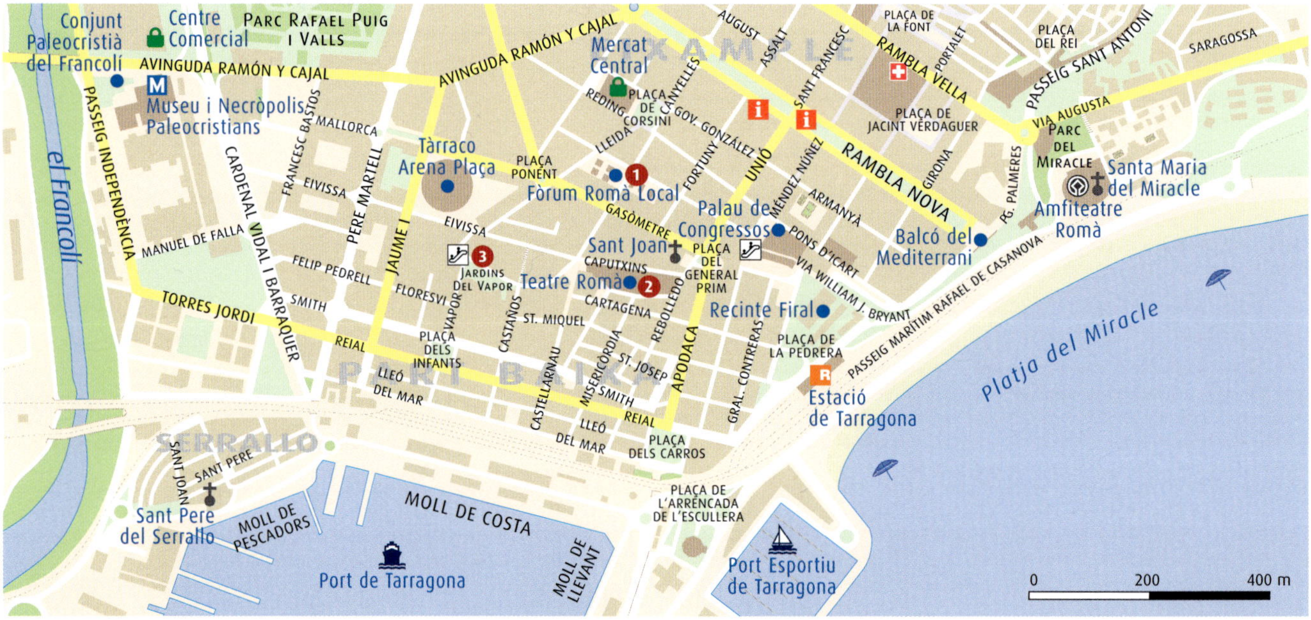

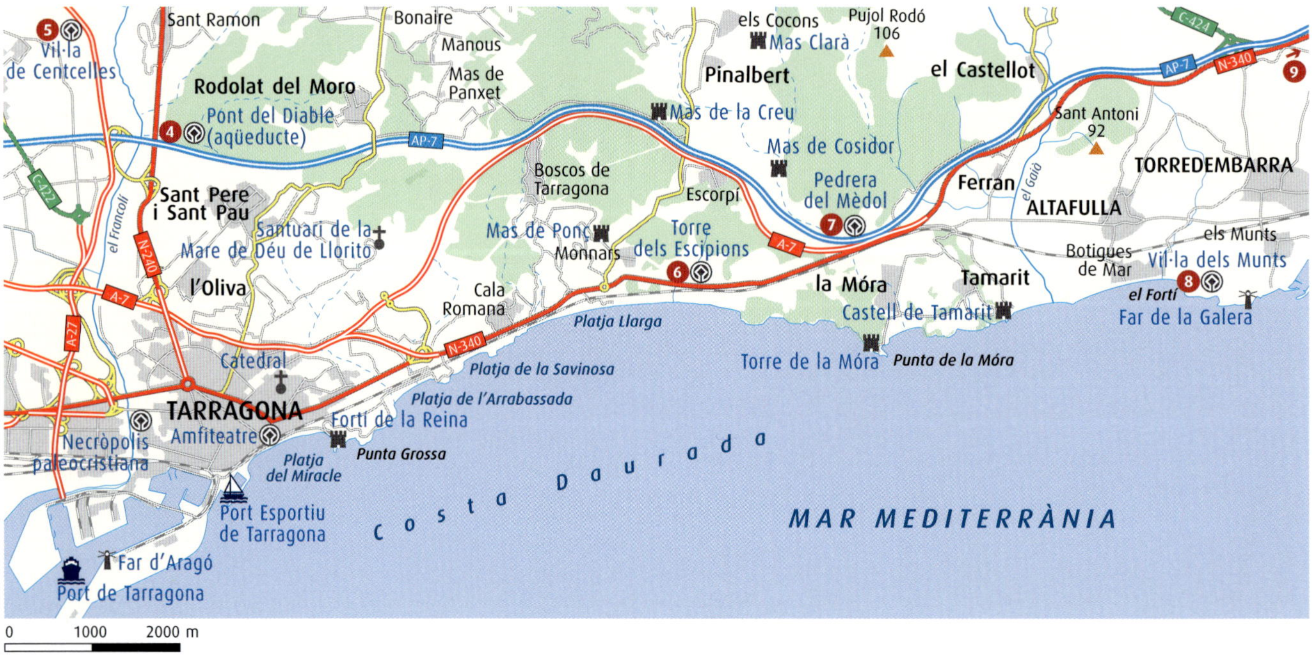

Medieval route

This route takes you through the Part Alta and the splendour of the Middle Ages. After the Christian resettlement of the city in the 12th century, the Roman area that was the administrative centre of Tarragona province became a higgledy-piggledy jumble of streets that survive today almost intact. The medieval route takes us away from the central area we have explored on foot. You'll need a vehicle to get to the point where the resettlement began, Tamarit, which marked the border with al-Andalus in 1118.

1 The walls - Torre d'Arandes, Torre de les Monges and Torre d'en Tintoré **2** Pla de la Seu - Old City Hall, Carrer de la Merceria and Casa Balcells **3** Carrer Major - Casa de la Generalitat **4** The Cathedral, the cloisters and the Museu Diocesà **5** Chapel of Sant Pau (Centre Tarraconense El Seminari) **6** Church of Sant Llorenç **7** Chapel of Santa Tecla la Vella and old hospital of Santa Tecla **8** Jewish Quarter **9** Church of Santa Maria del Miracle (Amphitheatre) **10** Walled village of Tamarit

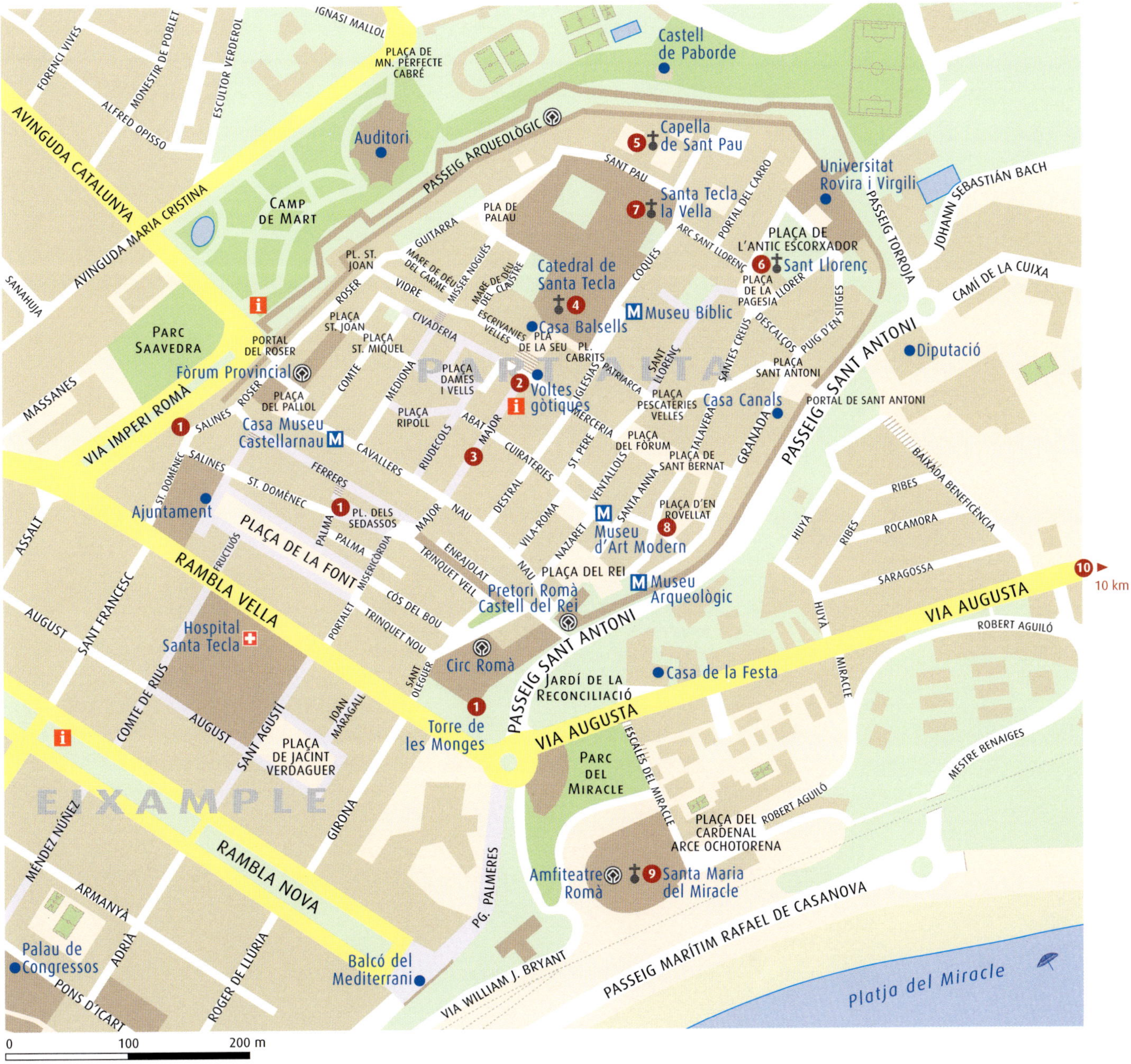

Modern and contemporary route

You can take as long as you want to explore modern and contemporary Tarragona which spans the 16th century to the present day and was a time of major urban growth. However, a day would be sufficient to get a complete overview of the process that has resulted in the modern the city as you explore its central neighbourhoods: from the Part Alta — where you've already seen the Roman and medieval quarters — to the Eixample, with a short trip to the Punta del Miracle, and the period of the War of the Spanish Succession.

1 Passeig de Sant Antoni: Gate and cross of Sant Antoni, and the Palau de la Diputació **2** Fortí de la Reina and Fortí de Sant Jordi **3** Carrer Cavallers - Casa Montoliu **4** Casa-Museu Castellarnau (Museu d'Història de Tarragona) **5** Casa Canals (Museu d'Història de Tarragona) **6** Museu d'Art Modern **7** City Hall and Plaça de la Font **8** Public Library **9** Plaça de Braus (Tarraco Arena Plaça, TAP) **10** Antiga Tabacalera

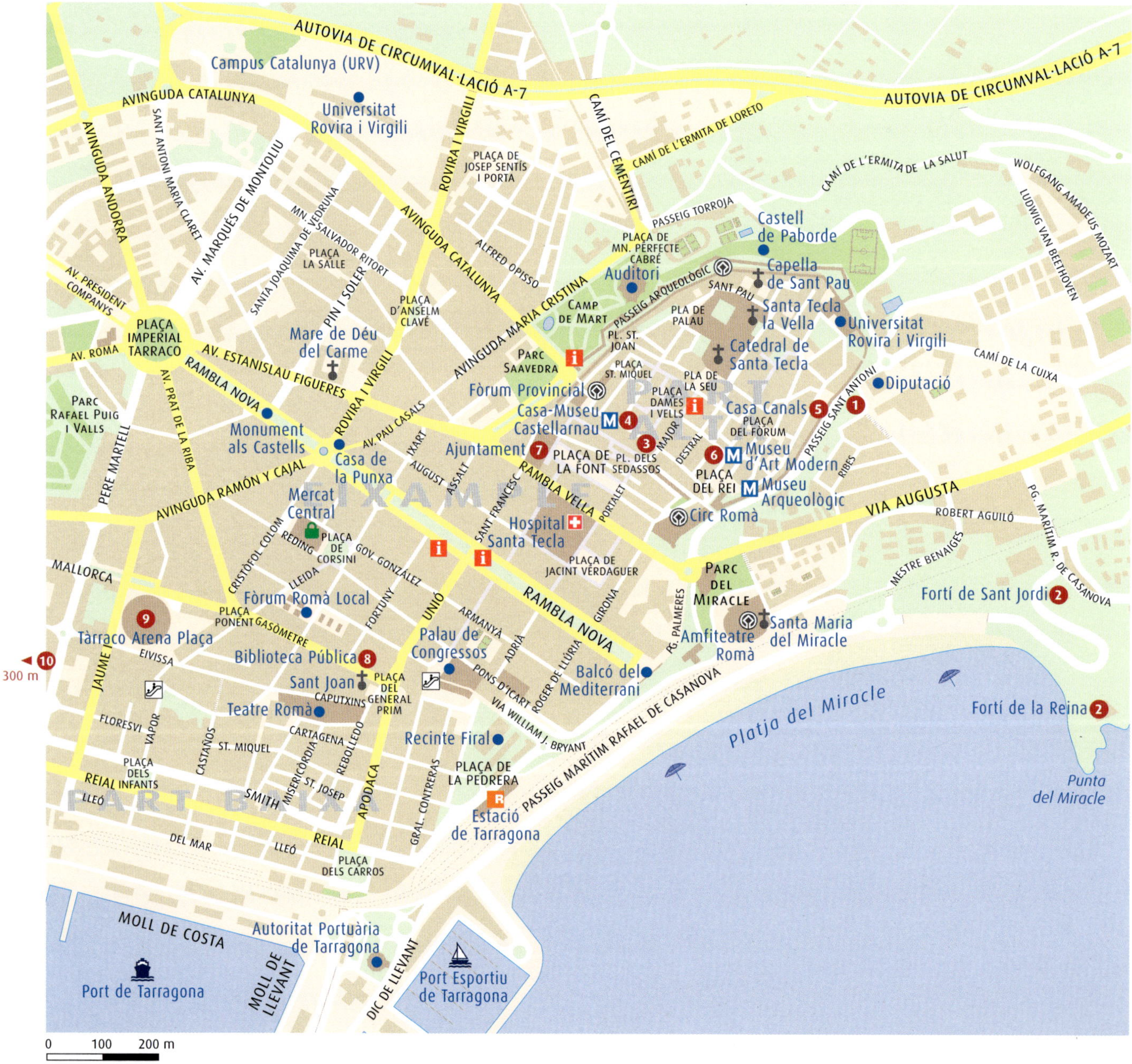

Modernista route

The *modernista* route will take you on a journey to discover the Catalan offshoot of art nouveau, *modernisme*. The city is home to countless *modernista* landmarks and the route could be even longer than the one proposed here: the *modernista* buildings on Rambla Nova are worthy of a route in their own right. Nevertheless, the route was designed to be done in a short space of time because it mostly looks at the exteriors of buildings and the streets. It also aims to bring great architects, such as the Tarragona-born Josep Maria Jujol, to a wider audience.

1 Teatre Metropol (Jujol) **2** Church of the Pares Carmelites Descalços (Jujol) **3** Chapel of the Church of Sant Francesc (Jujol) **4** Casa Ximenis (Jujol) **5** Church of Sant Llorenç (Jujol) **6** Chapel of Nostra Senyora del Sagrat Cor (Gaudí) **7** Mausoleum of Jaume I **8** Antic Escorxador **9** *Modernista* houses on the Rambla Nova - Casa Salas, Bofarull, Dr. Aleu... **10** Col·legi de les Teresianes **11** Cambra de Comerç **12** *Modernista* houses in the Eixample and other parts of the city - Casa Porta Mercadé, Casa Ripoll... **13** Mercat Central **14** Former Chartreuse Factory **15** Quinta de Sant Rafael **16** Balcó del Mediterrani

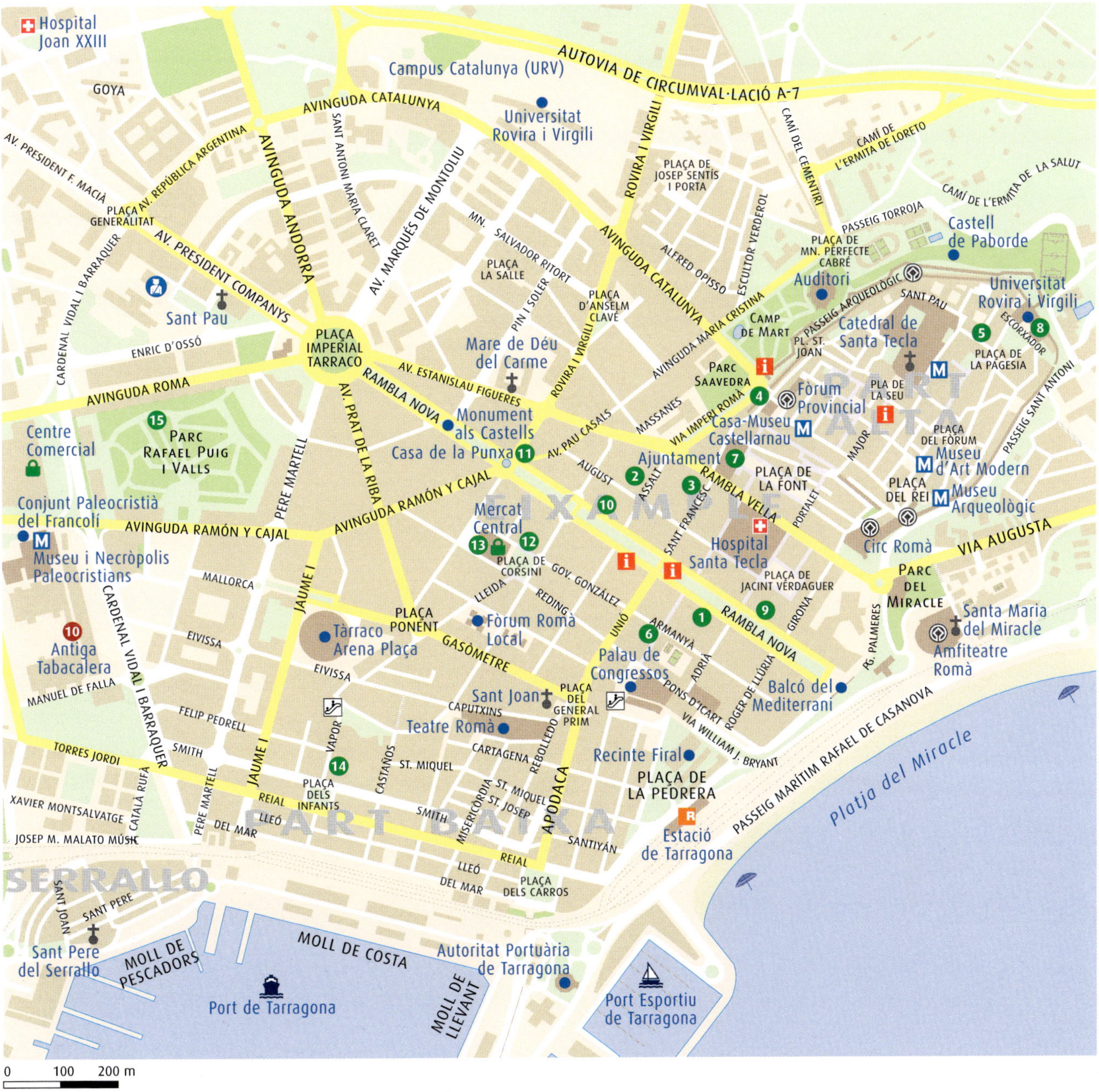

The Anella Verda circuit

Covering a distance of 34 kilometres, this is one of the many routes you can explore on the extensive Tarragona Footpath Network with its yellow signs and signposts. This one is particularly recommended because it goes all the way round the Anella Verda, the green ring that encircles the centre of Tarragona and some of its neighbourhoods. As this guidebook also points out, it can be divided into two parts or more: one along the coast, which can only be done on foot, and another inland, which you can explore by bike.

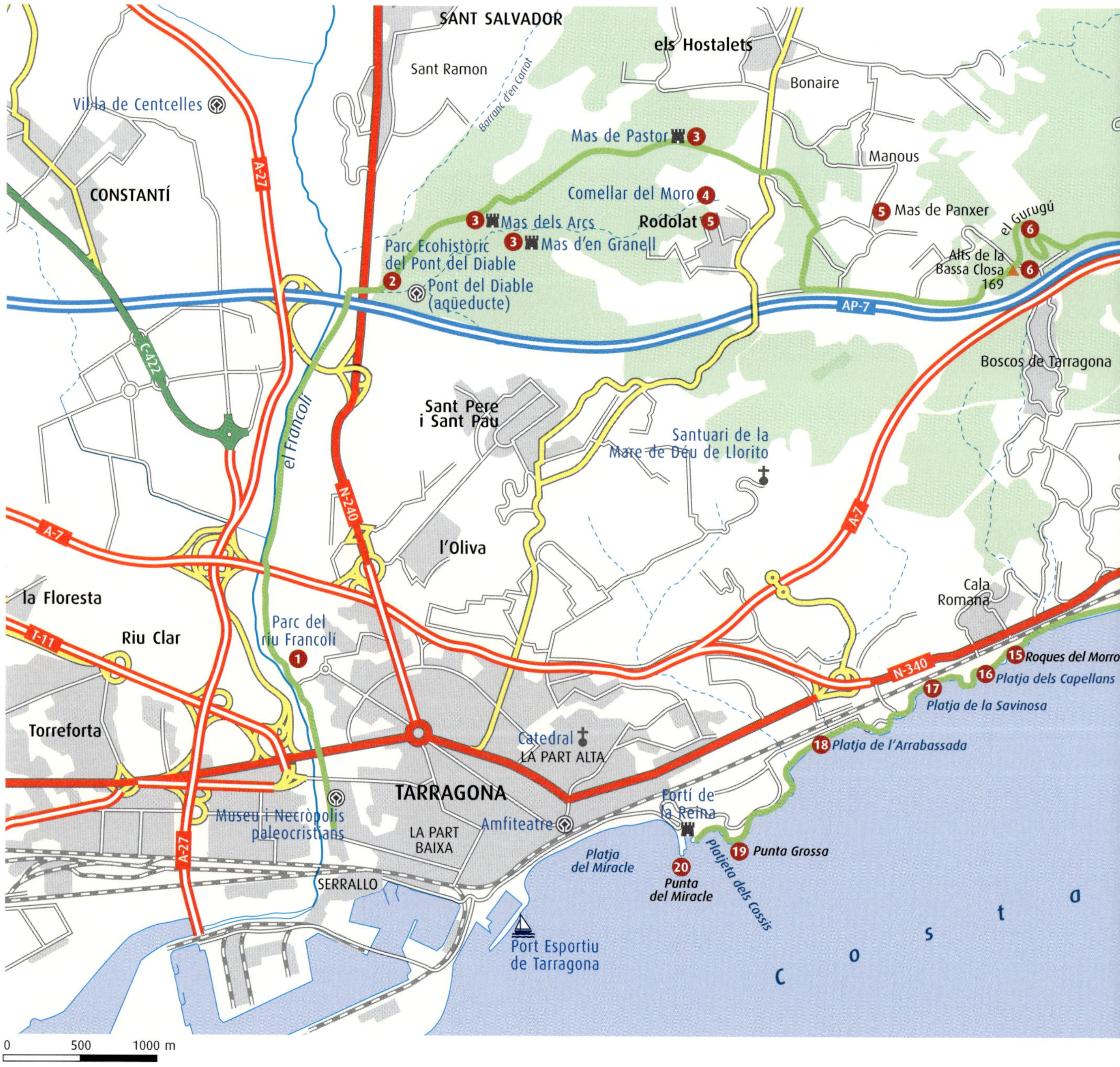

1 Parc del riu Francolí **2** Parc Ecohistòric del Pont del Diable **3** Mas dels Arcs, Mas de Granell and Mas de Pastor **4** Comellar del Moro **5** Mas de Panxer and El Rodolat **6** Alts de la Bassa Closa - El Gurugú **7** Mas de la Creu, Mas de Sorder and Mas de Cosidor **8** Ferran **9** Mouth of the river Gaià **10** Tamarit **11** Mountain of Sant Joan and La Móra beach **12** Marquesa woods **13** Punta de la Creueta **14** Platja Llarga **15** Els Morrots rocks **16** Capellans beach **17** Savinosa beach **18** Arrabassada beach **19** Punta Grossa and Cossis beach **20** Punta del Miracle

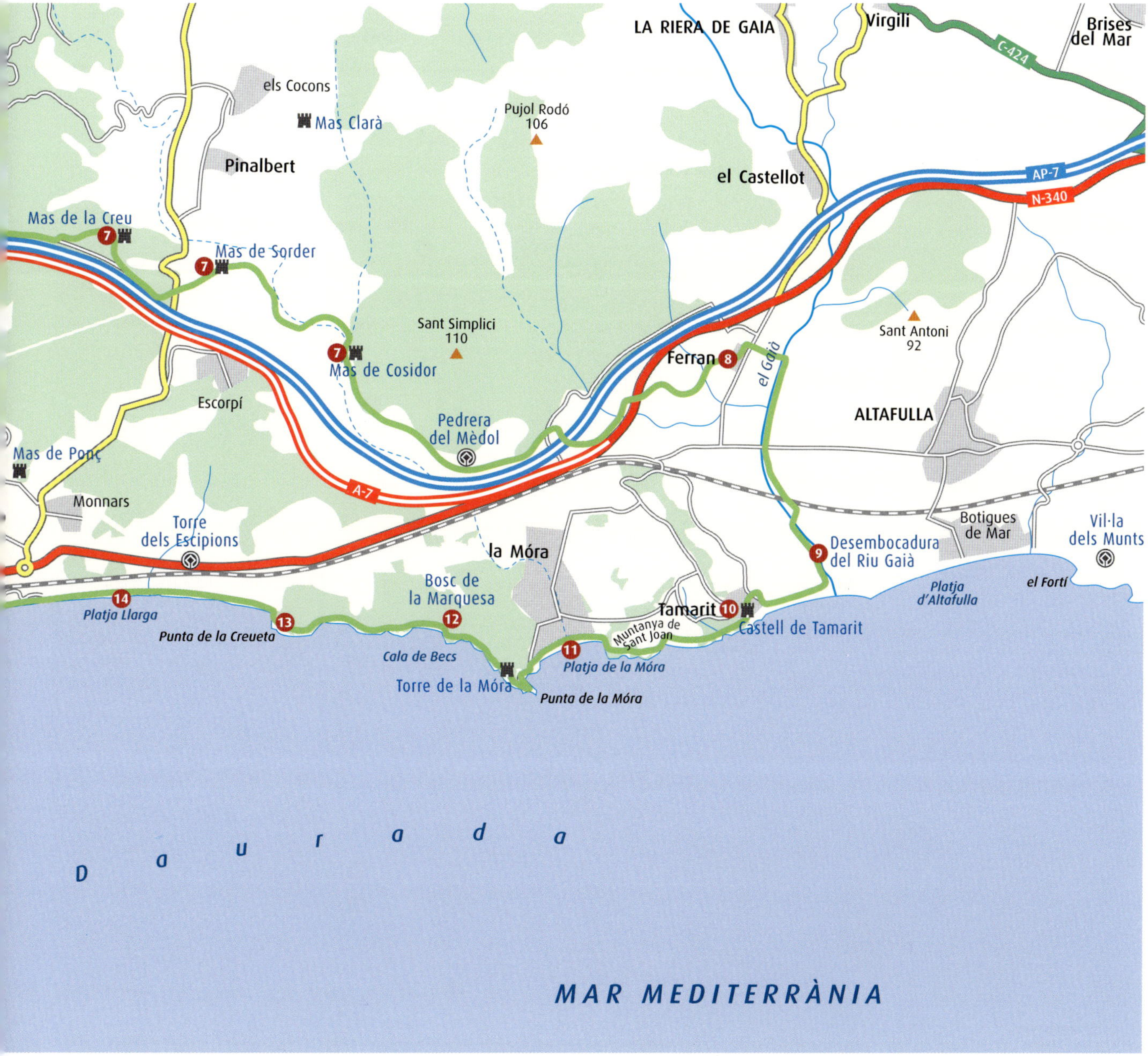

Port Heritage route

This route has explanatory panels describing each point of interest. It visits Tarragona's waterfront heritage landmarks and explores an important stretch of the city's seafront consisting of its commercial, fishing and industrial port. It begins at one end of the seafront and heads towards the sea along the Passeig de l'Escullera. We strongly recommend you follow the route and take the occasional detour to visit the other places of interest described in this book: the Museu del Port, El Serrallo...

1 Railway engine **2** Chain boat **3** Crane at the Club Nàutic **4** *Tinglado* 1 **5** Canon **6** Cranes **7** Derelict shipwrecked vessels **8** Torre del Rellotge **9** Geodesic point **10** Moll d'Aragó lighthouse **11** La Banya lighthouse

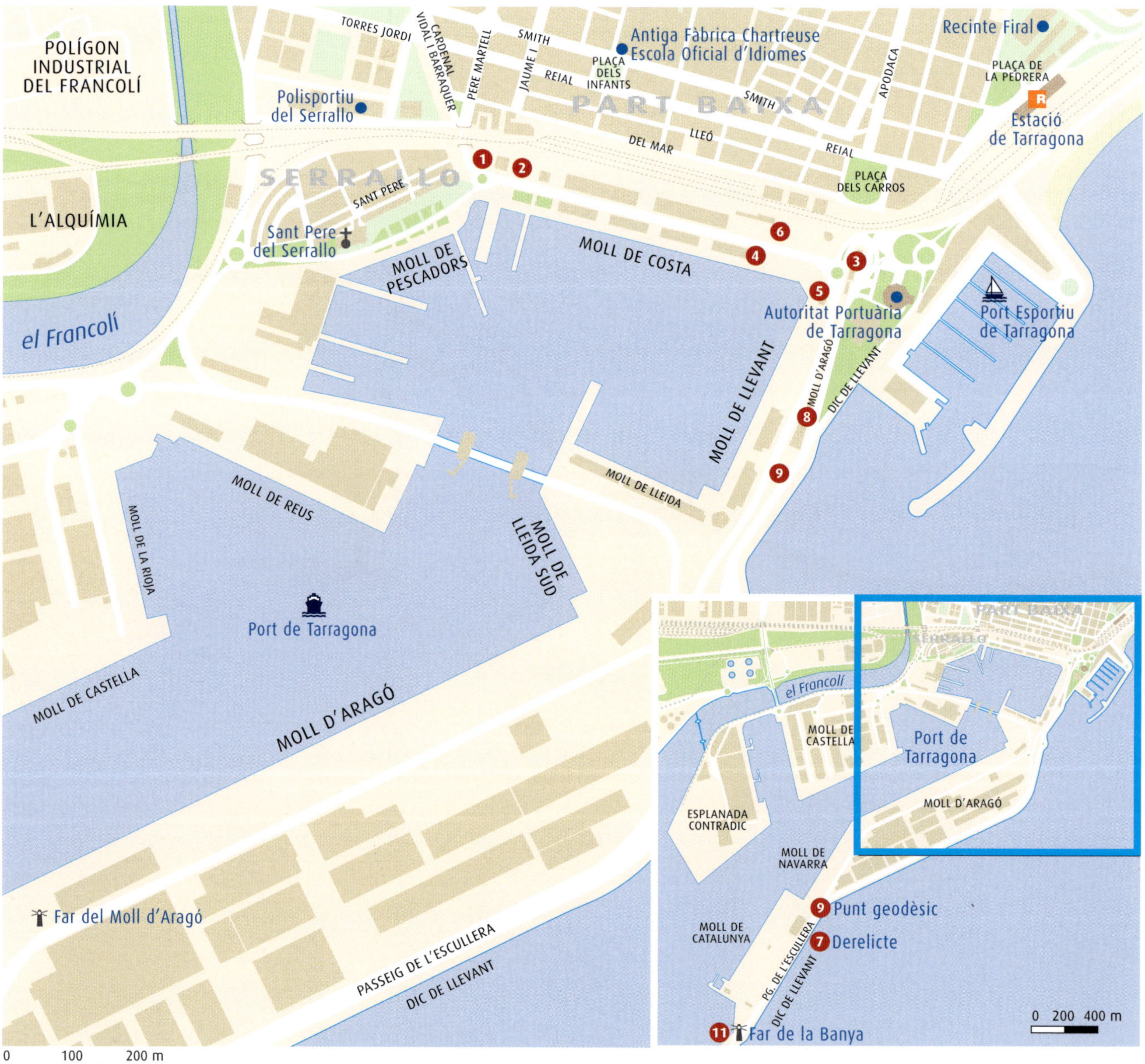